STEVE McQUEEN: THE COOLER KING

His Life Through His Movie Career

RICHARD SYDENHAM

Published by Big Star Creations
enquiries@bigstarcreations.com
Designed & Printed in the USA

Cover Photo Credits
Front: United Artists / The Kobal Collection
Back: Allied Artists / The Kobal Collection

"I'm just a kid who was on the wrong side of the tracks, had a hunch, got working and here I am. I don't get it, but I'm lucky as hell."

Steve McQueen

CONTENTS

AUTHOR'S NOTE

STEVE MCQUEEN...where do we start? Well how about first of all, why did I write this book? There were, I think, nine published books on McQueen when I began this painstaking yet rewarding stop-start journey in 1995. By the time this book reached the press, there were 24 in the marketplace, to my knowledge, and I'm sure mine won't be the last. I like to think, though, that the vast number of interviewees I have lined up in these pages will have answered more curiosities and revealed many more previously unheard anecdotes about this fascinating movie star. There are several reasons why this piece of work took so long to see the light of day and I will touch on them all. But what is most important for me to state is that I certainly would not have started this project or even finished this, if I felt that I did not have something new to say, with plenty more exclusive material to add to the legacy of one of the entertainment world's most complex, exciting and engaging personalities.

Believe me, writing a book whereby you arrange so many interviews and subsequently carry out those interviews with such distinguished figures from what can be a seemingly inaccessible industry in the main, then transcribe them all, write the chapters, not to mention all the research that is required, the reaching out to agents or publishers. It can be a tough slog, though enjoyable at the same time. Although this was partly an educational and rewarding labour of love in one sense, it was also incredibly time-consuming; especially given the fact that I conducted much research and many interviews pre-millennium, before the internet became such a natural part of our daily routines. I so wish I had the internet in the early days of this book. The amount of time I could have saved! I spent so long on the phone to the likes of the Screen Actors Guild (SAG) in Los Angeles and the British Film Institute in London and such like, attaining precious information required to help me carry on with this.

I despair at the absence of added background research that the internet provides nowadays that was not available for much of my early endeavours. For instance, the Texan writer Bud Shrake was a particularly fascinating interview regarding his times with Steve while recounting the penning of his screenplay (that he co-wrote) for *Tom Horn*. It was only after his passing in May 2009 – years after our interview, sadly, I read that he was apparently a highly-talented sports journalist who had worked for *Sports Illustrated* and authored one of the best-selling golf coaching books of all time. As a sports journalist myself – by trade – who has covered Open's and Ryder Cups, I felt an affinity with Bud that came only after his passing. We may have had so much more to discuss!

I was a 22-year-old, ambitious, fearless journalist / writer when I began this book, single, living with my parents, and with plenty of time to write into the night. Now I am a 39-year-old

Dad to Kiely and Isaac and Husband to Donna. I aim to ensure Kiely and Isaac at some point appreciate the McQueen magic and see beyond *American Pie* or *Penguins of Madagascar*! At least Donna now appears to enjoy McQueen movies when it was once a challenge, against a backdrop of the *Matrix* trilogy! My aspirations to write more books on Hollywood matters remain, while I also own a sports management and media company, Big Star Creations.

So why did it take so long to get to here? I suppose I can streamline many reasons into two basic categories: 1) Publishers' rejections and 2) In the absence of a literary agent my career commitments virtually precluded my efforts to acquire a publishing deal. I never gave up on this though because while I knew it was not a time-sensitive book, I also realised there were too many anecdotes, too many stories and far too many personal memories to give up on. I was surprised and obviously disappointed that several publishers did not believe in this project and I felt they considered McQueen an old story, not current enough, a financial risk, but it was strange to hear those knock-backs when his popularity seemed to be growing if anything with countless numbers of glossy magazines featuring him on their covers and with so many excellent websites cropping up dedicated to his memory.

I was two years into a sports journalism career when I started this book in the winter of 1995-96. I seem to recall my first few interviews were with Robert Wise, Don Gordon, Eli Wallach and Robert Relyea. That sports journalism career has since spawned into a third decade, after I started out from school as a British Gas engineer but left that job in '96 having realised it wasn't for me. By then, writing, interviewing and reporting was what inspired me. As I began writing, it seemed inevitable to me that I would one day pen something on McQueen – but it had to be fresh.

You may wonder, 'But why would a sports journalist write a book on Steve McQueen?' That's a fair question and probably an intriguing one. While all writers will know that once you're a writer you're a writer no matter what the subject matter, I accept it is something of a departure, having earned my living from cricket and soccer in the main yet I find myself here explaining away why I have written 150,000 words on a Hollywood icon. The answer is simple: passion, interest and curiosity for an actor and a movie star whose machismo, cool and screen magnetism hooked me from a relatively early age. I probably have my father, Derek, to thank for that. He is no film buff, just a typical everyman who appreciates a good flick, and as far as I can recall, he encouraged me to watch *Papillon* and *Nevada Smith* at first. Of course *The Great Escape* was always enjoyed annually at Christmas times, too. Even now, I don't think I have enjoyed a movie more than *Papillon*, possibly with *The Shawshank Redemption* on a par. Maybe it's a prison film thing? That would make sense as I have always loved *Cool Hand Luke*, *Brubaker* and *Midnight Express,* too! For McQueen not to have been nominated for an Academy Award in *Papillon* still shocks me. And his performance even caused the great Dustin Hoffman to feel insecure as Steve's co-star in that epic, as my chapter for that movie will expand on.

I didn't see *Papillon* for the first time until a decade after it was made, but who cares. A good movie is a good movie whenever you watch it, right? I was impressed by McQueen from then on; even as a young kid who had just lived through the *ET* phenomenon and was enjoying *Footloose, Rambo, Back to the Future* (I-III) etc. at the time and addicted to *Miami Vice*! Steve McQueen has that quality - that cool, timelessness that appeals no matter what age the fan or how disparate his/her usual screen tastes may be. The current new wave of Steve McQueen phenomena would suggest that he is still connecting with youngsters, and not necessarily those like me who needed their Old Man to show them the way. So many of his characters were effectively saying 'Up Yours' to the establishment (*Bullitt, The Sand Pebbles, Tom Horn, The Great Escape, The War Lover, Papillon* and more), but not in an unlikeable, playground bully or classroom jerk way but in a manner where you were with him and wanted him to win. Men love to identify with his supercool ways with the ladies, his ballsy non-conformism, his machismo and love of wheels – bikes, cars, dune buggies whatever. And the ladies enjoy his rugged sex appeal, his bad boy appeal on-screen or off. It has been interesting to investigate whether Steve's on-screen persona was like his off-camera character. Some say not, but most would say so, including Steve himself in most cases; certainly not in the case of Eustis Clay in *Soldier in the Rain*!

In more recent years, I have developed a particular admiration for a totally different character Morgan Freeman and his movies, but the McQueen appreciation is not a cyclical thing, it's permanent. I have, though, consciously not allowed that appreciation to bias my writing. My journalistic instincts, my yearnings to hear as much about the 'real McQueen' as possible and my recognition for a great anecdote no matter how weird or sensationalistic the memoir, I could never have watered anything down. This is a warts' and all account as told by the various interviewees; whether dealing with Steve's womanising, his awkwardness towards co-workers, his temper, his drinking, his drug-taking, his insecurity, his rudeness. There are enough stories of humour, compassion, love, loyalty, respect, skill and playful adventure to balance the negatives. This is written with honesty and intended to be another, important account in the life of Steve McQueen.

By the time I was fully engrossed with this venture, I had read most of the publications that were already out. *My Husband, My Friend* by his first wife Neile was a scintillating read and greatly revealing of the man behind the camera. Her memoirs told a wonderful story of how two people with similar backgrounds found one another in 1950s New York, fell in love, married, had kids, had fun, got rich and eventually divorced after the flower power and love culture generation turned Steve's head. *Steve McQueen: Portrait of an American Rebel* was also a credit to its author, Marshall Terrill. I don't know him but in my humble opinion it's the most in-depth, well researched general biography on McQueen, by non-family at least. His detail on the end of Steve's life, in particular, is unrivalled and a reason why I have chosen not to go over this well-trodden path. Likewise, Penina Spiegel's biography, *The Story of a Bad Boy in Hollywood*, a decade earlier in the 1980s was also greatly researched, especially on Steve's background in Slater, Missouri where he was raised by his Great Uncle Claude. However, I still saw gaps that needed filling and I set out to do things differently here. I knew I had to source many new people who had never or had rarely been quoted on McQueen. I feel the magnitude of new anecdotes and memories in here that show Steve in so many different ways, some good, some not so good, validate this book.

Of course some information will be common knowledge that tends to be recycled, though I felt there were still movies that had not been treated with much depth in previous publications and there were still many people who had not been asked for their memories of the various films. I always intended on chronicling Steve's movie career rather than his life in general, picture by picture, interviewing all kinds of industry professionals who interacted with him. Some I would have loved to have spoken to had passed away; some that I did speak to have sadly passed on since; others were not keen to talk; but thankfully enough were happy to comment and were generous with their time and their memories for me to be able to deliver more vital information on McQueen's life and career.

I feel honoured that all of my interviewees offered me their time and memories, whether receiving a letter from the director / producer Robert Mulligan, who directed Gregory Peck in *To Kill a Mockingbird*, whether sitting in the lounge of Academy Award-winning cinematographer Fred Koenekamp at his Los Angeles home (which was colourfully displayed with his collection of toy fire trucks), or whether speaking on the telephone to legendary actors such as Robert Vaughn, Martin Landau or Eli Wallach and famed director Robert Wise (*West Side Story, The Sound of Music*). There was John Michael Hayes, who wrote the screenplay to the Hitchcock classic *Rear Window*; and Horton Foote, whose screenplay was delivered so brilliantly in *To Kill a Mockingbird*. There are many more, all credited below.

I would also like to make special mention of the generous lengths of time that the late Robert Relyea afforded me during Trans-Atlantic phone calls answering a great deal of my questions related to the seven movies he worked on with Steve McQueen added to the other personal memoirs he had of his special times with Steve. I was genuinely depressed to hear about his passing in March of this year, as I was especially keen to send him a copy of this book with a note inside to express my heartfelt gratitude for his time and generosity. I will always be grateful for Robert's kindness, for sharing his memories so vividly, and for his guidance. Others who were especially helpful and who went beyond the norm to assist me in this project were Jeb Rosebrook, Barbara Leigh, Sharon Farrell, Robert Vaughn, Shirley Anne Field, John Leyton, Bob Bagley and Derek Bell.

I like to think every interview adds something new and unique. Thanks to everyone who helped to make this happen. It has been a long time coming, but we got here in the end!

THIS BOOK would never have been written were it not for the following who all agreed to be interviewed or contributed in some way towards this work. I would like to express my sincere gratitude to you all, and also pay my respects to those who have sadly passed away since speaking to me... Del Acevedo, Edie Adams, Bibi Andersson, Del Armstrong, RG Armstrong, Newt Arnold, Richard Attwood, Bob Bagley, Derek Bell, Jacqueline Bisset, Susan Blakely, Kathy Blondell, Sugar Blymyer, Bruce Brown (courtesy of Bob Bagley), LeVar Burton, Gary Cockrell, Jeff Corey, Gordon T. Dawson, Russell S. Doughten, Wendell Dowling, Louise Edlind, Blake Edwards, John M. Elliott, Donald W. Ernst, Sharon Farrell, Shirley Anne Field, John Flaxman, Horton Foote, William A. Fraker, Don Gordon, Charles Guggenheim, John Michael Hayes, Jeff Heininger, Chuck Hicks, Pat Hingle, Bo Hopkins, Peter Hyams, Steve Jaffe, L.Q. Jones, Vince Kehoe, Sheldon Kahn, Harry Kleiner, Fred J. Koenekamp, Buzz Kulik, Martin Landau, Ring Lardner Jr., Mert Lawwill, Barbara Leigh, Angus Lennie, John Leyton, Peter Lucarelli, Mako (Iwamatsu), Vitina Marcus, Mike Mason, Pete Mason, Ed Milkovich, Walter Mirisch, Robert Mulligan, Sir Stirling Moss, Mary Murphy, Don Murray, Ed Nelson, Kurt Neumann Jr., Chris Noel, Steve Nontell, Sir Michael Parkinson, Jack Petty, William (Bill) Pierce, David Piper, Bren Plaistowe, Michael

Preece, Paula Prentiss, Martin Ransohoff, Harriet Ravetch (otherwise known as Harriet Frank Jr.), Josh Ravetch, Robert Relyea, Jeb Rosebrook, Arnold Schulman, Lorenzo Semple Jr., Bud Shrake, Ray Summers, Robert E. Swink, Alan Trustman, Joe Turkel, William Tuttle, Robert Vaughn, Eli Wallach, Al Waxman, George Wells, Bert Williams, Jock Wilson, Robert Wise, Joe Wizan, Emanuel L. Wolf and Tim Zinnemann.

I am also grateful to the services provided by the British Film Institute, the Screen Actors Guild, the Motion Pictures Editors Guild, Zachary at the Make-Up Artists and Hair Stylists Guild, the American Society of Cinematographers, Gregg at the Writers Guild of America, the Costume Designer's Guild, the Directors Guild of America, the Producer's Guild of America, the British Racing Drivers Club, the American Motorcyclists Association Hall of Fame, Cheryl and Phil at the Kobal Collection Picture Desk and the many agents and assistants who helped to arrange interviews for the purpose of this book. And finally thanks to Marilyn Warnick at *The Mail on Sunday* for believing in this book enough to agree a pre-publication serialisation, in such an esteemed newspaper.

Richard Sydenham,
Birmingham, UK
October, 2013

THIS BOOK IS dedicated to all the Steve McQueen fans, industry professionals, his family and friends, editors, publishers' et al, who continue to appreciate and acknowledge the unique contribution of Steve McQueen to Hollywood and film, keeping his memory alive. His legacy is open to interpretation, but his all too short life was rarely dull

AND

TO MY FAMILY, who have always supported me in everything that I have ever done. Your faith means a lot

Robert Vaughn and Steve playing poker during
downtime on *The Magnificent Seven*
*(COURTESY: UNITED ARTISTS / THE KOBAL
COLLECTION)*

FOREWORD BY ROBERT VAUGHN

I USED TO see Steve around town in the late fifties; he looked like a glum James Dean. I was aware of him because he was doing *Wanted: Dead or Alive* at the time, although I had seen him before then. He was a down-beat kind of guy; we used to call him 'one of those New York actors.' I was not the kind of person that Steve normally hung around with. His buddies were mechanics, racing car people and biking guys - not actors, but for some reason he got to like me very much while doing *The Magnificent Seven*. We used to hang out together and go to bars and I'd go to race meetings with him. He liked me for no reason that I could understand but we got along well.

We really got to know one another on *The Magnificent Seven*. He was terribly paranoid about everybody and everything. Steve was a frightened man about all sorts of things from money, stardom, life in general, but he was especially insecure about his stardom. He never realised what a great star he was. He certainly never regarded himself as much of an actor, but in my way of thinking he is one of the greatest movie stars of all time because he had such an extraordinary personality on screen - it was so strong, so compelling and so sexual, yet he always thought himself inadequate as an actor.

I had a room at the motel where we were staying next to his. Charlie Bronson was on the other side of me. These rooms had connecting doors and I regularly had Charlie telling me about his childhood in one ear and Steve telling me about how Yul Brynner was taking over the movie in the other. Steve was very paranoid, as he usually was. He was constantly knocking on my door at six in the morning and he'd say, about Brynner, 'Did you see how big his gun was? Did you see how big his horse was?' He was always worried that Yul was going to steal the film from him. Although Yul was the star of the picture, Steve thought he was the star. The only thing Steve was ever secure about was his appeal to women. Even then when he was mainly a television star, women would still flock around him like he was God just so they could talk to him or shake his hand.

We had some fun times on that movie. I was never much of a swimmer and I remember Steve pushing me in the pool at the motel, fully clothed. I tried to tell everyone I couldn't swim but nobody believed me. Eventually, Steve dragged me out. Being down in Mexico together for a couple of months, we all got to know each other very well and we enjoyed every minute of it.

I was pleased to go on to make *Bullitt* and *The Towering Inferno* with Steve. Both of which were large-scale, unique movies in their own way. Of course you can read more about those in this book, which is a huge endeavour!

Robert Vaughn,
Connecticut, August 2013

(COURTESY: BRUCE BROWN - also pictured)

THE MAN BEHIND
THE MOVIE STAR

'He never held anything back. I don't think he left anything on the table. He lived his life every freakin' day' – LeVar Burton

STEVE McQUEEN IS remembered as many things: rugged and macho, paranoid and complex, loyal, tough, charming, rebellious, adventurous, among other things, but most certainly unpredictable. And maybe his quip to friend and co-star in three movies, Robert Vaughn, typified him. Vaughn was a guest at a rare glitzy party that Steve and his first wife Neile hosted in 1963 at their new imposing and spectacular stone house in Brentwood, Los Angeles, which had 18 rooms and spectacular views and which was aptly nicknamed 'The Castle'. Vaughn and McQueen were outside on the patio after midnight, looking towards the Pacific and the electric glow of Santa Monica in the distance. Vaughn broke the silence: "Steve, when you were back in New York in the fifties, living in a cold-water flat and courting Neile on your bike, did you ever think that you'd end up this way?" To which Steve replied crisply, after a characteristic pause: "What makes you think I'm going to end up this way?" Vaughn chuckled as

Steve walked off back to the party. Curiously, 15 years on and shortly before Steve's colourful life was prematurely ended by cancer, he was living up the coast in the most basic of conditions at an airplane hangar. His life was never predictable, but certainly full.

Terrence Steven McQueen was born at the St. Francis Hospital on March 24, 1930 in Beech Grove, Indiana to Jullian (originally Julia Ann) and William Terrence, parents who were never there for their son, and who would only appreciate him years later; when Steve had made it. By then it was too late for them to have any (meaningful) part in his life. While his mother tried to raise him – badly, and did try to stay in touch throughout, much to Steve's resentment, his father took off when Steve was just six-months-old. He never would meet his son, but was known to have wondered in later life whether the rising TV star playing Josh Randall in *Wanted: Dead or Alive* was in fact his boy. Steve's parents married almost as soon as Jullian's pregnancy was discovered, but it was about the only honourable thing 'Bill' McQueen ever did with regards to his boy. He was a stunt pilot for a flying circus and clearly parenthood and the responsibilities that went with it were not for him. This lack of a father figure had an immeasurable effect on Steve and left mental scars that he took to his grave.

Screenwriter Jeb Rosebrook detected these vulnerabilities when he worked with Steve on his own original screenplay *Junior Bonner* in 1971 (before its 1972 release). Steve was 41 at that time and one of the toughest men in Hollywood, but elements in the script revealed how he was still hurting inside.

It was a story that Steve adored about family values, and of a special relationship between rodeo legend Junior Bonner and his father Ace (played by Robert Preston), and the material touched a nerve. "In the original script I had Dad in there, not Ace, and I recall quite clearly from the very first rehearsal that Steve preferred to call Bob Preston's character Ace and not Dad," Rosebrook revealed. "Steve did not have a very happy childhood and did not even know his father so I can only think that considering this background it would have been very difficult for Steve to call Ace 'Dad'. There was one moment, with the cow-milking scene, where he does call him Dad. And the scene at the railroad station when Ace parted from Junior may be one of the only scenes in a Steve McQueen movie where he was either in tears or close to it."

Just months after his birth, Jullian and baby Steve shifted to Slater, Missouri, a city about 90 miles east of Kansas City. They went to live with her parents, Lillian and Victor Crawford. When the Great Depression took hold, they all moved to the farm of Lillian's brother, Claude Thomson, a hog farmer by trade but to Steve he soon became so much more; Great Uncle Claude had the most positive and lasting influence on Steve throughout his formative years and he learned values that stuck with him for life. After tasting the bright lights and the big city buzz in Indianapolis, Jullian quickly tired of farm life and took off once more. "I was a guest at Steve McQueen Week there in Slater," said Chris Noel, who co-starred with Steve in *Soldier in the Rain*. "I went to the farmhouse where Steve actually had lived with his grandparents and I saw the room that he slept in. He was basically a farm-boy and had to walk several miles to get into the city to go to his school."

Materially, it was a modest upbringing, but Steve grew to love and respect Claude, who taught him about discipline, hard work and the basic morals in life, giving him a solid base that his reluctant mother and absent father were never likely to. Steve did not always follow Claude's advice in terms of doing right by the law in later life having being raised with a clear knowledge of right and wrong – though much of that derived from his mother's wayward example, but Steve did learn from the old man about the ethics of hard graft. He knew a man had to give blood and sweat to provide financial security for his family. Steve went on to become many things in his life, not all good, but few would deny he worked his butt off to give his family a good life.

Steve first went to Slater when he was six-months-old, after the breakdown of Jullian's marriage to Steve's father. But as happened a lot in her life, Jullian grew bored by the pace of life in Slater and returned to Indianapolis. Financial troubles and the 'burden' of her young boy, though, saw Jullian return to Slater when Steve was three; only this time to leave him in the care of her parents and Uncle Claude. Steve was the proverbial weight around her neck; Jullian wasn't cut out for motherhood and it was a weakness that Steve never forgave her for to her dying day, when he was an established global movie star.

The upside to life on Uncle Claude's 320-acre farm was that it sparked a love for the Great Outdoors in Steve that remained with him until his death. During the shoot of *Tom Horn* in 1979, when he and third wife Barbara Minty slept in a trailer in the middle of nowhere in Patagonia, Arizona, it reminded Steve of his youth and the times with Uncle Claude. The old man had a 'work-hard, play-hard' reputation, which would be another trait that Steve would later adopt. For now, though, Steve had more work to do than play, which was just as well as Steve would later say that Claude "had no use for slackers". But he was not unappreciative of his boy's endeavours and would treat him to regular Saturday Matinees. Westerns would always be Steve's favourites. Claude also bought Steve a red tricycle for his fourth birthday, which Steve later revealed "started my racing fever"; he would race other kids on it for gumdrops. "I skinned my knees on it a lot but I sure won a lot of gumdrops." Despite this play time, there was always sorrow and a feeling of loneliness and abandonment. Steve would see other children around Slater with their parents and would wonder when his parents would return to claim him. They never did – for many years.

Before then, Steve attended the Orearville School, which meant a two-mile walk every day. School life was tough on Steve as he was hard of hearing in one ear, through a mastoid infection that was never treated. And he was later found to be dyslexic; quite a shortcoming to overcome considering he had to read scripts and had lines to learn in later life.

Jullian finally returned for Steve when he was nine. It was a tearful farewell between Steve and Uncle Claude, but the old man knew he belonged with his mother. Unsurprisingly,

Steve did not last long again with Jullian and her second husband in Indianapolis. Steve, incidentally, was asked to call him 'Dad' even though it was another one of Jullian's marriages that was destined for failure. Home life had an unsettling effect on Steve, who ran with hoodlums, broke into shops, stole hubcaps and played pool for fun. His stay there was short-lived and he returned to Claude's before long. Steve lived with Jullian again when he was 12, this time they shifted to Los Angeles, where she had married another man who Steve only knew as 'Berri', who was a drunk and a bully and would regularly beat Steve. To escape the bullying, he would run with the wrong crowd, getting involved in petty theft, soon attracting the attention of the local police. Jullian gave him an ultimatum: return to Uncle Claude's or it was reform school – he chose the former.

Claude promised Jullian he would straighten the boy out and put him on the right road once again. Things were different this time, though, as Steve had by now had a taste of city life and Slater was not enough for him. At 14, after meeting a pencil seller at a travelling circus in Slater, he was encouraged to go and see the world, which he duly did without too much thought. Nobody could have blamed Steve for escaping, with the parentage he had had. But Steve *was* culpable for taking off without telling his Uncle Claude, the one person in his life who was genuinely bothered about him. Claude was deeply upset by Steve's disappearance and did not know for some time that he was alive and well. The next time the two met again was 1957, when Steve, then 27, drove through with his new wife. Much of the reason for Steve's reluctance to return was the hurt and feeling of abandonment from his mother that he associated with Slater.

Steve never did make it on his own in the big, wide world as a pencil seller or anything else for that matter – at that stage. He ended up tracking down his mother and Berri in LA before the same cycle repeated itself. The beatings kept on coming from Berri and Steve therefore spent more time on the streets to escape his home life. He had to carve out a reputation for himself in his gang, who initially saw him as a country hick. He stole more hubcaps than any other to earn his top-dog ranking. But this existence had a narrow shelf-life. The police eventually caught up with him again and subsequently his mother had no apprehension in signing him into reform school at the Boys' Republic, Chino Hills, California. Steve just saw the move as another rejection from his mother, who was happier to send him away to the authorities to mete out the kind of example and discipline that she was incapable of.

Boys' Republic was good for Steve. He would not know it at the time but in later years he would view that experience as one that saved him from a life of crime. Steve began his 18-month term at Chino on February 6, 1945. The officers there recognised the potential in Steve and nurtured his character strengths rather than punishing him for his occasional want to self-destruct. But it was often a lonely place. Steve watched other young offenders leave for weekends with their families while he was left behind. These painful experiences, on the back of an already hurtful upbringing, cultivated a hatred of his mother but more, moulded him into a male chauvinist who had a suspicion of women for the rest of his life. Steve's three wives were all dark-skinned brunettes. When Steve had an affair with sexy blonde-haired actress Sharon Farrell during the making of *The Reivers*, he told her: "I've only been with one other blonde, and it was a mistake. I never am attracted to blondes. I don't trust blondes!" A shocked Farrell then inquisitively asked, "What colour was your mother's hair?" Steve shrugged and said, "Blonde."

One positive borne out of his own pain, though, was Steve's love of children. He was generous to kids throughout his life; rarely could he deny an autograph if the hunter was a kid, even when he did not sign autographs as a policy. He lived his life with an inherent motto of: 'I hope no kid has to grow up like I did.' Even when he had not granted a Press interview for a decade through the 1970s, it took a fearless kid, working for his school magazine, to scoop his interview when the world's most powerful media could not get near him.

Although Boys' Republic was positive for Steve, it was no holiday camp. He had to fight his way out of a fair few scrapes, just to survive the natural pecking order that exists in young male-dominated, confined environments. He once escaped but after being caught by police and spending the night in a proper jail, he realised Chino wasn't such a bad place and knuckled down. The boys largely policed themselves, as the officers tried to encourage responsibility and trust in one another. They had to work hard like digging tree stumps out of the ground, mixing cement or, as happened to Steve once after he stepped out of line, cleaning the urinals. "He told me a story on the set of *The Great Escape* one day about what a rough time he used to get in that Boys' School," co-star John Leyton said. "He had to have his name on the back of his jacket and apparently he discovered that one of the boys had eradicated the 'M' and 'C' from his name. He recounted that story with a fair bit of laughter. But it was obvious that he was far from happy about it at the time."

After his 18 months at Chino, Steve was released and sent to his mother, but this time in New York after she had moved once again. Still the rejection continued. Steve was expecting to share her apartment but instead was informed she had rented out another room for him. When Steve entered his new lodgings, two men were in one another's arms. Jullian had neglected to tell her son that his room-mate was homosexual. He wondered how his mother could be so thoughtless as to place her vulnerable son in the home of an unknown. He had now really had enough and at 16, Steve realised he was better off on his own and set out for what would become a colourful journey.

He first joined the Merchant Marines; then worked as a towel boy in a brothel, a labourer, sold pen and pencils at a fair ground, before winding up in Myrtle Beach, Florida, where he enlisted for the Marine Corps in April, 1947, aged 17. He became a tank driver in the Second Division of the Fleet Marine Force. His three years in the Marines taught Steve many positive values that would stand in him in good stead for the remainder of his life, notably his attitude to physical fitness. Throughout his movie career he usually worked out in a home-made gymnasium, whether it was at home or on location. Even when he was married, the disciplines of keeping a 'body beautiful' extended to his wives. Neile would have to pose for him while he inspected her body under lights and would make comments about how she could improve any 'imperfections'. Her South East Asian background that had moulded a compliant, tolerant nature meant she never would tell Steve where to go and went along with his chauvinistic ways. His second wife Ali MacGraw also later spoke about going through the same rituals.

Steve was discharged from the Marines shortly before the Korean War commenced in June 1950. His life may have taken a much-altered course had he still been in the forces then. His days as a drifter continued around Florida before realising there were more opportunities for him in New York: they were modest ones initially, such as a bartender and an encyclopaedia seller – anything that would help him pay the $19 rent at his cold-water flat.

Then in 1951, he made a decision that would change his life and set him on a path towards superstardom. But it was a long time coming yet. A girlfriend persuaded Steve to accompany her to acting classes at the Neighbourhood Playhouse. There, he was introduced to the respected Sanford Meisner and soon was accepted into Meisner's acting classes. He had to overcome his macho reluctance to embrace the Arts and what came with it, like wearing a leotard and taking dance classes to improve body movement and muscles. But once he realised he had something, he worked hard to make a success of it. He endured unbelievable levels of fatigue, keeping down a driving job through the night to fund his acting classes by day. It paid off for after two years, he earned a scholarship to the Uta Hagen-Herbert Berghoff School, where he was handed his first paid acting job, collecting $40 a week from performing at a Yiddish Theatre. "I really don't like to act," Steve commented in later years. "At the beginning, back in '51, I had to force myself to stick with it. I was real uncomfortable, real uncomfortable."

Steve's first proper role came in a production called *Peg O' My Heart* at Fayetteville, New York, which starred the *Meet Me in St. Louis* child actress Margaret O'Brien. His performance was described as "embarrassing" by a fellow actor. The honest assessment stunned him, but he wasn't about to quit and worked harder to improve. Steve added stage credits in *Member of the Wedding* in 1952 starring Ethel Waters, *Time Out for Ginger* starring Melvyn Douglas, and later *Two Fingers of Pride* starring Gary Merrill and *A Hatful of Rain* in 1956, which was Steve's big break after he replaced Ben Gazzara in the lead role of Johnny Pope. By then he had also started to work in live television, which was a new phenomenon of that generation. But undoubtedly the greatest triumph of this time in Steve's fledgling career was his breakthrough into the legendary Actors Studio, when he was one of two from 2,000 to successfully audition. The other was Martin Landau, who would later co-star with Steve in *Wanted: Dead or Alive* and more prominently, *Nevada Smith* in 1966. Landau was present when Steve first encountered James Dean, who was then the hottest property in New York. "I obviously knew Steve at the Actors Studio but I knew him prior to that because Jimmy Dean was my best friend," Landau recalled, "and the first time I ever saw Steve was when Jimmy was having trouble with his motorcycle. We drove into a garage between 9th and 10th Avenue on Manhattan and Steve was working there as a mechanic."

To be accepted into the Actors Studio was as good as 'making it'. Once you were in there you were part of the assembly line en route to screen notoriety. "If I hadn't made it as an actor, I might have wound up a hood," Steve later commented. That was the significance of his entry into the prestigious Actors Studio where he followed names that would soon become screen royalty, such as Paul Newman, Jack Lemmon, Walter Matthau and James Dean.

"Back in the fifties the Actors Studio was *the* place to study acting, to work with (Lee) Strasberg and (Elia) Kazan," said Academy Award winner Landau, who later helped establish the Actors Studio West in Los Angeles where he is a lead tutor. "To become a member one had to audition and it was real hard to get in. Geraldine Page auditioned six times before she was allowed in. Dustin Hoffman would tell you he auditioned nine times, but the truth is he auditioned six times before he was accepted. The year Steve and I were accepted, there were 2,000 applicants. Anyone who was ever in the Actors Studio was unique as there are lots of good actors who audition who do not get in. Steve had something, a real talent, and that obviously emerged when he went to film.

"Lee Strasberg was quite gentle on Steve at the Studio, and he was much rougher on me," Landau added. "The reason he was gentle with Steve was because of his previous experiences with Jimmy Dean. Jimmy stopped working at the Studio, he would go there but he wouldn't get up and do scenes any more. And Strasberg, aware of the pressure he put on Jimmy, was then less tough on Steve. I am not sure if Jimmy was over-sensitive with the critique of his acting or whether Lee was too tough on him but I do know that Lee could be very, very tough and when he was like that he was relentless. And Jimmy said, 'I'm not going to put myself in that position anymore'."

Those days in New York in the early fifties were competitive times when many talented actors were all hustling. Hollywood, though, was not then the be all and end all as it is now for most young thespians. Dean, Landau, McQueen et al were struggling young actors trying to get on. Everyone's dream at that time was to earn a play on Broadway. Television was in its infancy and was seen just as a way to make extra money. Live television plays produced in New York would not reach the West Coast until a week later. Plays were the be all and end all – Hollywood was 3,000 miles away and a different animal so ambitions then were not about getting into movies. "It was about developing as an actor so that you could walk across a stage and hold an audience for two hours," Landau said. "Make no mistake Steve's goal was to be a working actor on Broadway. Steve was one of the people trying to get work, who were wonderfully gifted, and years later became iconic and legendary. But at the time we were all kind of scrambling."

James Dean had a quiet, moody quality that set him out from what was around at the time. But Marlon Brando, Paul Newman and Steve were also identified as similar actors who looked cool in a pair of Levis and a white T-shirt and executed a silent mystique that appealed to the masses. It was said that Brando started the trend along with Montgomery Clift, before Dean came along and soon to be followed by Newman and then McQueen. It was as much a sign of the changing times in America. They answered the demands of what youthful America could identify with at that stage in society. After World War II, great social change was afoot. Teenagers started to influence the United States like never before. Different styles of music were introduced like rhythm and blues, and black music infiltrated the white world with Otis Redding being played by white disc jockeys. Elvis Presley came along later, after Jimmy Dean and Marlon Brando. Dean's trademark character of the young, rebellious boy epitomised what was happening in the US – and the world to a lesser extent. Landau commented: "In that period, people stopped wearing suits and ties and began wearing blue jeans and open shirts. The world had changed and Jimmy and those types of actors fitted in to that new world. The times dictated what was cool. Teenage youth was calling the shots; had that not happened the Gielgud's and Olivier's would have continued on. It was a change in style and Steve McQueen, Jimmy Dean, Montgomery Clift and these guys were the personification of the times in the USA. It was a perfect time for those actors. Beauty and handsomeness prevailed. The likes of Jimmy, Marlon and Steve opened doors for guys like Al Pacino, Robert De Niro, Gene Hackman and Robert Duvall in later years."

The Steve McQueen cool that may have metamorphosed from a Brando-esque beginning or developed from the moodiness of Jimmy Dean certainly found its own niche in time and when it did, it would have made a billion had it been packaged and sold. Even now, young actors try to 'do McQueen' – but it rarely works. "Actors can make fools of themselves if they are not careful," commented actor John Leyton. "I have seen people trying to do James Dean or Steve McQueen and it is not that easy. For them that way came natural; that's the difference."

It has been said that Steve idolised James Dean, especially after his breakthrough in *East of Eden*. The truth is that Steve admired Dean's skill but he was too driven and hungry to succeed himself to be overly distracted by the careers of his contemporaries. Steve was actually more impressed by Dean's early television work than his Hollywood movies. Dean did not struggle for work when many others did. He appeared in a lot of live television at the Kraft Theatre, such as *A Long Time Till Dawn* in 1953, something that director George Stevens saw before the actor had made *East of Eden,* but it had him in line for *Giant*. "Stevens told me that when I worked with him on *The Greatest Story Ever Told*," Landau added. "He had watched that play and then thought of Jimmy to play Jett Rink in *Giant*. So Jimmy was working on a lot of TV then, but Steve was not working as much as Jimmy was. So it was not so much the three movies Jimmy did that attracted Steve's admiration but more his TV activity in New York. He also did *See the Jaguar* (1952) and *The Immoralist* (1954), so Jimmy was making some noise in New York. Therefore, Steve noticed Jimmy long before he did *East of Eden* and his other Hollywood movies."

The year of 1956 was another watershed in the life and career of Steve McQueen. There was his first appearance in a feature film *Somebody Up There Likes Me*, albeit as a $19 a day extra, his breakthrough stage opportunity in *A Hatful of Rain*, and the not to be underestimated matter of marriage.

Steve landed a role as an extra in Robert Wise's production *Somebody Up There Likes Me* while still at the Studio. It was to star James Dean but after his tragic death, Paul Newman starred. From that moment on, Steve viewed Newman as the man he needed to catch. It was a race. And Steve always loved the competiveness of a race. It took 18 years for him to catch Newman, in terms of sharing top billing with him on *The Towering Inferno*, though he had by that time been an equal in Hollywood for many years, since *The Great Escape* in 1963.

The stage production of *A Hatful of Rain* starring Ben Gazzara and Shelly Winters opened on November 9, 1955, though Steve debuted on July 2 the following year. Its eventual success led to the movie version in 1957. It only came about as an experimental Actors Studio project. Steve McQueen was shunted forwards from relative anonymity at the Actors Studio into a fairly important role on Broadway as a first replacement to Gazzara, who was a far more experienced stage actor. "It was a big break for Steve," Landau said. "He stepped into that role well as Ben was a New Yorker and had been born and raised on the streets of New York and so he fitted easier into the part of Johnny Pope. Tony Franciosa, who played his brother, was also a New Yorker, but Steve wasn't and came from another part of the country yet he filled the role quite well. That performance launched him and gave him a degree of importance and somewhat of a name to kick his career off."

These were exciting times in Steve's life but he was still far from making it. One person around the New York scene, though, who was well on the way to stardom was a pretty young dancer by the name of Neile Adams. In fact, when she eventually got together with Steve, it was her money that kept them afloat in those early years. Initially, she would bump into Steve now and again in the regular hangouts like Downey's Restaurant on Eighth Avenue. The more their paths crossed the more there seemed to be chemistry between them. Typically, Steve was too cool to immediately ask her out on a date, in case she turned him down so he just relied on charm and sweet-talking her. That was until he saw her out about town with Mark Rydell, who would become Steve's director on *The Reivers* in 1969. It wasn't that Steve was shy – quite the opposite. The first words he said to Neile were, 'You're pretty.' His reluctance had more to do with the fear of rejection, and he'd had enough of that from his mother to last him a lifetime. But the sight of Neile out with Rydell shocked him into finally propositioning her.

Steve and first wife Neile Adams together in the early days
(COURTESY: THE KOBAL COLLECTION)

They soon realised there was something between them and they felt even closer for the similarities they had from childhood, as they talked late into the night on their first date. They were two lost and lonely souls coming together. While Steve's background was undoubtedly tough, Neile saw her share of struggle, too: born in Manila in The Philippines, never knew her father, and spent time in a Japanese concentration camp. She was, though, raised by a more able mother than Steve had. Neile and Steve were soon inseparable. Their busy work schedules meant they spent their most quality times together on Sunday's, when they would take in a double matinee and watch stars like Humphrey Bogart, Cary Grant, Gary Cooper and Steve's favourite James Cagney.

Steve had somewhat of a reputation with the ladies around the New York scene not to mention being a speed-freak, petrol-head. Neile was headed for stardom and her managers were far from happy at her new love, who would wait for her stage-side. But their connection was strong and it did not surprise their inner circle when they were married on November 2, 1956, after just four months together. They knew they were meant to be. It was a typically spontaneous Steve McQueen wedding, as he picked her up in a rented Ford Thunderbird and sped off to the romantic setting of San Juan Capistrano, before legal red tape meant they had to move on to San Clemente. Steve was waved over by two highway patrolmen for speeding en route. When he explained he was trying to find a minister to wed him and his wife-to-be, the officers sympathized and gave him an escort to a local

Lutheran minister, who was persuaded to open his Church and marry the young couple just before midnight.

The marriage sealed a relationship that became significant to many of Steve's decisions throughout his movie career, until their eventual divorce in 1972. Within two years of marriage, Neile shelved her own successful dance career to support Steve's. She was instinctive and knew what was best for her husband's career. Some of his best decisions were coerced by Neile, like his reasoning to bully Norman Jewison into giving him the seemingly incongruous part of Thomas Crown in 1968. "She has always been such a smart woman and she had a lot to do with Steve making the right decisions through much of his career, as he was an instinctive actor," commented actress Susan Blakely, who co-starred with Steve in *The Towering Inferno* but who also became a friend of Neile's through their charity work.

Married life was difficult on them both initially, for varying reasons. Steve was struggling to land meaningful parts, though his career began to take off once Neile convinced her manager Hilly Elkins and William Morris agent Stan Kamen to find work for her husband. He was living off her wages, though he hated that he was unable to provide for his wife – even if he did enjoy the spoils of new cars he would buy with her wages. Not long after this time, Steve befriended British racing car legend Stirling Moss. McQueen was not the type he would normally hang out with but they became friends and remained in touch for years after. "We met in the late fifties, after he called me up when I was over in America doing some racing," Moss recalled. "He asked me to go and see him.

It was interesting to see at that point that he had quite a small pad. But when I saw him a few years later he had a fantastic house in the Beverley Hills region. I remember thinking how his lifestyle had changed very much for the better. His personality never changed though, which was a credit to him given all the fame he was receiving at that time in his life. I thought he was a very likeable person – way-out and certainly not the kind of person who I usually went around with. He was just so keen on cars and racing that it probably gave us a closer bond as friends than with people outside of the racing world. I never saw him for years before he died but we always wrote to one another every Christmas."

Neile's urgent plea to find Steve work had the desired effect when the agents came up with *Never Love A Stranger*, *The Great St. Louis Bank Robbery* and *The Blob* (which Steve also pitched himself for, after a chance meeting with the producers). His career then gradually began to take off. They were low-budget movies but he was the star in the latter two, which meant a lot on a young actor's CV. Fourth billing in a Frank Sinatra picture *Never So Few*, in 1959, cemented his growing stardom in Hollywood.

The first three roles led to his major breakthrough, as Josh Randall on *Trackdown* spin-off *Wanted: Dead or Alive*. CBS initially ordered 28 episodes after a pilot show from an episode of *Trackdown* was deemed a success. Steve was paid $750 per episode initially and would go on to make 94 episodes from 1958-1961. The bulk of the money the show generated went to Four Star Productions, which was run by David Niven,

Charles Boyer and Dick Powell. As Josh Randall, the alternative bounty hunter, he perfected his method with his shortened Winchester 1892 gun that was nicknamed the 'Mare's Laig'. When the Beech Grove Public Library began their tribute to the city's most famous son in 2010, they focused on his time as Randall, given the launch-pad it became for his career. The Collection, though, does also possess a complete set of McQueen's film performances (television and movies) and biographies. "I noticed that folks tended to fly right by his three seasons on *Wanted: Dead or Alive* to celebrate his movie career," said Steve Nontell of the Steve McQueen Birthplace Collection, Beech Grove, Indiana. "I believed we could focus on the 'birth' aspect of his life by way of seeking only memorabilia from the TV show…this show was the 'birth' of his 'star' status, opening the door to the major movie roles. So it seemed, historically, an honorable way for us to celebrate our city's piece of his life."

Wanted: Dead or Alive catapulted Steve's name and image onto screens around the country and soon he was in demand from Hollywood producers. Although Steve began to resent the TV series because it was curtailing his opportunities in feature films, he also knew what it had done for him. His growing reputation meant he also had no hesitation in hounding producer and writer Ed Adamson into frequent script changes; something that would become a common theme in his career. The series ended on March 29, 1961 when the network switched it from Saturday to Wednesday nights, a move that ultimately failed.

Steve as Josh Randall on his breakthrough TV series
Wanted: Dead or Alive
(COURTESY: CBS / THE KOBAL COLLECTION)

The newfound riches enabled Steve and Neile to buy their first house on Skyline Drive, Laurel Canyon in Los Angeles in 1958. Times were changing and they moved apace further when their first child, a daughter named Terry Leslie McQueen, was subsequently born on June 5, 1959. Shortly after Terry's birth, Steve was compelled to find his father and his investigations eventually led him to a former girlfriend, who informed Steve he had died months earlier but enjoyed him on *Wanted: Dead or Alive*, and had always wondered if that was "my boy". Possibly the most tragic and heart-wrenching of all deaths in the McQueen family, though, came 18 years after Steve's own passing; when Terry died on March 19, 1998, aged just 38 as a result of haemochromatosis, an unusual genetic disorder of the metabolism. During her youth, she led a happy life despite the unfortunate split between her parents when she was 14. Steve was always there for her – and for that matter her brother Chad, Steve's son, who was born on December 28, 1960. Steve was as loving and caring a father to them, and to step-son Joshua, as absent and unloving his own parents were to him. Terry told UK magazine *Hello* in an interview in 1989, "I don't think any daughter could be closer to her father than I was to my Dad. We'd talk every day on the telephone; I'd be with him every weekend. There was never a time when he wasn't there when I needed him." Even Steve's industry colleagues understood what family meant to him, irrespective of how wild he could live his life at times. "Steve enjoyed a beer, I know he dabbled with drugs and that he smoked a lot of grass in his life and he screwed around with women behind his wife's back," said Bo Hopkins, Steve's co-star on *The Getaway*. "But despite all of that, one thing that nobody could ever dispute was his love for his children. He really loved his kids and I think he must have been a terrific father to them."

Steve's first hit movie was *The Magnificent Seven* in 1960, which was directed by John Sturges. The director had earmarked Steve's potential when working with him on the Sinatra picture *Never So Few* a year earlier. Yul Brynner was the star of *The Magnificent Seven* but McQueen did his best to be noticed, and made a pretty good fist of it. In the winter of 1960-61, the McQueen's expanding family and bank balance meant they were in the market yet again for a new home, this time a $65,000 house on Solar Drive, Nichols Canyon in the Hollywood Hills. Steve would later name his production company Solar, after this property. Only months later Steve and Neile bought a vacation home in Palm Springs, where they liked to go for relaxation. It also gave Steve an excuse to go off and ride his dirt bike in the desert – an excursion he would never tire of. Despite his burgeoning career, Steve never chose his friends depending on their status. He enjoyed hanging out with those who had so-called ordinary jobs like bike mechanic Bud Ekins or hairdresser Jay Sebring. But when he liked to play up his movie star status he would joke that, "We film stars shit crushed pineapples."

Another low-budget movie, a frothy farce comedy called *The Honeymoon Machine*, came next, which did little to help

Steve build on his growing reputation. His next four movies were all War films, though three were commercially unsuccessful – *Hell Is for Heroes, The War Lover* and *Soldier in the Rain*. The third picture of that quartet was the kind of hit from which careers are made, exactly the result *The Great Escape* brought Steve in 1963.

His fee for that United Artists production would enable Steve and Neile to buy their dream home in February 1963 on Oakmont Drive, Brentwood, which they would refer to as 'The Castle'. It was Fortress McQueen! But for Steve, materialism never really meant much other than security for his family and was actually a kick for him to think that a street hustler of some seven years earlier had made it to this. It was a game he was winning.

And that same childish sense of fun and adventure was soon felt by his neighbours, notably his co-star in *The Great Escape* James Garner, who was also housed on Oakmont. Steve liked to lob his empty beer cans into Garner's neat and tidy garden. He could not resist it, with the flowers so perfectly trimmed and with no newspapers lying around. Garner knew where the beer cans were coming from but never let on. "That was Steve," Garner said. "Deep down, he was just a wild kid. I think he thought of me as an older brother and I guess I thought of him as a younger brother; a delinquent younger brother." Steve insisted 'The Castle' had a gym to maintain his daily workout routine. Even when on location, he would always insist in his contracts that the producers provide him with training apparatus.

While savouring his newly-found status as a Hollywood star, Steve always found time for racing – cars or bikes. It was the fix in his life that he craved. "He was nuts about anything that had four, six, eight or 12 pistons, anything with four wheels or two wheels," commented friend John Leyton. "He absolutely loved anything to do with motor racing. I visited Steve at his house in the Hollywood Hills once and he was like a little boy at the time because he had just bought a D-type Jaguar and he thought it was wonderful."

At this time, while making *Love with the Proper Stranger* with Natalie Wood, Steve told hairdresser Sugar Blymyer (also known as Maryce Bates) of his and Neile's extravagant plan to extend their family by adopting Mexican children. Steve was known to fantasise at times and this may well have been such an example. McQueen had enjoyed his time in the country while making *The Magnificent Seven* but it was little known that he wished to adopt. "We had a Mexican lady that watched our kids as we had three daughters at home," Blymyer said, "and it was such a shame that while she was looking after my kids in California, she had four daughters of her own back in Mexico. I felt kind of bad, so we put in the papers to adopt them and they got to come up and live with us. They later became (American) citizens. Steve was taking in this story of mine backstage; he was really interested and was talking about how he and Neile might also do something like that." Although that never did happen, Steve and his third and final wife Barbara Minty adopted a street kid from the Chicago slums while he was making *The Hunter*. She shifted to California for improved schooling and opportunities and made a success of her life, thanks to Steve's generosity.

An exhausted Steve and Neile took most of 1964 off after three movies came out the previous year, while *Baby, the Rain Must Fall* hit the box-office on January 15, 1965. Steve's greatest thrill of the year and indeed one of the best of his lifetime was representing the USA motocross team in the International Six-Day Trials in East Germany. Prior to arriving behind the Iron Curtain, the team first arrived in England to collect their Triumph motorcycles. Jock Wilson, an employee with the manufacturer, remembered how Steve impressed everyone by his down-to-earth manner. "The first day in England, he arrived as a megastar; after that he was a motorcyclist like everyone else, just one of the boys. If anybody had tried to treat him like a movie star, he wouldn't have liked it. He never acted as though he could walk on water or anything like that. He was quite a modest guy." Wilson was surprised at Steve's easy-going nature and was therefore happy to oblige when the movie star asked him if he could arrange for a sign-writer to paint the Stars and Stripes on their van, which they used to transport the bikes. Steve poured himself into preparations for the Trials, to the same degree as if getting into character for a movie. He worked at Bud Ekins' workshop in an effort to become more proficient with spanners and such like, so that he could change rear tubes and other components in a reasonable time. Wilson recalled a tale of the movie star's garage experience. "These burly biker types would turn up for assistance, to get their puncture or whatever fixed, and Steve McQueen would show up and go to work. That sums the guy up."

Steve proudly carried the American flag at the pre-event parade and was accompanied by his good friend and stuntman Bud Ekins, and the remaining three team members Dave Ekins, Cliff Coleman and John Steen. Steve was rider No. 278 on a 650cc Triumph. He was set for a gold medal until he was cut up by another rider that sent him and his bike flying into the air, before landing on mud and rocks, sustaining a split chin and beat-up knees. His bike was far worse off and spelt the end of his race. Dave Ekins and Coleman, though, collected gold medals and Steen silver. "I was plenty disappointed at not being able to finish," Steve said later, "(but) I'd proved that I was capable of holding my own against world-class riders, and that was my *real* satisfaction."

Steve's appearance at those World Trials was partly acknowledged and honoured 35 years on, when he was posthumously inducted into the American Motorcycle Association Hall of Fame in 1999 after being nominated by the general public, and especially an appreciative motorcycling community. He earned his place on two fronts: for his off-road biking ability as demonstrated in Germany, and for being an ambassador for the sport, for which there can be no question after his daredevil and exhilarating riding in *The Great Escape* and then his input to *On Any Sunday* in 1971. "There is no doubt on this second point," said Jeff Heininger, chairman of the American Motorcycle Heritage Foundation, which oversees the AMA Motorcycle Hall of Fame. "McQueen's well-documented rise to stardom in the 1960s and 70s occurred at the same time that the popularity of motorcycling in the U.S. was exploding. He was a true riding enthusiast and off-road competitor and not, in the words of motorcyclists, 'just a poser.' His reputation as an independent person who forsook tradition and conformity resonated not only with his millions of film fans, but also with motorcyclists who pursued their love of riding in the face of criticism from family and friends during an era when the general public still associated motorcycling with hooliganism. There are many motorcyclists who have enjoyed successful careers in film and television. Peter Fonda, who produced and starred in *Easy Rider*, and Marlon Brando, James Dean, Clint Eastwood and Lee Marvin were also riders. But McQueen was certainly one of the most skilled motorcyclists to achieve international film stardom."

Steve always felt more comfortable in the company of bikers and car racers than movie producers or actors. He was a star from his acting but he never quite felt at ease in that world as he did when chilling with his buddies at a race meet or biking for fun in the desert. "That is not even debatable," former biking World Champion Mert Lawwill said, after he struck up a friendship with Steve during the making of *On Any Sunday*. "That is 100 per cent a fact. When I was doing my rehab at Steve's after a serious accident I had, Steve would be practicing his motocross and asked me to teach him to ride. He was obviously an excellent rider already but just wanted some expert feedback I suppose. It was funny because I would say, 'Well you're turning a little late here and turning too soon there,' and he looked at me and said, 'Sure, it's easy for you to say!' He wanted the advice but maybe didn't appreciate what I had to say, but it was all in good fun."

Photographer friend William Claxton had similar fun with Steve as far as bikes were concerned. Biking was Steve's release from the world, when he needed the company of buddies he could relax around and enjoy a few beers and a joint or two. "It wasn't unusual to receive a phone call at about 5am on a Sunday morning," Claxton said. "I'd roll over, half-awake, and answer the phone. On the other end I'd hear: 'Hey, Clax. It's Steve. What's happenin'? Want to go out with us? I'm meeting Bud (Ekins) and Don (Gordon) and some of the other cats up at Palmdale. You know, DuPar's greasy spoon. Bring your axe (camera). We'll load our bikes on Bud's truck. Scarf some breakfast, eggs, sunny-side-up, bacon, hash browns. It'll be a blast. Smoke a little grass. Watch the sun come up over the desert.' All of this in rapid, hushed tones – 'We'll chase some jackrabbits across the Mojave; do some wheelies in the sun; we'll have a ball. I know your old lady's going to be pissed. So's mine. How 'bout it? Meet you in Palmdale in 52 minutes. Ok'?"

Steve was never happier than when he was
riding his dirt bike in the desert
(COURTESY: THE BRITISH FILM INSTITUTE)

The mid-sixties was Steve's golden era. After *The Great Escape*, his star was already riding high but a run of five box-office hits from *The Cincinnati Kid* through *Nevada Smith, The Sand Pebbles, The Thomas Crown Affair* and *Bullitt* cemented his iconic status. In February 1965, Steve became the first man to be featured on the cover of the trendy fashion magazine *Harpar's Bazaar*. In 1966, he received his only Academy Award nomination, for *The Sand Pebbles*. His lack of recognition was generally attributed to his anti-establishment nature that did not sit too well with those on the Academy board. Steve once told co-star on *Pebbles* Joe Turkel during the making of that movie, "I found out one day that I could do something pretty good so I work hard at it'. Turkel added: "What does that tell you? He was abused as a kid, he was told he couldn't do anything (good) as a kid, he never had a father every day to guide him. He was aware that he was a troubled kid, and that sentence, 'I found out that I could do something good' really struck a chord with me. It buttressed him up and made him feel good. He then put his heart and soul into acting and he was damned good at it." Steve was never phoney about anything, maybe apart from hiding his womanising behind his wives' backs. But generally he was a straight, honest and upfront guy and this was also the case with his acting ability. He knew he wasn't a Cary Grant or a Jimmy Cagney, but he also knew what worked for him. Steve once commented: "I am a limited actor. My range isn't that great and I don't have that much scope. I'm pretty much myself most of the time in my movies and I have accepted that."

Although Steve was no one's angel, far from it, he did hold some old-fashioned values as far as his movies went and opposed gratuitous violence, swearing or nudity in movies. That was one of the reasons why he did not support director Sam Peckinpah after he was axed on *The Cincinnati Kid* after just four days, as the controversial film-maker had shot a nude scene with aspiring actress Sharon Tate. Incidentally, neither Peckinpah nor Tate had any involvement with the eventual picture. The aftermath of *The Cincinnati Kid* was significant for Steve in that his mother passed away from a cerebral haemorrhage. The psychological pain from his unfinished business with her, in never having the deep conversations he so wanted, to discuss the pain he had caused in shunning her and no doubt the upset she had caused him years before, haunted him for years after.

Steve followed many other Hollywood greats on March 21, 1967 – three days before his 37th birthday – by becoming the 153rd star to put his hand and footprints in cement at the famous Grauman's Chinese Theatre in Hollywood. Curiously, though, Steve only received his star on the Hollywood Walk of Fame on June 12, 1986. From the moment *The Great Escape* hit the screens to the time Steve took a time-out after *The Towering Inferno* in 1974, Steve McQueen was the hottest movie star in the world. LeVar Burton was a kid in those days and although he got to star alongside Steve on his swansong movie in 1980, *The Hunter*, he well remembers the impression that Steve made on him and the world during those times when Hollywood producers were tripping over themselves to sign him to their projects.

THE MAN BEHIND THE MOVIE STAR

"I was born in the fifties, and in the sixties he was the quintessential movie star," Burton enthused. "He was the icon of the era. He was the guy everyone wanted to be and have a beer with and he was the guy who every lady wanted to bed. I don't know why but I never did talk about his career with him. He was the kind of guy that when he was with you he just wanted to be in the moment. This conversation, this can of beer, this time. This is where we are. Here and now."

One element of Steve's character that was constant from his youth to his latter days was his appreciation of the opposite sex. To put it bluntly, Steve could not say 'no' and cheated on all three wives, though less so and before marriage in the case of Barbara Minty. He had a macho, rebellious charm that women knew they should probably resist, but rarely could. His movie star image only added to the attraction as the years passed. Steve loved all his three wives deeply and he was a devout family man. Nothing was ever more important to him than his 'Old lady' and his kids. But he also had double standards and a shameless want to sleep with any woman that attracted him. Of this there is no doubt.

Neile's forgiveness for his flings was admirable. Steve told her about some of those times when the guilt weighed heavily on his shoulders, but he kept most of his philandering to himself. Neile commented: "I was McQueen's queen and there was no denying that. The man loved me, and I knew it. And yet, on the other hand, there was this quirk, this need in his personality to flex his muscles outside the marriage bed. At first he was not indiscreet, and I doubt I would have found out about his extracurricular activities were it not for his need to confess them to me to relieve him of his guilt...I knew that his bed-hopping meant no more to him than a drive around the block. As he used to say, 'You can only say 'no' so many times'."

Steve's flings were usually more casual than full-blown affairs. He was like a little kid in a candy store as far as women were concerned and if he wanted to enjoy some something sweet, he often helped himself. Steve McQueen worried about nothing or no one. Even after his divorces to Neile and Ali MacGraw, Steve once said to Neile that he was building a ranch and why couldn't all three of his wives go live with him under the same roof! He was joking, of course, but Neile detected a slight grain of seriousness. Joe Turkel said: "Steve loved southern California, he loved motorcycles but he also loved girls. There's a story that one of his friends told me: He was riding along on his motorcycle and happened to see this pretty girl standing on a street corner in LA. He just whipped over to her and said, 'Come on honey, I'm Steve McQueen, let's go and have a little bit.' And she was thrilled and jumped on this motorcycle and off they went. His wife didn't know, nobody knew, so that was ok!"

Steve could be choosy when it came to women. After all, with his status, he had the pick of the bar, the restaurant, the grocery store or the movie set. His co-star on the 1972 picture *Junior Bonner* was Barbara Leigh, and they shared a love affair before, during and after that film. Barbara came to understand Steve's taste in women. "Steve only liked very beautiful women, mostly exotic looking women," commented Leigh. "I know because one of my girlfriends was Miss New Mexico and third runner-up to Miss World, and she hit on Steve but he turned her down. She was a blonde, blue-eyed beauty. People make Steve out to be someone who chased every girl in a skirt – ugly or not – but in reality he was a spoiled brat in his movie star years and he only settled for what he thought was the most beautiful."

Cracks began to appear in Steve and Neile's marriage from the late sixties onwards, to their eventual divorce in 1972. She had noted that he began acting more like a "spoiled brat" like when he demanded a pool table be moved into his twelfth floor rented apartment in San Francisco while making *Bullitt*. The table could not fit into the elevator and a crane was hired to swing it into his room, after the window was removed to accommodate it. He had that kind of power and wasn't afraid of using it. These times also coincided with his increased use of drugs, though Neile had been accustomed to these habits for many years, and was encouraged to find hiding places at their home in case they were ever raided. Marijuana was his regular drug of choice, but he took cocaine and LSD frequently, too, but more so in the Love and Peace 'flower power' generation, which Steve felt a connection with. "Steve was beginning to alarm me," Neile wrote in her memoir *My Husband, My Friend*. "His use of grass was escalating steadily. What used to be indulged in after work or after dinner and before bedtime was now being used freely at all times of the day. Coke was also becoming part of his daily consumption.

He seemed to find a drug connection everywhere – in and out of the country."

An anonymous phone call that Steve took at that time also had a significant effect on his behaviour, and his marriage. The voice on the other end told Steve there was a list being published of all the gay people in Hollywood and his name was on it. Despite police and FBI checks on the call and the list, nothing ever came out, but the thought that his masculinity and sexuality could be brought into question disturbed him – deeply. Subconsciously his womanising outside of his marriage increased. "That fuckin' list had twisted my head so bad, baby," he would later tell Neile, "that I felt I had to prove to the whole goddamn world I was Steve McQueen super-stud."

The final nail in the coffin of Steve and Neile's marriage was a row that took place in France, back at their chateau while he was filming *Le Mans*. He managed to persuade her to snort a line of cocaine, even though she was dead against drugs, as he quizzed her over and over as to how she could possibly have remained faithful all these years when she knew he had strayed many times over. The effect of the drug meant she surrendered her rebuttal and admitted to a one-off fling with a Hollywood star. Even though he had slept with literally hundreds of women during their marriage, behind her back, he could never accept Neile's sole indiscretion. They tried to salvage their marriage for the following 18 months but his violent temper towards her, fuelled by her affair that he could just

Steve and friend from *On Any Sunday* Bruce Brown
during a fishing trip in Alaska
(COURTESY: BRUCE BROWN)

not move on from, meant divorce was inevitable. Both saw psychiatrists to ease their own pain, hers stemming from a husband who was becoming ever more abusive and unforgiving towards her, and his from a betrayal of loyalty by a woman he loved more than anyone. The history of his relationship with his mother likely sparked a dis-trust in women within him. He could not handle the realisation that the one woman he saw as dependable as could be had been unfaithful to him. Few would have blamed Neile for her fling, which was merely to escape the increasing torture of her disintegrating marriage, especially considering the amount of 'fuck-flings' he had over the course of their marriage, but Steve never saw it like that. Their divorce was officially ratified in Santa Monica on April 26, 1972. They remained in touch almost daily to discuss matters pertaining to the children. Admirably, despite their own initial discomfort together as ex-husband and wife, both Steve and Neile never used Terry or Chad to gain any parental brownie points and allowed them to live with whichever parent they wished, and to freely come and go between them.

Although Steve had pretty much driven Neile to the situation of divorce, it was not something he was happy about. He loved her dearly and had lost his soul mate. The split hurt him deeply. Bruce Brown, the director and creator of *On Any Sunday*, which Steve appeared in and was an executive producer on, encouraged Steve to get away from the gloom of his private life. The two had become good friends during their time making the film and were alike in many ways. It turned out to be quite a trip for Steve, who was unable to keep his rebellious instincts at bay. "Steve and Bruce went to Alaska on a fishing trip around the time when Steve's divorce to Neile was going through, when he was really down and depressed," said Bob Bagley, a long-time friend of Brown's and also the cinematographer and production manager for *On Any Sunday*. "Bruce suggested they went fishing to take his mind off his divorce, and Steve agreed.

"One of their guides had a front-wheel drive car, which Steve wanted to test drive to see how it handled. After a day of fishing, in the wee hours of the morning, he and Bruce took the car to a mall parking and put it through its paces. The police arrived and put Bruce and Steve on the hood, cuffed them and took them to the local station where they were arrested (Steve had to return to Anchorage for the subsequent hearing). While the cops gave them a grilling, Steve asked them, in a self-effacing manner, 'Hey you guys, didn't any of you ever see *The Blob*?' It was interesting that he would ask them about one of the worst films he ever did and that he didn't say *The Great Escape*. That was Steve; he wasn't glorifying himself but was having fun at his own expense. And another thing Steve did while in that police station was to introduce Bruce as his personal assistant, and said if mug shots were forthcoming, Bruce was the only one who could take his picture, which he did! This was typical Steve. He was a fun-loving guy who, deep down, really didn't take himself too seriously. I find it hard to believe that he was mean-spirited as some have tried to make him."

The hurt from his divorce was fuelled by rejection, a fear that extended across all axis of Steve's life. When directors Robert Wise and Norman Jewison snapped at him during *The Sand Pebbles* and *The Cincinnati Kid* respectively, in response to Steve's badgering and questioning, he never spoke to them for days, licking his wounds like a scolded infant. And he had friends and colleagues who received the same child-like but strangely endearing treatment. Steve was the most loyal of friend's, but if he felt that loyalty was not reciprocated, that was it. He had known Robert Relyea for over a decade by the time their shared Solar Productions' empire and indeed their friendship hit troubled waters during *Le Mans*. Steve never forgave Relyea for his flippant remark, unknowingly in the company of a CBS employee that the film "was out of control". This comment was followed by heavy-handed treatment by the studio to complete the movie without losing any more money on it, as they saw it. McQueen did not speak to Relyea for years after the film, and even when they did meet again, things were awkward.

Similarly, Tim Zinnemann, the assistant director on *Bullitt* and *The Reivers* was also offered Steve's cold shoulder when he dared turn Steve's offer down to work on his beloved racing movie. "He was a very loyal friend and a great guy to be around," Zinnemann said. "He asked me to be on *Le Mans* and I said 'yes' at first and then later turned him down to work on *Carnal Knowledge*. It was something that I handled badly at the time. And he never spoke to me after that. Because of his extreme loyalty to his friends he took my knockback as a personal insult." Actor Don Gordon was a close friend of Steve's from his TV days in the late fifties right up until his death 20 years later. They acted in three movies together – *Bullitt, Papillon* and *The Towering Inferno* and although McQueen never admitted it, Gordon is well aware some of his best parts were because of McQueen's influence. Their bond wasn't always so close and the suspicious McQueen made Gordon earn his friendship. "He didn't trust anybody," said Gordon. "At first, before we became real good friends, he used to play games with me. He would give me a piece of information that he had obviously made up, which was quite outrageous, and he would wait to see whether it appeared in the newspapers. Of course it never would appear in the Press because it was nobody's business and more importantly because he was my friend. Eventually, he came to trust me and I trusted him."

Steve was infamously paranoid and troubled from as far back as his New York days in the fifties, but certain things that happened to him through his fame only strengthened those feelings. One such incident was his narrow escape that saw only fate steer him away from certain death. He had been invited to an intimate party by his hairdresser friend Jay Sebring, who was a friend and former lover of actress Sharon Tate. She was hosting the gathering at her husband Roman

Polanksi's home, while he was working on a movie in London. A casual rendezvous with another girlfriend saved Steve's life, for Charles Manson's brainwashed cult led a frenzied series of murders at the Polanski home on that August evening in 1969. The fine line between death and his good fortune shook Steve and made him all the more private and paranoid thereafter. He was rarely comfortable in crowds or amongst fans who demanded a piece of him, and for the final decade of his life, right up to his premature death in 1980, Steve shunned the limelight when possible. Sure, he had times in his life when he would wear a false beard and a baseball cap so not to be hassled by fans, but he would tire of people NOT recognizing him after a while and quickly remove his disguise. But in the latter years he was genuinely content with anonymity.

"I remember when we had dinner in Paris," recalled *Le Mans* co-star and Steve's off-screen love interest of the time Louise Edlind. "It might have been a great experience for me but maybe not for him as we were unwise enough to have a window table. We were like monkeys in a cage. It made me realise just how famous he was because people just stood and stared at him. But he didn't run out of the restaurant scolding people; he just sat there. I laughed at him because I suggested that he should like being recognised as a big star. He didn't seem to agree." Biking champion and colleague from *On Any Sunday* Mert Lawwill observed an equally uncomfortable side to Steve when confronted with the real possibility of a screaming public. "We were at LA airport one day and Steve just took off and I thought, 'Whoa, where's he off

Steve and co-star and off-screen girlfriend Barbara Leigh
embrace on *Junior Bonner*
(COURTESY: ABC / BARBARA LEIGH)

to in such a hurry?' We were walking as a group and Neile
and the kids were there too. But he just took off and went
on ahead. I asked him about it later why he took off on us so
fast. He explained that if he hung around long enough to get

recognised he would be mobbed and would not be able to move. That frightened him a lot."

Steve's paranoid instincts did not always serve him well, especially with regards to his work. He turned down the chance to star in many films over his career, and rightly so in most cases, but one he always regretted was *Butch Cassidy and the Sundance Kid*. He only lost out on the brilliantly-scripted film by William Goldman because of stubbornness of ridiculous proportions – borne by paranoia that Paul Newman might be getting a better deal than he, even when an equal cut and equality on the credits had been offered. Although Steve had first suggested flipping a coin for top billing, they then agreed to share top billing whereby McQueen's name came first but Newman's was higher on the right-hand side. It was all set until Steve thought about it some more and said, 'No. I want to flip a coin instead', which of course the sensible Newman was never going to agree to. Instead, Robert Redford came in and the film was a huge hit. Steve would say in later years, 'Every time I look in my rear-view mirror, I see Robert Redford.' At least the shared billing proposal *was* eventually used, on *The Towering Inferno* in 1974.

Actress and model Barbara Leigh was one of the first serious girlfriends Steve hooked up with once his marriage with Neile hit the rocks and was subsequently to end. He met her initially in the planning stages of *Junior Bonner*. She detected very quickly, on their second date in fact, Steve's impatient nature at being disturbed in public and his penchant for privacy. "During dinner Steve was twice asked for photographs," Leigh said. "The fans were nice enough and sweet, but Steve wouldn't give them his autograph. He really hated giving autographs, especially when he was eating, and he wasn't particularly nice about it either. It embarrassed me that he wouldn't just quickly sign a piece of paper for people who appreciated and acknowledged him as a movie star. He was a little mean-spirited about it. He explained to me that it wasn't he who was being rude, but the fans. He pointed out that it was they who interrupted his dinner, with no regard for his privacy. It wasn't how I would have handled the matter, but then again, he was the superstar."

Steve's relationship with Leigh was serious enough for him to introduce his children to her during the location work on *Junior Bonner* in Prescott, Arizona. They as good as lived together for the six weeks she was required but they continued to see one another once back in California also. Leigh claims Steve asked her to move in with him several times but her predicament was complicated somewhat by the fact she was also dating Elvis Presley and film executive James Aubrey at the same time. Their relationship fizzled out once Leigh became pregnant – with Steve's baby, though she never did tell him it was his and instead said it was Aubrey's. Steve was keen for a third child and what further added to Leigh's anguish was that Steve could not have been more supportive and friendly to her as she arranged to have the child aborted – to appease her real love at the time, Aubrey. That relationship was also soon to end. "Did I choose the right man: Jim over Steve? Absolutely not," Leigh reflected painfully. "But that is what I did at the time and in hindsight we would have probably broken up anyway, even with a baby. I was not mature enough or confident enough to hold a man like Steve, when at that time he could have any woman he wanted – and did. But we stayed in touch until he started breaking up with Ali and I moved to New York City and got married. I never told Steve that I was pregnant with his child; they are bad memories for me that have haunted me till this day. I've asked for forgiveness and I have gotten it, so I cannot dwell on that part of my life. Some things are best not talked about. But I do regret some choices I made in my life, like not moving in with Steve when he asked me to. I might have had his child and have a son today but it didn't work out that way, so again, I can't go there or dwell on that. Most people in life can reflect back and wish they had made different choices at some point or other. The answer is to move on, move forward with love in your heart and remember life is not always what you think, but what you make it."

Ali MacGraw came into Steve's life in early 1972, when she was his leading lady on *The Getaway*. He was single and she was married to Paramount Pictures executive Robert Evans, who it was said was a great producer and lovely gentleman and maybe was married to his job a little too much. The result of these twin circumstances was an almost immediate off-screen affair that blossomed through principal photography and thereafter. They would eventually marry on July 13, 1973, at Cheyenne, Wyoming. Over time, Steve's insecurities and preference that Ali stayed at home and shunned the movie world that was at her feet following three hits *Goodbye Columbus, Love Story* and *The Getaway* would seemingly create trouble for them as a couple. Steve never *forced* her to give up acting; that was Ali's decision alone, but he certainly made it be known he wasn't keen on her continuing her career as it was heading. Steve once said, "They call me a chauvinist pig. I am, and I don't give a damn!" That was Steve's take-it-or-leave-it attitude on life and most people took it.

His old-fashioned virtues were endearing in some ways, in that he wanted to be the breadwinner for his family, but in other ways, his philosophy was terribly outdated. But this was their marriage and Ali went along with Steve's wishes because she loved him. "I was willing to bet that Ali would never get to do a film without Steve," Neile said. "It would be ok if they worked together, but if she did, trouble would be sure to follow. My feeling is that Steve systematically went about destroying Ali's career because of his need to have her in his hip pocket at all times. He wanted her at the house because his mother hadn't been there when he had needed her." Psychological scars can sometimes stick around. Ali has since spoken out that their marriage was not all about "Bad Boy Steve and Saint Ali" and that a lack of communication was as much to blame for their eventual break-up as anything. They were just complete opposites in terms of their cultures with art student, museum-appreciating Ali trying to fit into the life of bike-loving, beer-swilling, dope-smoking Steve.

"With Steve I learned the rules early," Ali wrote in her autobiography *Moving Pictures*. "(He would say) 'Baby, you look great in jeans and a T-shirt. You have a great ass, but you better start working out now because I don't want to wake up one day with a woman who's got an ass like a 70-year-old Japanese soldier.' That put the fear of God in me, and sent me scurrying off to exercise classes with my dancer-choreographer friend Ron Fletcher, with whom I worked obsessively four or five days a week for five years."

Through his marriage to Ali, Steve gained a step-son Joshua, the son of Robert Evans. Steve came to love Joshua as his own and even after his marriage with Ali officially ended in 1978, he would still spend weekends with him, while living with his third wife Barbara Minty. It was tough on Ali that her years with Steve coincided with his hermit era, when he made so much money from three hits movies in a row *The Getaway, Papillon* and *The Towering Inferno* that he felt he did not need to work anymore and subsequently took two years out – it was a semi-retirement, until his yearning to get back into a film project snapped him out of that lethargic existence. This was merely the way he chose to live, he had had enough of Hollywood and of people in general and just wanted a quiet life with his wife, kids and his many bikes and cars that littered the street outside of his new home on Broad Beach Road, Trancas, northern Malibu.

"In the seventies I bought a house on Broad Beach Road where Steve lived – I lived next door to my good friend Jack Lemmon," recalled then neighbour and Steve's co-star on *Love with the Proper Stranger* Edie Adams. "Every once in a while Ali would talk Steve into going to the local property owners' meetings where you would discuss things like beach access and local events. I always felt that Steve was on Ali's case...'Don't get fat, don't gain weight, don't do this or don't do that.' I think that marriage was a rough go for Ali. He wouldn't let her go anywhere or have any friends. And he really didn't want her to gain any weight. So therefore I used to see her at the local exercise class a lot.

"Steve just sort of flaked out in the seventies. I didn't know whether it was to do with booze or something more but he just didn't want to socialise with anybody. He wasn't as direct or alert as he used to be. It was hard to get his attention. When he used to pass my house while walking his dogs, he'd sometimes wave but he never wanted to come in and socialise. He was a complete hermit. Steve never talked to too many people, until he found out that I was living there. And Chad and my daughters then became friends. Steve would pick up his mail from the nearby gas station as he didn't want anybody round at his place – not even the mail man. My kids went round to his place because Steve knew me. I used to see him at Trancas Market doing his shopping. He would usually

Ali MacGraw and Steve pictured during
The Getaway, when they fell in love
(COURTESY: NATIONAL GENERAL)

have a bottle of beer in his hand and a funny looking beach
hat on so nobody would recognise him."

Steve was still good company to his friends. He had got to
know Bill Pierce on *Junior Bonner* in 1971 and they remained
friends intermittently thereafter. Pierce was a film executive in Arizona and had made Steve's life easier during the

shoot and Steve never forgot and invited him to his home. "I went over to Malibu a couple of times and visited, and the last time he was with Ali MacGraw," Pierce said. "I first went to see Lucien Ballard, who was the cinematographer on *Junior Bonner* (*Nevada Smith* and *The Getaway* too), as he also lived on Malibu beach. He said, 'Steve's next door, he's waiting for you.' So I went over and knocked on the door. The door opened and there was this most gorgeous thing you have ever seen in your life without a stitch of clothes on. It was Ali; a beautiful woman. She said, 'Oh you must be Bill, come on in, we are out on the deck'. We talked about all kinds of different things but there was never any movie talk. We'd talk about what was happening in our lives, how our kids were doing, that type of thing. They seemed very happy." Ali looks back on that time as an era when a star's privacy was pretty well respected, and she despairs at how a private man like Steve would have coped in modern times with paparazzi's, 24-hour news and the never-ending feeding frenzy that is the media's insatiable appetite for celebrity gossip. Papers like the *National Enquirer* led the way with published gossip and news exclusives, but there were not dozens of cable news channels and websites all competing with one another for stories like there is today. "I think it is absolutely horrendous that there's no privacy now," she commented. "I think something will soon have to be done to protect people from hacking and blogging and lying and spreading rumours and chasing you down the street. Lives are wrecked that way. I feel very lucky that I was at the tail-end of some ability to control my privacy. After all, I was married to the biggest movie star in the world and when we went to live in Malibu, we were just people who lived there. Nobody was sitting outside of a Starbucks waiting to see if there was something going on. I don't know how people handle it."

Steve barely spoke to the media in the 1970s and refused all Press interviews. The media was just another invasion of his privacy. Even later in his life, when learning to fly, Steve issued a polite warning to his 20-year-old flying instructor Pete Mason, after he requested a photograph. "He didn't like photos or photographers," Mason recalled, "but that was what (his third wife) Barbara did. I asked his permission to take a picture from the front seat of an airplane over my head to the back seat while we were in flight. He said, 'Yeah go ahead. But if I see anything in the *National Enquirer*, you're history!' He really did not like the *National Enquirer* one iota. He didn't want anything to do with that rag."

Like Neile, Ali was beautiful and smart, but she could also be feisty and upfront with Steve in a way that Neile had often been tolerant when maybe a more aggressive reaction would not have been unreasonable, given some of Steve's antics over the years. Executive producer on *Papillon* Emanuel Wolf recalls one exchange between them that he felt demonstrated Steve's controlling, paranoid nature and also Ali's dry sense of humour in dealing with her husband. "We had a final cut screening of *Papillon* in Los Angeles and of a 40-minute documentary that we put together," Wolf said. "Although I had the word on final cut I also needed Steve's approval. So we watched the footage and came outside and we're standing there chatting when Ali says, 'Well I'm going to leave you boys to talk about the picture. I've got a few errands to run.' Steve was visibly disturbed by this. He turned to her and said, 'Where are you going?' She said she had just a few things to do. He came back again and asked, 'Well, can't you tell me where you're going?' And she'd had enough of this and said, 'Well I'm going out to get laid.' (Director and Producer) Franklin Schaffner was a very straight guy, I'm standing next to him and Steve's agent Freddie Fields was also there – we didn't know where to look and were looking up at the sky while he and Ali were having this diatribe. It was very funny, but very awkward."

Ali suffered a miscarriage during their marriage, which occurred on the studio lot during filming of *The Towering Inferno*. Tragically, it was the third occasion within three years that Steve almost had a third child but circumstances ruled otherwise. Steve was fully in agreement about Neile's abortion in 1970 when her pregnancy was discovered during the filming of *Le Mans*, in the middle of their darkest days; while he never knew about Barbara Leigh being pregnant with his child. Ali's sad loss made for a shocking day in their five-year marriage. Who knows how the arrival of a child may have impacted on their relationship and whether it may have brought some calm and permanency to their marriage?

Steve took on an apartment at the Beverly Wilshire Hotel in late 1976 supposedly to be closer to the studios for his new movie project *An Enemy of the People*, but another reason was so that he could date women more freely as his relationship with Ali dismantled. Eventually, in November 1977, Steve filed for divorce and it went through the following year, without Ali receiving a single penny, even though she had forgone her once-burgeoning career for the time of their being together. Ali admitted years after that she was too proud in not asking for any financial settlement from Robert Evans or Steve, as she adjusted to a life that could and should have been much more comfortable. As Ali moved on with her life, Steve moved Barbara Minty into the Trancas beach house, which Ali had renovated so tastefully with her artistic talents.

Steve first caught sight of model Barbara Minty when he was on a plane and she was adorning one of the inflight magazines. Never one to miss an opportunity, he phoned her agent and requested a meeting with them, supposedly to discuss a role in his next movie. But all along it was purely an excuse to have a date with her. They first met on July 4, 1977 for a lunch at the Beverly Wilshire. He soon removed his camouflage and Barbara, then 24, was gradually seduced by the charming movie star, who was 23 years older than her.

Barbara quickly learned that times with Steve would never be boring, and usually involved road trips for fun and adventure. They would travel light and arrange their accommodation as they moved around. On one particular trip, when they passed through Lolo in Idaho, looking for somewhere to lodge, Steve was mesmerized by watching a normal family scene through the window of this one house. Barbara had to break him from his stare and Steve insisted on an introduction. When the owner of the house answered the door, Steve, from his position on the doorstep, took little time in commenting on the delightful culinary smells drifting through from the kitchen – and was happy to join this family for dinner when the offer came. This was at a time when Steve had a bushy caveman beard and matching hairstyle and therefore he went unrecognized. Barbara and Steve had so much fun with this family they ended up staying a few days for more dinners, drinking and even some fishing. Steve never had that stable family life when he was a young boy, and it may just be that his time around this family gave him a taste of what he had missed in his youth. He also enjoyed being treated as just another guy and appreciated how this family treated him and Barbara generously because they were kind and not because he was a film star. That was, until he missed the attention of being recognised! When that happened, he was always happy to unmask the movie star.

Steve had mellowed considerably by the time Barbara came into his life and he was not as paranoid or competitive as had been the norm for so many years. He was secure in himself for what he had and for what he had achieved. There was still the odd flash of the old Steve once in a while, though. *Tom Horn* screenwriter Bud Shrake recalled: "I was round at Steve's beach house one day and he got really pissed with Barbara. She was doing the washing and had put all the pink towels in with the white. So they all became pink. I don't think it took much for Steve to get irritated with people; though he was always great with me. I liked him a lot."

Steve sold his beach house in June 1979 and eventually shifted to Santa Paula, about an hour's drive north of Malibu. He and Barbara lived in an airplane hangar for six months until a suitable property became available. Steve was never one to live the typical glitzy Hollywood lifestyle and he would likely have been happy to remain in the hangar, though Barbara put her foot down and she had her house, though was not sorry to experience the primitive yet charming adventures that the hangar brought them. Their age gap made little difference to their intimacy and the fun they shared. They got along like an old married couple. They would spend Saturday nights watching *Benson, Loveboat* and *Fantasy Island*, while Steve also loved to watch classic old movies from the 1930s and 40s. They were happy times.

Steve had by now left the bikes and cars and his old buzz of racing behind; he had a new love – flying. He started flying seriously in 1979, and even persuaded Barbara to fly too. Steve loved the freedom that aviation gave him. There is a possibility he also wanted to emulate the father he never knew, who he had been told was an ace pilot. Steve bought a $35,000 bright yellow PT Stearman airplane, which was built in the 1940s for the US Navy. He saw it advertised in the local classifieds, which he ritualistically used to thumb through each morning with coffee in-hand. Steve loved to hoard antiques such as old toys, motorcycle parts, road signs, furniture and more. He was so enamoured with anything old and charming or just plain quirky he insisted that his contract for *The Hunter*, his final movie in 1980, had a clause that allowed him to keep all the props in the movie.

Pete Mason, now a manager at Santa Paula Airport, remembered how Steve tracked down his father when intent on taking to the skies. "Steve, evidently, wanted to fly and he was walking around Santa Paula Airport one day and wandered into a hangar owned by Perry Schreffler (a retired U.S. Air Force Lieutenant Colonel)," Mason recounted. "Perry didn't know who this guy was because when Steve wasn't working, he had this scruffy beard and long hair. Perry advised Steve the best way to learn was with a military instructor in a Stearman and recommended my Dad (Sammy Mason). That night my Dad got a phone call – I was 20 then and was still living at home. I heard my Dad say on the phone he wasn't taking any more primary students and was concentrating on aerobatic flight mentoring. After five minutes of politely saying 'no', he got off the phone and came to me and said,

'Have you ever heard of an actor called Steve McQueen?' I said, 'Yeah Dad! One of your favourite movies is *The Great Escape*. Remember the guy on the bike who got caught up in the fence? Well, that was McQueen.' I told my Dad that as I was also an instructor I would be happy to do it. McQueen wouldn't take no for an answer and when he called back ten minutes later, my Dad said he would do it if he could team up with me and we could both teach him. McQueen wanted to do a lot of flying so my Dad did the intense instruction and I did the fun stuff, flying to places like Portabella, Watsonville and flying over his (old) house in Trancas before doing a loop back from there and a bit of cross-country flying, too."

Steve was a natural pilot, though there was one aspect he struggled to grasp. When on the ground in a Stearman, it requires the pilot to steer the rudder pedals with the feet, so when you want to turn left you push with your left foot and when you want to turn right you push with your right. And it requires a quick reaction, too, after landing. Steve just could not master this one thing and it really annoyed him. That was until he realised why he was having problems. It transpired that when he was a kid he used to ride a homemade go-kart and to steer that, it was left foot for right and right foot for left, and decades on it was still his instinct to steer that way. Once he was able to address this small issue, he flew expertly; even becoming as determined a pilot as he was a racing driver. He couldn't resist a challenge and when Pete Mason offered to take the controls on a particularly gusty flight, Steve refused to back down and subsequently performed one of his best-ever landings.

Steve enjoyed the quieter life up-coast and would almost certainly have spent many more years there had his terminal illness not so cruelly struck him. Pete's nephew Mike recalled how Steve would clown around with him. "I was only about 12 at the time, and when I first met Steve he taught me a funny handshake he said he learned from some local hooligans while filming one time. He always welcomed me into his hangar to look at his motorcycles and various cool stuff. He had a .22 Gatling gun that I really liked. He was always generous to me with his time but not having seen many movies, I did not then grasp that he was such a famous guy."

Pete Mason's father Sammy became a close friend to the McQueen's and was also a key influence on Steve becoming a born-again Christian in 1979, a year before his death. He and Barbara started attending the Ventura Missionary Church Service every Sunday. "I suspect Steve knew something wasn't quite right health-wise in that time frame – maybe that had something to do with it," commented Pete Mason. Steve's old friend from *Junior Bonner* Bill Pierce offered another reason for his late switch towards Christ, saying: "Steve became very spiritual towards the end, and I am sure he had some regrets about the things he did in life, like fooling around with women while he was married, but we all have regrets, don't we."

Friend and instructor Sammy Mason tutors
Steve in his beloved Stearman biplane
(COURTESY: WENDELL DOWLING)

Russell S. Doughten, associate producer on *The Blob*, recalled how Steve was not all that enamoured with religion when he worked on the film in 1958 despite a crew who were all devout Christians, though Steve was always willing to listen and learn about their faith. "We were making a horror film yet we were a Christian film company," Doughten said. "I had spoken to Steve about the Lord and the Scriptures and although he did his own thing much of the time and kept himself to himself, he heard me out. When we finished on the movie I gave him my copy of the Bible, which I had marked up. That was my way of wishing him well. Later on, when we met up in California as we were both working out there, he indicated to me that he was reading a Scripture. Then much later on, after he died, I was told that the copy of the Scripture I had given him was on his bedside table in his bedroom. That to me seemed a curious thing and perhaps suggested that he cared more for religion all those years ago than he let on."

The mischievous Steve McQueen was never far away, even during these worrying times when his declining health was concerning him, privately. After one practice flight to Monterrey with Pete Mason, he said to the young man, 'Come on, we're going to church as I promised your Dad I'd take you.' Mason recalled: "We found this random Catholic Church and Steve did something with water, he knelt on a pew and prayed for a couple of minutes, and I followed his lead. As we were leaving, he said, 'I might be a Christian, but there's something I want you to know. I'm never gonna give up beer and I'm never gonna give up women! I have told all my friends this and if they see me getting married again they are supposed to come and drag me away.' So when he got married to Barbara, it was a surprise to me."

Steve felt ill during the filming of *Tom Horn* in early 1979 and assumed he had pneumonia. However, towards the end of filming he had begun to cough up blood. On December

17, 1979, almost a month after principal photography had finished on his final movie *The Hunter*, he was diagnosed with an incurable cancer. This at a time when Steve had made his money, made his life, and found happiness. He had once commented, years before: "I just want the pine trees and my kids and the green grass. I want to get rich and fat and watch my children grow." Sadly, fate had other ideas. It was a particularly violent form of cancer too: mesothelioma is a rare form that attacks the protective lining covering many of the internal organs of the body, especially the lungs. It is most commonly caused by exposure to asbestos, which Steve could trace back to his Marine Corp days when the ship on which he worked had asbestos lined in its ceiling. He also wore fireproof suits and hoods so often when racing cars in the 1950s and 60s, with the old-fashioned ones containing traces of asbestos.

On December 22, a biopsy at Cedars Sinai Hospital revealed a massive malignant tumour in his right lung. Only Barbara, his trusted friend Sammy Mason and ranch-hand Grady Ragsdale were present and were sworn to secrecy. While doctors and specialists told him to prepare for the worst, giving him months to live, Steve's instant reaction was one of typical determination with a will to fight it and beat it. Steve wanted to keep the grim news private, from media, friends, and especially his children. He spent Christmas in hospital and, sadly, would never get another chance for one at home with his family, even though he made grand plans for all of them to be reunited for Christmas the following year. Steve tried courageously to beat the disease by opting for alternative medicines like vitamin infusions and bizarre dietary concoctions, courtesy of Doctor William Kelley's controversial treatments. This after conventional doctors had given up on him.

Although Steve received the deadly news in late 1979, many felt he had known something was not right for a long time before then. Neile believed his problems may even have started as early as 1972 when he had a potentially dangerous polyp removed from his vocal cord after endless bouts of coughing. *Tom Horn* screenwriter Bud Shrake spent six months with Steve in 1978 and remained adamant that McQueen was going to reveal his deepest health worries. "Initially, Steve had told me that he had walking pneumonia but said not to tell anyone because he didn't want the insurance companies to find out as they might have cancelled the insurance on the movie," Shrake commented.

"One day Steve said to me, 'Bud, I want to tell you a big, big, big, major secret. Come into my study.' So we went into this room, which was about the size of a boxcar and he then closed the door and locked it. The walls were absolutely covered with pictures of Ali MacGraw. There were also lots of guns, pistols, rifles, ammunition, all sorts of shit lying around. So then Steve got ready to tell me this big secret and first asked me if I wanted some coffee. I said, 'Yeah, sure,' and as he went to press this buzzer that opens the door, the electricity went out and we were stuck there until one of his aides came and got us out. He never did tell me that secret but after he died, I realised that he was going to tell me he thought he had cancer. I can't think what else would have been so important. It would have killed the movie had it got out that he was sick, and he knew it."

On finding out his unofficial death sentence that was the dreaded 'Big C', Steve set about calling his old buddies and trusted colleagues. He wanted to speak to old friends he had lost touch with but also smooth over relationships that had suffered bumpy times over the years. "He called lots of people up and was making his peace with us all, and wanted to say hello before it was goodbye," said English actress Shirley Anne Field, who co-starred with Steve on *The War Lover* in 1962 and who Steve had not always been over-friendly to. But there was another reason for his call to her, out of the blue. "Our conversations were mostly about his health. He had remembered that I lost my sister in 1967 to cancer and he thought he could talk to me without me giving him away, which of course I didn't. Steve told me he was going to try this health clinic in Mexico; I thought he was very brave through his illness."

Another to receive the McQueen farewell call was his old friend and business partner Robert Relyea. They had fallen out and lost touch after the disaster that was *Le Mans*, but Steve knew the history they had together was more meaningful than what now seemed a petty squabble given his predicament at that time. "Out of the blue Steve rang and asked if I fancied having dinner with him the following evening – just as if we'd gone out the night before when in fact it had been years," Relyea recalled. "We ate at the

Beverly Wilshire. After dinner we walked around the block and spoke for a couple of hours about nothing in particular. We then shook hands and that was the last time we ever spoke to one another."

Perhaps one of the most moving of all Steve's goodbyes was with his former co-star and close friend Don Gordon. "Just before he got sick I was having dinner with him over at my beach-house and he said to me, 'You know Don, I've got this cough and I can't get over it and I don't know what the hell is the matter with me.' Anyway, about two weeks later I had to go to Europe to do a movie and I called him up to say goodbye. He invited me round to his place – the airplane hangar where he was living. We chatted there for a while and he said, 'When you get back you will have to come up and fly with me.' I told him I would love that. Then we said our goodbyes and it was then that he did something that he had never done before; he put his arm around me and hugged me and said, 'I'll see you later.' I realised after that he must have known he was quite sick and that he was on his way out. It was his way of saying goodbye – forever – and it touched me a great deal. I still find it hard to deal with. It's like I lost a brother."

Steve married Barbara Minty on January 16, 1980 at their Santa Paula home, three days before Neile re-married. "Barbara was not a gold digger, he was attracted to her and they were good together," Pete Mason said of the couple. "I remember at a motel in Portabella, he was sitting down in this chair and she was snipping away at his hair and they just looked like a real happy couple in love."

Steve and third wife Barbara Minty, in March 1980
(COURTESY: AP)

Their 11-month marriage was sadly dominated by the ordeal that confronted Steve, as he faced the toughest battle of his life. Many, especially Neile, felt Steve made a mistake in employing the services of Dr. William Kelley's experimental methods, but he was playing the best hand he felt was available to him. "Who has the right to judge?" Steve's late daughter Terry commented years after his passing. "There was nothing at home they could do; his cancer was inoperable. Doctor after doctor said, 'All we can do is make him comfortable.' Someone gave him light at the end of a very dark tunnel – and so he went there." Steve had a special diet, such as raw liver blended with apple or pineapple juice, while additional food packages were flown down from California to the Mexican border, where it would be couriered across to him. It wasn't uncommon for a few bottles of beer to be included.

During Steve's painful, last few months, he was being pressed by the clinic to publicize their work and what they were doing for him. Neile, for one, was furious that they would seek any sort of endorsement without any obvious, positive results being seen. In essence the fact Steve agreed to be treated at the clinic under their rules, was an endorsement in itself; he didn't need to be giving media conferences about it. Three months before Steve's death, People magazine hailed Doctor Kelley as 'McQueen's Holistic Medicine Man.'

Steve returned to Santa Paula two weeks before his eventual death, seemingly to others he was returning home to die in his beloved California. But on his way back he stopped off for a CAT scan that revealed the cancer had spread viciously.

He was persuaded to undergo surgery at the Santa Rosa Clinic in Juarez, Mexico to remove huge tumours in his neck and stomach. The way he saw it, he was going to die anyway so why worry about the risk of surgery. He underwent the operation on November 6 in the presence of his two children. Terry and Chad departed later on, having been told his body had responded well to the surgery. But at 3.45am on November 7, 1980, Barbara and the children learned that Steve had lost his brave fight and died, due to heart failure, aged 50. His heart, which had withstood tremendous pain and hardship through a gruesome illness, had finally given out. His death may have officially been attributed to heart failure, but cancer was truly his killer.

The news stunned the world, even though his illness was already out there. It never made it any easier on his fans, his family or others who knew him. "When I heard of Steve's death I was at an awards night for the Actors Studio," said Steve's old co-star and friend Martin Landau. "It was a sad moment."

LeVar Burton, who Steve had taken delight in mentoring during his final movie *The Hunter*, was shocked and saddened when the news came. "Nobody wanted to acknowledge it when it came," Burton said. "After we finished *The Hunter* everyone went their separate ways and it was some months later that I heard that he had gone down to Mexico for the experimental treatment. That showed he was still fighting, he was still hanging in there and looking for another round. When he did go it was a real punch because you can't help thinking to yourself, 'If anyone can beat it, he can.' Cancer is not a pretty way to go out."

Cinematographer Fred Koenekamp worked with Steve on three movies and stayed in touch from first till last, *The Hunter*, which he worked on. Steve's passing left him numb. "The day Steve died I was on a picture working in the Californian mountains - it was snowing and very cold - then about ten in the morning a member of the crew came up to me and said, 'We've just heard Steve McQueen died.' It could have been anybody else and I would probably have not thought much about it, but it hit me like I had lost a real good guy - we shared some good times. The news really shook me up. It was a bad day."

For Steve's daughter Terry, the pain understandably lasted long after he was gone. "It was difficult to watch Dad's movies," she told *Hello*, nine years after his passing. "I'd feel the pain, remember those difficult months. Now I get a warm feeling. Very few people are fortunate enough to be able to turn on the TV and see someone they loved very much who has passed away." She went on to dedicate some of her own time working for the National Institute for Cancer Research before her own tragic, premature death in 1998.

Steve's funeral/memorial was held in the garden of his ranch at the base of the mountain in Santa Paula. It was more a celebration of Steve's amazingly eventful but all too short life, than a morbid affair, according to Pete Mason. He and his father performed a fly-by overhead tribute in Steve's beloved Stearman, before meeting with Ali MacGraw, Lee Majors and

LeVar Burton among others. "After the service, my Dad and I climbed into Steve's favourite yellow Stearman and flew a couple of miles along the shore," Mason remembered. "I took the controls at the front while my Dad carefully emptied Steve's ashes out into the air over the ocean. It was terribly sad."

Burton was honoured just to be invited to the occasion, which he recalled as being a very intimate affair. Many of Steve's former industry friends and colleagues would have loved to have paid their respects, but just as Steve would have wanted, this was for his nearest and dearest. "I was happy to be included as I knew a number of people who wanted to be there," Burton commented. "I felt like I was standing in for a lot of people whose lives he had touched throughout his life and career. It was sombre and sad as those occasions tend to be, but it was also really heartening. Having his airplane buddies do a flyover was really inspiring. It was sad but also liberating. We were at the house for the most part but afterwards I remember it being a long, quiet drive back to LA. That seemed really appropriate."

Steve's passing affected the lives of millions. Of course, primarily his family; Terry, Chad and step-son Joshua had lost a father who was always there for them as his own was not for him. Neile had lost her long-time husband but also one of her best friends, a soul mate, after they had long patched up their differences; Ali lost her ex-husband of six years, and had to deal with the pain of being shut out of Steve's life, post-divorce; and third wife Barbara Minty McQueen had known Steve for less than four years, was married not even a year and their loving, adventurous relationship that was in its infancy, was cruelly taken away by the deadly disease. By then Steve had shaken off the insecurities and paranoia that plagued much of his life and just as he found contentment and love once more, the end was near. Barbara wrote a beautifully, warm-hearted memoir, published in 2007, about her time with Steve, when they would spontaneously take off in his old pick-up and tour all over the country. Her website barbaramintymcqueen.com stands as a memorial to her all-too short marriage but, nonetheless, of a relationship that was loving and seemingly destined for a bright future.

LeVar Burton felt the last shot of Steve McQueen in a Hollywood movie, when he was holding his screen baby at the end of *The Hunter,* was a wonderfully, touching but appropriate image for Steve to bow out with. "That freeze frame shot at the end, with this grin on his face at the thought of him having this little baby in his arms; it's magic, it really is magic. That was it, the end of a life well lived, and lived fully. He never held anything back. I don't think he left anything on the table. He lived his life every freakin' day."

Paul Newman in *Somebody Up There Likes Me*. Steve
had to wait 18 years until he shared top billing with
his friendly rival, Newman
(COURTESY: MGM)

SOMEBODY UP
THERE LIKES ME

(MGM) 1956

'I can't honestly say I saw Steve was going to be a big,
tremendous talent' – Robert Wise

WHEN A YOUNG Steve McQueen, desperate for work, stepped into the office of director Robert Wise, he made a lasting impression. The distinguished film-maker, who went on to direct Academy Award-winning pictures *West Side Story* and *The Sound of Music,* was looking for a handful of small-time actors that would be cast in bit-parts, portraying a posse of New York street kids. Steve McQueen had by now learnt his trade at the Actors Studio and had clocked up several stage roles, but he was in search of that foot-in-the-door, where he could finally boast an appearance in a feature film; *Somebody Up There Likes Me* gave him that – just about.

Although he was paid only $19 a day for his miniscule role as street kid Fidel, his film career had begun. Wise remembered vividly the impression that Steve left on him during their first meeting. "He walked into my office with this cap on and a little jacket. He had a real cocky attitude, which caught my eye. Not fresh, just nice and cocky. I took to him right away."

The star of the picture was Paul Newman - another product from the Actors Studio assembly line. Tough, cool and donning the white T-shirt and Levis, Newman was the latest target of comparisons with James Dean and Marlon Brando; a trait that Steve had to contend with later. At this point, the divide between Newman and McQueen was off the scale. They were completely at opposite ends of the casting sheet. It was Newman's second feature release after making his debut in ill-fated *The Silver Chalice* two years before. His powerful portrayal of boxer Rocky Graziano in *Somebody Up There Likes Me* received great acclaim after its release in July, 1956.

Based on the fighter's autobiography, written by Rowland Barber, the picture is an accurate study of one of the sport's most famous sons. MGM was only able to cast Newman because of an agreement with Warner Brothers, where he had an existing commitment but they released him while they had nothing for him. The original choice to play the lead role was James Dean but his tragic death in a car crash at age 24 the previous year, meant Newman was offered the role. Many felt that Newman's career, and Steve's to a lesser extent, was able to flourish because of Dean's trailblazing of the young, rebellious movie star type, but also ultimately from Dean's passing.

"Both Paul and Steve had careers, in a sense, because Jimmy died," commented Academy Award-winning actor Martin Landau, who had gone to the Actor's Studio with Dean, Newman and McQueen in the mid-fifties, and was in fact best friend's with Dean. "Paul took on several things because of Jimmy's death. While Jimmy was filming *East of Eden,* Paul was doing *The Silver Chalice.* Jimmy used to visit his set a lot. When *The Silver Chalice* was released it was horrifically reviewed. Paul had a contract with Warner Brothers and they willingly let him go because it was so bad; whereas Jimmy in *East of Eden* skyrocketed. Paul screen-tested with Joanne Woodward for *East of Eden* the same day Jimmy did with Julie Harris – they did the same scene – and Jimmy and Julie got the parts. So when Jimmy died Paul did *Somebody Up There Likes Me.* Paul's career was boosted then, at a time when his career was almost blacklisted in Hollywood because of *The Silver Chalice.* And then Steve emerged. It was a perfect time for them."

Wise was anxious to show theatre-goers the 'real Rocky Graziano.' Thankfully for the producers, boxing legend Graziano obliged in helping refine Newman's characterisation. Wise recalled: "We had a great advantage, though Paul more than I, of spending some time with Rocky. We met him in New York and went around with him. We went down the Lower East Side of New York, met a lot of his old buddies and saw the candy store where he used to hang out. He gave us some old photos of himself, which helped us for when we came to choosing Paul's wardrobe. Also, there had been a long inter-view with Rocky a year before in *Look* magazine and we got hold of this tape so Paul could practise on his accent, trying to speak like Rocky more naturally. That helped us a lot."

It was a convincing performance by Newman, who spent hours at a gym with boxer Tony Zale (who appears in the film) trying to get into character. Wise was moved by Newman's portrayal and he felt McQueen would have struggled in such a role. Curiously, though, a year or two further down the line, this may have been a perfect vehicle for McQueen given the similarities between his and Graziano's upbring-ing. Graziano had a slum childhood – McQueen was carried around by his runaway, alcoholic mother when not being cared for by his grand-parents or great uncle; Graziano had a drunken father - McQueen didn't know his at all; both had a helplessly rebellious nature and were no strangers to juvenile delinquency (McQueen ended up in a reform school); both ultimately arrived at the sensible realisation that the resolve of spirit influencing their destructive and troublesome ways, could also be used well if channelled into something posi-tive, whether boxing or acting. However, Wise never felt McQueen would have been able to deliver this portrayal like Newman did.

"Paul had more range," Wise said, "though I don't really think Steve was ever put to that test. If you look at Newman in *Somebody Up There Likes Me* - I thought that was such a marvellous characterisation, which was so far away from himself: raised in

Cleveland, Ohio, Shaker Heights, well-to-do background, college-educated; for him to cut the character of Graziano the way he did, playing a rebel and almost a criminal, was just beautiful. Now Steve was great, but he never had that range."

Steve's ever-supportive wife Neile had not been impressed with her husband's cameo performance and was concerned for his future. She was always trying to help him perfect his approach that would best showcase his unique talents but it took him some time to get there. She commented in *My Husband, My Friend*: "Paul (Newman) was already a star. He had zeroed in on his screen personality, and was busy defining and sharpening it with each succeeding film. Steve on the other hand was floundering. He had no idea how to transfer his personality onto the screen. I knew that there was only so much that acting school could teach him. The answer for him was screen time. But how? When? Nobody was banging down his door. He had not turned in a good performance as Fidel in *Somebody Up There Likes Me*. Would he be given another chance? I became determined to get him out of this Brando-Dean mould, otherwise he would never make it."

Wise, nonetheless, was delighted by Steve's cameo role. "It was an almost unrecognisable part, but it was his first feature. Steve was very good in the part and, although he definitely had a quality about him, I can't honestly say that I saw this was going to be a big, tremendous talent." Ten years later, McQueen starred in *The Sand Pebbles,* produced and directed by Wise. By then, he was not earning $19 a day, but $650,000!

Main Credits:

Cast: Paul Newman, Pier Angeli, Everett Sloane, Eileen Heckart, Sal Mineo, Harold J. Stone, Joseph Buloff, Sammy White, Arch Johnson, Robert P. Lieb, Theodore Newton and more uncredited such as Robert Easton, Clancy Cooper, Dean Jones, Michael Dante and Steve McQueen (uncredited, as Fidel).

Director:	Robert Wise
(Assistant Director)	Robert Saunders
Producer:	Charles Schnee
(Associate Producer)	James E. Newcom
Cinematographer:	Joseph Ruttenberg
Writer:	Screenplay by Ernest Lehman, based on the autobiography of Rocky Graziano, with Rowland Barber
Editor:	Albert Akst
Make-Up:	William Tuttle
Music:	Bronislau Kaper

REVIEWS:

NEW YORK TIMES, July 5th, 1956

Let it be said of Mr. Newman that he plays the role of Graziano well, making the pug and Marlon Brando almost indistinguishable. He is funny, tough and pathetic in that slouching, rolling, smirking Brando style, but with a quite apparent simulation of the former middleweight champ.

VARIETY, July, 1956

For Paul Newman (the film) is a showcasting that should help remove the Brando look-alike handicap. His talent is large and flexible.

TIME OUT

A disappointing biopic of Rocky Graziano, East Side delinquent turned World Middleweight Champion. The trouble is that Wise forsakes the terse economy and unpretentious naturalism of *The Set-Up* for a rather straggling narrative which spends far too long throwing up mildly socially-conscious observations about poverty, and trying to turn the whole thing into a movie with a message about hope and determination. It's still not that bad a film, however. Newman's performance, though inflected by Method mannerisms, is powerful

Steve as Jewish lawyer Martin Cabell, on
Never Love A Stranger
(COURTESY: ALLIED ARTISTS)

NEVER LOVE
A STRANGER

(Allied Artists) 1958

*'Steve had a rough adolescence and childhood and had been
a juvenile delinquent...This picture gave him an
opportunity to do something different'* – R.G. Armstrong

THE ROUTE TO success in the film industry is rarely straightforward and therefore incorporates career moves actors would
not always have made with the benefit of choice. This is one
such film for Steve. For a guy who was very particular about
his characters, playing Martin Cabell, a vulnerable yet educated Jewish boy who becomes district attorney, was not the
ideal role for the macho, motorcycle-riding McQueen. Steve
would have been better suited to the lead part, portrayed by
John Drew Barrymore: an orphan who learned to fend for himself, and who soon became associated with those on the wrong
side of the tracks, eventually running all the underworld rack-
ets as head of the New York Mafia. McQueen was fresh out
of the Actors Studio and, despite the incongruous role, didn't
take long to assert his method on *Never Love A Stranger* - a film

directed by Robert Stevens and based on Harold Robbins' debut novel (Robbins also co-wrote the screenplay).

It was actually Robbins' original intention for Steve to play the lead role that was handed to Barrymore. Steve was aware of Robbins' plan too and the switch was just one of a few issues that left Steve with a negative impression of studio Allied Artists. And even after all his subsequent success he never forgot those early experiences in New York with Allied. Emanuel Wolf was President and Chairman of Allied Artists by the time Steve worked with them again 15 years later on *Papillon* (though he did also make *Soldier in the Rain* with Allied in 1963). Wolf remembered how Steve was still deeply troubled, bizarrely, by those days in the 1950s with Allied: "We were filming *Papillon* in Jamaica and we're on the set and about to shoot a scene when Steve comes over to me...

McQueen: "I've got to talk with you, but I have to shoot this scene, can you wait?"
Wolf: "I can wait."
McQueen: "You're not going to go away are you?"
Wolf: "No I'm not going to go away Steve."
(Half an hour later after Steve finishes shooting the scene, he invites Wolf to his motorhome trailer for this chat. They sit down.)
McQueen: "Do you want a drink?"
Wolf: "Yeah sure, what have you got? As long as it's cold..."
McQueen: "Look I don't get drinks for people but if you want anything the refrigerator is over there."
Wolf: "Fine, I don't have to have a drink. What's the problem Steve?"

McQueen: (leaning forward seriously) "We've got to change the logo."

Wolf: "What do you mean we've got to change the logo? What logo?"

McQueen: "Your logo is old-fashioned, this is a new time and a new era, we have got to have an up-to-date logo."

Wolf: (now realising Steve is referring to the Allied Artists company logo) "Steve don't worry there is a new logo, it looks professional, up to date and it will look terrific."

"That's what this whole meeting was about! Here was me worrying that there was going to be some big issue and all he wanted to discuss was the Allied Artists' logo. I only realised about five years later why all that meant so much to Steve and it went back to his first (credited) feature back in 1958, *Never Love A Stranger,* based on Harold Robbins' book. Harold was a very good buddy of mine so when I did *The Betsy* (based on another Robbins book) with him in 1978, he explained some of the things that had happened on that picture. Only then did it hit me why Steve had this negative image of Allied Artists and the logo etc. I realised why he had these things on his mind in Jamaica. It's quite incredible that he never forgot about those experiences that had occurred some 15 years previously."

Wolf recalled the day when he tried to give Robbins a birthday treat only to inadvertently discover not only his pain that still lingered from *Never Love A Stranger* but the anguish that Steve would have suffered also. The fact McQueen was a rookie and desperate for his first feature credit back then in the late fifties meant he was unlikely to make much of a fight against the treatment he received by those in charge on the movie. The ballsy, obstinate McQueen came later.

Wolf recalled: "Because it was Harold's birthday I had got him a print of his very first film, *Never Love A Stranger*, with the intention to watch it together in my own screening room where I had my office in New York. The idea was to watch the movie and then go for some dinner. Anyway, Harold and I start watching the movie and about halfway through he gets up and says, 'I can't watch this anymore; it's too painful for me and reminds me what the problem was back then.' Harold then explained to me that he was the one who discovered Steve McQueen back in New York and that it was he who had recommended Steve to Allied Artists for this picture. But they got the casting all wrong and made Steve the Jewish District Attorney. The way Harold told me was that Steve was meant to play the lead, not John Drew Barrymore."

The picture was filmed in New York, Steve's former playground, and the tragedy is that the angst-ridden lead part was made for him, as Robbins had clearly identified. Co-star R.G. Armstrong said: "Steve had a rough adolescence and childhood and had been a juvenile delinquent. He played that type of person a lot – the rebel. This picture therefore gave him an opportunity to do something different." At this stage in his career, Steve was hungry for recognition and *Never Love A Stranger* gave him fourth billing behind Barrymore, Lita Milan and Robert Bray. The movie was shot in 1957 but withheld for a year because of financial problems. Incidentally, Steve would later inform his new wife that he had had a fling with Lita Milan during the movie. "She would be the first in a long line of 'flings' that would plague us – me – throughout our married life," Neile said.

Steve's assured approach and dedicated preparation made for some nervous moments on the set and agitated the often-troubled Barrymore. The lead star was less confident about his own role, according to Armstrong, who knew Steve from the Neighbourhood Playhouse: "Every time they'd get a scene all set up to go after they had rehearsed it and practiced it, Barrymore used to walk away and reconsider his approach," Armstrong recalled. "He would often ask the director to reset it. John was insecure of his part, but Steve was ready to go every time - he had his character nailed down. I think John was a little worried that Steve was taking the scenes away from him, the lead star, and that's why he was constantly interrupting the shoot and talking with the director. We could hear him saying things like 'McQueen's trying to steal my movie'. Steve was very patient while all this was going on. He was good, as he'd been studying hard at the Actors Studio."

Ironically, Steve's scene-stealing attempts cropped up again and again in other films, most famously on *The Magnificent Seven,* causing a rift with star Yul Brynner. And by 1963 during *The Great Escape*, it was McQueen who was worried about co-stars seemingly taking 'his' movie away from him. But here, in his maiden picture, he was a dedicated rookie doing his job and keen to get on, which just fuelled Barrymore's insecurities.

John Drew was the son of actor John Barrymore, considered to be one of America's great Hamlet's. Barrymore Jr. failed to live up to his father's standards and did not make much of an impression on the film industry. He encountered personal troubles throughout his life, which included four divorces, estrangement from his children and drinking and drug-related issues. At that time, Steve was clean and most certainly hungry for success and knew of his destiny, according to Armstrong. "He was tremendously ambitious and he really wanted to be a big star, but he would never come out and say it. That wasn't his method. We used to hang out together sometimes and you knew what he was saying just by the way he'd look at you. He was heading for the top and I felt he knew he was going to make it big. It wasn't a surprise to me when he did become a star because I knew he always had that star quality and such a charisma that came from the depths within."

The picture failed to make an impression at the box-office and did little to further Steve's career, but it was another pay cheque and his first all-important credit.

Main Credits:

Cast: John Drew Barrymore, Lita Milan, Robert Bray, Steve McQueen (as Martin Cabell), Salem Ludwig, R.G. Armstrong, Douglas Rodgers, Felice Orlandi, Augusta Merighi, Vincent Barbi, Abe Simon, Vitina Marcus and more uncredited such as Richard Bright, Walter Burke, Gino Ardito and Dort Clark.

Director:	Robert Stevens
Producers:	Richard Day, Harold Robbins
(Assistant Producer)	Peter Gettinger

Cinematographer:	Lee Garmes
Writer:	Screenplay by Richard Day and Harold Robbins, based on Robbins' novel
Editor:	Sidney Katz
Wardrobe:	Ruth Morley
Music:	Jack Shaindlin / Raymond Scott

REVIEW:

THE HOLLYWOOD REPORTER, June 27th, 1958
In addition to Barrymore's good performance, Robert Bray and Steve McQueen are more than acceptable as a gang leader and a district attorney, respectively.

THE FILM DAILY, June, 1958
… Other players who do well by their roles are Robert Bray, a racketeer baron and Steve McQueen, a law enforcement officer who knew the hero when they were kids.

Steve in his first role as a lead star, in The Blob
(COURTESY: PARAMOUNT PICTURES)

THE BLOB

(Paramount) 1958

*'For some reason Steve wasn't too pleased with The Blob,
he thought he was above it. He only came to
appreciate it later...This movie was undoubtedly a
big step for his career' – Russell S. Doughten*

AT THE AGE of 28 and with only one film credit behind
him, Steve was desperate for a vehicle that would bring
him some kind of success and with it bigger and better
movie deals. Surprisingly, coupled with his hit television
series *Wanted: Dead or Alive*, *The Blob* helped him to achieve
just that. The amazing success of this horror, science-fiction
picture astounded many, not least Steve himself. Prior to its
release, he had the choice of accepting a flat fee or ten per
cent of the film's profits. He chose the former, believing
the B-grade production would bomb. It was a decision that
cost him about $1.2 million as the film flourished after its
November release. "It was a low-budget film compared to
most, even at that time, at about half a million dollars," said

associate producer Russell S. Doughten. "Steve wanted his money straight out, he didn't want any deals. His salary was $1,000 a week for six weeks. I remember that because we were getting over budget and we asked him if he could help us for the last week and maybe work something out, but he said, 'No, nothing doing, I want my fee'. That was a costly decision on his part as it ended up grossing a lot of money but I didn't get any of it and neither did Steve. It made lots of money at the box-office and still plays regularly now on Cable. It would have made well in excess of $10 million."

The cast smacked of youthful exuberance and refreshing innocence and had no real star to boast, but it was compensated by an energy that keeps the movie running at a fair pace. Plot-wise, we learn that a shooting star has left behind a man-eating, gelatinous monster. Steve and his girlfriend, played by Aneta Corsaut, soon discover the mass of jelly (the blob), constantly swelling with every fresh victim. The majority of the film follows their plight in trying to end its existence. Incidentally, Steve had dated Corsaut previously but, despite his boast he would use in later years that he sleeps with all his leading ladies, she told the producers that there was no longer any romantic liaisons between her and Steve.

Steve was embarrassed by the film after its release, but before shooting began he was desperate to be in it when the producers started casting. In fact, he was his own agent in winning the part and convinced the film company to hire him. "'Shorty' (Irvin) Yeaworth, the director, and I were in New York trying to cast young people in *The Blob* and we had taken a walk at Central Park when we saw a young man walking a dog. This man looked up and said, 'Oh hi, I know you guys.' It was Steve McQueen. He had visited our studios once before because there was a girl he was interested in. We had a studio in Chester Springs, Pennsylvania and were filming a picture with a young actress from New York playing the lead role. And while we were filming he came to visit our set in this little, remote town. I was standing out on the porch and I heard this sound, 'vroooom' going through the woods – I think he was driving an MG at the time. He asked me if this young lady was present and I pointed him in her direction and that's how we came to know him.

"On this particular occasion he asked why we were in New York and we told him we had come to cast *The Blob*. He said, 'Oh yeah, tell me about it, I'm an actor, I can help you. Come back to my place, meet my wife and I can look at your script and see if I can do a part for you.' We thought it wouldn't hurt us to do that much. Steve was a known actor then and he was a bit older than we had in mind, but he convinced us because he read the script very enthusiastically and said he would have no problem playing a younger guy. So he had earned himself a reading, as we hadn't cast any of the younger parts yet. We thought we could carry on casting younger actors and cast around him. We liked his enthusiasm and his experience as an actor."

It wasn't a picture Steve necessarily wanted to be associated with, but it provided a change of direction. In fact, later in his career when he set up his own production company he had a promo poster of *The Blob* hanging proudly in his office. Of the movie Steve commented: "I usually played a killer or a delinquent, and I did a lot of snarling. Producers would tell me I had 'mean' eyes. That's when I began to sweat over being pegged as a heavy. Once they hang that label on you, it can knock out your chances for a lot of other stuff. So I began looking for something to improve my image - and what I got was *The Blob*... The main acting challenge in this one consisted of running around, bug-eyed, and shouting 'Hey everybody, look out for the Blob!' I wasn't too thrilled when people would tell me what a fine job I'd done in it."

Although a fairly amateurish melodrama, it's now a cult movie that is still shown across the world. Steve's contribution was a major factor. For producer Jack H. Harris, McQueen always appeared a precocious talent, right from the first moment he saw him on television. "He electrified me," Harris said. "I was sitting in my chair half asleep and he woke me up and I couldn't get over how Steve McQueen looked and acted on the tube." But Harris soon discovered the darker side to the artist. "Steve had a reputation for being a trouble-maker and he earned it sincerely - he was very hard to deal with. Whenever we had a problem, the director would call me and say, 'your star is acting up.' I would run out to the set, sit down with Steve and when I got past the 'I'm gonna call my agent, I'm gonna call my manager, I'm gonna call my lawyer' routine, we were able to talk out what was wrong. In the end, we came to terms. What he was looking for was not to tell everyone what to do, he wanted approval and some-one to be daddy that would say, 'You're a nice guy and I like you'." Doughten believes those antics were rare and recalls Steve as a reliable operator on the set. "He was a professional actor, he was always ready and delivered when required, he was a very dependable and direct-able actor. Steve just didn't want any horsing around with his part, he wanted to get in there and get the job done."

While on location in Chester, Pennsylvania, the cast and crew stayed in a large, ancient building where folk once vis-ited to swim in the nearby fresh spring water. Make-up artist on the movie Vince Kehoe said it was the perfect residence for the film company, who were all devout worshippers. "Nearly all of the crew were part of a religious group - the camera-man, the director, the producer, all except me. They were not one of those crazy religious groups; they were very nice peo-ple. We would have our breakfast together, our evening meal together and generally, there was a very pleasant atmosphere amongst us all."

Steve, though, was his own man and chose not to get too close to anybody. He was seen as a loner, who stayed in a separate apartment and when he wasn't on the set he was in his car, burning up the curving roads in the nearby woods. Steve was affable, but he made it clear he wasn't there to have a good time with the others. Kehoe recalled: "Steve McQueen wasn't a warm person; he never had a warm personality. He kept himself to himself pretty much and was very solo, but I think that was part of who he was. I don't think it was a fault; that was just Steve McQueen. He had a car that he drove like a maniac. He'd roar around these country lanes like a mad man. They asked him not to drive when he was doing the picture because they were afraid he was going to kill himself, and then they'd have been stuck, but he still drove anyway. He just used to shrug his shoulders as if to say 'Hey man, I'm going to do what I want to do'."

On the set, though, Steve (credited as Steven McQueen for the only time in his career) was revelling in his first starring role. He appears strained in a role that was almost too 'nice' for the man we came to know as the 'King of Cool' but this was at a time when he was still in search of that magic formula on screen. Kehoe sensed an insecurity in Steve that plagued him all through life. "He was not greatly sure of himself and, though he eventually developed a persona that worked for him, at that time during *The Blob*, he didn't strike me as star quality. And by then I had worked on a lot of films with a lot of good actors." Steve's forthcoming TV series, *Wanted: Dead or Alive*, soon allowed him to master his craft. But for now on *The Blob*, he was pleased to lose the 'next James Cagney' tag. The movie was released on September 12, 1958.

"For some reason Steve wasn't too pleased with *The Blob*, he thought he was above it." recalled Doughten. "I think he only came to appreciate it later in his career. *The Blob* probably helped him to get his role on *Wanted: Dead or Alive* though he didn't like to think so. This movie was undoubtedly a big step for him in his career. But whatever I or anyone else says, he was a guy with a lot of drive so it's not surprising what he ended up accomplishing. He was very motivated."

Main Credits:

Cast: Steven McQueen (as Steve Andrews), Aneta Corsaut, Earl Rowe, Olin Howland, Stephen Chase, John Benson George Karas, Lee Payton, Elbert Smith, Hugh Graham, Vincent Barbi, Audrey Metcalf, Jasper Deeter and more uncredited.

Director:	Irvin S. Yeaworth
(Assistant)	Bert Smith

Producer:	Jack H. Harris
(Associate Producer)	Frank Fuhr, Russell S. Doughten
Cinematographer:	Thomas E. Spalding
Writers:	Theodore Simonson and Kate Phillips (also known as Kay Linaker), based on a story idea by Irvine H. Millgate
Editor:	Alfred Hillmann
Make-Up:	Vince Kehoe
Music:	Ralph Carmichael, Burt Bacharach (composer)

REVIEWS:

NEW YORK TIMES, November 7th, 1958

If the acting is pretty terrible itself, there is becomingly not a single familiar face in the cast, headed by young Steven McQueen and Aneta Corsaut.

THE HOLLYWOOD REPORTER, September 10th, 1958

Jack Harris and his associate producer, Russell Doughten, seep in on the low-budget horror trade for teenage audiences. The results should please the blue jeans set. *The Blob*, as impersonal and as overwhelming as a lava flow, is a good deal more scary than the familiar character men flaunting rubber fangs and pasteboard foreheads.

DAILY CINEMA, January 30th, 1959

Although the plot sidetracks in an effort to keep suspense going, the cast work hard to give it a sense of urgency.

VARIETY, September 10th, 1958

With the science fiction cycle still in orbit, *The Blob* has good prospects of turning a profit for both its producer and distributor. McQueen, who's handed star billing, makes with the old college try while Miss Corsaut also struggles valiantly as his girlfriend.

MOTION PICTURE HERALD, September, 1958

It is good standard science-fiction fare worth an extra push because of the teenage angle, an approach pointed up by a chief and sergeant of police, one of whom has faith in teenagers and the other who believes them all bad. Encouraging too for the future of the industry are the direction and the performances by the youngsters.

Steve in his second starring role, but was another low-budget
film that did little to further his career
(COURTESY: UNITED ARTISTS)

THE GREAT ST. LOUIS BANK ROBBERY

(United Artists) 1959

'Steve had magnetism. If you see him on the screen, you look at him and nobody else' – Charles Guggenheim

THIS WASN'T TO be the picture that would make a rich man of Steve, but there again, he probably knew that when agreeing to take it on. It was more an excuse to star once again and take a closer step towards the big time. Of the film, McQueen said, "the only *great* thing about this one was the title. Most of the gang gets wiped out while I surrender to the cops. Nothing really worked in the film, but it was another screen credit. And each credit helps get you the next one. You're young and you're hungry and you grab what comes along." Charles Guggenheim, co-producer and director, remembers just how keen McQueen was to be involved with his project. "He took a side-track to work with me because he had already signed a contract to do *Wanted: Dead or Alive*. Steve did the film because he liked the vehicle."

The picture is based on real-life events and was filmed over six weeks at the actual location in Missouri, the state in which he was raised, on the farm in Slater. *The Great St. Louis Bank Robbery* was budgeted at just $110,000 and Steve was to be paid a modest couple of hundred dollars a week. Guggenheim revealed that mid-way through shooting, Steve's agent contacted him and demanded a raise for his client of up to $400 a week. Incredibly, even this modest request couldn't be accommodated because of the picture's already miserly budget.

The film grossed modestly, but more importantly McQueen received encouraging feedback from the Press, which helped build momentum for his burgeoning PR that was slowly growing along with his success on *Wanted: Dead or Alive*. Guggenheim, though, refused to take any credit in Steve's turnaround in fortunes and didn't believe this film had much impact on his career. "I don't think it helped him at all; that came with the TV series. I'm sure in retrospect his agent would have preferred him not to have been in my movie."

The film was certainly a slow burner, and Steve's infamous cool, as the reluctant getaway driver, was not quite there at this stage, yet his performance was polished enough. It is hard to consider that over the next two years he would go toe to toe with hotshots like Frank Sinatra and Yul Brynner – and retain his growing reputation on and off-camera. It clearly illustrated the pace at which his acting and confidence was growing.

Co-director John Stix, a cousin of Guggenheim, was the man responsible for securing McQueen for the picture. He had been impressed by Steve in New York when plying his trade off-Broadway. Guggenheim said: "John recommended him and I have a feeling Steve would not have done the picture without John's involvement. I could see Steve's potential was very great. He had come out off-Broadway with very good reviews and I knew I was fortunate to have him even though he wasn't a great star at that time. He always had that star quality which is hard to define. Steve was himself and people saw him as a genuine, believable person whatever part he played. He had magnetism - there is no doubt about it. If you see him on the screen, you look at him and nobody else."

As a movie icon Steve commanded a reputation for being a non-conformist, an anti-authoritarian; another in a line of Hollywood renegades. Things were no different even in these early days. He could be troublesome and difficult for directors, as Guggenheim found to his cost, but there was also a boyish innocence that cried out for affection as opposed to the wrath of the boss's tongue. Notes Guggenheim: "It was the first time that I had met him and it soon became obvious that he had eccentricities. Sometimes he didn't arrive on the set on time and wouldn't be dressed properly and ready to go. Quite often, when I turned around he wouldn't be there. Instead he'd be racing his automobile around the parking lot like a maniac. He could have a real lack of respect for what he was doing at times. But I didn't give him a bad time though, when maybe other directors might have. Although I knew I'd lost some money waiting around, I felt lucky to have him on the film and he wasn't the kind of guy that you wanted to get mad at. He lived a very difficult childhood and was a maverick who served some time at reform school. Steve adapted extremely well to a fairly organised, accepted way of doing things, in light of the fact that there was nothing stable in his life for a long while. We got on well together."

Steve duly appreciated and respected the man-management tactics that Guggenheim employed with him on the film; evident when the two met up years later in Hollywood and McQueen encouraged the director-producer to come up with properties for them to work on together. Although such never came to pass, this picture remained a triumph for the producer, who had both extracted a good performance out of the developing actor, while somewhat taming the fires within a hot-headed, but maturing talent.

Main Credits:

Cast: Steve McQueen (as George Fowler), Crahan Denton, David Clarke, James Dukas, Molly McCarthy, Martha Gable, Larry Gerst, Boyd Williams, Frank Novotny, Nell Roberts, Bob Holt, May Kohn, Jay Elliot, Robert Klauss, Barney Bennett, Nancy Lyon.

Directors:	Charles Guggenheim, John Stix
Producer:	Charles Guggenheim

(Associate Producer)	Richard T. Heffron
Cinematographer:	Victor Duncan
Writer:	An original screenplay by Richard T. Heffron
Editor:	Warren Adams
Music:	Bernardo Segall

REVIEWS:

MOVIE FILM BULLETIN, September 20th, 1960
Based upon actual incident and filmed on the spot, this low budget independent production has an amateurish look and its attempt at documentary realism results in a rambling narrative and fuzzily recorded dialogue. Nevertheless, the treatment is fresh, sometimes - as in the Fritz Langish finale - brilliant, and the whole takes on a savage authenticity implicit in Victor Duncan's scarred and grainy photography. Steve McQueen plays the weak youth with a distinction owing nothing to Method mannerisms.

VARIETY, February 25th, 1959
Steve McQueen as the youth and David Clark, Crahan Denton, and James Dukas in criminal roles manage to make parts fairly persuasive.

Steve with Gina Lollobrigida, Frank Sinatra and Richard
Johnson in *Never So Few*
(COURTESY: MGM / BRITISH FILM INSTITUTE)

NEVER SO FEW

(MGM) 1959

'Steve knew this was his big chance. He recognised very clearly that it was an increased opportunity to launch himself because it was a Sinatra film' – Robert Relyea

STEVE'S CAREER MAY never have enjoyed the success it did had it not been for *Never So Few*, which wasn't a hit at the box-office but, simply, it was a Frank Sinatra movie and Sinatra movies got noticed. This World War II picture, about a small group of men who wage a futile battle against the Japanese army on the Burma-Chinese border, was directed by John Sturges and starred 'Rat Pack' leader Sinatra and his good friend Peter Lawford, while Gina Lollobrigida played the female lead. Fellow gang member Sammy Davis Jr. was also set to appear but mysteriously pulled out over an alleged disagreement with Sinatra. When Steve was named as the replacement for Davis, it surprised many connected with the project, though this was the big break that McQueen had longed for.

Assistant director Robert Relyea was shooting location footage in Ceylon (now Sri Lanka) and was astonished by the news. "When I received a telegram from LA telling me that Steve was the replacement for Sammy, I thought they had got to be kidding. Not only because we had shot a hell of a lot of doubles for Sammy, but because at that time the name Steve McQueen meant nothing to me but *Wanted: Dead or Alive* - he was just a very good television actor." With his TV show, Steve was making a name for himself in Hollywood, on the back of some promising performances in low-budget movies. *Never So Few* was not the epic picture that would make an instant legend of the young actor, but the connection to Sinatra was significant. "Steve knew this was his big chance," said Relyea. "He recognised very clearly that it was an increased opportunity to launch himself because it was a 'Sinatra film'. You could see in his eyes that he thought it was neat, as Frank went to his own drummer and Steve thought he was studying under the master."

The clause in Steve's *Wanted* contract allowed him to make films as long as shooting did not interfere with the schedule of the TV programme. It was his intention to be a movie star in any case. Even when riches and popularity came his way through *Wanted: Dead or Alive*, his aspirations remained constant. Although Steve's manager Hilly Elkins recommended him to John Sturges for the picture, it was the opinion of revered talent scout Stan Kamen that influenced Sturges. "Everybody highly respected Kamen's ability to recognise whatever the hell it is that we talk about that special thing in an actor," Relyea said. "I believe and I know John Sturges believed that Stan Kamen had the best eye in Hollywood for recognising a talent." Steve remained loyal to Kamen for the next decade, before firing him during the bloodbath that was *Le Mans*. The very fact that Steve replaced Sammy Davis Jr. - an established movie star - was enough evidence of just how highly he was regarded by Sturges. It was to be the beginning of a fruitful combination, as Sturges and McQueen went on to make another two films together, and both of which prospered a lot more than this one.

Sinatra's stardom could intimidate co-stars. Even his friends and pack members looked to him as 'the leader'. When Sinatra laughed, everyone laughed. His personality had a presence that made people around him feel inferior. Relations between him and Steve were always going to be interesting, given that both were strong-willed, macho and proud of their reputations as toughs. From the outset, when the picture began shooting on the MGM lot at Culver City, Sinatra was keen to see how far Steve could be pushed without retaliation. It was his way of testing the new kid on the block and seeing if he was going to threaten his 'position'. After a battle scene, Sinatra threw a firecracker at Steve, as they were used as ammunition in the picture. Not to be outdone or beaten, McQueen then responded by letting an even bigger firecracker loose in Sinatra's dressing room, which almost blew the closet right out. Steve preceded this act by firing a full clip of blanks from a Tommy gun around

Sinatra's feet. It sent a deathly silence around the set. The whole cast and crew wondered how the famous 'Rat Pack' tough would accept these antics from the youngster, who was keen to stand up to this heavy and make a point of his own. "Everybody was watching Frank to see what he'd do," McQueen told author William F. Nolan. "He had a real bad temper and I guess they all figured we were gonna end in a punch-out. I wasn't sure myself, as we stared at each other. Then he just started laughing, and it was all over. After that, we got along fine. In fact, we tossed firecrackers at each other all through the picture. Off-camera, that is. I'd done the right thing. Once you back down to a guy like Sinatra, he never respects you."

MGM were going to send Steve a bill for the damage to Sinatra's dressing room but Stan Kamen's expert diplomacy skills advised them against that course of action, for Kamen foresaw what Steve's reaction would be – certainly not an apologetic one. *Never So Few* had a relatively modest budget at $2 million, though MGM were still keen to recoup any funds they could having spent a great deal already on the movie set. Despite opting not to make the film overseas, at a significant saving, they still sent Relyea and Sturges to Thailand and then to Kandy in Ceylon with camera crews to film background footage, as those locations doubled for the Burmese jungle. Back at Culver City studios in Los Angeles they drained a river that was used in *Tarzan* and *Meet Me in St. Louis* and used that space for filming airfield scenes and for building a mock jungle on. "When the bulldozers came to remove the eight foot of mud from the bottom of that river," Relyea recalled, "they found a number of dead animals!"

When the cameras were rolling, Sinatra was less competitive. His attitude bordered on magnanimous. The healthy screen relationship between Sinatra and McQueen had a lot to do with Steve's astuteness, as Robert Relyea explained: "Frank treated Steve very well, though it wasn't a big brother or father-son thing. Sinatra was just a very professional guy and I don't ever remember him being discourteous to anyone. With Steve - the young TV star - Frank could have thought, 'I wonder if this young man is going to try and showboat now.' But rather than that, in a very straightforward way, he just embraced Steve as another actor and let him do his stuff. Sinatra was a very bright guy, never jealous and he never worried about who was getting all the close-ups. He knew when certain actors were making the movie better. Also, I think Steve got along very well with Sinatra because he was bright enough to understand that he wanted to be noticed, but at the same time, he was too smart to say 'I'm gonna challenge this guy', who was King of the Hill."

Sturges was sold once Steve's name was put forward to replace Sammy Davis Jr. However, because of the power Sinatra commanded and as it was 'his' picture, MGM needed to have his blessing. After several screenings of *Wanted: Dead or Alive*, the Rat Pack leader agreed that Steve should be cast for the role. His salary was just $20,000 though, and some $55,000 less than what Davis was to collect, but at this stage the cheque was less important than the exposure. The movie for Steve was a marketing exercise. He was showcasing himself on the big screen, and it paid off.

Says Relyea: "Steve had a look, a movement, a couple of words and the eyes that would achieve more than a melodramatic speech and John Sturges knew it right away. When Steve got out of a car, he floated; when he cocked a machine gun – it looked natural. It's like with footballers, you can tell those that have been coached and those that are just natural and Steve was natural to acting."

One of Steve's racing buddies at that time was Kurt Neumann Jr., who worked with him on *The Cincinnati Kid* as the assistant director. He also worked with Sinatra on *Some Came Running* as an uncredited second assistant director in 1958. He felt there were interesting similarities between Sinatra and McQueen. "Frank Sinatra and Steve were very much alike - they both had a similar personality. Frank would do some of the most outrageous things that would cause you to literally despise him for what he had just done, or had done to others, like having someone fired or physically hurt. But then he would turn on the charm and very quickly you would find yourself humming while he sang or something. It was quite ridiculous how he could charm you so quickly. You would think to yourself, 'My God, he's just done that awful thing to that guy and I'm being taken in by the Sinatra charm already'. And Steve had that same kind of x-factor, if you want to call it that, which seduced people. He didn't have to try very hard, he just exuded this charm."

In *Never So Few*, Steve played Bill Ringa, a cocky young-ster who Captain Reynolds (Sinatra) takes an instant liking to and promptly acquires his services for battle in Burma. There were other co-stars in the picture who, like Steve, were also desperate for industry acclaim; like Charles Bronson and Dean Jones. It was McQueen, though, who received the greatest praise from critics. John Sturges was also delighted by Steve's contribution. "John used to say, no matter who was the lead of the picture, watch out for 'the gut' or the mid-section because that's where you really need your strength, and in the case of *Never So Few*, Steve McQueen was the gut, along with Charlie, Dean and Richard Johnson. Steve had a quality that shone through and when we came to look at dailies, we could see it. That cut-off sweatshirt he wore (an idea conceived by wife Neile) just gave him a look that set him out from the rest. John Sturges was well known for his ability to work with big stars and he told me after this film was made he knew Steve was going to be a big star. He knew he had a tal-ent that was maybe not definable at that stage, but was so enormous."

Main Credits:

Cast: Frank Sinatra, Gina Lollobrigida, Peter Lawford, Steve McQueen (as Corporal Bill Ringa), Richard Johnson, Paul Henreid, Brian Donlevy, Dean Jones, Charles Bronson, Philip Ahn, Robert Bray, Kipp Hamilton, John Hoyt, Whit Bissell, Richard Lupino, Aki Aleong.

Director:	John Sturges
(Assistant)	Robert E. Relyea
Producer:	Edmund Grainger
Cinematographer:	William H. Daniels
Writer:	Millard Kaufman (based on the novel by Tom T. Chamales)
Editor:	Ferris Webster
Wardrobe:	Helen Rose
Make-Up:	William Tuttle
Music:	Hugo Friedhofer

REVIEWS:

THE HOLLYWOOD REPORTER, December 7th, 1959

In *Never So few*, Edmund Grainger has produced what promises to be a box-office smash in which the elements of sex, adventure and humour are excitingly blended... Sinatra latches on to a hell-for-leather jeep driver from Hell's Kitchen (Steve McQueen). Some of the sight gags used by McQueen in a brush with the M.P.'s date back to Mack Sennett. But his general performance displays a casually sparkling personality vital in upholding the entertainment merit of the entire production. Kaufman has given him some very funny lines, which he delivers admirably. While functioning in a high gear as a laugh-getter, McQueen is always a believable soldier and never a dragged-in comedian.

THE FILM DAILY, December 7th, 1959

An unusually fine cast bolsters the picture, and included (behind Sinatra and Lollobrigida) are Peter Lawford, Steve McQueen, Richard Johnson, Paul Henreid and Brian Donlevy...John Sturges has directed effectively for producer Edmund Grainger. Lawford contributes a major role as the medical captain who goes along on the missions, and Steve McQueen as the two-fisted soldier.

VARIETY, December 9th, 1959

The Edmund Grainger production, directed with theatrical flourish by John Sturges, is also loaded with good young stars. It will be a good box-office attraction...The film may provide a catapult to stardom for Steve McQueen, hitherto known principally as a television actor. He has a good part, and he delivers with impressive style.

115

Steve, far left, pictured as one of 'The Magnificent Seven'.
Others from the left: Yul Brynner, James Coburn, Horst
Buchholz, Brad Dexter, Robert Vaughn and Charles Bronson
(COURTESY: UNITED ARTISTS)

THE MAGNIFICENT
SEVEN

(United Artists) 1960

'Both (Steve and Yul) were very similar in that they just had to win; they had the same competitive spirit that a sportsman would have. I don't know why but there can be a lot of insecurity in people who achieve that kind of status' – Shirley Anne Field

AFTER RECEIVING CRITICAL acclaim alongside Sinatra in *Never So Few,* Steve continued his ascent up the Hollywood ladder in *The Magnificent Seven.* Again acting in the company of screen royalty, Steve's frantic plight to remove his 'television star' tag resumed. This time, Yul Brynner was the latest in danger of being upstaged by McQueen, who had by now tasted a small measure of fame and success and desired more of the same. Assistant director Robert Relyea admitted: "Steve saw *The Magnificent Seven* as a major rung in the ladder to hit towards the big time. I think Steve was then recognised for his talent but at that point I don't think he was classed as a star." All that changed in this now legendary western which today ranks chiefly in the history of the genre.

The story depicts seven good-willed mercenaries who are each hired for a $20 pittance by a group of Mexican farmers, tired of seeing their village preyed upon by ruthless bandits, headed by Calvera (played by Eli Wallach). Their task is to protect the vulnerable villagers from Calvera's men and restore harmony to the lives of the hardworking farmers who know little of violence but much of survival. They are reluctant to continue their regular charitable donations while threatened at gun-point, so choose to fight fire with fire. The Seven, led by Brynner, develop a spirit of admiration towards these people and their virtues, which only fuels their battle with the scavenger-like predators - making for a captivating war of morality. The movie is based on Akira Kurosawa's *The Seven Samurai*. Director John Sturges - who had previously made *Bad Day at Black Rock* and *Gunfight at the O.K. Corral* - contacted Kurosawa prior to shooting and explained how he intended to adapt it, making clear how he wanted to copy as opposed to change the original classic. The Japanese director, being a huge Sturges fan, gave his blessing.

Before shooting began, Sturges had to overcome politics that threatened the picture. At the time, the Screen Actors Guild was planning a strike in the United States which questioned the position of many films, but the reputation of Sturges ensured the survival of *The Magnificent Seven* as Relyea explained: "John Sturges was *the* most honourable man ever born and he insisted the SAG blessed this picture, which was always planned for a Mexico location. The Guild then told John to cast the picture in the next two weeks and if he did that, they would acknowledge that the film was always scheduled for Mexico." Sturges then sent out blank contracts to the cast and because of his trustworthy background the actors duly signed the documents without seeing a script of any kind. Once the cast was assembled, there was still a major hurdle to overcome as Sturges was left with *The Magnificent Six*, but after agent Stan Kamen's advice, James Coburn was drafted in when he was originally set to play the part of the victim in the knife fight. He joined Brynner, Steve, Charles Bronson, Brad Dexter, Robert Vaughn and the young German Horst Buchholz, who was appearing in his first American picture. The movie was funded by United Artists and cost them $3million. Their interest in the project was based purely on the presence of Brynner and they were not too concerned who else featured. Further casting responsibilities lay with Sturges, who eventually assembled a cast of virtual unknowns. Most went on to enjoy successful careers, which could be partly attributed to their participation in this vehicle.

Industry politics initially threatened Steve's participation. He was still under contract with Four Star Productions and they were not prepared to release him from his television work on *Wanted: Dead or Alive.* Executive producer Walter Mirisch recalled: "Steve's agent Stan Kamen and the head of William Morris, Abe Lastfogel, arranged for me to meet with him at a little restaurant across the street from the studios where Four Star were based. Steve had seen the script and was very anxious to be in the film, but getting him free from the television show was a big problem because they had more shows to do to fulfil their commitment to the network they were making the show for. Their shows conflicted with our starting date and there wasn't much that we could do about it."

What could have been disastrous to Sturges's plans merely resulted in a minor hiccup, due largely to Stan Kamen's business skills and to the director's resilience. "Right from the beginning of developments for *The Magnificent Seven,* John wanted Steve to play that role," remembered Relyea. "He went to the William Morris Agency about Steve being in the movie and they in turn went to Four Star who said 'No - it can't be done' – words that John Sturges could not and did not accept. He then worked on Four Star through William Morris but Four Star kept saying, 'This is the contract and that's that.' But Sturges stayed with it like a bulldog and said 'I will not give in - Steve is going to be in the movie'." Walter Mirisch will never forget just how determined Steve was, also, to be involved with the project. "Steve put a tremendous amount of pressure on the Four Star people, particularly Tom McDermott who was running the business for them. He gave poor Tom a real tough time. Steve knew the story; he liked the script and was really keen to be in it. He had to extend himself for this movie and he knew it would be good for him; the evidence is in the pressure he put on McDermott to make him available for the picture."

McQueen's name in the film was now assured and his salary was $65,000. He played second in command to Brynner, though in reality, the role of understudy was not in Steve's nature - he was always determined to be the star of the show and he was not alone with this concept. Apart from Brynner, who had won an Academy Award for *The King And I* in 1956, the remainder of the cast were also ravenously hungry for their own piece of screen success. Robert Vaughn admitted: "We were all very ambitious and tried to take the film from one another. Brynner was the only star then so we were all competing." During preparation it became evident at just how fierce competition was. Explained Relyea: "Sturges took all seven guys to Western Costume and there, laid out, were hundreds of outfits including hats, boots, shirts, guns and so on. John liked to see them in their chosen outfits and stand them together to see if anybody had the same shirt or whatever. Those rooms were always mirrored and I was amused to see that they were all looking at each other just like John was looking at them. It was as if they were saying to themselves 'I want a hat like his hat' or 'I want spurs bigger than his spurs,' which in the right spirit and under a good director, is healthy competition to have on a set." Robert Vaughn echoed: "I think John loved that competitiveness that we all had, thinking it could only improve the magnitude of the film."

The rivalry might easily have exploded out of hand but for the experience of Sturges, who observed the signs before they became troublesome and promptly told the seven there was to be no repeat. It all happened on the first day of shooting on location in Tepoztlan, near Cuernavaca. Eli Wallach wasn't required that day and he stood next to the director and watched the activities evolve. "Each one of them did something as they passed the camera so that you would remember them. I was very amused by it all." Relyea was also on hand to witness the comical events. "I will never forget that first day. It was a typical John Sturges scene, filming from low angle, as the seven up above all cross this stream in single file. We rehearsed it several times and it went fine, but when John called 'roll 'em' for real, all hell broke loose. As Yul passed through, behind him Steve leaned out of his saddle and scooped up water in his hat, Charlie Bronson undid his shirt, Brad Dexter started scratching - it looked like *Hamlet* going on behind Yul. John looked at me and said, 'What are they doing? What the hell's going on here? This is going to be a long picture!' Of course after John spoke to them it all settled down eventually and everyone went to work. They were just letting out their oats and thinking 'Gee, he looks good on his horse, what am I going to do'?"

These events worried Brynner, who was concerned that these guys were trying to steal *his* picture. He viewed Steve in particular as a threat and rightly so as his screen presence shone bright enough to disturb Brynner's cool exterior. Eli Wallach recounted, with a chuckle: "When Steve and Yul were driving the funeral wagon, Steve takes out a shell from his rifle and shakes it next to his ear - so your eyes automatically go to him, he was scene-stealing. Steve was a clever actor." McQueen stretched the boundaries of his craft without ever going too far, as Wallach confirmed: "According to the script, Steve had to be the lieutenant to Yul who ran the thing and in that sense he was obedient, but all Steve had to do was give a look, to steal the scene, and Brynner knew it!"

English actress Shirley Anne Field, who co-starred with Steve on *The War Lover* in 1962 and also appeared with Brynner on *Kings of the Sun* a year later, detected obvious traits in both men that were freakishly alike, which made for an inevitable personality clash. "Both were very similar in that they just had to win; they had the same competitive spirit that a sportsman would have. I don't know why but there can be a lot of insecurity in people who achieve that kind of status.

"They both fabricated stories all the time to romanticise their past. Steve would tell me that his wife was a Polynesian Princess, when in reality she was a Filipino dancer raised in New York. He would lie like crazy and embroider all kinds of stories. Yul Brynner was the same; he told me he had no relatives and was a Mongolian orphan, he wasn't. One day I was sitting in Yul's caravan playing Gin Rummy with him, as he didn't have the concentration to read a book, and this woman came in once or twice and he'd refer to her as Marjorie. I asked him who she was and he said, 'Oh she's my mother (real name of Marousia Dimitrievna).' I said, 'But you're an orphan?' He and Steve were both so alike in that sense. It all comes down to insecurity; they didn't like something about themselves so they re-embroidered their history."

Relations were tense between the two on set, but Relyea had a close eye on proceedings as Sturges's assistant and denied the oft-spoken gossip that there was feuding between Yul and his hungry co-star. "They came from totally different backgrounds and were never going to be buddies or hang out together. McQueen and Bronson had more in common but weren't bosom buddies either. Yul and Steve gave each other room. In his spare time Yul would play cards with Brad Dexter, while Steve would be teasing Charlie and vice-versa. Bobby Vaughn mixed with who was around but was more of a loner and Horst Buchholz was playing catch-up because he was getting his first American break. Coburn got along with everybody. It's normal with a picture, when you put seven or eight stars together, some will get along with certain actors better than others. It's happened on a lot of pictures where somebody would go to somebody else and say 'He's getting all the close-ups' or 'The picture's centred too much on him.' But that never happened in my presence or John's and if there were these confrontations, we would have known."

Behind the scenes, though, there was clear tension and Steve, especially, was desperate to stay ahead of the rest. In later years during the making of *The Sand Pebbles*, Steve told co-star Joe Turkel about his tense relations with Brynner: "When they were riding in the stagecoach, Yul Brynner had a chance to talk to Steve and he was obviously feeling a little uneasy by Steve's presence and said, 'Hey Steve, just remember, I'm the star of this picture so don't get over-acting or stealing any scenes'. To which Steve replied: 'Fuck you'. Steve told me that and I also heard it from a number of people who were there."

Executive producer Walter Mirisch spent a lot of time on location and felt that despite the ambitious nature of the co-stars, Brynner was secure in the knowledge that he was the big man on the movie – no one else. "Yul was then a very big star and knew he was *the* star of the film. Yul was not a man lacking in self-confidence and was not shaken by Steve's presence, or anyone else's. From where I was standing, he got along okay with Steve, who treated him with respect most of the time. I was alone with the two of them many times and their relationship was fine; Steve was the young, aspiring actor who was doing everything he could to make his part better and be noticed, while Yul always knew that he had the commanding role - he was a thorough professional."

Similar events would be mirrored countless times in Steve's career, though curiously a relationship that was to unravel on a set in later years but in reversed format was during the filming of *Papillon*, when Steve had to compete with the equally ambitious Dustin Hoffman. They too got along for the sake of the film, but had no real connection as people. Of his relationship with Brynner, McQueen told writer William F. Nolan: "I knew something about horses by then, and quite a lot about guns. Brynner didn't, and it made him nervous. Word got around that we didn't much care for each other. I remember we were well into production when he walked up behind me after a scene and grabbed me by one shoulder. 'Now listen,' he says, scowling at me. 'There's a story in the paper about us having a feud. I'm an established star and I don't feud with supporting actors. I want you to call the paper and tell them the story is completely false!' He was *ordering* me to phone that newspaper, so I told him what he could do with his orders. He was a real uptight dude."

Each of the main players in the movie had their own personal driver and the stars requested that they were driven to the same restaurant just about every night, as it was not only the best eatery in Cuernavaca but the low-end motel where they were staying did not have a bar. Therefore, they would stay out at the restaurant until late, for beer and tequila.

Robert Vaughn revealed in his autobiography *A Fortunate Life* that he and McQueen shared some female company on one particular night, after Brad Dexter had introduced them to a local brothel. After too many tequilas, and after Dexter had departed, it was just the two of them and Steve made a request to the venue's Madam that all seven remaining 'hostesses' joined them in the veranda. Vaughn quipped, "Due to the effects of the tequila (which caused Steve to be 45 minutes late for filming the following morning), we did a hell of lot more laughing than humping."

Despite Steve's rivalry with Brynner and his ongoing paranoia about Brynner's pearl-handled gun and more,

Robert Relyea said if their relationship was as bad as what was often reported it would have had its affect on the film. "Take the scene for instance, where Steve and Yul are taking the hearse up the hill; there you see two guys working together, doing a scene very well and although they never went out and had dinner that night, I think you'd be able to tell if there was serious friction between them. They couldn't play scenes alone together that well if they were at each others throat - it would show. Keen and on their toes - yes, competitive - yes, but they were never growling. Those two guys understood each other."

The occasions where Steve did become a handful for the director, whether it was over-playing a scene in order to get noticed ahead of Brynner or just plain balking, were usually out of concern for the shallow part that he had in the film. Steve complained about his lack of dialogue, which was strange as he usually preferred reactions than dialogue. Walter Mirisch noted: "John Sturges and Steve developed a great relationship. John was a wonderful guy and I think a sort of father figure to Steve." If Yul Brynner didn't like Steve, he certainly respected him. This was obvious when he asked McQueen to again portray Vin for *Return of the Seven* in 1966 - a sequel to their 1960 box-office success. Steve said he was too busy but promised that he would co-star in his next picture. When Yul took him up on that offer, Steve sent Brynner a telegram reading, "I'm truly sorry that I can't be with you but my horse refuses to swim the Atlantic."

The cultural differences between Steve McQueen and Yul Brynner were huge. In Mexico, Brynner stayed in a large house while Steve resided at the motel with the rest of the cast and crew. "Yul lived very well, like a sultan in his big house," Wallach recalled, while Vaughn noted: "Brynner had an entourage with him ranging from secretaries to arrange his affairs to his personal hair-dresser, who would shave his head almost every day. Yul kept himself to himself pretty much." A further point of disparity was the fact that Brynner disliked riding horses. Steve had become quite adept at this following his experience as bounty hunter Josh Randall in *Wanted: Dead or Alive.* He later furthered this skill in *Nevada Smith, Junior Bonner* and *Tom Horn.* It was something that definitely riled Brynner, who was by no means a novice horseman, just a reluctant one. When Eli Wallach appeared with Brynner in a later picture, horses were still not his favourite companions. "We were in Yugoslavia making *The Romance of the Horse Thief* and we got on very well again," Wallach said. *"The Magnificent Seven* was never mentioned but Yul did say to me one day, 'Oh my, here we are with horses again,' because I was the horse thief. I don't think he liked them too much." *Seven* was an introduction to westerns for Wallach, who went on to appear in *How the West Was Won* (1963) and *The Good, the Bad and the Ugly* (1968).

As Wallach (and his wife Ann) befriended a group of gun-toting Mexicans who really took to him and showed him local cultures like cockfighting and tequila, Steve was usually up to mischief. On one occasion, Robert Relyea had to convince the Mexican police that he wasn't the psychotic kleptomaniac they believed him to be, when a parking meter was found in his hotel room; Steve had swiped the meter from town and kindly found it a home in the form of the assistant director's room! A similar thing happened again, but this time with a bus-stop sign, on the night of Steve's 30th birthday celebrations. It took the diplomacy skills of Walter Mirisch to rescue Relyea from the barrage of questioning at the local police station. "As we got to know one another more, the laugh's increased," Relyea admitted in good heart.

Walter Mirisch echoed: "We all had a great time and it was basically a trouble-free picture. Some real good friendships developed down there, particularly with Steve, Charlie and Jim Coburn, who we brought together again for *The Great Escape* later on."

Wallach, who remained in touch with Coburn until the latter's death in 2002, added: "I really did enjoy doing that film, it's like when you put on a pair of shoes in a store and they fit. I had the same feeling with *Baby Doll* and *The Good, the Bad and the Ugly*. When television ratings are down they put on *The Magnificent Seven* to bump the figures up. Even now, when I'm walking down the streets of New York City, people whistle the music behind me!" Wallach reached screen stardom late, making his debut in the Tennessee Williams story *Baby Doll* in 1957 at the age of 42. He was more accustomed to the theatre, where he first noticed an ambitious young man named Steve McQueen. "As a stage actor, I never thought

he'd be great in the movies, but he had a quality, a silent quality that came off over the screen. You felt he was thinking and
one of the hardest things about acting is to think on screen.
He was a very skilful film actor - very."

After working on *Never So Few* with Steve and John Sturges,
also as first assistant director, Relyea detected a different, more
workmanlike atmosphere in Mexico, fuelled mainly through
an ambitiousness that made for a tense shoot, notwithstanding the night-time fun. "In *Never So Few*, it was more like the
club getting together, but in this film, it was seven individuals
and Eli getting together, not with the same 'let's go to the set
and have a few laughs' attitude like on *Never So Few*. Here, it
was more like 'let's go to the set and do our jobs and I better
watch out for myself because he looks pretty good'."

In assessing westerns as a whole, Relyea believes *Seven*
will fair high among the greats. "Of course I'm biased but I
think history will look back kindly on *The Magnificent Seven*
and place it among the best westerns ever made." Wallach
acted with several legends of the western genre and is ably
qualified to judge McQueen's talent in comparison. He co-
starred with Clint Eastwood in *The Good, the Bad and the Ugly*
and also with James Stewart and John Wayne in *How The West
Was Won*. He reasoned: "Clint and Steve were alike in the
way neither enjoyed talking that much. They were the typical, strong, silent actors who were great western stars. Both
were wonderful horsemen and natural with guns; they could
flip their gun into the holster without looking, where as I had

to look. All these stars were big personalities and each one remained strong in what they did."

It was clear soon after the movie was released on October 23, 1960 that Steve McQueen had made his mark on Hollywood.

Main Credits:

Cast: Yul Brynner, Eli Wallach, Steve McQueen (as Vin), James Coburn, Robert Vaughn, Charles Bronson, Horst Buchholz, Brad Dexter, Jorge Martinez de Hoyos, Vladmir Sokoloff, Rosenda Monteros.

Director:	John Sturges
(Assistants)	Robert Relyea, Jaime Contreras (uncredited)
Producer:	John Sturges, Walter Mirisch (executive)
(Associate Producer)	Lou Morheim
Cinematographer:	Charles Lang
Writers:	Screenplay by Walter Newman (uncredited) and Williams Roberts, based on *The Seven Samurai* by Akira Kurosawa
Editor:	Ferris Webster
Wardrobe:	Bert Henrikson
Make-Up:	Emile Lavigne
Music:	Elmer Bernstein

REVIEWS:

THE FILM DAILY, October 6th, 1960
An outdoor action drama set in a little Mexican village, *The Magnificent Seven* packs a solid entertainment wallop. It has style, substance and a story that is unusual and powerful. Heading the cast of this Mirisch Co. presentation are Yul Brynner, Eli Wallach and Steve McQueen...Each man is seen in a test of his fighting mettle and it comes across the screen graphically. They are all specialists in the art of dealing out death...Performances are impressive from beginning to end.

VARIETY, October 5th, 1960
Until the women and children arrive on the scene about two-thirds of the way through, *The Magnificent Seven* is a rip-roaring, rootin' tootin' western with lots of bite and tang and old-fashioned abandon. The last third is downhill, a long and cluttered anti-climax in which *The Magnificent Seven* grow slightly too magnificent for comfort...McQueen, an actor who is going places, brings an appealing ease and sense of humour to his role.

MONTHLY FILM BULLETIN, April, 1961
Supporting performances are of an unusually high standard. Particularly notable are Charles Bronson as the neolithic-looking strong man with tender paternal instincts. James Coburn as the tensely commanding knife expert, Steve McQueen as the most relaxed of the group, and Robert Vaughn as the one whose black gloves and nightmares serve

as a constant reminder that *The Magnificent Seven*, unlike *The Seven Samurai*, is also and perhaps sadly a Freudian Western.

THE DAILY CINEMA, February, 1961
Superbly told and gripping tale of rough justice in Mexico, shrewdly blending brain and brawn. Acting, production, photography - magnificent.

MOTION PICTURE HERALD, October 8th, 1960
Beside him (Yul Brynner) most importantly is Steve McQueen, who has a notable television following for his leading role in the highly successful *Wanted: Dead or Alive*. He has a homely, taciturn sort of appeal which is of a high order.

Steve in a scene with his leading lady Brigid Bazlen
(COURTESY: MGM / THE KOBAL COLLECTION)

THE HONEYMOON MACHINE

(MGM) 1961

'To put Steve McQueen, an actor who had just bro-
ken through as a rugged, tough gunman in a western, in
this farce comedy was an unusual piece of casting'
– George Wells

JUST WHEN STEVE had finally made his first 'big' movie
with *The Magnificent Seven* alongside Yul Brynner, it was
important he maintained the credibility that he had earned.
This picture, though, did nothing to improve the impression he had made on Hollywood. It might even have set him
back a couple of rungs on the ladder to stardom. His manager Hilly Elkins admitted years later that this film was the
wrong move for Steve. Although at the time, it appeared to
be a good opportunity for McQueen to branch out and display his versatility in a comedy. Hindsight has proved that
The Honeymoon Machine was anything but a useful tool to help
escalate Steve's name to the lofty heights of Hollywood great-
ness. Even Lorenzo Semple Jr., who wrote the original play

The Golden Fleecing from which the screenplay was based on, said: "It wasn't very good and was actually quite feeble, and though the film was okay, it was still one of the few Steve McQueen pictures that failed to make any money." The movie was released on July 10, 1961 to a lukewarm reception, after a frantic three-week shoot at MGM Studios, Culver City.

The story portrays three conniving sailors from a US Navy Cruiser. While docked in Venice, they use the ship's computing machine to work out a system for beating the local casino's roulette wheel. The eventual mayhem almost causes World War III when the Morse Code used to convey the winning formula from the ship to the hotel room that Steve's character, Lt. Fergie Howard, is staying in, is intercepted by the hierarchy of the Russian Navy. While all this is going on, Lt. Howard falls in love with the Admiral's daughter, played by Brigid Bazlen. Years later, writers speculated there had been a real life romance between Bazlen and McQueen, but co-star and second leading lady Paula Prentiss refutes such claims: "No, I really don't think so," she said. "Steve was often on his own, in his own world. It certainly didn't strike me that there was a romantic relationship between them." There were also rumours of quarrels between McQueen and Bazlen but they were also unfounded. There was plenty of anxiety on the set but that was between Steve and the director or writer, either over the script or his approach to the character.

An experienced crew was assembled by MGM and veteran writer George Wells was asked to write the screenplay from the Broadway play. Larry Weingarten produced and the director was the experienced and no-nonsense Richard Thorpe, best known as the original director on *The Wizard of Oz*, before he was fired after two weeks for making Judy Garland appear too old for the part of Dorothy. He also made *Jailhouse Rock* with Elvis Presley and *Prisoner of Zenda*, the Stewart Grainger picture. The cast was relatively green and relied heavily on Steve's involvement for success. Co-stars included Bazlen, Prentiss, Jim Hutton, Dean Jagger and Jack Weston, who later appeared in *The Cincinnati Kid* and *The Thomas Crown Affair* with McQueen.

Steve had a real difficult time in getting along with Thorpe, a director from the old school. Explained Wells, "He wanted to arrive on set, get to work, get filming and go home. This never suited Steve, who always wanted to spend lots of time talking scenes over and finalising his approach." Most discussions relating to the movie were held between McQueen and screenwriter Wells. "Dick Thorpe stayed out of it and allowed me to handle his star. He was a little impatient with Steve's insecurities and just didn't want anything to do with Steve's analysis of how he should play everything out. But Steve and I got along well. However, I do remember Steve once telephoning me at my home at three in the morning to air his concern at the previous day's shooting. This never occurred again after I told Steve in no uncertain terms that I didn't work at that time of day."

Steve's uneasiness in his ability to execute comedy accounted for the vast majority of discussions. "To put Steve McQueen, an actor who had just broken through as a rugged, tough gunman in a western, in this farce comedy was an unusual piece of casting," Wells observed. "Steve was a very sincere actor who took his work seriously and though he knew it wasn't a perfect vehicle for him, he was still determined to conquer the comedy genre. He told me that he tried to relate everything in his character to things that had happened in his life." Contrary to wider opinion, co-star Paula Prentiss felt *The Honeymoon Machine* was a good career move for Steve and she disagreed with Steve's manager Hilly Elkins that this was a project he should have skipped. "I thought Steve was capable of doing it all: action, drama, comedy, whatever. And his great strength in this film was that he didn't try to act funny; he played it very straightforward. I genuinely believe this film did help to enhance his career as it showed he had more range than many people gave him credit for." Still, the finished product was not to Steve's liking as he walked out of its first preview such was his distress at his performance.

After three days of shooting, Thorpe, producer Weingarten and Wells looked at the dailies and saw just how slow Steve and the film were. They knew it was unacceptable and that something had to change so crisis talks were called with their uneasy star. "Steve was methodising everything and with this kind of comedy, he needed to be spontaneous otherwise audiences would soon become disinterested," Wells said. "The plot was so thin that they couldn't get away with the long pauses Steve was giving. I drew the short straw and was delegated to speak with Steve about it. We chatted on the set and discussed how to approach things." McQueen then told Wells he was very worried by the way things were going – he was close to walking. "Steve thought everybody was on his back and that something was wrong and he didn't have any answers," Wells recalled. However, the writer felt he knew how to treat the insecure star and he explained that it was taking longer for him to say the line than it took to write it. With a smile, the actor understood the situation and revamped his attack.

"I wouldn't say there were major problems between Steve and Richard Thorpe," said Paula Prentiss, "but he was certainly a very tough-talking kind of director and wasn't the type who wanted to stand around discussing scenes all day. That's why we ended up shooting the picture in something ridiculously short like 15 days!" Wells, then, had to be the mediator between McQueen and Thorpe. Things were much more relaxed off-screen, and Steve used to enjoy the sanctuary of his family. On one occasion he invited Prentiss round to his house. "I spent a day at Steve's place and met his wife Neile and his little daughter (Terry). He struck me as a fantastic father to that little girl. In the time that I knew him, Steve was a very gracious, wonderful man and I liked him a lot; he was a lot of fun."

A generous tribute considering her first meeting with Steve: *The Honeymoon Machine* was only her second movie and she was still finding her way in the film business after college. Steve had just come off *The Magnificent Seven* and had earned rave reviews, so the young actress was excited about her first meeting with him. In quite anti-climatic fashion, though, the first thing the actor told her was: "Baby, I think you're too skinny to be in the movies!"

Main Credits:

Cast: Steve McQueen (as Lt. Fergie Howard), Brigid Bazlen, Jim Hutton, Paula Prentiss, Dean Jagger, Jack Weston, Jack Mullaney, Marcel Hilliare, Ben Astar, William Lanteau, Ken Lynch, Simon Scott and more.

Director:	Richard Thorpe
(Assistant)	Ronald Florance
Producer:	Lawrence Weingarten
Cinematographer:	Joseph LaShelle
Writer:	George Wells (based on the play *The Golden Fleecing* by Lorenzo Semple Jr.)
Editor:	Ben Lewis
Wardrobe:	Helen Rose
Make-Up:	William Tuttle
Music:	Leigh Harline

REVIEWS:

VARIETY, August, 1961

Once again Metro is wagering its chips on fresh rookie talent and light romantic farce material. The combination paid off in *Where The Boys Are*, and this one looks like a modest, but tidy, follow-up pay off…Almost every scene has a few good comic jolts and there are other compensations. Among these are the performances of

McQueen, who reveals a promising flair for romantic comedy and Jack Weston, who chips in a gregarious characterisation of a drunk to overcome some pretty brittle material.

THE NEW YORK TIMES, August 24th, 1961

Retooled by George Wells into a screenplay and adorned with a new and youthful cast, this erstwhile stage-bound exposition is reaching the same conclusion on screen. Indeed, if you'll kindly permit us to reach a conclusion of our own, we would say this display is demonstrating that it is even tough to fool some of the people some of the time (after the Broadway play suggested you can't fool all of the people all of the time).

Steve was perfectly cast in the role of hard-bitten soldier,
Rees, in *Hell Is for Heroes*
(COURTESY: PARAMOUNT PICTURES /
BRITISH FILM INSTITUTE)

HELL IS FOR HEROES

(Paramount) 1962

'Hell Is for Heroes was almost autobiographical; Steve was
his own man. He was very private, though I don't mean he
was aloof, he just liked to do things his way' – L.Q. Jones

AFTER THE HONEYMOON MACHINE, Steve was desperate for a gritty role that would put his career back on track. He got exactly that when he was handed the role of Rees in this uncompromising World War II drama, also starring Bobby Darin and Fess Parker. The movie opens by introducing McQueen to an amateurish-looking outfit. It's a chalk and cheese scenario: they are friendly, talkative and hopeful of returning home. He is cold and merciless, who lives for combat. When Fess Parker delivers the news that they are to go to war and defend the Siegfried Line in France, Rees is unmoved, receiving the order in workmanlike fashion. The soldier is a loner, a real tough cookie who would be lost in an organised society. When Paramount opted for Steve for the role of Rees, it was a stroke of casting genius. The steely eyes and intense personality of McQueen gave his character the perfect definition.

Co-star L.Q. Jones, who later appeared in *Casino* with Robert De Niro, was stirred by how Steve engrossed himself into the part of Rees. He said: "You often see a picture and you say, 'He did a very good job,' but there again a number of other actors could have done just as well. But if you look at many of Steve's films, who could you substitute him for? He's there, that's him, either because the part was tailored that way or he made himself so good in it that you said, 'Aha, that is him, can't be anybody else.' *Hell Is for Heroes* was almost autobiographical; Steve was his own man. He was very private, though I don't mean he was aloof, he just liked to do things his way."

Prior to shooting, the picture endured much political conflict. The first scriptwriter Robert Pirosh, who wrote the story from which the movie was based on, was to direct. But after clashing with studio executives and more to the point - McQueen, he was fired.

Steve wanted more involvement with script decisions and the duties of the director. He had cajoled and bossed his way to running the set on *Wanted: Dead or Alive* as his success soared and, John Sturges apart, he was yet to meet the director who would stand up to him; but when Don Siegel was hired, that man had arrived. Siegel directed Elvis Presley in *Flaming Star* before this movie and went on to direct the likes of Henry Fonda (twice, including *Madigan*), John Wayne (*The Shootist*) and Clint Eastwood (five times, including *Dirty Harry* and *Escape to Alcatraz*).

In their first meeting at a Paramount office, McQueen immediately made his *position* known:

McQueen: (to Siegel) I hope you don't mind if I look through the camera on every shot.

Siegel: I don't mind. The cameraman might though.

McQueen: (Modestly) Now, I throw ideas at the director all the time; maybe four or five hundred. I don't say they're all good. Maybe only one hundred and fifty are usable.

Siegel: I don't care who I get the ideas from - the grip, the electrician. My name goes on the screen as director. But there's one thing you better be damn sure you understand (hitting the desk hard). I'm the director! Come hell or high water.

Steve was left red with anger. Someone had actually matched him blow for blow. Siegel was used to handling star quality and never took any nonsense no matter how big the actor thought he was. It took a while for things to settle between them, before and into the shoot, but eventually they gained a mutual respect for one another.

"Don and Steve made a hell of a team actually," said L.Q. Jones. "They had a little bit of trouble at first, but it's not unusual for a few sparks to fly when two very talented people are finding each other out. By the time they got into it after a couple of weeks, they were each other's biggest fans."

L.Q. appreciated how Steve had become so intent on controlling matters, but also states how clever he was to quickly evaluate the skill of Siegel and subsequently offer him due respect. "Soon as you do one or two pictures, you realise that if you've got a shit script, you're up the creek from the start. But whatever the quality of the script, it's in the hands of the director and he is the only person that can see everything that's going on, so you've got to trust him. At that point Steve had finished doing a lot of television and felt he knew what they could do. He wasn't ready to trust Don, but once he realised Don knew exactly what he was doing and exactly what he wanted and was going to get it, Steve was tickled to death and went to work. It's a different cup of tea once you hit the big screen and Steve was wise enough to realise this. He didn't back off and give himself over, but he was certainly willing to listen. They had a lot of fights and it wasn't unusual to see them shouting each other out, almost coming to blows, but that's not always a bad thing - the film is all you care about. Neither really cared for one another's feelings - it's the picture that counts."

There is a strong anti-war theme to *Hell Is for Heroes:* at the end, after Rees's heroic attempt at blowing up a German pillbox, the film fades out with his fellow soldiers continuing in battle. It suggests war is futile and that hell really is for heroes.

In one particular scene, Steve was required to walk from a long shot into an extreme close-up, where he would be crying by the time he passed the camera. It was Siegel's idea, but the scene never quite went to plan, as the director noted: "We shot it and nothing; absolutely nothing in those bitter blue eyes. Not a glimmer of a tear. We didn't give up. When Steve walked into his close-up, we blew chopped onion shreds directly below his eyes. It might as well have been chopped liver. Steve probably had the strongest eyes in the world. I decided on desperate measures. This time when I yelled 'Action', as steely-eyed Steve started walking I slapped him sharply across his face - then dived over an embankment, expecting him to tackle me. Instead, he walked on and, as usual, nothing happened. My eventual solution wasn't what I wanted, but it worked. We put drops into Steve's eyes to make him look as if he was crying...I felt great empathy for him."

Hell Is for Heroes was shot on location in Redding, at the north end of California, in temperatures exceeding 100 degrees. A retired Army Major, who was technical adviser, refused to take responsibility for the health of cast and crew when shooting was forced to continue, despite the extreme heat, even in the shade. To get around it, they occasionally shot at night when it was cooler.

Stuntman Chuck Hicks noted that although McQueen was still making his name at the time, his growing aura after *Wanted: Dead or Alive* and *The Magnificent Seven* created a certain fear around him from the crew. "I only had one scene with Steve, when I was a German soldier running towards where Steve was in a trench. While I was running I had a rifle that kept jamming. The prop man who was in charge of the rifle kept saying it was my fault and I didn't know how to shoot it right. My character then gets shot and they pull me in a pillbox to try to get information from me. Then they turned the camera on Steve using the same gun. Now Steve is having the same problem I had, but now it's the gun's fault. There was a lot of apologizing from the prop man to Steve, though there were no apologies to me. There was a pecking order in place and Steve was right at the top of it." The ongoing malfunctions with the firearms were apparently due to the blanks used, all stemming from budget cuts and money problems experienced on the movie.

Paramount studio executives arrived on the set shortly before shooting ceased with a directive to bring the film back to the lot in Los Angeles, due to the escalating costs. The picture was budgeted at $2.5million, but costs continued to rise alarmingly for what was supposed to be a low-budget production. McQueen and Siegel, though, stood united and fought to complete the picture on location. They were a match for anybody. All through his career, Steve resented interference from studio "suits".

Siegel could be equally awkward given the right circumstances. L.Q. Jones made four films under the direction of Siegel and he came to understand the man. "Don had a biting sense of humour, was a little laid-back, didn't come on very strong but when he did you knew you were in trouble because he'd have you by the throat in five seconds," Jones said with a chuckle. "He ran his set, he was an old-time director; it was *his* picture. He wouldn't take shit from anybody. If you contributed and if you paid attention to him he adored you, but if you started fucking around and not doing things that should be done, he was on your case. Other than that he was a terrific man and could be a kick in the head himself."

From what began as a volatile relationship, devoid of that imperative mutual trust, flourished into a tremendous actor-director comradeship. Siegel appreciated McQueen's qualities and utilised them perfectly. It remains one of Steve's best performances, though Paramount had less faith in the movie and promptly released it on June 26, 1962 as a double bill with *Escape From Zahrain* starring Yul Brynner. Inevitably, with such a marketing strategy, the picture was destined for failure at the box-office - as it proved. If the reviews were anything to go by, the picture was worthy of much greater faith by the Paramount executives. *Variety* was particularly positive about Steve's performance, writing: "McQueen plays the central role with hard-bitten business-like reserve and an almost animal intensity."

Main Credits:

Cast: Steve McQueen (as Rees), Bobby Darin, Fess Parker, James Coburn, Bob Newhart, Nick Adams, Harry Guardino, LQ Jones, Stephen Ferry, Mike Kellin, Simon Prescott, Joseph Hoover, Robert Phillips, Bill Mullikin, Don Haggerty and more.

Director:	Don Siegel
(Assistants)	William McGarry, James A. Rosenberger
Producer:	Henry Blanke
Cinematographer:	Harold Lipstein
Writers:	A screenplay by Robert Pirosh and Richard Carr, based on a story by Pirosh
Editor:	Howard A. Smith
Make-Up:	Wally Westmore
Music:	Leonard Rosenman

REVIEWS:

NEW YORK TIMES, July 12th, 1962

An arresting performance by Steve McQueen, a young actor with presence and a keen sense of timing, is the outstanding feature of *Hell Is for Heroes*. In the impressive new war drama that opened yesterday at neighbourhood theatres, Mr. McQueen sharply outlines a provocative modern military type. Surly and unpredictable, a dangerous misfit among the normal soldiers in his platoon, he is the kind of anti-social citizen unable to function in a civilised society. But, at the moment of combat when decisive action must be taken, it is his socially adjusted comrades who hesitate, while the maladjusted private takes command. For better or worse, he is the stuff of which heroes are made.

MONTHLY FILM BULLETIN, June, 1962

Steve McQueen gives an unvaried performance as a sullen, unshaven incarnation of the death-wish in this conventional American war story of the rebel against military authority who is finally justified, though in a more qualified and roundabout way than usual.

VARIETY, May 30th, 1962

Producer Henry Blanke has framed and mounted a gripping, fast-paced, hard-hitting dramatic portrait of an interesting World War II battlefield incident in *Hell Is for Heroes*. The Paramount release should be a popular attraction with male audiences and filmgoers who prefer an emphasis on explosive, nerve-shattering action in their war dramas...McQueen plays the central role with hard-bitten businesslike reserve and an almost animal intensity, permitting just the right degree of humanity to project through a war-weary-and-wise veneer.

Steve McQueen was not too dissimilar to his character in
The War Lover, Buzz Rickson, according to leading
lady Shirley Anne Field – pictured
(COURTESY: COLUMBIA PICTURES)

THE WAR LOVER

(Columbia) 1962

'Steve told me, "I'm going to be the biggest star in the world."... I wasn't surprised when he did become the big star he aspired to be, on his next movie The Great Escape... There was no doubt that when he was on the screen, you couldn't take your eyes off him.'
– Shirley Anne Field

AFTER MAKING EIGHT movies in America, Steve opted for a change of scenery. He was by now a notable personality in Hollywood, but still only one of his pictures had really been successful – *The Magnificent Seven*. In an attempt to rectify this, he agreed to star in another World War II picture, with Robert Wagner. He hoped the English location might provide the spark his career so needed. The signs appeared to be good considering the engaging yet complex character he took on: Captain Buzz Rickson is a respected, yet overly competitive, insubordinate, hard-bitten, hot-headed and insecure pilot but a selfish individual, whose sole interest is his own existence. The ending, though, does everything to disprove this when he commits hari-kari after his colleagues have already bailed out following a bombing raid. Buzz dies a hero, but his reasons for taking his own life stem from his personal insecurities in life.

Curiously, Buzz Rickson resembled shades of Steve McQueen, according to leading lady Shirley Anne Field: "There were similarities," she commented. "Steve would never let you steal a shot; he was ultra-competitive and had to win in every way. I would be having a love scene with Robert Wagner, and Steve – about six feet behind us – would pour a pint of lager over an extra's head, to distract the camera away from us. And he would say to me about RJ (Wagner), 'You might think he's the prettiest but just you wait till after this film when you see us both on the screen – you'll never look at him again.' There was no doubt that when he was on the screen, you couldn't take your eyes off him. I felt his competitiveness was understandable given his background in television. He had a chance here in the movies and he was determined to grab it."

Co-star Al Waxman, better known for his role as the Lieutenant in TV police series *Cagney and Lacey*, felt the picture was merely a stepping stone to better things for Steve. "During *The War Lover* he was on his way from being a successful television actor still and this movie just helped to springboard him." Steve was paid $10,000 a week, which added up nicely considering he was in London from September 1961 through Christmas. Within a year, though, he had more than doubled his earnings with a fee of $400,000 for his next film *The Great Escape*.

The War Lover was set in 1943 London and filmed at Shepperton Studios outside London, as well as on location at an

RAF base near Cambridge. Steve savoured the whole experience of shooting in England and particularly enjoyed carving up the English countryside in a race car or on his motorcycle – usually when he should have been on the set. "If a scene was being set up and was taking a long time, Steve would take off on his bike across the fields while it was pissing down with rain," recalled Waxman. "He'd come back splattered in mud and they'd have to get him a different costume. They would be waiting to shoot again and he would just get on the bike and disappear again. He was juvenile but not in an unattractive way; people seemed to like him for it. I certainly enjoyed his company."

Steve's on-set behaviour sometimes mirrored that of the stereo-typical school-kid, who would run amok when handed the freedom to do so, with a lack of authority in place. But given the presence of a respected, firm director who lays down the law, Steve generally responded and would go to work with minimal fuss. On *The War Lover*, Philip Leacock directed and although he had a history of working with notable stars as Dirk Bogarde, Shelly Winters and Alan Ladd, McQueen didn't respect him as he had John Sturges, Robert Wise or a tough guy director like Don Siegel. Subsequently, Steve misbehaved, argued and basically had his way with most things, but never in a nasty way and effused enough of the McQueen charm to get away with it, says Waxman: "Steve was just a guy who knew what he wanted and would sometimes dictate how he thought a scene should go. But that's not uncommon with big stars, though his next film *The Great Escape* was the one that catapulted him to major stardom. On this movie we had Phil Leacock directing and he was a very mild and gentle man and I don't think he was a fighter or the kind of guy that would say, 'This is my territory and I'm running it.' Without speaking ill of him, he probably gave in to the star more than other directors might have. Steve, though, to be fair to him, wasn't the kind of person that said, 'Right, this is how we're going to do it.' I acted in another picture with Phil Leacock, which Ben Gazzara starred in and he was a pushy, ballsy kind of guy. He took over from Leacock, who just had to swallow it. Steve wasn't any less strong than Gazzara, but he never ran rough on the director like Gazzara, who basically took things over."

Shirley Anne Field, then a 23-year-old fresh from co-starring in hits such as *The Entertainer* with Laurence Olivier and *Saturday Night, Sunday Morning* with Albert Finney, agreed that Steve was a challenge for Leacock. "Philip was a nice, darling man but he didn't have the strength to deal with the likes of Steve McQueen," she commented. "He was a good director but I think *The War Lover* could have been better if he had been more objectionable at times, but he was just so worn out in trying to direct Steve and placated him too much when firmness was needed."

Leacock later claimed to have enjoyed the experience of working with Steve, though to onlookers during the movie, his experience appeared far from an enjoyable one: "Directing Steve McQueen before he became a super duper star was a treat," Leacock said in an interview, before he passed away in 1990. "He took direction well and added his own charisma which contrasted with Bob Wagner's more repressed way of looking at things. It was more character study than actioner and McQueen liked playing the anti-hero very much."

Field admired Steve's boyishness and cocky ambition, but also saw a darker side – and not just in his dealings with the director. Steve cheated behind his wife Neile's back habitually throughout their 15-and-a-half-year marriage and he did so on this movie, taking advantage of her brief absence after she had been with him for the most part.

"Steve didn't behave well to all women socially, though he was fine around me," Field said. "While his wife was away for a short time, he went off to the Embassy Club and picked up a girl, who was a friend of mine. She went home with him and he badly hit her. I was horrified when she told me. I told Steve what I thought about it but he said, 'It's different to what you think.' He didn't say any more and I just left it at that. I still know that girl to this day and she has never mentioned it since and speaks about him in glowing terms. People remember what they want to remember. Steve tried it on with me also but, as my defence mechanism, I politely asked him to come back to me after we'd finished the film knowing he never would. I never quite knew if he was being genuine or if he was trying to compete with Robert Wagner. But I was wary of Steve after what my friend had told me. I didn't want to go out with anyone who I was going to get into a fight with physically."

It was not only violence that fired Steve's darker side. His uncontrollable insecurities also affected many scenes and relationships. In one scene Buzz visits Daphne (Field) at her home.

The climax shot required him to rip off her dressing gown, leaving her half-naked. The rehearsals went fine, but when the cameras rolled for real, the gown wouldn't split. It transpired that the wardrobe designer had been told by Steve to reinforce the stitching so it wouldn't come apart. He did not want her standing there half-naked commanding the audience's attention. He may have attended reform school and lacked all the standard educational qualifications, but Steve McQueen had an intelligence of a different kind – one that belonged to the street, which prepared him well for a career in films, where cunning scene-stealing was the norm.

Not all of McQueen's acting ability was about being crafty, and much of his work meant throwing himself into character with some good old fashioned blood and sweat. "Steve worked hard; he was incredibly professional about his work," co-star Gary Cockrell said. "During *War Lover* he was on his way to being a big star – he was an empire builder. He was a hard guy and could be hard for others to work with, but maybe that had more to do with others being jealous of him. At this time, Steve was on his way to being a great, big star and therefore he didn't suffer fools greatly."

Away from the set, the cast and crew mixed well – even if the crew did choose to leave McQueen stuck in the mud during one high-speed adventure in the English countryside. Steve initially resided at the Savoy Hotel before he was politely asked to leave when he set his room on fire trying to cook late one night. He then stayed in a rented house in Eton Square, where he threw several parties, most notably pre-Christmas, which coincided with the completion of the movie. "The morning after that party," Waxman remembers, "Steve asked me, 'Was I rude to you last night?' which I thought was kind of funny. I'd say, 'No, you were not,' but in fact he may well have been. He then said, 'If I was rude to you it was probably because you were speaking into my deaf ear.' I asked him which ear that was, but he would never tell me!" Steve could be rude, but more often than not, people wouldn't hold it against him. It was his lovable rogue personality that people found enchanting. McQueen loved shorting folk out of money he owed them. Those street tricks from his boyhood New York days were difficult to leave behind. Waxman suffered from these antics at first hand. "I had a habit of collecting umbrellas and walking sticks. Steve saw me coming to work one day with a cane and he asked me what was wrong. When I told him it opened out into an umbrella, he asked me to get him one and promptly gave me five pounds. I don't think he understood the meaning of money over there in England. I told him he still owed me 30 bucks, 'Okay I'll pay you,' he said, but I never did see the money!"

Steve again demonstrated his customary paradoxical behaviour at the movie wrap party. He could be unfriendly at times to Field – overwhelmed by the role she played of an upper-class English lady, even though actress and character were quite dissimilar, and he could certainly be challenging for director Leacock. But Steve also showed enough of that sweet-natured charm to seduce those around him. He presented Cockrell with a wind-up musical toy and told him to give it to his son.

And during the shoot he went out of his way to make Cockrell feel at home on what was a grand Hollywood movie, even if it was being filmed in the UK. "Steve was very kind and very nice on the movie from what I saw of him," Cockrell said. "We were both from Missouri and so that gave us a common bond.

"One day he asked me to go riding, as he had two dirt bikes over with him. He still took me along even though I told him I had never ridden before. We rode out to this gravel pit on the edge of London. Steve was obviously very good as the world would soon discover on *The Great Escape*, but I was not so good and lost control of the bike and went over the edge of this pit. Steve was shitting himself that the movie was going to be over, because my character, Lynch, was the sympathy part and Steve knew the implications if I got badly hurt. Fortunately, while the bike had dropped to the bottom of the pit, I was able to grab on to the edge and get out of there unhurt. He was very relieved and was certainly more bothered about me and the movie than his motorcycle."

Steve was also there to comfort Wagner, at a time when his suave co-star needed a good friend. Wagner may usually have appeared ice cool on the outside but within he was suffering. During *The War Lover*, Wagner was enduring a painful divorce from Natalie Wood and Steve felt his pain and was a great support to him. Wagner considered Steve overly competitive as an actor and hugely self-conscious; but that did not prevent him from appreciating his better qualities. "Steve was a good friend at a difficult time in my life," Wagner commented. "The subject of Natalie came up often, and he knew I was broken-hearted. He was very sympathetic, and I grew to like Steve a lot." They came to trust one another and, over the ensuing years, became occasional biking and drinking buddies. They would again act together 12 years later on *The Towering Inferno*.

McQueen and Wagner would have many deep and meaningfuls over a beer, at the local pub, according to Field. "They were fairly anonymous in Shepperton so they liked the fact they could melt into the crowd, with everyone minding their own business. They would not have lived that English pub ambience much in Hollywood."

The War Lover opened on October 25, 1962. The Premiere in Dallas was attended by Steve, Robert Wagner and Shirley Anne Field. It was an extravagantly presented event by Columbia. But an insecure Field squirmed and sank lower into her seat, embarrassed at what she felt was not her best performance. Steve noticed her pain and swapped seats with his friend and publicity agent Dave Resnick so that he could coax her through. Field was overwhelmed by this other, caring aspect to McQueen's character. "I saw a different side to Steve in Dallas; a kindness that I had not known from him. I was in tears because I couldn't get my character up there on the screen and Steve saw that and got me through the night."

Field had been more accustomed to the confident, arrogant Steve McQueen. He had told her during filming, 'I'm going to be the biggest star in the world.' She laughed when he said it, given that he was only just fresh out of television. But she also sensed a burning desire within him that convinced her he just may be right. "If I'm honest I didn't see the electricity at that point. Not until I saw him up there on the screen;

and it was then I could tell he had true star quality. I wasn't surprised when he did become the big star he aspired to be, on his next movie *The Great Escape*. When he was well cast, he had that great presence on-screen. There was a magnetism."

Main Credits:

Cast: Steve McQueen (as Captain Buzz Rickson), Robert Wagner, Shirley Anne Field, Gary Cockrell, Michael Crawford, Bill Edwards, Chuck Julian, Robert Easton, Al Waxman, Tom Busby, George Sperdakos, Bob Kanter, Jerry Stovin and more.

Director:	Philip Leacock
(Assistant)	Basil Rayburn
Producer:	Arthur Hornblow Jr.
Cinematographer:	Robert Huke
Writer:	Howard Koch, based on the novel by John Hersey
Editor:	Gordon Hales
Wardrobe:	Elsa Fennell
Make-Up:	George Partleton
Music:	Richard Addinsell

REVIEWS:

NEW YORK TIMES, March 7th, 1963
The fellows who sit in the cockpit of the one plane on which the action centres are a dull pair and are rendered even duller by poor acting and weak direction.

MONTHLY FILM BULLETIN, March, 1963

Buzz, is, in fact, a psychopath, and the film is a chronicle of his collapse as his confidence is gradually sapped, and finally broken. His end is a combination of suicide and madness, and enough of this comes across, especially through the excellent playing of Steve McQueen, to emphasize the general discursiveness of the film and its lack of a firm overall pattern.

VARIETY, October 24th, 1962

The story transpires in 1943 England and focuses on B-17 bombing raids over Germany, with the title character Steve McQueen a pilot of one of the planes. That the central character emerges more of an appealing symbol than a sympathetic flesh-and-blood portrait is no fault of McQueen, who plays with vigor and authority, although occasionally with too much eyeball emotion.

The Great Escape made an international superstar of Steve,
but it could have been very different had Steve not fought
for crucial script changes to improve his character, Hilts
(COURTESY: UNITED ARTISTS / BARBARA LEIGH)

THE GREAT ESCAPE

(United Artists) 1963

'Steve handled stardom very well throughout his career, right from
The Great Escape. A typical Sunday would be for us to take our kids
over the park and play football. On a Saturday night he might have
had a couple of people over to shoot pool. You rarely heard about
Steve McQueen at the big Hollywood parties'
– Robert Relyea

THIS WORLD WAR II picture, shot in the summer of 1962, was
a blockbuster smash for Steve and the producers. Serious issues
with the script, though, meant it proved a tough challenge for both.

It is predominantly based on fact from Paul Brickhill's
book, which was adapted for the screen; first by three-time
Academy Award nominee Walter Newman (uncredited), then
the novelist Bill Burnett (credited as W.R. Burnett), though it
was Australian writer Jim Clavell, who had been a former prisoner of war in Japan, who actually produced the finished script
that was exciting enough to satisfy the producers. Still, though,
there were huge problems with the script while on location –
mostly involving Steve's character – and a fourth writer Ivan
Moffat was drafted in. There were 12 script versions in total.

The sequence whereby Steve escapes and is then intentionally apprehended to acquire information to benefit the '*The Great Escape*', was conceived by additional scriptwriter Ivan Moffat to appease Steve's demands to strengthen his part
(COURTESY: UNITED ARTISTS / BRITISH FILM INSTITUTE)

The Great Escape chronicles how 76 men escaped from the high-security POW camp Stalag Luft III in Germany in 1944. Once the majority were recaptured, 50 were shot in cold blood by the SS. In fact, Brickhill had been a POW in the real camp after his Spitfire was shot down over Tunisia. Sturges bought the movie rights to his book as early as 1951 but it took him a decade longer to bring the picture to fruition, with a $4 million budget.

The project was a gamble for Steve given that he had just come off two War films that did not do great business at the box-office. This wasn't a typical War film though, as there was no combat, no battles over territory – just an adventure about escape. Nonetheless, in the knowledge that Sturges was directing, who Steve had worked with before when he received his only major acclaim (on *The Magnificent Seven* and *Never So Few* to a lesser extent), he jumped in. It proved to be the best career move he ever made considering its eventual global success. The film personifies everything about Steve McQueen, the King of Cool. He employs those distinctive mannerisms that he became synonymous with and in doing so he received fame and recognition like never before. The potential, the precocity, the promise - it was all realised in *The Great Escape*. His trademark reluctant smile; his contempt toward superiors, his throwing of a baseball while in a prison cell, and of course his carving up of the Bavarian countryside on his Triumph TR6 Trophy motorcycle (posing as a German BMW R75). It really was vintage McQueen. The influence of John Sturges once more was no coincidence in the way

A reunion from *The Magnificent Seven*: from the left,
James Coburn, director John Sturges, Steve McQueen and
Charles Bronson
(COURTESY: UNITED ARTISTS / THE KOBAL COLLECTION)

McQueen's stardom escalated thereafter. Sturges recognised
Steve's talent and he simply gave him the camera.

"It was a great chance for Steve to show his qualities,
even more so than *The Magnificent Seven*," assistant producer
and second unit director Robert Relyea commented. "After

this picture, the path was open for him because the industry and the public recognised him for what he was - a star."

Initially, McQueen and second lead James Garner were seen as a gamble by the studio United Artists as both had never carried a big budget movie on their own before and had only been stars in television series. McQueen was a huge success in *The Magnificent Seven,* and *Never So Few* before it to a lesser extent, but those pictures were carried by Yul Brynner and Frank Sinatra respectively. Here, McQueen was *the* star in his own right. Steve McQueen and James Garner was not the first choice star combination for executive producer Walter Mirisch and producer John Sturges. They wanted Kirk Douglas to play Hilts and Burt Lancaster to play Hendley, as Sturges had directed them in *The Gunfight at the O.K. Corral* and was confident they would commit to the picture. When their significantly larger salaries proved a stumbling block, McQueen and Garner were eventually decided upon at a saving of over $1 million.

The lack of Steve's universal fame, at least in a global way, was evident in how he was viewed by the English actors. English co-star John Leyton had to inquire about Steve's background to understand why he was playing the lead. "During the shoot, it never felt like this film or Steve would be a huge hit, to me," he commented. "Those feelings changed later. But during filming I thought the biggest star was James Garner. He had just come off a huge TV series, *Maverick.* I know this sounds terrible but in 1962 I wasn't so sure who Steve McQueen was. Somebody had to prompt me and tell me that he was one of the stars in *The Magnificent Seven.*"

Steve's attempted escape on his motorcycle is one
of the most iconic movie moments
(COURTESY: UNITED ARTISTS)

Mirisch was relieved that their eventual star line-up was well received after the safe option of Douglas and Lancaster was shelved. "I am eternally grateful that it worked out the way it did," he said. "Steve McQueen and Jim Garner were much younger and I think that made it more realistic and better for the picture. This was the best that we finally fell upon; although it was a gamble because they were not considered stars at that time."

Competition to be noticed on *The Great Escape* was fierce amongst what was a multi-star cast. As well as Steve, there was Garner, *'Big X'* Richard Attenborough (after Richard Harris had to withdraw through his commitments with *This Sporting Life*), Charles Bronson, James Coburn, Donald Pleasance, James Donald and David McCallum. In such respected company, Steve knew he had to be good, and to ensure he maintained his status as the lead actor on the movie, he used every trick he knew and every idea he could think of. And he needed to, given his insecurities about the size and importance of his character, Captain Virgil Hilts. Lengthy delays occurred on the set while additional writers were drafted in to improve his part as Steve felt his co-stars were stealing *his* movie from him. Steve refused to work for the first six weeks of the shoot, until his part was enlarged. There were frustrations and hushed groans about the delays and of Steve's reticence to execute the original script, but nobody can deny that whatever tactics

Steve used, he ultimately made a legend out of what was, initially, a nothing role.

"To be fair to Steve, Hilts was an insignificant character," co-star John Leyton commented. "Quite what that part was doing in the film I have no idea. If Steve was cast first as the star, why didn't they cast him as the scrounger? I guess if that had happened James Garner wouldn't have been in the film. As it was James Garner played that role beautifully. They invented Hilts's role for Steve from the original true story. Everything he did was fictitious. Everybody had a role in the film – apart from Steve McQueen's character. I don't know why Steve would have taken on this film given those circumstances. It has always been a mystery to me. Maybe he was offered things that didn't materialise? It is obvious that John Sturges just wanted Steve in the movie, no matter what his role was. And it's equally clear that Steve trusted Sturges to do right by him, which he did."

Steve twice came close to quitting the picture over his character's lack of substance and it needed the diplomacy skills of his agent Stan Kamen, who flew over from the States, to prevent him from walking out on this movie. Garner and Coburn also advised him not to quit. Any other director might have refused to tolerate such antics from his star, but Sturges knew what McQueen meant to the film and, subsequently, he was prepared to change the script to meet Steve's demands.

"He had to find his niche," says Relyea. "Steve didn't feel he had his *thing*. Charlie Bronson had his shovel and his pick as 'The Tunnel King'; Jim Garner could work on his part as 'The Scrounger'; but Steve didn't have anything and he felt he couldn't work without a defined character to play. So we shot around him for six weeks and eventually we came up with 'The Cooler King'."

There was a time, briefly, when Sturges had resigned himself to losing Steve on the film and he approached Garner to take on the lead role. Garner regarded Steve as his "delinquent younger brother" as the two hung out together, racing bikes or cars and later became neighbours. Garner was not comfortable with the idea of the lead and he invited fellow co-star Coburn and Steve to his rented house in Munich and tried to persuade him not to quit Germany and *The Great Escape*. This rendezvous had the desired effect when Sturges eventually agreed to flesh out Steve's part more and give Hilts some added substance. But reaching that stage of compromise was a tough slog on Steve, Sturges and the rest of the cast, who had to shoot out of sequence.

"Munich was nowhere near as big a city then as it is today and I remember you would bump into cast or crew members from the film out at a restaurant regularly," John Leyton recalls. "I saw Steve a few times at one of these restaurants and he would be in pretty deep conversation with John Sturges – just the two of them. The rest of us were out socialising and having a drink in our own groups, but Steve was still 'at work'. It soon became known that Steve had a problem with his role and he did what he could to change it. To Steve's credit he never mentioned it once to me that he was unhappy with his role. And as far as I know he never mentioned it to anybody else. Other people may have made a song and dance out of it. So in that respect he was very professional and only aired his opinions to the director and producers."

Steve's wife Neile admitted that Steve was a "nervous wreck" generally when trying to get a fix on his character just prior to principal photography on whatever film he might be working towards. But for *The Great Escape*, he was especially anxious and concerned. These feelings were not exactly helped when the editor cut a 20-minute montage early into shooting to maintain morale amongst the cast and crew and Steve had not even shot a scene at that stage and he instead had to watch how cool was James Garner in his well-defined role. Steve was boiling over and was adamant that Hilts had to find his niche and quick. "The part of Hilts was still ambiguous," Neile commented. "Hilts had no real personality. He was bland and he was boring. Steve knew that, given this cast, unless he came up with something interesting for this role he would blend in with the scenery. He had absolutely no intention of letting that happen. He did, after all, have top billing and he didn't want to lose face. John Sturges, who was Steve's mentor, was trying to solve the problem. Together with writer Ivan Moffat they laboured until all hours of the night trying to do justice to Steve's presence in the film."

Walter Mirisch acknowledged that Steve's issues with his character's lack of scope posed a grave problem while the shooting went on without him. "It troubled us and it troubled Steve, too," Mirisch reflected. "Actually in order to try and buttress up both Steve's role and his importance to the movie, several ideas were added like the sequence where Big X asks Hilts to escape and allow himself to be recaptured so that he can come back and give the information to everyone else (contributed by Ivan Moffat). That was all written in just to buttress up Steve's role. That was done to show Steve's self-sacrifice. It added footage to an already long film, which was something John Sturges and I were concerned about. But as often happens when making movies, after a while we began to like it and thought it was a real good idea, which we should have thought of earlier! Despite all the troubles, I really don't think Steve was ever close to quitting. He liked being in the picture; he had a good instinct for it and knew this was going to be a successful picture. Steve had great confidence in it and of course he was right because it is certainly one of the best pictures of his life."

The Cooler King was just right for Steve. It allowed him to play the rebel, which was when he was at his best. Winding up in a prison cell for long periods might seem like a way of eliminating scope to shine in the film, but Steve had the creativity to get the best out of his characters, and Hilts was no different. It was his idea to bounce a baseball against the wall while incarcerated, and it was something that furthered the definition of his character. Says Relyea, "I spent a whole day in that cell with Steve when he wasn't working, just practising his method, throwing that baseball. It became a symbol that he was thinking once again at how he would try to escape next time." Like his character in *Papillon*, which he made a decade later, Hilts has an unrelenting desire to escape and his cocky nature is even flaunted in front of the Nazi camp officials when he tells the Commandant that he hasn't seen Berlin, yet he hopes to do just that 'before' the war is out.

The additions that were made to the script for Steve's benefit caused delays and some of the other actors became annoyed with what some viewed as prima donna antics. Charles Bronson would later be quoted as saying: "For *The Great Escape*, Sturges had many problems with Steve McQueen. He's not a truly professional actor. We filmed almost two months and when we saw the rushes, he (McQueen) was horrible. We had to get a new scriptwriter and begin again from scratch. Sturges had confidence in him, totally, because he had worked with him before and thought it was unnecessary to give him too much instruction."

Steve and Charlie were friendly rivals on *The Magnificent Seven* and were wary of the other's success. That verbal attack on Steve attributed to Bronson was a surprise to John Leyton. They performed most of their scenes together as the 'tunnel kings' and socialised in Munich on most nights after work but Leyton never recalled any anti-McQueen whingeing from his friend and co-star, Bronson.

Robert Relyea acknowledged there were voices of discontent at Steve's behaviour. "I think the irritation was that we actually started to shoot before the situation with Steve arose, when we had to shoot around him. That made some of his colleagues irritable as we were drifting away from the drive of the themes and the outspoken ones, like Charlie, would say, 'I don't quite understand it; I've got my script and I know that my character has to be worked, why can't he work his?' But the situation never got out of hand, though. You must remember half the cast were English professionals and guys like Dickie Attenborough and Donald Pleasance would never allow themselves to become involved with an unhappy cast."

Undoubtedly, the sequence that most people identify with *The Great Escape* is Steve's hair-raising escape by motorcycle while an endless amount of German soldiers are in pursuit of him following the mass exodus from the camp. The footage was filmed around the mediaeval town of Fussen, on the Austrian border, to the South West of Munich. This was another of Steve's own ideas that he felt would enlarge his part, while adding real drama to the picture, so Sturges was happy to oblige. Steve even doubled as some of the German soldiers, chasing himself. In the goggles and full uniform, it was impossible to spot him. Even Sturges was unable to identify him when Steve, in Nazi costume, approached the director with the idea.

The highlight of the sequence was the now infamous jump towards freedom. Although McQueen carried out all the daredevil riding over the German countryside, it was his close friend and stuntman Bud Ekins, who he had befriended at Ekins' motorcycle shop since 1961, that actually performed the finale jump courtesy of a ramp that the crew positioned at the foot of one of the hillocks. The producers felt the jump was too dangerous for Steve. He accepted this, though reluctantly. Says Walter Mirisch, "Steve really wanted to do it, but we were afraid he'd hurt himself and delay the production of the picture. But typically of Steve, I was told later that he did do the jump off-camera just to prove to everyone that he could do it! He wasn't being necessarily macho, he just loved his bikes and his reputation meant a lot to him. I think he felt that his reputation was on the line and he wasn't one to be outdone by anyone. He was hugely competitive with Bud and needed to get even." Bike enthusiast John Leyton also did the jump with Steve, as did James Coburn, who fell off in the process.

On McQueen's creative input, particularly his own role, Relyea said: "Once those additions to his part were made, Steve really flushed it out and went to work. He thought all the time and he often said: 'I shouldn't be comfortable when I'm working because that's not when I do my best.' Eventually, he would become comfortable when he had found the tools to work with, like the motorcycle chase."

One of the casualties of the pulsating motorcycle footage near the end of the movie, which was of course added into the script at the last minute to appease Steve, was a sequence between James Garner 'the scrounger' and his onscreen room-mate Donald Pleasance, 'the forger'. The two shared a touching scene during a blackout with explosions visible outside of their cell window. Sturges thought it was one of the best scenes filmed but, over a lunch he had arranged, he explained to Garner during the editing process that it had to be left on the cutting room floor to accommodate Steve's heroics on the bike. Garner appreciated the gesture and agreed the motorcycle footage made the movie better.

The common perception of this picture when studied in hindsight is that Steve McQueen was a pain in the ass and played the sulking, spoiled movie star all the way to get what he wanted. Maybe some of that is true but as co-star John Leyton pointed out, initially the part of Hilts was a nothing role and without McQueen's histrionics he and the film would surely have suffered terribly. How could anyone imagine *The Great Escape* without the bike chase and The Cooler King, throwing his baseball back and forth into his mitt? McQueen not only stood his ground for a bigger role but played a major part in conceiving these exciting additions to his character. Even executive producer Walter Mirisch now admits that Steve's actions were vindicated by the eventual success of the movie and of his own performance. His fierce protests in Germany, when he threatened to quit, may only have been posturing and just a game ultimately, but the tactics had the desired effect when the Hilts character was bolstered significantly to elevate Steve McQueen to Hollywood stardom.

"I guess the bike chase was mostly Steve's idea," Mirisch admitted. "We were looking at ways to dramatize the escapes of each of our principal characters. We had Big X and Gordon Jackson caught in the street, the plane crash with Jim Garner and Donald Pleasance, so it just seemed natural that Steve's escape would be on a motorcycle.

"The extra ideas did make the film better but they also made the film longer, which may or may not be an asset to it. It is certainly a fair argument to suggest that Steve's additional sequences did make this movie better. I would not quarrel with the possibility that that was the case. In hindsight, his intuition about the necessity to build up his role was probably valid, despite how disturbing his behaviour was at the time."

Given all the pressures and confrontations on the picture, it proved to be quite a stressful movie for Steve. Also for Sturges, the producers, the rest of the cast and the writers – they all had something to prove, as the film company were apprehensive about the project throughout. Their feeling was, 'You're making a movie about a prison camp where we shoot

50 at the end - what's this about?' It was important for Steve that he had his family around him. Their influence relaxed him after a tough day's shooting.

"Steve felt the pressure on that film more than anyone because he was the star," says Relyea. "So if there is a little bit of home or a family to go to at night, it helps. I should think Neile spent many nights being the listening wall. She was very good at being the sympathetic one, doing her best to stay away from confrontation because she knew he had that all day from the directors, writers, producers et cetera."

Steve had another way of venting his frustrations and it usually meant he was on two or four wheels at breakneck speed. "Steve went nuts over there," James Garner wrote in his memoir. "He was always getting into scrapes. When he wasn't working he would race that motorcycle with the swastikas on it all over Munich just to annoy the Germans. And people would yell. He also totalled a Mercedes Gullwing; stuck it right into the pine trees. The police finally set up a roadblock and nailed him. They put him in jail for a few hours and took his driver's licence away."

Steve also relished a leisure day that one of the crew arranged as a way of building camaraderie early into what was a mammoth six-month shoot. The fact this particular excursion meant a legitimate excuse to put pedal to the metal, Steve was able to demonstrate his 'thing' and showboat a little.

"Quite early into the shoot we went kart racing," John Leyton recalled. "They were nippy little things too so I was surprised they allowed us to do it; especially when you consider Steve wasn't allowed to do 'the' jump in the movie for insurance purposes. One of the assistant directors arranged it at the weekend and those I can remember who definitely went were Steve, Jim Coburn, Jim Garner and myself. I don't remember any of the other English actors being there. But as you can imagine Steve loved it – anything on two wheels or four wheels and Steve was there. He was always competitive, but the karting was funny because we both came a cropper on this tight corner. He came off first and ended up in no man's land. I was behind him and did exactly the same thing; nearly sent him flying and he had to jump out of the bloody way to miss me. I was worried that I might have seriously hurt him, but Steve found it very funny; he wasn't at all worried about getting hurt."

With Neile and the children around him having reached Germany in May 1962, Steve was always far happier and while the likes of Leyton, Coburn, Bronson and Garner socialised most evenings around the bars of Munich, the lead star kept his distance.

"Steve was very much a family man," Leyton said, "which goes against the reputation and persona of the wild and rebellious Steve McQueen."

Realising just how important it was to keep their star happy, the film company found the McQueen's a beautiful chalet in Bavaria, near to Munich. Every morning Steve had an hour's drive to the Geiselgasteig Studios, where the prison compound had been built as a replica to the original. It wasn't unusual for Steve to alert the attention of the local police when on his way to work, as speed limit signs to him were merely an extension of the landscape than to be adhered to. John Sturges had to use his diplomacy skills on more than one occasion to free his star from the clutches of the police, when they caught up with him at the studios after trailing a dust cloud for most of the journey.

The Great Escape is now one of the most iconic movies in Hollywood history and what it did for Steve's career was near immeasurable. His name was white-hot and every studio wanted a piece of him. He was still searching for that major breakthrough beforehand, but with *The Great Escape* he had found it and promptly received the adulation he had craved, despite the odd negative review, most notably The New York Times, who considered his baseball throwing as "one of the most moronic running gags in years". Steve was paid $400,000 for this picture and he delighted in his newfound riches, which gave security to his family and in terms of material gain a Brentwood mansion on Oakmont Drive that he and Neile called 'The Castle'. He once said in an interview, "Stardom equals financial success, and financial success equals security. I've spent too much of my life feeling insecure."

McQueen did well to maintain a down-to-earth manner for much of the time and refused to get sucked in to the Hollywood trap where artificial personalities are frequently manufactured by the persuasion of riches. "Steve handled stardom very well throughout his career, right from *The Great Escape*," said Robert Relyea, who would later become a business partner of Steve's.

"The time I worked with him, a typical Sunday would be for us to take our kids over the park and play football. On a Saturday night he might have had a couple of people over to shoot pool. You rarely heard about Steve McQueen at the big Hollywood parties. He was a family man and when he started earning a lot of money, he just bought a big house to put that family in. He was more comfortable sitting around with non-industry people talking about motorcycles. He was interested in anything mechanical like bikes and cars; you would never see Steve McQueen on a yacht in the marina - he just wasn't like that."

Main Credits:

Cast: Steve McQueen (as Captain Virgil Hilts), James Garner, Richard Attenbrough, James Donald, Charles Bronson, Donald Pleasance, James Coburn, Hannes Messemer, David McCallam, Gordon Jackson, John Leyton, Angus Lennie, Nigel Stock, Robert Graf, Jud Taylor, Hans Reiser, Harry Riebauer and more.

Director:	John Sturges
(Assistant)	Jack N. Reddish
Producer:	John Sturges, Walter Mirisch (executive, uncredited)
(Assistant)	Robert Relyea (and second unit director)
Cinematographer:	Daniel L. Fapp
Writers:	Screenplay by James Clavell and W.R. Burnett - Walter Newman and Ivan Moffatt were uncredited (based on the book by Paul Brickhill)
Editor:	Ferris Webster
Wardrobe:	Bert Henrikson
Make-Up:	Emile LaVigne
Music:	Elmer Bernstein

REVIEWS:

THE NEW YORK TIMES, August 8th, 1963

I find it artificial from the outset - from the point where a string of trucks arrives in the new prison compound and disgorges a crowd of swaggering bucks, nondescript British and American fellows, snarling rudely and pointedly casing the joint. There's Steve McQueen, surly and sophomoric, tediously whacking a baseball in to a glove, which he continues to do at intervals throughout the picture, providing one of the most moronic running gags in years...*The Great Escape* grinds out its tormenting story without a peak beneath the surface of any man, without a real sense of human involvement. It's a strictly mechanical adventure with make-believe men.

VARIETY, April 17th, 1963

Mirisch Co. and United Artists have hit the jackpot with *The Great Escape*, a film of blockbuster potential...There are some exceptional performances - histrionic and cinematic. Probably the most provocative single impression is made by Steve McQueen as a dauntless Yank pilot whose 'pen'-manship record shows 18 blots, or escape attempts. McQueen has a style, an individuality, that is rare in the contemporary scene. He is a throwback to the personalities of earlier screen eras. He is the possessor of the kind of unique star quality with which such performers as Cagney and Bogart captured the public imagination. And he is further endowed with the agility and daring spirit of the athlete, as attested to by his motorcycling manoeuvers on this occasion.

THE HOLLYWOOD REPORTER, April 17th, 1963

The Great Escape is a great adventure picture, tense with excitement, rich in character, leavened with humour, novel in setting and premise...McQueen, with his unique capacity for projecting both spitting meanness and easy charm, continues his steady, unwavering climb to the highest stardom. He also does some frightening motorcycle stunts in the chase scenes, which, as star, he should not have done, but having done them, they're terrific.

FINANCIAL TIMES, June 21st, 1963

The players, who include James Garner, Richard Attenborough, James Donald, and Donald Pleasance, all fall into conventions - schoolboy heroic - to suit the material. All, that is, except Steve McQueen, who is becoming an admirable player. Engaging sympathy for a start by having a tousled face practically the double of the late Thomas Mitchell, he is virile without being a thug, tough and yet with a strange grace. And he has the relaxation and interior quality of a fine actor.

Steve bravely took on another comedy role in *Soldier
in the Rain* but it was not one of his best performances
and he appeared somewhat miscast
(COURTESY: ALLIED ARTISTS /
THE KOBAL COLLECTION)

SOLDIER IN THE RAIN

(Allied Artists) 1963

*'Steve informed me that he went to bed with all of his lead-
ing ladies. He wasn't the kind of man you got upset at...He tried
me out, or maybe I tried him out, and that was pretty much
it. It wasn't as though Steve wined and dined me; we just used
to go back to the hotel or one of our trailers' – Chris Noel*

STEVE WAS CONSTANTLY looking for a change of pace
or a different role, just to prove to the world and to himself
that he had the range to carry it off. He was often credited
for his macho, dominating screen presence but rarely praised
for his acting skills. After playing Hilts, possibly the coolest
POW ever seen in a movie theatre in *The Great Escape*, Steve
looked for a variation to the norm. *Soldier in the Rain*, a light
drama-cum-comedy, became that diverse character selection
he sought. But despite his best intentions, this movie did not
come together for him or build on his growing reputation. In
fact it more likely set him back after the huge success of *The
Great Escape*.

"He looked uncomfortable in the movie," said his co-star and lover Chris Noel. "I liked Steve, but in this film he was not a good actor. I don't think Jackie Gleason or Steve were all that good in the film and I believe it was because they both had attitudes towards each other. It was supposed to be a funny movie and had (writer and producer) Blake Edwards have directed, I am sure it would have been. But frankly I feel this turned out to be a sad movie."

Steve played Supply Sergeant Eustis Clay, who was a simple, over-friendly dreamer that belonged anywhere but an army base, where the majority of the picture was set. Eustis Clay is a close companion of Master Sergeant Maxwell Slaughter the barracks head, played by Jackie Gleason. The two men are total opposites in character, but they share a dream that, one day, they will leave the army and both enjoy the luxuries of life on a desert island, surrounded by naked women "with flat stomachs...whose breasts tilt up". It is a warm friendship. Maxwell is a father figure to Eustis and feels an obligation to watch over him like an unofficial guardian, as well as best friend; a frothy, buddy movie, but with an undertone of sadness and vulnerability. Like in *The Honeymoon Machine* two years earlier, McQueen was never really comfortable with comedy, and again in this picture he seems uneasy in a part where he over-acts. "It was a hard kind of picture for him," said co-star Ed Nelson, "because he usually played the big, intelligent, stud tough guy. But here he was playing a wimp."

This incongruous screen image of Steve never impressed the masses and co-star Chris Noel, who played Steve's girl-friend in the picture, shared that view. "He did a great job, but I have to admit that I preferred to see Steve as a man of adventure in movies like *Bullitt* and *The Great Escape*. A lot of people could have played Steve's role in *Soldier in the Rain*, but with most of his other films there's no one else who could possibly have done a better job or carry off the film in the same, exciting way that Steve often did."

This picture saw the first involvement for Steve's newly-formed production company, Solar, named after the street on which he lived. Blake Edwards was writer and co-producer though said he had very little to do with Steve on the film. This was an irritation to McQueen as he wanted to work with Edwards, who had made *Breakfast at Tiffany's* two years prior. "Steve and Jackie (Gleason) were not happy at first because they expected Blake Edwards to direct, but at the last hour Blake decided he wanted to work on a *Pink Panther* movie and so he pulled off the film and had nothing to do with it," Chris Noel revealed. "They then offered Jackie the chance to nominate who he wanted as director and he opted for Ralph Nelson (as they had made *Requiem for a Heavyweight* together a year ear-lier, which starred Anthony Quinn). I believe Jackie had a clause in his contract that gave him the ok on the director. Once Steve knew that Blake Edwards would not be direct-ing, he played up.

"Steve had a bit of attitude about him after coming off *The Great Escape*," Noel added. "Jackie Gleason and Steve did not like each and feuded quite often throughout the picture. They were opposites in character and it was pretty interesting to watch them interact with one another. Because Steve wasn't happy with the director he would show his disrespect to him, and indirectly Jackie, by turning up late on the set. And in doing so he kept Jackie Gleason hanging around and that really annoyed him so he started doing the same for the golf course scene. The feud got so bad that they had to shut filming down for two days because neither one of them showed up. The director had a real struggle controlling these two big egos. Eventually he persuaded the two stars to settle their differences. Steve and Jackie actually went out for dinner in Los Angeles. It was meant to be a peace-making exercise and Steve invited me along, presumably to help take the tension out of the meeting. They barely spoke all evening and it was a very tense and boring meal to be part of."

McQueen and Gleason were magnanimous about one another during publicity afterwards, but their compliments of each other's talents masked a personal dislike between them. "Jackie kept himself to himself pretty much off the set," Noel added. "We never saw much of him away from the camera, but one thing I did notice was that he really liked to *drink*."

Off-camera, Steve's flirting was infamous and while shooting this picture he wound up in bed with both female leads, according to one of those 'conquests' Chris Noel, who revealed that fellow leading lady Tuesday Weld also spent intimate times with Steve after her own affair with him ended. Although home life with Neile, Terry and Chad meant everything to Steve and supporting them was, in fact, the very reason for his hard toil in the industry, he saw womanising almost as recreation. Sometimes he would even hint at his misdemeanours to Neile as if to relieve himself of the guilt. His affair with Chris Noel began almost immediately on the set, as she instantly fell for his charm and sexual magnetism. They first met during a screen test and began a month-long affair that drifted halfway into principal photography.

"Steve was a pretty cool guy and was hard for me to resist after seeing him in *The Great Escape*," Noel recalled. "He never got called 'The King of Cool' for nothing. I didn't know anything about him before *The Great Escape* because I was only 22 at the time; this was my first Hollywood movie. It was very exciting to get to know him and be around him. I walked by his trailer early on and he invited me in. Straight away Steve informed me that he went to bed with all of his leading ladies. Maybe you would take offence from some men saying that to you but Steve McQueen wasn't the kind of man that you got upset at.

"I just thought that he was an exciting, sexy, vibrant, adventurous, amazing man. He used to tell me great stories, like when he lived with two prostitutes in his younger days in New York. He told me that he learnt a lot from them -

and he wasn't talking about acting skills! He really was great to talk to. You could talk to him about anything. In the month we were together, he treated me very well; he was very nice, sexy and was a very good lover. He was only interested in me when we were together – we didn't talk about the movie, we just had fun. I remember one time we went up in a hot air balloon. Steve just loved adventure, but especially his fast cars and bikes.

"The reason why, I think, Steve liked me at first was because I told him that I had seen him in *The Great Escape* at a special preview in New York - before it had been officially released. He was very impressed with that as I had gone to a special screening in New York City. He was stunned that I knew about this movie and that I had the opportunity to see it at this early stage, before its release. Nobody in Hollywood had even seen it. That won me Steve's favour and almost certainly got me the part."

When the gossip of Steve's latest infidelity was leaked to Neile, she was understandably furious and drove up the coast to find out what was going on. Noel added: "When we were shooting at the barracks, his wife arrived on the set because she thought that Steve was having an affair with me. Although we did have an affair, by that time he was seeing Tuesday (Weld), not me. I knew he was married and I didn't want to be going around with a married man. He tried me out, or maybe I tried him out, and then that was pretty much it. It wasn't as though Steve wined and dined me; we just used to go back to the hotel or one of our trailers. The strangest thing about all that was the way Tuesday reacted to me: while I was seeing Steve, she never spoke to me. I think she saw me as a rival to her intentions with Steve. It didn't bother me that Steve saw Tuesday after me; I was just glad that I was no longer messing around with a married man. When I heard she would be coming on to the set I thought, 'No more, goodbye!' Steve just moved on." Interestingly, Neile wrote warmly of Tuesday Weld in her book *My Husband, My Friend* and intimated that her personality was like a female version of Steve's.

Sugar Blymyer (credited as Maryce Bates) was hairdresser to both leading ladies on the movie but was not aware of either of Steve's affairs, though acknowledged it was not unusual for this kind of fraternizing to be kept secret. "I was doing Tuesday Weld's hair on this film and she was a full-time job - Tuesday was a lot of fun but she was a handful," commented Blymyer "She was a wild child. She drove me down the coast road by Monterrey one day and I was hanging on for dear life. Another day she went down to the beach and got seaweed and threw it into the swimming pool so people would think there was a monster in there. You could never quite get her to do what you wanted her to do but she was fun. I also took care of Chris Noel and those two took up all my time. But I never did hear any gossip that they were running around with Steve McQueen, who I thought was happily married. But it doesn't necessarily mean nothing happened as actors were paranoid in that way in case they ended up in some gossip column. I worked with Natalie Wood for 17 years and I had to read a book after she had died to realise half of what she got up to."

When he was not required to shoot, McQueen regularly took off in his sports car (usually with one of his female companions) and would exploit the spacious roads of the Monterey location in North California. Part of the reason for his frequent disappearances was his strained relationship with veteran director Ralph Nelson, according to co-star Ed Nelson (no relation): "Steve and Ralph had a misunderstanding right away. Steve took over the picture more or less. After a few days it became obvious just how things were going to be and Ralph didn't argue. He wanted to do the picture and get the hell away. I believe he was building a house and I think he just couldn't wait to get back there and be well away from the demands of trying to direct Steve McQueen. He still acted as the director but anything Steve wanted, he got. He called the shots, as nobody knew what worked better for him than he did, that's why they hired him. Gleason was the same. You must remember that this was an odd character for Steve and he didn't want to trust the advice of anybody else."

Steve's dogmatic nature with the director was not the only behaviour he showed on the picture that led some to question whether he had allowed his ego to expand beyond allowable proportions. He had reached the summit of his industry with *The Great Escape* and some felt his head was still in the clouds of leading an epic cast when he pitched up to this movie set – though veteran Gleason hardly tolerated any movie star nonsense from him. "On this film Steve wasn't as nice as he was on *Love with the Proper Stranger*, which I also worked on with him," said hairdresser Blymyer. "He had a totally different attitude. Jackie Gleason was really funny because when Steve got too big for his boots Jackie would have a nice understated way of putting him down a little bit. I don't remember how exactly Jackie might have done that but I do recall that Jackie put Steve in his place when he needed to. Jackie was King on this movie.

"When we'd all go out to dinner he would order six partridge pies. And Steve would sometimes try to match him as he was very competitive and didn't want to be outdone on anything. It wasn't just eating where Steve was competitive; he just wanted to look important when Jackie was *totally* important. It's shocking how Steve behaved on this movie considering how sweet and nice he was on *Proper Stranger*, when I really liked him. But sometimes actors are like big kids and let their egos run away with them. Maybe Steve thought, 'I've done *The Great Escape*, I'm important,' but Jackie didn't care, he'd seen it all before. Actors do have very tender egos and want to be important."

McQueen and Gleason, though, gelled well enough as a pair of buddies on screen. One scene called for a bar brawl where Eustis and Maxwell become involved in a fight with soldiers from the base; it took three days to shoot. While filming this sequence, McQueen sustained a black eye but he was not unhappy as this kind of method acting was more his style: "I'd rather do this kind of action stuff than the heavy emotional scenes," Steve told author William F. Nolan. "For those you have to turn yourself inside out and empty all your emotional pockets." McQueen was a tough cookie in his movies and in real life, but this counted for nothing in these scenes, where professionalism was everything. "Steve McQueen was a very convincing actor who knew how to fight and make it look good, but he also knew how to act," Ed Nelson commented. "He never once hit anybody (by accident). His technique was very good because, like me, he was brought up on westerns and so he knew how to fight on camera."

Solar Productions' involvement allowed Steve more creative input, but even with that additional executive power, he was unable to help make this movie click into a commercial success. On the movie, he commented: "I hadn't done any comedy since *The Honeymoon Machine* and I felt it was time to do something different. But the picture just didn't come together. I really don't know why, because all the elements were there." Ed Nelson felt it was not the right vehicle for Steve, though acknowledged his contribution. "I don't think Steve approached it as a comedy. If you would have told him he was very funny I think he'd have been shocked and would not have enjoyed that. I think he looked at it more as Pathos:

a simple guy who depended on another guy so much. It's certainly not my favourite Steve McQueen film; I prefer *The Great Escape* and that kind of thing. I don't know why he wanted to do this movie. It's like with John Wayne, when you find out what the audience likes - give it to them and don't go fooling around with this other stuff. But Steve made a brave choice and I respect him for that."

This was not a commercially successful picture for Steve after its release on November 27, 1963, and it did little to strengthen his star status after the success of *The Great Escape*. But it did illustrate he possessed more range, however effective, than simply playing the tough soldier or cowboy types he previously excelled at. By the same token, it also showed just how good he was in the films he was more suited to; he fitted into the action-adventure genre in pictures such as *Papillon* and *The Getaway* so comfortably that it caused his less dynamic films to pale in comparison. However, *Soldier in the Rain* has not been forgotten, as Ed Nelson explained: "The film was never a big money maker, although it has attracted some kind of a cult following. I have had so many people say to me, 'You're in one of my favourite pictures.' What picture was that, I ask them, expecting them to say anything but *Soldier in the Rain*. Then they say that and it makes me think there's obviously something more to the picture than we first realised."

Main Credits:

Cast: Jackie Gleason, Steve McQueen (as Supply Sergeant Eustis Clay), Tuesday Weld, Tony Bill, Tom Poston, Ed Nelson, Lew Gallo, Rockne Tarkington, Paul Hartman, John Hubbard, Chris Noel, Sam Flint, Lewis Charles and Adam West.

Director:	Ralph Nelson
(Assistant)	Austen Jewell
Producer:	Blake Edwards and Martin Jurow
(Associate Producer)	Dick Crockett
Cinematographer:	Philip H. Lathrop
Writers:	Maurice Richlin and Blake Edwards, based on William Goldman's novel
Editor:	Ralph E. Winters
Wardrobe:	Jerry Alpert (men), Shirlee Strahm (women)
Make-Up:	Bud Bashaw Jr.
Music:	Henry Mancini

REVIEW:

THE NEW YORK TIMES, November 29th, 1963

The principal character in this flimflam is a simpleton soldier whom Steve McQueen succeeds in making just about as unattractive as any poor, bumbling simpleton could be. And the big, fat sergeant who protects him and fills his head with rosy dreams isn't a great deal more beguiling as Jackie Gleason plops him onto the screen. Both actors are really quite unpleasant in this broad and insensitive display of human stupidity and duplicity at an Army training base. The picture flops uncertainly between two irreconcilable intents. It's neither good knockabout comedy, which it struggles most frantically to be, nor is it trustworthy sentimental drama along the lines of *Of Mice and Men* …Mr. McQueen is simply callow with his striking of foolish attitudes, his butchering of the English language and his sporting of hick costumes. And Mr. Gleason is merely offensive (unless you happen to be conditioned to his style) as the nonchalant pater familias whose greatest admirer is himself. Blake Edwards as the producer and Ralph Nelson as the director are responsible for this farce.

Steve was in awe of Natalie Wood's acting ability. The two
shared a healthy respect but no off-screen romance, according
to Steve's wife Neile, despite her attempts to seduce Steve
(COURTESY: PARAMOUNT PICTURES)

LOVE WITH THE PROPER STRANGER

(Paramount) 1963

'Steve came in and imitated Jimmy Dean imitating Brando - with the same jeans, same T-shirt and the same arrogance. It was an interesting progression to watch that happen'
– Arnold Schulman

PITCHING STEVE WITH Natalie Wood for this romantic drama was the hottest male-female duo that a studio could buy at this time. After Steve's major breakthrough in *The Great Escape*, his popularity had soared, while Natalie Wood's superstardom was established already. She had previously appeared in *Rebel Without a Cause* with James Dean in 1955, *West Side Story* in 1961, and in the same year *Splendour in the Grass* with Warren Beatty, for which she received an Academy Award nomination. It was rumoured that Wood had initially wanted Beatty - her lover at that time - to appear with her in *Love with the Proper Stranger*, but for director Robert Mulligan, that was never an option.

The director felt the casting was perfect, and his two lead stars became a great team. "Steve was everyone's first choice and that includes Natalie," said Mulligan, whose alliance with producer Alan Pakula had spawned *To Kill a Mockingbird* beforehand. "We sent the script to Steve in Palm Springs on a Friday. He read it over the weekend and said 'yes' to the movie on Monday. He loved the screenplay and was very enthusiastic about working with Natalie. Throughout the production, Steve performed like a true professional. He rehearsed with Natalie and the entire cast. He was supportive in every way and did everything I asked of him. Natalie, too, was always a pleasure to work with. She and Steve hit it off right from the start and it comes across on screen. They were great together and we had a great time making the movie. There was no 'movie star' nonsense. I never had much patience for that kind of behaviour on a movie set. They showed up every day ready to do their best. A director can't ask for any more." Mulligan impressed the whole cast, especially Steve, with his ability to make everyone feel important and involved. Steve respected him and gave him his full attention.

Wood and McQueen were an interesting combination given their backgrounds: McQueen had a rough upbringing devoid of a loving family, while Wood was just the opposite. Co-star Edie Adams already knew both stars prior to the film. She had got to know Wood through her close friend Warren Beatty. Says Adams, "She was a very nice and sweet girl, mother-dominated early on, but when she found her true voice she did what she wanted to do. She was a very talented, natural, fearless actress." Steve, though, was rough and ready, hung out with his motorcycle buddies for fun and avoided the Hollywood scene. McQueen was never confident of his acting ability unlike the assured Wood. He always maintained a level of paranoia as to whether he was good enough to keep churning out films that people would pay to watch. He thought his wealth and lifestyle would be taken away from him at any time; hence the reason why he would occasionally order two steaks at a restaurant, and why he could be incredibly tight with his money – a trait that stayed with him throughout his life.

Off-camera, relations between Steve and Natalie could have been much more intimate had the leading actress had her way. She was taken by Steve's macho cool and though she was with Beatty at the time, it didn't stop her going after Steve, according to his then-wife Neile, who wrote in her memoir *My Husband, My Friend*. "Natalie tried every which way to ensnare Steve short of using a butterfly net, including resorting to adolescent tricks like sticking her leg out of her trailer steps, pretending she was talking to someone inside just as Steve would pass by...Steve was amused by the methods she employed and actually looked forward to the next day's shoot to see what her next move would be."

Steve couldn't deny Natalie's beauty; his refusal to buckle was more out of loyalty - not to his wife but to friend Robert Wagner, whom Wood had been married to. Steve liked Wagner a lot and had been a good friend to him during *The War Lover* when their divorce was ongoing. Loyalty amongst friends meant a lot to him. Years later, after Steve had split with Neile, the Hollywood rumour-mill made out that he did eventually succumb to Wood. But during *Love with the Proper Stranger*, he was the *Proper Gentleman*.

The material of the film centred on abortion, which was illegal in those days, and such a theme was controversial back in sixties' America. Writer Arnold Schulman, who later wrote *Goodbye, Columbus* that ironically starred McQueen's second wife Ali MacGraw, had problems getting the film made because of the delicate subject matter. Wood plays a naive young woman (Angela Rossini) from a religious New York-based Italian family. She falls pregnant after a one-night affair with Rocky Papasano (played by McQueen), a jazz musician enjoying his freedom in life. When she tells him of the pregnancy, he refuses to claim any responsibility, though his guilt becomes too much for him to ignore. When he arranges a back-street abortion, the insensitive nurse causes Rocky to renege on the idea and in the harsh situation, he realises his love for Angela. This isn't your standard love story - more an anti-love theme. For the time, it was extremely risqué and certainly ground-breaking in terms of the material. Comments Schulman: "It was very controversial because abortion was illegal then and also, when a woman got pregnant it was common for the man to say, 'Okay, I'll marry you.' But in this case she said, 'I want the baby, but I don't want to marry you.' The studios thought nobody would buy the concept. It was thirty years ahead of its time and an absolute miracle that it got made. I think the fact that Alan Pakula and Robert Mulligan were so hot at the time after doing (*To Kill a*) *Mockingbird* was the main reason the studio accepted the story."

Doubts were raised by cynics as to whether Steve possessed the sensitivity to portray such a part, as his previous successes had come from action pictures. He had never acted in a serious romantic drama before, though his performance in *Proper Stranger* was well acclaimed. Mulligan commented: "I had directed Steve years before in live television when he was just a young actor, and I liked him. At that time he was struggling, studying and doing theatre, and I knew he had a light, easy comedic tough as well as a natural charm when he wanted to use it."

Writer Schulman also had previous experience of working with Steve at the Actors Studio in New York. In those days, writers would study with actors so both understood their respective roles. He observed an intriguing pattern in how the moody actors of that time all followed one another. "I was attending the Actors Studio when Brando came along, who had this walk, the jeans, the T-shirt - very cool. Then Jimmy Dean came along and imitated Brando. After that, Steve came in and imitated Jimmy Dean imitating Brando - with the same jeans, same T-shirt and the same arrogance. And Paul Newman had probably done it before McQueen. So it was an interesting progression to watch that happen. But I must say I found Steve wonderful to work with and he brought a great deal to the part. He did extremely well in understanding what was between the lines and his looks and reactions were terrific."

This was a welcome discovery for the writer, having listened to the usual horror stories that seemed to be synonymous with McQueen's name. "We got along very well," said Schulman. "I heard that he was a real pain in the ass but I found him to be nothing like that. Once or twice he would say to me, 'I want to change this line or that line, I don't like the way it goes.' But I would just explain to him that's what the character would say and Steve accepted it; he was great. He'd never question the characters; he just wanted to know more about the environment because Steve didn't know too much about the behaviour of Italians in the area. Nowadays, you wouldn't cast Natalie Wood and Steve McQueen as two Italians in The Bronx; maybe a young Stallone and Cher."

By now, Steve had gotten used to being a genuine star and didn't have to showboat to flaunt his star quality. He was comfortable, therefore, to effectively play second fiddle to Natalie Wood. There were no complaints that she was given top billing, as Steve felt she fully deserved it. "Steve was so cute on this film, he sat around on the set and you could see that he really looked up to Natalie," said hairdresser Sugar Blymyer, who worked with Wood for the first time on this film before a 17-year spell as a regular member of her entourage. "Steve was huge after *The Great Escape* but he was still in awe of Natalie; everyone was all over her. Even I felt special when I was chosen to do her hair. She was a total professional; she could learn to do anything and was always on time. She had an entourage of about seven of us to support her but was an amazing person because she was so professional. And Steve had so much respect for her."

For Edie Adams, who played Barbara, Rocky's promiscuous girlfriend, *Love with the Proper Stranger* was great fun and an opportunity to study how Steve had matured since she first met him in 1957, when she was dancing on Broadway with Neile, who Steve had married the previous year. McQueen would hang backstage and Edie shared several insightful moments with Steve in New York and also in Las Vegas, while he was still a struggling yet enthusiastic actor just out of the Actors Studio. Steve was always uncomfortable around the cabaret lifestyle of the Vegas glitter. He'd have far preferred to have been riding his motorcycle in the desert. "I had great talks with Steve backstage on acting as he was never part of the Vegas scene," recounts Adams. "He was very intense, the silent type, but I could see he was a very dedicated actor. He dressed very casual and tough-looking like in 'the beat' generation - a fashion of counter-culture - a far cry from the Vegas scene. Steve didn't seem to want to talk to many people. He noted that not many people were friendly and he was happy that I was friendly to him. I was a keen student of acting too and I was interested in what he had to say. I could talk theatre with him, but not many people in Vegas wanted to talk theatre. Steve made it well known that he didn't want to be part of the Vegas scene, which was all gold chains and glamour; not his kind of raw, emotion on-screen and race cars thing."

By the time Steve and Edie met up again for *Proper Stranger*, not much had changed. "Steve and Neile were not part of the Hollywood party scene, where as I was out every night where there was a party under a tent and when swimming pools were emptied and made into dance floors. However, Steve was still the cool, tough guy who didn't speak all that much. He changed more by the time I saw him again in the seventies."

Steve never enjoyed being in the public eye, as his reclusive years in the 1970s would be a testament to. On *Proper Stranger*, he was spooked by a fan that got in his face during his downtime one evening, which was the kind of behaviour that fuelled Steve's dislike of fans' intrusiveness throughout his life. "Natalie and Steve went out to dinner in New York City and were enjoying a private conversation when a fan rudely pulled up a chair at their table and started questioning them," Blymyer said. "It really freaked Steve out as he was very private. It's horrible to think that people bothered these stars like that and they could not have their own privacy. They were two very private people and they didn't like that at all."

In *Love with the Proper Stranger*, Steve coped well in a role he was not too familiar with, and he particularly enjoyed the chance to play a man so close to the masculine ideal who is promiscuous until he meets the right girl. The movie, released on December 25, 1963, received five Academy Award nominations; Steve was overlooked while Natalie Wood received a nomination for her performance. Writer Arnold Schulman, also nominated for his original screenplay, was delighted with

Steve's work and he felt he had cut the role perfectly in what was thought to be an incongruous part for him, which at least earned him a Golden Globe nomination for Best Actor. "I was very pleased with how the film came out. The only thing I was displeased with was the ending. I said from the beginning to Robert Mulligan that under no circumstances will it be the kind of movie where the two lovers kiss at the end. I had been on location every single day and the one day I wasn't there, they shot it. I was really furious. It was a conventional ending to an unconventional love story. I would have preferred an ending where they walked off quarrelling, but you knew that they would end up getting married. I thought that would have been a bit more believable. It was just a typical Hollywood ending in what was meant to be a very un-Hollywood film.

"Steve, though, was perfect and a writer couldn't have asked any more from him. During the making of the film, he asked me if I wanted to form a company with him, but like an idiot I asked him why and nothing came of it. That proved to be a very poor business decision, but I'm just pleased to have known Steve McQueen and to have worked with him. He was one of the best."

Main Credits:

Cast: Natalie Wood, Steve McQueen (as Rocky Papasano), Edie Adams, Herschel Bernardi, Anne Hegira, Harvey Lembeck, Mario Badolati, Penny Santon, Elena Karam, Virginia Vincent, Nina Varela, Tom Bosley, E. Nick Alexander, Marilyn Chris and more.

Director:	Robert Mulligan
(Assistant)	William McGarry
Producer:	Alan J. Pakula
Cinematographer:	Milton R. Krasner
Writer:	An original screenplay by Arnold Schulman
Editor:	Aaron Stell
Wardrobe:	Edith Head
Make-Up:	Wally Westmore
Music:	Elmer Bernstein

REVIEWS:

MOTION PICTURE HERALD, December 25th, 1963
Natalie Wood and Steve McQueen make an outstanding romantic team in *Love with the Proper Stranger*, a comedy-drama set in New York City today. Not only does the pairing of the stars have obvious box-office advantages, but it has worked even better than one might have expected in the way their personalities complement each other in the film.

THE DAILY CINEMA, August 17th, 1964
As the improper strangers who discover that what started out as a messy fling has become a marriage-worthy relationship, Natalie Wood and Steve McQueen are ideally cast. Edie Adams scores as Rocky's tart-tongued but kindly ex-girlfriend.

THE HOLLYWOOD REPORTER, December 19th, 1963
Miss Wood and McQueen are superb in their roles. They make a handsome couple, flip and hip. They personify today's

rootless young people. They also make credible the decency that is there, the strength in reserve when it is needed... McQueen slips into his role with deceptive facility. His bewilderment is keen, his disinclination to pay the piper heartfelt, but his strength of character is dominant and triumphs. McQueen does a fine job all around, a puppet in other's hands, and a live person taking the reins in his own hands.

VARIETY, December 25th, 1963

The more substantial portions of Schulman's script are capitalised on by director Mulligan and his cast, notably his two stars. Miss Wood plays her role with a convincing mixture of feminine sweetness and emotional turbulence. McQueen, now firmly entrenched, displays an especially keen sense of timing. Although he's probably the most unlikely Italian around, he is an appealing figure nevertheless.

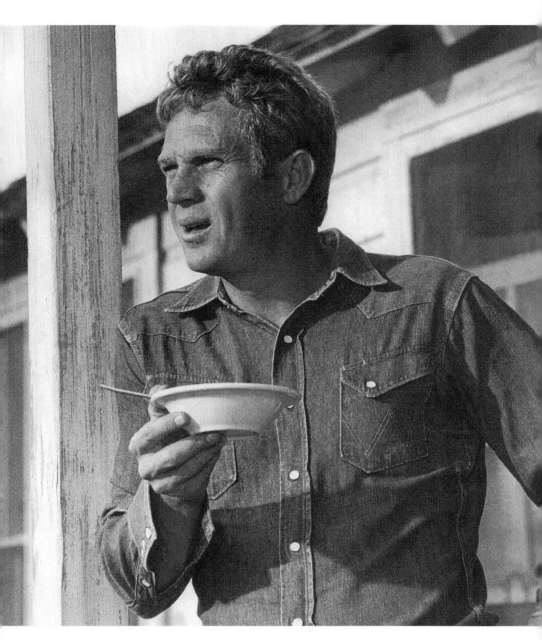

Steve gave a powerful portrayal of the troubled Henry Thomas in
Baby, the Rain Must Fall, though felt uncomfortable with the musical
aspects of the character
(COURTESY: COLUMBIA PICTURES / THE KOBAL COLLECTION)

Baby, the Rain Must Fall

(Columbia) 1965

*'Steve was uncomfortable with the singing and guitar playing and
I was disappointed he didn't spend more time and energy studying
and rehearsing to become more comfortable with what he had to do.
Unfortunately, by that time in his career he'd become a 'star' and was
distracted by all the attention he was getting'*
– Robert Mulligan

THIS MOVIE WAS arranged during the final stages of *Love with the Proper Stranger*. As soon as the Pakula-Mulligan pairing came up with this property they knew it was another perfect vehicle for Steve. He plays Henry Thomas, a troubled singer/guitarist who lived a difficult childhood and eventually wound up in jail after a bar fight he was involved in led to a man's death. While in the confines of his cell, his wife and young daughter await his release. Henry, an angry and confused character, is eventually paroled, thanks to the permission of his lifelong guardian mother - an old disciplinarian spinster whose bitter ways helped

215

create his painful existence. Immediately, he struggles to cope with life on the outside, particularly in his role as husband and father, and before long he is back in trouble once more. Lee Remick plays his wife and she gives a powerful performance as the lonely, over-understanding spouse. The only other star of any major fame is Don Murray, who had previously appeared as the male lead along side Marilyn Monroe in *Bus Stop* in 1956. Murray is cast as the sheriff in the small Texan town, who knew Henry from his childhood.

The movie, Steve's final black and white picture, was shot in and around Wharton and Columbus in Texas. It was based on the Broadway play *The Travelling Lady,* which was written by Horton Foote, who had also written *To Kill a Mockingbird* three years prior for the Pakula-Mulligan team. After the success of that Gregory Peck movie, producer Alan Pakula and director Robert Mulligan were both keen to involve Foote in their next project, and he promptly accepted the role of adapting his play into a screenplay. Every studio in Hollywood was interested in their next movie because they were a hot proposition after *Mockingbird.* Securing McQueen for the male lead only added to the anticipated box-office attraction. Although the elements for a hit appeared to be there after its release on January 13, 1965, the dollars trickled in as opposed to a flood.

Mulligan manfully shouldered the blame for the lack of commercial appeal and felt its shortcomings were down to him. "I was not happy with the movie or with my work on it, although there were some good moments with Lee Remick and Steve," Mulligan said with a refreshing honesty. "I hold no one responsible but myself for the fact that it failed." Horton Foote, a Texan himself, was less certain why it bombed. He was happy with the finished package and was particularly pleased with how McQueen and Remick played together. "I don't know why it failed," said Foote. "A lot of people love the film and it's still playing on television. It was a big mystery to me. I was very pleased with the film and felt it captured the sense of the place and the period and came out really well."

Steve's wife Neile wrote in her memoir *My Husband, My Friend* that Steve had an affair with Lee Remick (who died of cancer in 1991) during the picture, alleging that Steve had unburdened himself with the revelation by telling her so. But in Marshall Terrill's biography *Portrait of an American Rebel*, Remick flatly denied any affair occurred.

The role of Henry Thomas was ready-made for Steve, who was also a complex individual. Foote did not know McQueen was to be the star when he wrote the screenplay, but the casting could not have been better, he felt. "I admired Steve as an actor. It was a wonderful part for him because he had a lot of anger in him. I thought there was a kind of rebellion in Steve that a lot of guys down here (in Texas) have. He had an enormous talent and this was a wonderful role for him, which he worked very hard at. Steve understood this guy; he bummed around the country and also had a terrible childhood so I think he felt very rebellious and understood the anger in Henry."

Steve shares a moment off-screen with co-star Lee Remick.
Steve's wife alleged the two had an affair, but Remick denied
this before her death in 1991
(COURTESY: COLUMBIA PICTURES)

Don Murray felt the likeness between Steve and Henry helped his own performance. He was able to think of the relationship between Slim (the policeman) and Henry almost as though it was he and Steve in real life. "He reminded me of some of the kids that I had grown up with - the typical, pugnacious street kid. Everything worked from the standpoint of reality. Steve played a guy that was always getting into trouble; he was a troubled youngster and he became a troubled man when he came out of prison. My character in the film was the sheriff that grew up with this kid and so my feelings towards Steve were very much like the character he played. In real life Steve was a guy I liked, but he too had a troubled childhood, was in reform school and I knew kids like that so I was able to relate to his character in the film real well, in a similar way I could relate to him in real life." The on-screen relationship between Murray and McQueen was further strengthened by the encouragement from Mulligan. He knew how both actors felt about one another in real life and he prompted them to project these feelings into the movie. Their relationship was a friendly one, though there were aspects that each of them disliked about the other. "Bob is what I'd call an inspirational director," says Murray. "He'd draw upon the things that I felt about McQueen to use in my character. He did the same with Steve, who probably thought I was a square."

Murray could never allow himself to be fully enamoured by Steve due to his boisterous antics that occurred on and around the set in Texas. Put simply, they were total opposites. Socially, it was a happy atmosphere; one day Steve invited Don and some members of the crew to go riding with him in a car he was afforded by the film company. It was to be a forgettable experience for the co-star, though an enlightening one. Recalls Murray, "We were going down the highway, then all of a sudden he takes off across the fields, hitting speeds around 100mph. Nobody had seat belts on, so we were all bounced around the car. I told him to slow down but he wasn't paying any attention, then the car caught fire and we all had to bail out. We all stood around in a state of shock, watching this brand new car burn up. But Steve couldn't stop laughing. I found it appalling the way he had a real disregard for other people's property. That was the sort of thing about him that I didn't like, which tempered the other aspects that I admired him for."

Steve's childish humour and sense of fun appealed to many but not Murray, who was also angered at how Steve had fun at the expense of the assistant director, who was nursing a broken foot. Steve would send the hapless assistant on a countless number of errands. "Climb up that hill and get me this, or go over there and get me that," McQueen would ask. "I didn't like that," says Murray, "and I told him so. He would laugh, but he looked slightly embarrassed at the same time as I think he knew I was right." These were

BABY, THE RAIN MUST FALL

typical examples of how the irrepressible child inside Steve would often surface. He loved having fun, though not everybody always appreciated it - and this included the Texas Police Department. "At the weekends," recalled Horton Foote, "Steve was always out driving his car and dodging the cops most of the time, because they were usually out looking for him - to get him for speeding. He loved to outrun them."

Despite the obvious similarities between Steve and Henry, there were also aspects to Henry's character that were a huge departure for Steve to execute - most notably, playing guitar and singing. This particular role was an incongruous one for McQueen. It was something he never quite felt at ease with, even after receiving tuition from musician Billy Strange. This led to some heated clashes between the director and the star. Says Mulligan, "Steve was uncomfortable with the singing and guitar playing and I was disappointed that he didn't spend more time and energy studying and rehearsing to become more comfortable with what he had to do. Unfortunately, by that time in his career he had become a 'star' and was distracted by all the attention he was getting. Though he continued to perform professionally in every other way on that film, he neglected to do what he knew he had to do. We had a series of bad moments during the shoot about this. They were always in private and Steve promised to do better. It never happened."

Englishman John Leyton, who had co-starred in *The Great Escape* two years earlier, was also a singer with a No.1 hit *Johnny Remember Me*, though few were aware of his singing fame on the movie set. He became a buddy of Steve's in Germany, but said he could never picture him with a microphone in his hand. "I can't imagine Steve singing at any time," Leyton commented. "I'm not surprised to hear that he was dubbed." Don Murray was aware of the problems between Steve and the director and he too thought that Steve did not devote himself to the guitar and singing aspect of Henry's make-up, mainly because of self-consciousness. "I felt that Steve disparaged the singing part of his character - it wasn't macho. He learned to devote himself to a motorcycle chase or a bar brawl sequence because all that's considered macho; but a singer wasn't just something he felt embarrassed at because he couldn't do it, but also, to me, he never thought it was the macho thing he should be doing."

Away from that part of McQueen's work in the film, his commitment was first-class and he duly enjoyed the opportunity to work with Alan J. Pakula and Robert Mulligan again, after *Proper Stranger*. He announced to Murray, "I've gotta behave well because you've gotta respect people like Pakula-Mulligan. They've done *To Kill a Mockingbird* and are top-notch people." Murray, who had worked with Mulligan in live television in the fifties, had great respect for the director and was slightly concerned prior to shooting that McQueen didn't run rough on him, given the notorious bad-boy stories he had listened to in passing. "I had heard that Steve bullied directors and I was a bit worried, as I didn't want him to do that with Bob, who I really admired. As it was, Steve had the good sense to recognise Bob's talent and, subsequently, he was always respectful."

Off-camera, there were plenty of social events to keep the cast and crew in good spirits. One activity that McQueen and Murray got up to, behind the backs of the producers, was boxing! Hardly the average pastime for actors on a movie set, but these two really got into it, using Don Murray's own equipment. "It started off as just sparring but it got to be kind of vigorous," admitted Murray, "and that was when the production staff stepped in and took it all away." There is one scene in the movie where Murray and McQueen fight one another at a graveside. This scene went perfectly after they had both got used to each other's moves. Murray later wished he had thought to tell the producers that they were boxing to practise for that scene, although, "I don't think they would have bought it," he says, "and it would have been a good job as well because I'm convinced we'd have ended up breaking one another's nose!"

It was the boxing that brought the two actors closer on the set. When that stopped, Don organised a Mini-Olympics with events like golf, basketball, swimming, diving and touch football. Such an enterprising idea did not go down too well with the star. "I don't think Steve ever really bothered much with sport. The only thing he was into was auto-racing. I remember once, he must have felt a bit left out when we were playing all these sports, because he came to me with an article about him in an Italian racing magazine. He asked me to translate it as he knew I could speak Italian, and this article was praising him, saying how his reputation as a good driver wasn't Hollywood hype, it was true. Afterwards, I thought, 'Was that really the first time somebody had translated it for him?' I think deep down, because I was organising all these sports, it was his way of saying, 'You might be good at your football, but here's my thing.' He wanted to impress me."

Baby, the Rain Must Fall wasn't all recreation despite the good morale on the set. Steve poured a lot of himself into this heavy role in what was a downbeat, sombre movie. The picture may have missed the big bucks, but it wasn't because of any deficiency in Steve's performance. Murray concludes: "He took his work very seriously and I think it's the best acting he ever did in his career."

Main Credits:

Cast: Steve McQueen (as Henry Thomas), Lee Remick, Don Murray, Paul Fix, Josephine Hutchinson, Ruth White, Charles Watts, Carol Veazie, Estelle Hemsley, Kimberly Block, Zamah Cunningham, George Dunn, Glen Campbell (uncredited).

Director:	Robert Mulligan
(Assistant)	Joseph E. Kenny

Producer:	Alan J. Pakula
(Associate Producer)	Isabel M. Halliburton
Cinematographer:	Ernest Laszlo
Writer:	Horton Foote (based on his own play *The Travelling Lady*)
Editor:	Aaron Stell
Make-Up:	Ben Lane
Music:	Elmer Bernstein
Technical Advisor:	Billy Strange

REVIEWS:

FILMS AND FILMING, July, 1965

The performances are impeccable, and they are performances without any trading on personality. In particular, Steve McQueen contributes a quieter, stronger performance, quite free of his easy-going personal mannerisms. It is a study in boyish confusion, a mixture of defiant courage and inner fear, that is put across without tricks and is perhaps the best study of this kind of character that Hollywood has yet given us.

THE DAILY CINEMA, May, 1965

Slow-burning tale of a born loser, smouldering with stifling Southern small town atmosphere: sympathetically handled and persuasively acted; but theme doom-laden and motivation confusing. Ticklish popular attraction, but with undeniable star pulling power...The feeling between Henry and

Georgette (Remick) is tenderly conveyed by Steve McQueen and Lee Remick. The former suggests impressively the bottled-up tension of the hero and though the tones of the gusty singing aren't his own, he gives the illusion that they are and that's all that matters.

SIGHT AND SOUND, Summer, 1965
Lee Remick, temperamentally ideal for her role, gives a kind of faultlessly low-key performance that is, in itself, a sufficient recommendation to see the film. Steve McQueen, less comfortably cast, emanates a kind of strength and goodness slightly at odds with the unbalanced character he portrays.

VARIETY, January 13th, 1965
Chief assets of Pakula-Mulligan's *Baby, the Rain Must Fall* are outstanding performances by its stars and an emotional punch that lingers. Steve McQueen is exactly right as irresponsible rockabilly; Lee Remick portrays his wife sensitively, and newcomer Kimberly Block is charming and unaffected as their six-year-old daughter. But box-office draw of this Columbia release depends on stars, because it's sombre, downbeat story meanders and has plot holes that leave viewers confused and depressed.

FILMS IN REVIEW, January, 1965
(McQueen) is a handyman by day and a folk singer by night, and has told no one he is married. He greets his wife with a mixture of bravado, irritation and affection that is

unbelievable and the picture's chief fault, i.e. his character is so inconsistent it's impossible to become interested in him. Some of this is the fault of McQueen, an earnest but unfinished actor. Most of it, however, is the fault of how the part is written....Despite these failings, *Baby The Rain Must Fall* has emotional power, and brings about in the beholder the catharsis which is the sibe qua non of effective drama.

The Cincinnati Kid heralded a golden period in Steve's career,
sparking five consecutive hit movies between 1965 and 1968
(COURTESY: MGM / BRITISH FILM INSTITUTE)

THE CINCINNATI KID

(MGM) 1965

'I don't ever remember Steve being close with anybody on The Cincinnati Kid. He got along fine with people on the set, but he just had this capacity to take care of himself. Maybe that had something to do with the way he grew up' – Jeff Corey

STEVE'S INITIAL COMMITMENT to *The Cincinnati Kid* was driven purely by an ambition he was desperate to fulfil – to work along side the great Spencer Tracy. McQueen had already shared the screen with Frank Sinatra and Yul Brynner, but for Steve, neither compared with Tracy. The combination of Tracy and McQueen was a hot deal that promised huge rewards for the producers and was set up by Abe Lastfogel, the head of the William Morris Agency. Producer Martin Ransohoff, of Filmways, owned the movie rights to the book by Richard Jessup, and Lastfogel wasted little time in approaching Ransohoff with his dream-ticket idea. "How would you like Tracy to play 'The Man' and McQueen to play 'The Kid'," he said teasingly. Both actors belonged to William Morris so the producer knew it wasn't just executive hokum.

MGM were alerted of the project and no way were they going to miss out on such a bankable prospect. "Wrap it up straight away," studio head Bob O'Brien told Ransohoff. McQueen was paid $300,000, while Tracy, in the twilight of his career, commanded $250,000. These commitments were made without a script and without a director in place. Tracy agreed on the fact he loved the book so much. While McQueen also enjoyed the book, his primary reason of wanting in was just so he could work with the acting great. As soon as the ink had dried, though, Tracy had to withdraw from the movie due to health reasons. It was a bitter blow to the studio having formed such a powerful duo, but it was an even bigger disappointment for Steve. "He was very upset about it," says Ransohoff, "which was understandable because he badly wanted to make a movie with Spencer Tracy."

The news that Edward G. Robinson was the replacement comforted Steve, as he knew he was still going to be acting with a class performer. The relationship between the two, though, deteriorated quickly and was an uncomfortable co-existence that each tolerated for the sake of the movie. Steve was encouraged by the experience and talent recruited for the rest of the cast: Karl Malden, Ann-Margret, Joan Blondell, Tuesday Weld, Rip Torn, Cab Calloway – all were established stars. Meanwhile, a raw director by the name of Sam Peckinpah was hired who, at that time, had only enjoyed success in television.

The script was still being drafted by Ring Lardner Jr. at this late stage and over dinner one night McQueen gave his backing to Ransohoff, but not without a word of warning. "I know things are still up in the air, but I'm cool about everything," Steve assured him. "But just tell your writer – I'm better walking than I am talking." It was a short statement but said so much and was a veiled criticism of Lardner. Steve was forever cutting dialogue from his scripts; he knew he could say more with a squint of an eye than he could through a monologue.

McQueen's flippant comment on Lardner's script helped get the writer fired, at the same time that Peckinpah was also dismissed. Commented Lardner: "I met Steve only when we had a reading aloud of the script, during which I made a few changes to suit the particular actors. Then I went off on a trip to New York, confident that for once, both the director and the actors were happy with my screenplay the way it was, and I could count on a reasonably faithful rendition of it. A few days later, I learned that the producer had fired the director, Sam Peckinpah, ostensibly for shooting a nude scene with Sharon Tate (in a screen test, before her part went to Tuesday Weld), and replaced him with Norman Jewison, who had also brought Terry Southern with him for a rewrite." Incidentally Lardner Jr. had not been the first writer to contribute to the script. Paddy Chayefsky submitted a draft version first, but it was not well received by Ransohoff, who replaced him with Lardner Jr.

Troubles with the director added further disruption to this movie early on. The talented yet stubborn Peckinpah had hardly got going before he clashed with producer Ransohoff over creative issues relating to the picture, while some members of the cast were also unhappy. "We had very serious disagreements," admitted Ransohoff. "He had talked me into making the movie in black and white, with a sort of documentary feel. That was against everything I had seen in the film. I wanted an entertaining film, like a gunfight with a pack of cards. I wanted the humour and the fun of it to dominate the picture – and that needed colour. I was disappointed with the early rushes and I knew things had to change. There were too many differences between what Sam and I wanted from the film, so I had to shut down production after one week." Eddie Robinson was also upset after two days of shooting when Peckinpah had shot a sequence that Eddie felt was not in character for him. Such events caused Steve further anguish. First Tracy was gone and now Peckinpah was gone.

During that temporary break, in between directors, Steve went on a drug-fuelled bender, according to his then PR man Dave Resnick. It was Resnick's way of protecting Ransohoff from having a restless star on his hands so rather than risk having McQueen sitting around idle making demands on his production company, Resnick suggested they paid for him to head out to Las Vegas to get the feel for gambling. Well, that was the company line, at least. "Just give him some money, let him go to Vegas, get the feel of this gambling thing while you guys get the picture going," Resnick was quoted as telling Ransohoff in Penina Spiegel's *The Story of a Bad Boy in Hollywood*. "Next thing I know I'm called into the Rogers & Cowan office. MGM wants to hire me out to go with Steve to Las Vegas for two weeks. Now they paid me $1,500 a day, they paid Rogers & Cowan $1,500 a day, that's $3,000 for each day.

Here we are Steve and I, taking off with like $25,000 in cash. We bought a lot of coke. We went to Vegas and partied for two weeks. It was a bizarre time. Oh shit, we had a great time."

Just before they left for Nevada, Steve's old racing buddy Kurt Neumann Jr. was drafted in as assistant director to help sort out the ailing movie. Steve and Neumann became friends after Steve shifted from New York to Los Angeles in search of work. Neumann was working on *Rawhide* while Steve landed the part of Josh Randall in *Wanted: Dead or Alive*. They would then meet up for race weekends at a time when Neumann drove a Lotus 11.

As soon as Neumann arrived, Peckinpah was out the door. "The producers' Filmways (ran by Ransohoff and John Calley) were having terrible problems with *The Cincinnati Kid* when Sam Peckinpah was the original director," Neumann recalled. "Things were not going well so I finished *The Loved Ones* on the Wednesday and started *The Cincinnati Kid* on the Friday. I joined them on their fourth day of shooting and Sam was still there then and seemed pleased to have me on board as we knew one another. I was only with Sam for one day though when we shot a riot scene down at the train yards. I took a call halfway through the day from John Calley, who told me that Sam had just been fired, though he didn't even know it yet. They wanted him in the first car off the set. I had to get Sam into the car but I didn't tell him why otherwise he would have had my head! Sam was quite a character, but I liked him a lot. When we wrapped that night I had to tell all the key people that we were shutting down for a few days. By that time Norman Jewison was on board but none of us knew it then."

Despite the early mishaps, it was felt that Jewison's arrival brought a calmer, more settled atmosphere and also allowed the producers to make the film they had always intended on. "Marty Ransohoff was quite a character himself, a bit like a bull in a China shop, he wasn't frightened to make decisions," Neumann said. "He actually loved Jackie Gleason and Paul Newman in *The Hustler* and that was somewhat of an inspiration for this film as this was a bit like *The Hustler* but not with pool, with cards."

Canadian Jewison found a way to work with Steve just fine, but only because he diplomatically placated his insecurities and protests. Not only did Jewison go on to direct Steve in *The Thomas Crown Affair* three years later, he also had success with *The Russians Are Coming, the Russians Are Coming* (1966) and *In the Heat of the Night* (1967), which won him an Academy Award and landed Best Picture also. He was a smart operator and he soon developed a good working relationship with the anxious star. By this time, Terry Southern had been hired to complete the script. Finally, everything was in place and the movie was able to continue.

The story tells how a young card sharp becomes the hottest stud poker player in the area, cleaning up against whoever cares to accompany him on the table. His reputation soon travels far and wide. The word is that he's the best around, nobody can beat him. Nobody that is, except for the veteran Lancey Howard (Robinson) – who is genuinely regarded as the 'King of the table.' Shooter, played by Karl Malden, arranges the ultimate showdown between 'The Kid' and 'The Man'. While this clash shapes up, we see Steve and Tuesday Weld develop the romantic side to the picture, while Melba (Ann-Margret), Malden's girlfriend, continually tries to lead 'the Kid' to her bed. Critically, there were negative murmurs about the way in which Robinson beat McQueen's full house at the end. Says Ransohoff: "Real gamblers from Vegas kept calling up and saying, 'He'd never have stuck with that hand in real life'." This was compensated in the picture by the dialogue executed by Edward G. Robinson: "It's all about making the wrong move at the right time, kid."

The movie was mostly shot in New Orleans and set in the 1930's. There was, generally, a friendly atmosphere on the set. This was due largely to Jewison, who had the ability to create that kind of spirit. In the first few days of shooting, though, Steve was feeling a little tense, having not been on a film set for a long time. "I'd been away from the camera for a year and the depth I was trying for in this role just wasn't coming for me," Steve said. "For the first three days on the set I felt like I'd never acted before in my life. Then things got better. I loosened up and began to get my juice back."

Karl Malden observed Steve's initial behaviour with interest. He recalled: "Steve McQueen realised he had a big challenge when he did *The Cincinnati Kid*. I have a feeling that he felt he had got into the big league." Norman Jewison echoed: "He was a little nervous about Eddie Robinson, as Eddie was a star." The chemistry between Robinson and McQueen was superlative. Even if you removed the dialogue from their scenes together, the body language would still give the intended message. McQueen is all cocky, who has learnt his trade in the underworld of stud poker, yet there is a visible respect for Robinson, who has conquered the tables nationwide. Lancey Howard oozes sophistication and a professionalism that the 'The Kid' can only aspire to. However, he is insecure of his age, his game and his title.

It was ironic that these personal characteristics and the relationship between the two mirrored real life. Steve was very much like 'The Kid' and had actually played stud poker successfully in his New York days to earn extra bucks while studying at The Neighbourhood Playhouse. Robinson, meanwhile, was reflected by aspects of his character too. He wrote in his autobiography: "There was a line I had to say to Steve: 'As long as I'm around, you'll always be second best; you may as well learn to live with it.' I could hardly speak the words. I knew they weren't true. It was I who had to live with it. He was the star, I was second best. Steve comes out of the tradition of Gable, Bogie and Cagney, and even me – but he's added his own dimension. He is a stunner, and who knows what glory the future holds? But surely he is already an honourable member of the company of players."

Despite Robinson's generous praise and the natural chemistry that both exuded playing opposite one another, their relationship off-camera was non-existent. They had nothing in common. "Not many people realise just how strained things were between Steve and Edward G. – they really did not like each other," assistant director Neumann revealed. "Off-camera they simply did not have a relationship, as they were complete opposites. Edward G. was an absolute marvel as a person and Steve was horribly jealous of him, while Edward G. just could not be bothered with Steve.

"For example, we had the entire facilities of MGM at our disposal and the sets were just beautiful. The libraries were stocked with novels and Eddie would peruse the book shelves. We also had some wonderful paintings that were hung on the wall and Eddie was quite an authority on art. On one set we went into, Eddie climbed on to a table and lectured the entire cast and crew on this one particular painting hanging on the wall; what he had to say was absolutely wonderful, yet Steve was rude to him, which is probably the most polite thing to say. He made a nasty remark, never shouted out or directly challenged Eddie, it was more little comments under his breath. Steve would never have confronted him head on as he knew Eddie would have made him look very small – in an intellectual way and Steve was too smart to have done that. Eddie was very tolerant of this behaviour.

"Steve was street-wise though and knew that Eddie would be seeking his revenge in his own way and this was bothering him quite a bit. In fact, one night after we got down to New Orleans there was just the two of us and Steve said he wanted to grab a coffee with me. He said: 'Eddie is going to destroy me because I know I have really pissed him off. I don't know how or when, but he's going to destroy me.' For Steve to predict that was very interesting. It showed how perceptive and instinctive he was. I told Norman what Steve had said and we agreed that we'd just have to watch out for it. And happen it did, when the card game progressed to a two-man shootout between 'The Kid' and 'The Old Man' – though I'm not sure it made it past the cutting room as there were a few alterations from the script. But Steve had some dialogue and was looking uncomfortable when Eddie reaches into his inner breast pocket and pulls out the biggest kitchen match you've ever seen and lights up his cigar, as the audience's attention is transfixed by this huge flame – all going on while Steve is talking. Eddie is so interested in what Steve is saying that two or three times he tries to light that cigar, but hesitates each time, while that match is burning lower and lower. Eventually he lit his cigar and threw away the match. While all that was going on Norman and I were looking at each other, thinking this is getting very tense. The crew were picking up on it also. After that scene Steve got up and left and we didn't see him for an hour or two. It was one of the cleverest scene-stealing moves of all time and Steve knew it. He had been destroyed by a master."

As ever, Steve was particularly concerned with his character and the dialogue. Although he turned in a good performance, McQueen was naturally insecure and he needed to see for himself that things were okay. He badgered Jewison to see the 'dailies', to check he was coming across right on screen – he wasn't yet ready to trust Jewison with his part. But the director found a way to placate Steve and still keep to his policy of not showing the dailies. It was the show of authority that Steve needed to see; he could then respect him – as a film-maker and as a man. "It's normal for an insecure star wanting to see the dailies, but Norman put a stop to that and wouldn't let him see anything," Neumann recalled. "I also never thought it was a very good idea to allow that as actors get too many ideas about how they could have shot that scene better or this scene better, and it can just cause problems. A perfect example of that was *Le Mans*. Steve had control of that movie and it was a disaster, it was absolute madness."

McQueen always insisted on being believable in every non-comedy character he played, and while his professionalism is commendable, it frustrated the hell out of his co-stars and directors. "Generally, we never got to do a shot until noon because Steve liked to discuss his role with Norman at length, and we would all be waiting on the set," co-star Jeff Corey remembered "Steve was very careful. He wanted to know why and when, and what's the alternative to shooting it this way and that sort of thing." Martin Ransohoff added: "Steve was a very complex guy. He had a lot of anxieties and basically was a complicated man."

While these lengthy discussions were going on between Jewison and McQueen, the other members of the cast learned to entertain themselves with activities such as scrabble and table tennis. When shooting wrapped for the day, Steve rarely socialised with cast and crew. "I don't ever remember Steve being close with anybody on *The Cincinnati Kid*," Corey reflects. "He got along fine with people, but he just had this capacity to take care of himself. Maybe that had something to do with the way he grew up. I didn't get too close to Steve, but I found he was very interested in acting. All our conversations were about motor-bikes. He would invite me to his dressing room to show me catalogues about this bike and that bike. He was naturally possessed with bikes and speed, absolutely crazy and demonic about motor-bikes."

Co-star Ann-Margret was also passionate about motorcycles and this shared interest gave the two some familiarity, for which the actress was grateful as she was not a drinker or a smoker and instead got her kicks from riding bikes. She was leaned on heavily by MGM not to ride her bike during the movie, which greatly annoyed her, and she turned to Steve for advice, which was naturally of the anti-establishment variety: "So what did you do (about the studio orders)," she asked Steve. "I kept riding the bike," was his typically fearless reply. When she suggested that the studio executives might not take too kindly to that response and what does he think she should do, he concluded: "Keep riding the bike!" Margret not only appreciated Steve's penchant for motorcycling but also his acting ability. "Steve McQueen was a real tough guy," she said. "Full of machismo, a man who made his own rules, but both of us got along really well. He was a truly gifted actor, insightful, sensitive, intelligent, and believable in every scene we did together."

The other leading lady Tuesday Weld was said to have had an affair with Steve on *Soldier in the Rain* two years earlier, but this time there was no romantic carry-on, according to Kurt Neumann: "I had heard the same stories about them on their last picture, and I knew and liked Tuesday very much. But there was nothing going on between she and Steve during *The Cincinnati Kid*, whatever had happened before. These kinds of romances do occur on location but they're usually turned off as quickly as they're turned on."

Steve was eternally paranoid and he had actually carried one such insecurity into this picture from five years prior on *The Magnificent Seven*, just going to prove how he never did take a defeat in one-upmanship very well. "I questioned Steve on the size of his trailer that he or his agent had insisted upon," recalled Neumann. "The damn thing was so big it had to be moved in daylight hours only as it required a special escort and signs saying 'wide load' and things like that.

"I said, 'Steve, what the hell is this?' He said, 'What you mean?' I told him, 'This ocean liner on wheels that you've got for a dressing room is the silliest thing I've ever seen. If you had got a smaller motor home you could have driven it yourself.' He hadn't thought about that and then went on to tell me why he wanted that ridiculous trailer. It turns out that down in Mexico when they were filming *The Magnificent Seven* all the actors' trailers were lined up and one stuck out, which was considerably bigger than the rest – it was Yul Brynner's. That really pissed Steve off and he never forgot about it. This was his way of getting even. But when he came to realise how ridiculous it was what he had insisted on, it was too late for him to back down. It was a huge ego thing for Steve but I think it was only out of insecurity. Being a star can be tough for some people, not everyone knows how to handle that pressure and occasionally these types of things crop up."

Steve's insecurities could be about the most trivial of matters. Producer Martin Ransohoff shared a healthy working relationship with Steve, but still managed to unwittingly upset his star on the set of *The Cincinnati Kid*. Ransohoff was producing two other pictures at the same time and therefore spent only eight days from fifty in the studio or New Orleans. This was something that McQueen picked up on eventually and he confronted the producer, who was also spending time in Paris on *The Sandpiper* starring Richard Burton.

"I know why you're spending all this time in Paris," Steve commented. "You think Burton is a bigger star than I am!"

The producer was astounded by Steve's insecurity, but at the same time, empathised with him. "It was fair enough as I was the person who had got him to do the movie, so it was right that I maintained an interest in the picture, which I did."

The film was a pleasing end result for all concerned, for Steve especially. It triggered the beginning of a golden era for him, as his next four movies were also hits at the box-office, as this was, yielding $16 million worldwide from a $3 million budget. *The Cincinnati Kid,* released on September 21, 1965, was the perfect vehicle to continue Steve's escalating reputation. "I feel it was one of his better movies," Ransohoff concluded. "He was absolutely terrific and so natural. There was always a bit of danger about him which, I think, made him so attractive and appealing and perfect for this role."

The official Premiere in New Orleans was hit by Steve's absence. He had to fly to San Francisco to visit his sick mother, who subsequently died at the Mount Zion Hospital, shortly after his arrival. She had suffered a cerebral haemorrhage. The dysfunctional relationship that Steve shared with his mother was not something he remembered fondly. Even when she had moved to northern California to be closer to him and his family, he stayed away and allowed Neile to visit her with Terry and Chad. But when she passed, the pain finally told; he was openly upset at not being able to say the things he wanted to tell her. "Jullian's death produced heart-wrenching sobs and left him guilt-stricken and bereft," Neile said of Steve. "He had hoped she would recover if only to ask for her forgiveness for the unhappiness he had caused her. He was not able to unburden himself to her and he carried the pain around for a very long time."

The Cincinnati Kid's eventual success provided a degree of solace at an upsetting time in his life, but could never ease the kind of pain inside of him that had been developed over many years since his difficult childhood.

Main Credits:

Cast: Steve McQueen (as Eric Stoner, 'The Kid'), Ann-Margret, Karl Malden, Tuesday Weld, Edward G. Robinson, Joan Blondell, Rip Torn, Jack Weston, Cab Calloway, Jeff Corey, Theodore Marcuse, Milton Selzer and more.

Director:	Norman Jewison
(Assistant)	Kurt Neumann Jr.
Producer:	Martin Ransohoff
(Associate Producer)	John Calley
Cinematographer:	Philip H. Lathrop
Writers:	Ring Lardner Jr. and Terry Southern, based on and adapted from Richard Jessup's novel
Editor:	Hal Ashby
Wardrobe:	Donfeld
Make-Up:	William Tuttle
Music:	Lalo Schifrin

REVIEWS:

NEW YORK TIMES, October 28th, 1965

The Cincinnati Kid is strictly for those who relish – or at least play stud poker. Here is a respectably packaged drama of a young card sharp, played by Steve McQueen, with a capable enough cast, that pungently projects the machinations and back-room temperatures of the side-street professional gambling world and little else.

VARIETY, October 20th, 1965

Martin Ransohoff has constructed a taut, well-turned-out production in his latest bid to come up with something off the beaten path. In McQueen he has the near-perfect delineator of the title role...McQueen's particular style of acting fits this role well, his mutterings and his sometimes-incoherency adding to the strength of his character, for which he is given occasional bursts of wry humour.

THE DAILY CINEMA, October 22nd, 1965

Irresistibly gripping poker-playing battle between the wary champ and the wily contender: relishingly acted and stuffed with fascinating thirties atmosphere, human conflict, gambling eccentrics and the hot-eyed fever of the game. Outstanding box-office star attraction...The men are just superb. Steve McQueen is the ideal Kid.

THE HOLLYWOOD REPORTER, October 14th, 1965

The Cincinnati Kid is a superb picture, one of the year's best. It is a realistic drama, flirting the edges of crime and violence. It is a poetic and symbolic story, with elements of tenderness and compassion. Martin Ransohoff's production for MGM will be a smash box-office success, and it deserves to be. Norman Jewison's direction stamps him unmistakably as an important movie director, daring, imaginative, assured. *The Cincinnati Kid* is a thoroughly satisfying picture in every way. Most memorable are the performances: Steve McQueen and Edward G. Robinson are a brace of actors at their best.

Steve in one of his best roles, and most demanding
(COURTESY: PARAMOUNT PICTURES / BRITISH FILM INSTITUTE)

NEVADA SMITH

(Paramount) 1966

'Henry Hathaway didn't dare offend Steve. He did not want a situation where Steve might not come out of his dressing room as wasted minutes cost thousands of dollars. Henry treated Steve with kid gloves and was softer on him than he was with others'
– Martin Landau

THIS WAS STEVE'S first western since *The Magnificent Seven* in 1960. The genre proved then to be a suitable one in which Steve could exhibit his natural, rugged persona. *Nevada Smith* was no different. A further similarity lay in the fact that he was to work with another respected veteran director as he had with John Sturges before. In this picture, Henry Hathaway was director and he brought with him a fearful reputation. He was an infamous disciplinarian who never took kindly to movie star bullshit. When Hathaway worked with Robert Mitchum on *White Witch Doctor* in 1953, on the first day of shooting, Hathaway took Mitchum to one side and said, "Bob, I can get real angry and call you all kinds of names on the set that might upset you, but I just want to reassure you that fifteen minutes later it'll all be over and forgotten." To which Mitchum replied, "Thank you Henry for telling me about yourself. Now I want to tell you about myself: when people talk to me just like you have, I knock them right on their ass, but fifteen minutes later it's all forgotten!" Steve and Hathaway never quite shared the same moment but there was early tension, until the director quickly realised Steve McQueen was not a man to be pushed around, and they subsequently enjoyed a healthy, respectful relationship.

Not many stars stood up to this tough director like Mitchum. Given Steve's previous history with directors, this relationship promised to be a lively one. Steve was never one to be intimidated, even by an experienced film-maker like Hathaway, but he was also very clever and perceptive in assessing people. When McQueen had previously misbehaved on a set, it was usually out of disrespect for the director. His best work prior to this film was in the presence of a strong director: *Never So Few*, *The Magnificent Seven* and *The Great Escape* - John Sturges; *Hell Is for Heroes* - Don Siegel; *Love with the Proper Stranger* and *Baby, the Rain Must Fall* - Robert Mulligan; *The Cincinnati Kid* -Norman Jewison. All such movies were good for Steve in some way and the directors received the relevant attention from the star.

By the time *Nevada Smith* started shooting on July 1, 1965 (it was released a year later on June 23, 1966), Hathaway was 67 and well past the age of tolerating uncooperative actors. However, on this movie set there was no need for him to worry. McQueen gave the director everything he had. John

Michael Hayes, who wrote the screenplay and who had previously written Hitchcock films *Rear Window, To Catch a Thief* and *The Man Who Knew Too Much*, said: "Hathaway and Steve got along famously. Steve knew he couldn't push Henry Hathaway around, as he was a very tough director so Steve respected that and was a good boy." Co-star Pat Hingle, who knew McQueen when he was an acting student in New York, feels the hard-man reputation of the director got slightly overestimated through the years: "Henry was a soft-hearted person who had this facade that made him yell and growl at you, but that was just to conceal his soft heart. He didn't fool me."

Co-star Martin Landau, who played Jesse Coe – one of the three men that Steve's character was seeking to avenge for the gruesome murder of his parents, viewed Hathaway as an explosive, maniacal director but certainly not a stupid one. "Henry was crazy and screamed a lot but was one of the gentlest people in the world if you met him away from the set," Landau explained. "But on the set he was wild and would really scream, especially at Arthur Kennedy. He loved people to be his goats to pick on. I didn't let him do that to me because I knew about him. And he and Steve got along pretty well; he treated Steve well compared to others. Henry was tough but Steve was the star and Henry didn't dare offend Steve. He did not want a situation where Steve might not come out of his dressing room as wasted minutes cost thousands of dollars. Henry treated Steve with kid gloves and was softer on him than he was with others."

Make-up artist Del Acevedo also saw Hathaway as a toothless tiger: "He was a good director to work for and a great guy most of the time, though sometimes he got a little nasty and could blow up on a set but he was usually a good guy. He had a nickname that was said behind his back, which was 'Horrible Henry', but it was only a bit of fun. He could be very nasty but he could also be very generous."

According to Steve's then wife Neile in her memoir, Steve looked at the director almost in a fatherly way. "Steve and Henry Hathaway took a deep liking to each other," she wrote. "Hathaway, the veteran western director, called Steve 'son' and went to special pains to make this film the best thing Steve had done to date. For Steve, in turn, this crusty, love-able old man with the twinkling eyes and ruddy cheeks was the father he never had. It was not uncommon to find Steve on the set a full half hour before Henry, just sitting there in his chair and teasingly greeting him with a 'Where've you been, Sir?' Reporting to the set early was his way of showing the old man his respect."

The movie was based on *The Carpetbaggers*, a Harold Robbins novel that had been adapted previously and starred Alan Ladd. Within that film was a character named Nevada Smith, which was a role expanded for this picture. It tells how Max Sand, a young man with a white father and an Indian mother, sets out in pursuit of three men who murdered his parents in cold blood. Revenge is the central theme to the movie, but along the way, Max, who changes his name to Nevada Smith, is taught a harsh lesson about life. The film dealt with some controversial issues for its day. Casting a white man in wedlock to an Indian woman was a relatively taboo subject in 1966 America. Also, the scalping of Smith's mother was particularly gruesome, though most violence was left to the imagination. At the time, there was a new boss at the censoring body, and this change in personnel coincided with a relaxing of the censorship laws.

The other stars of the picture were Arthur Kennedy (five-time Oscar nominated), Karl Malden (an Academy Award winner, for *A Streetcar Named Desire*), Martin Landau (an Oscar winner, for *Ed Wood*, and nominee in later years) and Brian Keith (acclaimed for *The Parent Trap* and TV sit-com *Family Affair*); all big names in their own right, which was something that appeared to motivate Steve. "He tried to come up to their level," screenwriter John Michael Hayes noted. "Steve worked very hard; he was a naturally hard-working, conscientious fellow. He didn't take his work lightly, he tried to match everybody and be as good as he could." Pat Hingle added: "Although Steve worked extra hard, he wasn't worried by the presence of the other experienced actors. By this time, Steve was one hell of a name in Hollywood himself."

Hayes' screenplay compacted Nevada Smith's revenge plight of finding these three men (Landau, Kennedy and Malden) before attempting to expose them to his own version of justice. It almost feels as though there are three chapters to the film. For the revenge mission of Arthur Kennedy's character, Nevada Smith purposely commits a clumsy bank robbery, knowing his punishment would be a prison sentence, exactly what he intended. It gave him the opportunity to confront Kennedy. This segment of the film provides some gritty location photography in the swamps around Baton Rouge in Louisiana. The swamps provided testing, difficult conditions for the cast, though McQueen relished the challenge. He was used to being head to toe in thick mud through riding his bike in the dirt. *Nevada Smith* was just another day at the office to him. "Steve took it in his stride, it was his kind of story," Hayes said. "He loved to be able to show off how sturdy and macho he was and he did very well at it." Make-up artist Del Acevedo added, on those awful conditions: "That was a real tricky shoot for Steve and the others because there were so many damn snakes in that water. They were told to tighten their pants at the ankles, to button their sleeves and put rubber bands on them to keep the leaches out. That was a nasty shoot." Co-star Suzanne Pleshette, a friend of the McQueen's, was reduced to tears in her muddied costume when a smiling Neile McQueen showed up on the set to visit her hubby, looking pretty and pristine in her bright white pants.

Steve didn't interact socially with the cast too much, chiefly because the film was so episodic and that meant a demanding shooting schedule as he was involved with almost every scene. He was together with Landau, Kennedy and Malden at the start, but then it was Brian Keith's section, before Suzanne Pleschette's section et cetera. There was no let-up for Steve, though, whereas Landau, Malden and Kennedy were able to hang out together quite often.

"Steve kept himself to himself pretty much," Pat Hingle said, "but it wasn't out of arrogance or anything like that. Playing the leading role for sixteen weeks can be very tiring and you don't want to be socialising all the time. Although, when we did have the odd country and western party, he'd turn up. Steve gave himself whole-heartedly to the picture and there was never any prima donna behaviour from him, when he was a big enough star to have got away with it if he chose to behave that way."

His schedule also prevented Steve from straying too far from Neile, when she was not around on location. Throughout their 15-year marriage he struggled to remain faithful, especially when middle age, free love and the flower power culture took such a strong foothold in California in the late 1960s. But during *Nevada Smith*, he was on his best behaviour. "Steve was very popular with the ladies because he was a good looking guy," Acevedo said. "And he also had an eye for them, but he didn't wander too far during this picture because Neile was around on the set quite a bit. She was a nice lady. It didn't stop the ladies from chasing him though because he was a hunk but he behaved himself on this picture. People rumoured that something might have gone on between him and Janet Margolin but I know that just wasn't the case; she had a guy out there with her pretty much all the time, so she played it pretty cool with Steve."

Landau and Steve were friends from way back in the mid-fifties in New York when they attended the Actors Studio. Landau also shared an episode of *Wanted: Dead or Alive* with Steve when he played an elephant trainer in a travelling circus and got stamped on at the end and was killed. But other than that they had not seen much of each other since, despite offers for Landau to appear in *The Magnificent Seven* and *The Sand Pebbles*. "I wound up working for John Sturges on *The Hallelujah Trail* instead and we talked about Steve quite a bit actually; we were both big fans of him and what he brought to his movies. Robert Wise also spoke to me about doing *The Sand Pebbles*, as he wanted me for the role that Dick Crenna played. So I might have been in another two movies with Steve if circumstances had been different.

"Steve and I got along very well but many other people felt he was very paranoid. We enjoyed catching up on *Nevada Smith*. We shared the same barber – Jay Sebring – so at the start of shooting, we all had a barbeque together in California. Jay had his girlfriend with him, Sharon Tate, who I had met before. She was beautiful and was trying to be an actress at the time." Tate was murdered on August 8, 1969 when Charles Manson's brainwashed crazies went on the rampage at the home of Tate's husband, Roman Polanski, who was filming overseas. That night, Steve had been invited to join them but a rendezvous with another woman freakishly spared his life.

Steve and Landau's big scene together was the knife fight in a cattle station, as Max Sand made Jesse Coe his first target on his spree of vengeance. They filmed through the night and the challenging scene was executed by the two actors without stunt men or stunt coordinators. "Steve and I choreographed it and acted 95 per cent of that scene ourselves, when we got to Lone Pine," Landau revealed. "We would frequently be out of breath because of the altitude at that location. We needed rest in between takes and Henry was very human and gave us that time to recover before shooting the scene from a different angle. It was a lot of huffing and puffing but we were close to a mile high in terms of the altitude so we'd take ten minutes out in between takes. We filmed the whole scene in one night and it was pretty hairy at times as I was sitting amongst a thousand steer, and we didn't use any stuntmen."

Another scene, in the swamps, called for Arthur Kennedy to face a multiple lashing from the bull-whip after a failed attempt at escape. Hingle, who played the trustee prisoner whose task it was to do the lashing, recalled one spontaneous moment during that shoot, which Steve instigated. "After his lashing, Arthur Kennedy fell to the ground like he was supposed to, and then we all expected Henry to shout 'cut' but he didn't. All of a sudden, Steve broke rank with his leg-irons on, ran down this muddy bank to Arthur, who was pretending to lie dead in the water, picked him up and carried him up the bank - as Nevada Smith didn't want him to drown there and then, as he had his own plans. Arthur must have weighed 225 pounds, while Steve couldn't have been heavier than 160. I had never seen such an impressive display of physical strength than this. The whole display was totally off-the-cuff and when you get something unprepared that looks so natural – it really is gold and Hathaway knew it. It also shows just how much Steve had immersed himself in to his character, as he even thought like him when he wasn't in the scene!"

Steve was able to pull that scene off because he remained strong and fit since his military upbringing. He had his weight training equipment fitted into his trailer and would often be spotted pumping iron to keep his body in shape, during what was a very demanding film with its various location shoots.

Steve's travelling arrangements to and from the set became a controversial area of debate, which involved the industry's union chiefs. As usual, he wanted to ride his beloved motorcycle over the rugged terrain around the various location sights, in the mountains of California and Louisiana. The studio didn't take kindly to their star placing himself in danger, as they saw it, and demanded that he stopped riding his bike and travel in the chauffeur-driven car provided him. Steve's anti-authoritarianism meant he was not going to lie down and accept these orders from Paramount. In the event, a compromise was reached that more suited McQueen than it did the film company. Pat Hingle explained: "Although the insurers (who were separate to Paramount) would not allow Steve to ride his bike, he still went ahead anyway. He would arrive in his limousine to the set of a morning, while his motor-home towed his motorcycle. Then, at the end of the working day, he rode his bike back, while his stunt double sat in his limousine. We all knew what was going on, but if the insurers arrived they would have thought that Steve was playing ball. The producers didn't like the situation but they were too scared to say anything to Steve. What do you say to him when he gives you those big blue eyes? 'No Steve, you're not going to ride your bike'. Like hell you would!"

Acevedo, who Steve nicknamed 'Avocado' but more often 'Ace', hit it off with Steve, who was true to his word when he said he would have Ace hired for his next movie, *The Sand Pebbles*. Steve was never one to spend too much time with make-up artists as it wasn't the macho thing to do; he was more akin to hanging out with the stuntmen. But these two got along and Steve was generous to him. "Steve had a slight temper and could be a bit impatient and grouchy in the mornings before he had his coffee, but we always got on great," recounted Acevedo. "In fact, almost 50 years on, I still wear an engraved gold bracelet on my wrist that he gave me at the end of *Nevada Smith*. On the front it has my name and on the back it says, 'Nobody's Perfect.' That was because I designed his make-up stubble and when I put it on his face one day he didn't like it and thought it was too long. But when we went and got Henry Hathaway's opinion he took one look and said, 'It's perfect.' So we turned around and as we were heading back to his trailer, Steve looked at me, screwed his face and said with a smile, 'Nobody's perfect'."

Steve's work on *Nevada Smith* made a huge impression on writer John Michael Hayes, who had much experience working with big-name actors like James Stewart, Grace Kelly, Cary Grant, Clark Gable, Bette Davis and Elizabeth Taylor. "Steve never thought of himself as a big star, he thought of himself as a work-a-day actor doing the best he could. He didn't feel that he was a big celebrity; he was kind of modest like that."

Nevada Smith proved to be another box-office hit. His career was on a roll.

Main Credits:

Cast: Steve McQueen (as Max Sand & Nevada Smith), Karl Malden, Brian Keith, Arthur Kennedy, Suzanne Pleshette, Raf Vallone, Pat Hingle, Martin Landau, Janet Margolin, Howard Da Silva, Paul Fix, Gene Evans, Josephine Hutchinson and more.

Director:	Henry Hathaway
(Assistants)	Daniel J. McCauley, Joseph Lenzi
Producer:	Henry Hathaway, Joseph E. Levine (executive)
Cinematographer:	Lucien Ballard
Writer:	A screenplay by John Michael Hayes, based on Harold Robbins' novel *The Carpetbaggers*
Editor:	Frank Bracht

Wardrobe:	Frank Beetson Jr.
Make-Up:	Wally Westmore
Music:	Alfred Newman

REVIEWS:

VARIETY, June 1st, 1966

In *Nevada Smith*, produced and directed by Henry Hathaway, a good story idea - boy avenging his murdered parents and maturing in the process - is stifled by uneven acting, often lethargic direction, and awkward sensation-shock values. Overlength serves to dull the often spectacular production values. Steve McQueen is biggest marquee lure.

SATURDAY REVIEW, June 18th, 1966

Fans of *The Carpetbaggers*, if such there be, may be elated to hear that yet another film - *Nevada Smith* - has derived from the book. But they will be disappointed to learn that, apart from being based upon one of the characters who appeared originally in Harold Robbins' overpopulated garbage heap, *Nevada Smith* has nothing in common with the earlier film save a few name similarities. Indeed, screenwriter John Michael Hayes, drawing on some background material from the book, has fashioned what is substantially an original and absorbing western based on the classic theme of revenge...Steve McQueen, as Smith, manages not only to make convincing this belated conversion to a better way of life, but to lend colour and credibility - even likeability - to what is essentially a one-dimensional character.

Steve received his only Academy Award nomination on
The Sand Pebbles, and duly earned it having braved an
arduous six-month location shoot in Asia
(COURTESY: 20th CENTURY FOX /
BRITISH FILM INSTITUTE)

THE SAND PEBBLES

(20th Century Fox) 1966

'Contrary to what I had heard before about Steve being temperamental and difficult, I found him to be very sincere and honest. It made me think, 'Hey, somebody's been jealous of his success'
- Mako

THIS PICTURE WAS undoubtedly one of McQueen's best. He gave a powerful performance yet had enough sensitivity to portray the fallibilities of his character Jake Holman. *The New York Times* described his performance as the "most restrained, honest, heartfelt acting he has ever done", while *Variety* said he was "outstanding". His acting was of the sufficient quality to earn his only Academy Award nomination. This success, which was accompanied by hot box-office reaction, was not bad for a guy who was initially seventh choice to play the lead role.

When director Robert Wise, who won Academy Awards for Best Director on *West Side Story* and *The Sound of Music*, originally commenced preparations on the film in 1962 Steve was not then the household celebrity he soon became. Incidentally, it was Wise who had cast Steve in his first

Candice Bergen and Steve were total opposites in real life
but that diversity helped create an interesting on-screen
chemistry between their characters
(COURTESY: 20th CENTURY FOX /
BRITISH FILM INSTITUTE)

movie as an extra back in 1956 in *Somebody Up There Likes Me*. "When I was going to do *The Sand Pebbles* originally," recalled Wise, "Paul Newman was my first choice to play Holman. I had about six or seven names down for the part of Jake Holman, and right at the bottom of that list was Steve McQueen. Newman didn't want to do it as he didn't feel it was right for him, so when we came to discuss the casting the studio bosses said, 'McQueen's not big enough, he couldn't carry the picture'." By the time *The Sand Pebbles* did eventually come around, Steve was a household name; but it was an elongated and complex process just to get the film made.

Wise had an interest in it for a long time. He was planning on starting *Pebbles* when he returned from England where he'd made *The Haunting* in 1963. Wise wanted *The Sand Pebbles* to be his next film. It was a project that he was passionate about, after reading the novel by Richard McKenna, but when the director returned to Hollywood, he discovered there were going to be problems putting the film together: In the early 1960's Americans were not allowed to visit mainland China, so he couldn't see the actual locations where the story took place. Therefore, Wise had to see how he could put the picture together using Taiwan and Hong Kong as location doubles. The delays meant the film was postponed. It was suggested that San Francisco could be used as a location double, and it would have saved the studio well in excess of $1million. "It was never really an option," Wise admits, "but I did go up to San Francisco once to scout the river that flows into the Bay to see if there was any possibility of using that as the Yangste River. It was not even close; it was awful. But the studio was urging me to take a look and see if I could find some way of doing it and not have to go abroad."

The film was in the blockbuster bracket with its eventual $12 million budget costs. Added to Steve's weighty $650,000 pay cheque - a far cry from his $19 a day in his previous appearance in a Wise production - there were other aspects that warranted great expense: Chiefly, the San Pablo itself...$250,000 was spent on rebuilding a replica of the original gunboat, including the recreation of its antique steam engine. Studio technicians also worked tirelessly in transforming two square miles of Taiwan's Keelung Harbour so it could pass as 1920's Shanghai, where the gunboat once patrolled along the Yangste. Its duty was to protect the lives of American missionaries living on mainland China, which provided the central theme to the movie. The story tells how China is finding its feet as an independent nation after generations of interference and humiliation from foreign powers. While the Chinese war-lords terrorise the natives and foreigners alike, Communists and Nationalists battle for power. The San Pablo symbolised the foreign stake in China. Along the way, Jake Holman meets a pretty female missionary played by a nineteen-year-old Candice Bergen, and the two develop an intimate friendship. Holman's individuality, stubbornness and refusal to comply with the accepted ways of life on the boat do not endear him to his comrades. Frenchy, played by Richard Attenborough, is his only genuine ally on the boat. The loneliness of the part seemed to inspire McQueen in delivering one of his best performances. He was forever in his element when he played a moody man of steel. *The Sand Pebbles* was no exception.

By the time preparations re-commenced on the movie following its troubles, when casting came round once more, the last-choice actor of before had by now enjoyed a meteoric rise to fame. "In the interim when I had to delay it," remembers Wise, "Steve did *The Great Escape* and became very hot, so when I got back from doing *The Sound of Music* and started talking about *The Sand Pebbles* again, Steve's name was right up there at the top. A couple of years had made all the difference." Co-star Joe Turkel even learned that McQueen's contract with Wise and the film company meant "he had the okay on everyone that was cast". That's some turnaround having initially been seventh choice for the lead. "Fortunately he took a liking to me and we got along well," Turkel added.

Holman, an engineer, rejected any offer of a position of authority, preferring instead to remain in the confines of his engine room that powered the gunboat along the Yangste River. It was a role Steve was passionate about and he soon immersed his own personality into the character. The fact Holman was an engineer pleased McQueen, as he had long been the kind to tinker with car and motorcycle engines, and this role gave him the chance to further his love for anything mechanical, which added to his professionalism in getting into character. Here, instead of working with fuel, he was working with steam. Steve spent a lot of time with a Scandinavian engineer who knew everything there was to know about the engine, familiarising himself with all the workings of the engine.

A Japanese actor by the name of Mako, who played Steve's assistant engineer in the film, also attended those briefings with Steve on the workings of the steam engine. Mako, too, went on to receive an Academy Award nomination, for Best Supporting Actor. The two played off each other with a wonderful chemistry. "Because he wasn't too talkative and I'm not too talkative, our relationship was an almost non-verbal kind of thing," Mako said. "One day he asked me to go motorcycling with him and his stuntmen buddies through the Taiwan countryside, and as I'd done my share of riding I agreed to go. I had heard that he was a speed demon before the movie, and they were right. I suppose that helped us to get to know one another for the film emotionally and psychologically."

Steve's reputation around Hollywood as a pain in the ass co-star preceded him and these tales were enough to give Mako sleepless nights when he thought of the six-month shoot that lay ahead of him in Taiwan and Hong Kong. "Contrary to what I had heard before about Steve being temperamental and difficult, I found him to be very sincere and honest. It made me think, 'Hey, somebody's been jealous of his success,' as I trusted him. We shared a very nice, harmonious working relationship. And watching how well he worked with Robert Wise also proved those other stories incorrect as far as I was concerned."

Another actor Joe Turkel, who played one of the sailors that turned against Holman, was used to awkward co-stars having endured uncomfortable times with Kirk Douglas on *Paths of Glory*. But he too was impressed with the Steve McQueen who pitched up in Asia; the supposedly difficult, spoiled brat who could make directors lives a misery. "Nobody knows this but every day we worked together he was always on time, he was always sober, he always knew his lines and was always ready to work," Turkel commented. "He didn't take his job as an actor lightly. I worked with Jack Nicholson (on *The Shining*) and he had a reputation as a basketball buff who was a loopy, crazy guy. He was also a fantastic actor. And Steve McQueen, in his own way, had the same reputation, as being a motor-cyclist and a drunk who would fool around with a million women and all that. But I tell you, Steve tried his damned-est and worked hard and gave it his all. He was a professional in every sense of the word. He was a conscientious actor. Steve had a tough life and knew he couldn't throw this (career) away."

Wise and the 20th Century Fox executives may not have considered McQueen good enough or big enough initially to carry the movie. But when he finally got his man in Taiwan, Wise knew he had the perfect actor to execute the part of Holman. "He was the best," the director acknowledged. "He had a great understanding purely for Holman, who was kind of a loner like Steve. Also Holman loved engines like Steve. And he loved firearms, and Holman had to have a gun, which was right down Steve's alley." The relationship was a healthy one between Wise and McQueen, though there were occasions when tempers frayed. One day, the director was busy lining up an important shot that Steve was not part of. However, McQueen wanted to get his costume agreed for his next scene and kept badgering Wise until he had his attention. This was too much for the director and he promptly snapped at him. Steve, who was proud, stubborn and surprisingly sensitive for a macho tough, reacted like a scolded child and didn't speak to Wise for three days thereafter. Although he took his direction, he ignored any other chit-chat. "I hurt his feelings," Wise said. "This tough, rough guy had been hurt."

Still, the harmonious times on the set outweighed the bad. Wise considered Steve's talent a special one, with his own defined strengths and an honest realisation of his limitations. "I've never worked with a star or any actor who knew what worked for him as well as Steve did. He must have studied himself on screen quite a lot because every so often I would be rehearsing a scene and he would say to me, 'Gee Bob, I think I could get that part over without that line and do it with a reaction', and he was right. He really knew what worked for him." It was vintage McQueen, asking the director to drop a line of dialogue, which he was never too keen on. He had enough confidence in his ability to execute a scene by using more reactions than words. Says Mako, "I used to think that when an actor had a lot of dialogue, he must have an important role, but Steve made me realise that being able to act without words is just as important."

There was a wonderful on-screen chemistry between McQueen and Mako, as they portrayed a close friendship between Holman and his keen-to-learn Chinese associate (or "slope-head"), Po-Han. They brought humour to the film, as well as sorrow. In the scene where Holman is teaching Po-Han the workings of the steam engine in order for his eager apprentice to clearly understand him, he would point to a pipe and say, 'Hot stim, stim hot.' Mako, as the confused pupil, used all the tricks in his book to provide sufficient emotion, and this was something McQueen immediately picked up on in rehearsals. "I was scratching my head," Mako recalls, "and Steve turns to me and says, 'Are you going to do that when we shoot for real?' I said, 'Do what?' Steve just passed it off. In a few days' time, watching him work, I realised what he meant. I had taken one of his tricks away from him." McQueen never became unreasonably competitive about it, but he knew he had to be on his guard as this young actor may just upstage him. Physical quirks like a scratch or a squint were skills that Steve himself used frequently in order to grab the camera's attention. Now, he was conscious Mako was doing to him what he had done to many actors down the years. Wise admired the way Steve handled the role. "I think the sequence where

Holman had to shoot Po-Han was my favourite. I thought his whole reaction, when he had to shoot his friend then throw his gun away was just great. Steve did that beautifully. It was clear he wasn't worried about repercussions from his seniors; only thinking of putting his friend out of his misery."

It was a tough shoot in Taiwan as the country was in conflict with Red China and was being used as an American military base, as the Vietnam War drew ever nearer. Stringent identification checks were forced on everyone connected with the film. Conditions in general, including the inclement weather, made the shoot all the more difficult. Added to the political turmoil, there were diseases to contend with, monsoon rains, tropical insects and a general language barrier that made things all the more exasperating. The production went over schedule by nearly three months. After beginning the shoot on November 22, 1965, Steve returned to California with his family in the spring of 1966. On his return, he said: "It's the roughest film I've ever made. I had my skull twisted a couple of times, got sick, inhaled tear gas, worked myself dingy and ended up exhausted. Believe me, whatever sins I'm guilty of I paid for 'em making this picture. I just hope something decent comes out of it."

Joe Turkel concurred that *The Sand Pebbles* would certainly have been one of Steve's roughest shoots: "It was a tough shoot as everything was in Chinese, the signs were all Chinese, everything seemed unfamiliar and we all longed to get home and be with our families, though Steve obviously had his family out there with him. But everybody got sick. When you ingested that fucking water, even doing things as routine as taking a shower or cleaning your teeth, you could be in trouble. The film people used to tell us, 'Don't let the water hit you in your face because it could get into your eyes, your ears, your mouth – let it hit you on the chest'. (Fellow co-star) Joe Di Reda was off the picture for a week in bed. Everybody got sick at some point. It was the longest location shoot I have ever been on and I dare say it was the longest Steve had been on."

Steve's relationship with his leading lady Candice Bergen was business-like at best, though with 16 years between them, they were never likely to be close. Steve invited her to his house that he shared in Taiwan with wife Neile and his two children to try to break the ice; though in truth the two of them were from totally different back-grounds. Bergen soaked up the local culture by reading a countless amount of books at her suite in the Grand Hotel on evenings or when not needed on set; Steve, though, was more interested in a different kind of fun, according to Bergen in her autobiography *Knock Wood*. She claimed that Steve once told her to "loosen up", which she took as mean-ing that she should "get it on" with one of his ex-marine stuntmen buddies who she described as "hard-drinking and hard-fighting". She added: "McQueen and his gang grew increasingly restless and often spent nights on the prowl, roaming the little city, drinking, heckling, picking fights and pummelling. Coiled, combustible, Steve was like a caged animal. Daring, reckless, charming, compelling; it was difficult to relax around him – and probably unwise – for, like a big wildcat, he was handsome and hypnotic, powerful and unpredictable, and could turn on you in a flash. He seemed to trust no one and tried constantly to test the loyalty of those around him, to trap them in betrayal. Yet for one so often menacing, he had a surprising, even stunning sweetness, a winning vulnerability."

Turkel also preferred to unwind back at the hotel with a relaxing dinner and prepare for the next day, than being one for the Taiwanese nightlife. While he accepts McQueen was a loveable rebel, he finds it hard to agree totally with Bergen's summing up of how McQueen spent his down-time over there: "I am not saying Candy is wrong but, picking fights? I don't think so. Steve might have run with a lively crowd and drank a little, maybe picked up the odd broad, even though his wife was out there with him; but in so far as fighting and drunk? I don't believe that. You can't stay out till the early hours having fun, then arrive on set at eight all clear-eyed and still perform as well as Steve did. I can spot a hangover or somebody who has been out all night in a minute. I don't want to disclaim what she said but maybe she was exaggerating. But I don't doubt that Steve had a crew of stuntmen who loved it (going out). They were riding motorcycles all over the place. In fact, Steve had one sent over to him; he would ride that sucker all over the place. He said to me one day, 'Hey Turk, you want to ride on a motorcycle?' I said, 'Pass. I've never been on one and don't intend to. You're crazy, just don't hurt yourself'. He said, 'I never have', and off he went."

Make-up artist and Steve's friend Del Acevedo (ex-Navy), only hired to the picture because of Steve's request following *Nevada Smith*, agreed with Bergen that Steve hung out frequently with the stuntmen. But he reasoned that it was not so much about hell-raising but more about security and knowing he could enjoy a couple of beers without being hassled. "Look, I know Steve could be short-tempered and was a pretty rugged guy," Acevedo said. "I would not have wanted to climb into a boxing ring with him, that's for sure. But I have a lot of sympathy for Steve because actors, especially when they are as big and famous as he was, are targets for show-offs. After work you might be in a bar having a drink and some punk thinks, 'Man, that's Steve McQueen over there. I would make headlines if I go over there and punch him.' That happened a lot. John Wayne told me it happened to him all the time. He would be in a bar and some guy would come over and take a swing at him. He said if you hit them back you're a bully and if you don't hit them back, you're a pussy. Steve was very popular with the stunt guys because he did some of his own stunts. And they took good care of him and were very protective of him. Not that he needed it, but more to help him stay out of trouble."

The Sand Pebbles was rushed into a December release, allowing it to qualify for the 1966 Academy Awards. It eventually grossed over $30 million. Its official opening was held on December 20th at the Rivoli Theatre on Broadway, New York. Steve was proud of his work on the movie, though it still wasn't enough to win him an Academy Award. That went to Paul Schofield for *A Man for All Seasons*. Mako commented: "Since Schofield was nominated, I had to go see the film. As an actor, Paul Schofield had something that Steve didn't have and Steve had something that Paul didn't, that macho movie star cool. So it was a close call." The snub by the Academy hurt Steve, and rightly so according to Joe Turkel: "Steve was sensational in *Sand Pebbles* and he never did anything better. But then Kurt Douglas never did anything better than *Paths of Glory* and he never got anything for that. Who knows what they want?"

After giving one of his best acting performances Steve desperately wanted some recognition. Mako revealed: "He was very pleased with what was done and particularly what he had done. After the Academy Awards ceremony, there was a party thrown by the studio. When I sought out Steve to say goodbye, he hugged me and he hugged my wife and he said, 'Ah fuck 'em all, next time we get 'em.' I think deep down it affected him. He wanted that award badly because he felt he deserved it."

It was the closest Steve got to Academy recognition, but he consoled himself with the knowledge there was no bigger movie star around then. The mid-sixties belonged to him.

Main Credits:

Cast: Steve McQueen (as Jake Holman), Candice Bergen, Richard Attenborough, Richard Crenna, Emmanuelle Arsal (credited under stage name *Marayat Andriane)*, Mako, Larry Gates, Charles Robinson, Simon Oakland, Ford Rainey, Joe Turkel, Gavin MacLeod, Joe Di Reda, Richard Loo, Barney Phillips, Gus Trikonis and more.

Director:	Robert Wise
(Assistant)	Ridgeway Callow
Producer:	Robert Wise
(Associate Producer)	Charles MacGuire
Cinematographer:	Joseph MacDonald
Writer:	Screenplay by Robert Anderson, based on the novel by Richard McKenna
Editor:	William Reynolds
Wardrobe:	Renie, Ed Wyniegear
Make-Up:	Del Acevedo, Bill Turner, Ben Nye
Music:	Jerry Goldsmith

REVIEWS:

NEW YORK TIMES, December 22nd, 1966

Holman is a lonely, alienated machinist's mate first class, whose only bond of attachment is with the engine of his ship. He is coolly distrustful of authority, he respects those who understand machines, and he stands off from a pretty missionary who would offer him symapathy and maybe love. And it is in the fate of this fellow, this non-hero, performed by Steve McQueen with the most restrained, honest, heartfelt acting he has ever done, that we see the ultimate reward for the kind of service he ruefully performs.

THE HOLLYWOOD REPORTER, December 21st, 1966

The Sand Pebbles is being released by 20th-Fox as a roadshow attraction. It has all the elements, large-scale action, conflict, romance, humour, and a meaningful story, that should guarantee a long run in this area. It looks very much like another winner for Robert Wise, who produced and directed...McQueen is a unique actor, one of remarkable conviction, and one who can project subtleties of character and development with a flick of his eyes or a slight shift of body English.

VARIETY, December 21st, 1966

The Sand Pebbles, based on a novel by the late Richard McKenna, is a handsome production, boasting some excellent acting characterisations. Steve McQueen delivers an outstanding performance.

FILMS IN REVIEW, December, 1966

There is some fine acting in *The Sand Pebbles*, and the performance of Steve McQueen cannot be overpraised. He plays a lone-wolf gob whose love for machinery slowly - very,very slowly - changes into love for a young American teacher in a school run by a fanatical US missionary. McQueen has a cerebral vitality which is absorbing to watch. No matter what the situation, he seems always to be possessed of more moral force than he's using.

Steve disproved the initial instincts of director Norman
Jewison and executive producer Walter Mirisch that he was
unsuitable for the role of the smooth aristocrat Thomas Crown
(COURTESY: UNITED ARTISTS / BRITISH FILM INSTITUTE)

THE THOMAS CROWN AFFAIR

(United Artists) 1968

*'When I heard McQueen was cast, I was furious as I thought
there was no way he could play an upper-class aristocrat.
But they told me to get used to the idea' – Alan Trustman*

WITH THE MAJORITY of his films, Steve was well cast.
That had a lot to do with the way he immersed his own
personality into the character, but the studios mostly got it
right over the years. He was perfect in *The Great Escape*, *Hell
Is for Heroes*, *The Getaway*, *Papillon*, *The Towering Inferno* and
Bullitt; the list goes on. *The Thomas Crown Affair*, though, was
a huge departure for him; a major stretch of the McQueen
range and he knew it himself but that represented a challenge, which he was up to. "I wrote it for Sean Connery
and Julie Christie," said Alan Trustman, who penned the
screenplay to fight boredom in his spare time while working as a senior partner in a Boston law firm. "They went
after Connery for many months. But it all ended one crazy
week in New York where (director-producer) Norman

Jewison and (executive producer) Walter Mirisch stayed at the Sherry Netherland Hotel and Connery was nearby at The Plaza. They all met for an hour every day but Connery couldn't make up his mind so they went back to Los Angeles and cast Steve McQueen as he was aware of the project and had been desperately chasing it for most of the year. When I heard McQueen was cast, I was furious as I thought there was no way he could play an upper-class banker. But they told me to get used to the idea."

Thomas Crown is a millionaire businessman bored by the comfort of his life. He needs a challenge, so he arranges the perfect bank heist; assembling a team of men who are strangers to one another, and he remains anonymous to them. With Crown cleverly masterminding the whole operation, a $2.6 million fortune is taken from the robbery, which he discreetly deposits into his Geneva account. Crown is a smooth, immaculately-dressed investment banker, possessing the kind of qualities that were relatively alien to Steve such as the expensive suits (McQueen wore Levi's and a shirt); Crown drove a Rolls Royce (McQueen was far happier in a sports car); Crown plays polo and golf for recreation (McQueen rode motorcycles in the dirt); Crown was a bachelor (McQueen was a family man). There were so many reasons to suggest why Steve was unsuitable for this role, and the studio thought so too. Norman Jewison, who had directed him in *The Cincinnati Kid*, agreed to make the movie, with the subsequent financial backing of United Artists. But he was steadfast in his refusal to involve McQueen in this project.

Trustman first sent his screenplay into the William Morris Agency, which also represented Steve. At that stage it was seen as an unsellable script and needed a great deal of attention before it was fit to be touted as a viable movie option. A young agent at William Morris by the name of John Flaxman was given the task of reading Trustman's work and advised to throw it in the garbage if he didn't think it was a bankable proposition. "We need to get this Boston lawyer off our backs," he was told. But within an amateurishly-presented script, Flaxman felt there was something to work with. It was then entitled *Blood on the Snow* and wasn't written in screenplay form as Trustman had never written one. "I had never seen a beginning to a story like it and was prepared to work with Trustman," Flaxman recalled. "I must have gone through eight rewrites with him over three or four months but still, I told him 'there's no ending and I can't sell this the way it is now'. The writer reacted badly and said, 'Well you write it!' So Flaxman had a choice of making this script work and justifying his months working with Trustman or expect to be fired. "I eventually came up with the ending and Trustman liked it and wrote it. The next development came when Norman Jewison was in town and he asked if I was excited about anything. I mentioned this screenplay but told him I hadn't done anything with it yet. I craftily told Norman that if I didn't hear anything from him by the next day I would take it that he didn't like it and I will offer it somewhere else. There is a story going round that I gave him five minutes to make up his mind but that's not true. But I did give him the impression there was interest in it elsewhere. Thankfully he called and said he loved it. The screenplay was written with a shared image between Trustman and myself, just to create a bond, that Cary Grant would play Thomas Crown and Julie Christie the female lead. Cary Grant was retired by then and we knew he wouldn't do it but that was the sort of person we had in mind for this character. But because Steve McQueen was also a William Morris client, he had gotten hold of this script and liked it and wanted to do the film. The rest is history."

It was at breakfast one morning in the McQueen household when Steve's desire to be in the movie began. Neile remarked to her sensitive husband, "I hear Norman Jewison is trying to get Sean Connery for *The Thomas Crown Affair*. What a shame that is, because I think you'd have been perfect for it." From that moment on, Steve had to be in the movie, just to prove that he could pull it off when it seemed nobody else thought he could. "I was advised not to do it," McQueen told author William F. Nolan. "They told me it would be like trying to make a silk purse out of a sow's ear. But I said, wait a minute, this dude wants to show he can beat the establishment at its own game. He's essentially a rebel, like me. Sure, a high-society rebel, but he's my kind of cat. It was just his outer fur that was different – so I got me some fur."

Kurt Neumann had been Jewison's assistant director on *The Cincinnati Kid* and was expected to work on *Crown* also, until another project came up which took him away from this picture. Nonetheless, he was involved long enough to glean just how determined Jewison was NOT to cast Steve McQueen for this role. "I spent a lot of time working on the preparations for *The Thomas Crown Affair* after Norman and I had done *The Russians Are Coming* together," Neumann said. "He sent me this script on *Thomas Crown*. I read it and it quickly became apparent who Norman had in mind for those roles. He told me the lead would be a 'Sean Connery-type' and the girl will be 'a Jeanne Moreau'. We had offices at Mirisch, left over from when we did *Russians*, and Steve heard about this script and he came to see Norman and I and the three of us went to lunch. Steve told us that he saw himself as Thomas Crown and desperately wanted the part.

"After lunch, Norman told Steve he would be in touch and Steve left. Norman then turned to me and said, 'Over my dead body will that guy play *Thomas Crown*. How can Steve McQueen possibly imagine himself in this movie'?"

Actress Shirley Anne Field felt Connery's oft-regarded image of smooth and sophistication was misplaced, and was as clichéd as Steve being limited to tough-guy characters. "I know Sean Connery well and I can tell you he's not sophisticated and was tougher and rougher than Steve," she said. "The image of him as James Bond – where people get that impression from – was produced; just a case of brilliant casting; not real. But like Steve, he had a real great presence on the screen."

When Connery turned the part down and other options came and went, and he also couldn't find his Jeanne Moreau, Walter Mirisch called Jewison into the office. Mirisch was renowned for his subtle way of dealing with problems and he was aware of everything that was going on and had eyes and ears all over the studio and didn't miss anything. He pointed out to his director and fellow producer that quite a lot of money had been spent already on preparations and that he did not want to spend any more money until the lead actors were set. Mirisch knew McQueen desperately wanted the part and he knew Jewison was equally enthusiastic for Steve NOT to be handed the role. Mirisch, though, was shrewd enough to realise that the film would make money if Steve McQueen played Thomas Crown. After that meeting Jewison reluctantly conceded, 'Ok, we've had it! Steve McQueen is going to be Thomas Crown!' "Norman ended up making a great, commercial picture but I don't think it was what he had intended at the outset, artistically," Neumann continued. "It wasn't that Norman had anything against Steve – he would have wanted Steve in many, many projects, but just not this particular one." Jewison had tremendous respect for Steve, and although he initially felt McQueen was not right for Crown, he warmed to the idea. He began to understand that Steve 'wanted to grow up' and take on a part he had never played before and that maybe there was a desire within him to be Thomas Crown, who was every-thing Steve wasn't: intellectual, college-educated, sophisticated, smartly-dressed and more. But one thing the two did have in common was a desire to beat the establishment.

Mirisch added: "Steve knew about the script and always wanted to play Crown. But we thought this is really not a Steve McQueen part – the neckties and high lifestyle. We were interested in Sean Connery because we needed a very sophisticated man to play that part. Norman and I met Connery in New York at the Regency Hotel where we had lunch with him. We were there all afternoon on this one day, trying to talk him into *Thomas Crown*, but he just wouldn't do it, so we had to move on. Interestingly enough, years later, I reminded him of this meeting and how hard we tried to get him to play that part and he said, 'Yeah, I should have done it' (after being type-cast as James Bond)."

Actress Barbara Leigh, who would later co-star in *Junior Bonner* with Steve and become his off-screen girlfriend for a brief time, understands why the executives just could not associate Steve with this role. She knew Steve as a man's man who cussed, drank beer aplenty and ate with his feet on the dinner table. "Steve didn't grow up with manners of much more than survival manners - manners to get by," she said. "But when he wanted, he knew how to play the game of sophistication, when it was called for – work-wise. I might have preferred him to be more like (my other boyfriend) Jim Aubrey, who was my Howard Roark in *The Fountainhead* – my hero. But I accepted Steve for who he was, which was pretty special no matter his manners."

With Connery ruled out, Jewison and Mirisch had continued to ignore Steve as they glanced down their list of targets. "We talked at length about Richard Burton as well but these desirables just never came off and we were forced to look again at Steve. We went for lunch with him and I told him again, 'You're not a neck-tie guy, Steve', but he said to me, 'Walter, I can do this and I know how to do it.' He was very, very persuasive and it's not easy to turn down Steve McQueen when he has set his heart on something."

Once the disappointment of failing to attract Connery and Burton had gone and the realisation that Steve McQueen was on board for Crown, people grew to accept him and worked towards making this casting an inspired accident. Writer Alan Trustman explained: "Despite my initial reaction, I decided it was time to embrace the situation so I went to United Artists and asked for every movie and TV clip on McQueen. I then went down to New York and spent 16 hours a day in a hotel room screening McQueen and making notes on what he could do and what he couldn't do, what made him comfortable, what made him uncomfortable. By the end of that week I felt I really knew McQueen and I rewrote the script for him. Steve went berserk he liked it so much. My favourite quote that he used in reference to me was, 'I don't know how, but the son of a bitch knows me'. Steve appreciated the transformation and for the next couple of years I was his boy, I was his writer. That continued through Crown, through Bullitt, until I refused to write his racing car picture

(*Le Mans*). That was the end of my writing career. But for a couple of years he was a superstar and I was his writer. He loved the advice I gave him on how to approach *Crown*; I said, 'You love girls but you are afraid of them' and he played it that way beautifully."

The female lead was played by Faye Dunaway, who had just come off the hit movie *Bonnie and Clyde*. She portrayed Vicki Anderson, the intuitive insurance investigator, who soon pinpoints Crown as the perpetrator of the crime. Her approach is blunt. She informs Crown almost immediately that she knows he is behind the robbery and that she always gets her man. The story is an interesting tale in the way that it's not a question of who-dunnit, more of whether she can prove her suspicions correct. Instead of detecting the obvious, the audience is in on the secret and rides along with her plight to nail the squeaky-clean businessman. Along the way, the two fall in love, which only complicates her task in hand. The scene which captures their first embrace - over a game of chess - became one of the great movie scenes, for it's dialogue, acting and photography, and of course 'the kiss' which is one of the longest ever filmed. It took three days to shoot the scene and a full day to shoot the minute-long kiss itself.

McQueen and Dunaway played off one another expertly. There was a good chemistry between them that gave depth to their relationship in the film. No better example than their chess game, which featured the now infamous kiss scene that spanned almost five minutes of screen time. Some clever camera work by Haskell Wexler, combining their flirting with concentrated facial close-ups, was driven by the intuitive vision of Jewison; and executed terrifically by McQueen and Dunaway. She was one leading lady who did not fall for his charms, physically; she was always one step ahead of him, which made for an intimate, respectful but slightly standoffish exchange that filtered through to their characters perfectly. Thomas Crown also knew he had to work hard to seduce Dunaway's Vicki Anderson, who was a tough, smart cookie. "Steve, friends said, didn't know how to deal with someone like me, who was intelligent and not inclined to the old male-female games that he knew how to win. For my part, I saw him as an icon. That shade of distance between us ended up working very well in creating the relationship between Vicki and Crown."

Dunaway enjoyed her screen relationship with Steve and noted how their backgrounds had similarities, although things were much different by the time they came together. "We had both grown up on the wrong side of the tracks, but by the time I got to *Thomas Crown*, I'd shaken off anything that might hint of that," she said in her autobiography *Looking for Gatsby*. "Steve, on the other hand, never stopped feeling he was a delinquent and any day he'd be found out. He worked for three weeks before he mastered life in a suit. And in *Thomas Crown*, the look was a good part of it. Steve was wearing $3,000 suits for the first time in his life. The Phi Beta Kappa key that hung on his vest he always said should have been a hubcap." The difference in how their lives had transformed meant they were never completely comfortable with

THE THOMAS CROWN AFFAIR

one another. "Steve had so much charisma and he seemed to trigger those nurturing instincts in women. He was a chauvinist – legendary in that he was - but a chivalrous one to me. There was a strange dynamic between us."

Although Steve threw his heart and soul into his character, he maintained a reluctance to totally become Thomas Crown. He couldn't wait to change into his own casual clothes after shooting had ceased for the day. Deep down, he never quite felt comfortable as this hotshot banker, despite pulling off a convincing performance.

For make-up artist Del Armstrong, it was a nightmare to deal with Steve. "He was very difficult to work with and very opinionated. He had that macho image with his motorcycles and so on. Right from the word go he was a pain in the ass. He gave the wardrobe people an awful time, as he never attended the fitting days when he was supposed to be measured up for those smart, rich suits he was to wear. They had to go to Palm Springs to just have a conference with him, and even then he was difficult; he didn't like the pattern or the colour. I think it was just the idea of those draped trousers and cut-away coats that put him off. I also had problems trying to get him used to make-up. He said to me, 'I don't know what you're gonna have to do but I don't wanna look made up.' On the set he never liked me to approach him patting him on the face, and of course the powder puff was entirely out of the question. We were in a nasty position because on the one hand we had to do what Norman Jewison wanted and on the other, we had to put up with what Steve McQueen didn't want."

Steve was less trying on writer Trustman and invited him to go and select his wardrobe with him after the producers laid out a six-figure sum for his clothing budget. Trustman was never one to enjoy such tasks and politely declined. He had his suits made by the high-end tailors Brooks Brothers and had no intention to trawl through clothes with the star. "I told Steve that I thought the budget for his wardrobe was ridiculous and that it was a waste of time, but he just shrugged and said, 'Well, it's got to be better than stealing hubcaps'. I then realised that while I was going to the best of schools, he was on the streets stealing hubcaps. That's who he was and sometimes it was easy to forget just how tough a background he had come from."

Steve was a stickler for detail and while some became exasperated with what they saw as petty time-wasting, others observed it as supreme professionalism. In an early scene, Steve was driving Norman Jewison crazy about the wrist watch he was to wear. He tried on four and hated all of them. He, the director and the wardrobe people eventually came to realise that Steve's own watch looked better on him than any of the luxurious ones specially purchased for his character. The next day, Steve had his agent Stan Kamen present Walter Mirisch a bill for $250 for "rental of wrist watch!" Mirisch was staggered at the lengths Steve would go to show he was the star, especially after agreeing a salary of $750,000 for the movie. Once again Mirisch was required to demonstrate the same diplomacy skills with Steve as he had with Jewison, when politely informing him that they needed to hire Steve for this incongruous role. So Mirisch invited Steve for "a little chat" on the set and managed to persuade him that submitting the bill was not exactly reasonable behaviour. The executive producer had a calmness about him that meant he was always able to communicate effectively with Steve and the upshot was that not a single cent was paid for the 'watch rental'. Mirisch was part of the establishment that Steve always resented, but somehow Mirisch had a non-combative way to reach Steve. He was well practiced, though, after *The Magnificent Seven* and, especially, *The Great Escape*.

"Steve was a complex figure," Trustman revealed. "Walter was a gentleman and knew all about him after those previous films they had done together and though they were successful movies I'm not sure he was all that enamoured about working with Steve again. Steve was always very insecure. On one of the rare days that I went on the set for *Thomas Crown*, I was wearing a brand new custom-made suit I had just picked up from Brooks Brothers. I noticed all this murmuring and someone eventually approached me to say that I couldn't stay on the set with that suit on, because it was better than the one Steve was wearing and I was politely asked to leave – orders which came from Steve, who had apparently said he wouldn't shoot until I left."

Steve was far happier at fleshing out the more physical aspects of Crown's character than prancing around in suits and expensive accessories. Polo was a totally new experience for him, but he developed a competence at it in no time, before it was shot at the Myopia Hunt Club. Though Steve never liked horses, he could ride well enough through his days on *Wanted: Dead or Alive* and with the two westerns he had made, but polo required different qualities. For a start, he had to sit an English saddle, which he had never done before. Norman Jewison was impressed with how he practised polo so hard that his hands were literally dripping with blood. Steve would go out some mornings for three hours before shooting began. He sustained blisters on blisters just to master a minute aspect of the role. "That's when I realized just how much he was giving for the film," Jewison commented years later. "Polo was symbolic of all the reasons why he wanted to play Thomas Crown." Learning to fly a glider and playing golf were other aspects Steve took to comfortably. Despite Jewison's respect for Steve's work ethic, he never did enjoy having to deal with the baggage that went with directing an insecure, paranoid, occasionally juvenile Steve McQueen. Steve's education wasn't learned in college; it was purely instinctive. Jewison felt Steve honed in on his own weaknesses, and when he identified the director was struggling with a particular scene, Steve would make his life harder, not easier.

Vince Kehoe, the second make-up man who had worked with Steve on *The Blob*, detected a marked change in the actor's personality over the course of a decade – and not for the better. Almost immediately at the hotel where the crew were staying on location in Boston, Steve appeared to

Vince as though he had let stardom go to his head. Kehoe re-introduced himself and McQueen barely acknowledged him. "By now he'd taken on a new persona from what I had known ten years earlier," Kehoe said. "He was playing the star all the way, flying in his own hairdresser and flying him back. He was a bit stand-offish and didn't really make a whole lot of friends on the set." Steve's movie star histrionics also extended to demanding 24-hour security to watch over his rented house where he was staying with Neile and his two children; despite the producers not being totally believing that Steve had seen an intruder when he offered this as the reason for the added expense.

The McQueen's rented property was a few miles away from the film company's temporary home. In order for Steve to get to work easily on his motorcycle and avoid the traffic, he was afforded a personal police escort every morning. McQueen revelled in the opportunity to have some fun with the cops. Explains Del Armstrong, "He delighted in giving this cop - who was escorting him - a run-around and losing him, and he thought he was riding free and unnoticed, before arriving on the set where he'd do a wheelie as his finale. But I got talking to a cop who was on the set one morning and I asked him if he was worried about keeping an eye on Steve. He laughed and told me the whole of the Boston Police Department knew where he was and what he was doing at every minute of the day. They had every intersection monitored from his house to the set, and a cop would get on his radio and say 'McQueen's just passed through so and so'. It was funny to think how

Steve thought he was giving the cops a run-around but, in reality, they were on to him all the time."

Steve also enjoyed further motorised chaos while the cameras were rolling. In one scene, it called for Crown to entertain Vicki in a dune buggy, in a scene filmed along Crane Beach in Ipswich, Massachusetts. Originally a stunt double was supposed to drive but there was no way Steve was going to stand by and watch a guy who was probably an inferior driver to him carve up the Boston sand. Jewison was quite happy to let his star do the driving as they could then zoom in for close-ups. With a double they would have had to settle for long distance shots. Steve exhibited all his driving skills as he gave Faye Dunaway the fright of her life with his acceleration along the oceanfront. On one occasion, the director requested a shot that would see the buggy head flat out for the ocean but turn off at the final second. However, when the time came to turn as the buggy was hurtling straight toward the ocean, the wheels locked and both stars ploughed into the water. Apart from saturation and shock, no damage was done, except that is, to the car, which had to be rebuilt before any further driving could be filmed. Dunaway took it all in good heart, which typified the tolerance between them.

The Thomas Crown Affair became Steve's fourth hit in a row and his performance did much to prove his range went further than all-action adventure films. Although, some people still did not accept his change in direction readily: "Knowing Steve as I did, I didn't buy it so much," Robert Wise, director of *The Sand Pebbles*, said. "I found it very hard to accept that movie knowing the character he was." For Walter Mirisch, it was a point proved by Steve after the executive producer's initial reservations. "He was just great the way he embraced it and became Thomas Crown. He surprised me at just how good he was in the movie. To put him in a western is easy, but this was quite a stretch for him. He certainly became one of the half dozen 'great' movie stars of the world."

Despite his ability to adapt to a different character like Crown, all the time the real Steve was not far away, as Del Armstrong recalled: "After spending all day in those posh suits, when Norman would wrap things up for the day, it never took Steve long to be back in his jeans and T-shirt and back on his motorcycle."

Main Credits:

Cast: Steve McQueen (as Thomas Crown), Faye Dunaway, Paul Burke, Jack Weston, Biff McGuire, Addison Powell, Astrid Heeren, Gordon Pinsent, Yaphet Kotto, Sidney Armus, Richard Bull, Peg Shirley and more.

Director:	Norman Jewison
(Assistant)	Jack N. Reddish, Walter Hill (second assistant)
Producer:	Norman Jewison, Walter Mirisch (executive)
(Associate Producer)	Hal Ashby
Cinematographer:	Haskell Wexler
Writer:	An original screenplay by Alan R. Trustman

Editors:	Hal Ashby, Ralph Winters, Byron Brandt
Wardrobe:	Alan Levine, Ron Postal, Theadora Van Runkle
Make-Up:	Del Armstrong, Vince Kehoe
Music:	Michael Legrand

REVIEWS:

VARIETY, June 19th, 1968

The Thomas Crown Affair is a refreshingly different film which concerns a Boston bank robbery, enginerred by a wealthy man who is romantically involved with the femme insurance investigator sent to expose him…Free of social-conscious pretensions, the Norman Jewison film tells a crackerjack story in modern cinematic terms, including multiple screen images. Well tooled, professionally crafted and fashioned with obvious meticulous care…As for the story itself and the players, McQueen is neatly cast as the likeable but lonely heavy.

NEW YORK TIMES, June 27th, 1968

The Thomas Crown Affair is just the movie to see if you want to see an ordinary, not wonderful, but highly enjoyable movie - of which there have been so few this year…McQueen is always special, and although this role is too indoors and formal, for him, he does get a chance to race across the desert, or fly a glider or lounge on the beach, in the casual-intense work he is best at.

THE HOLLYWOOD REPORTER, June 19th, 1968

For McQueen, it is less a change of image than of costume, the glove fit of an expensive Ron Postal wardrobe accomplishing a smooth transition from rugged rebel to rich rebel in a role that is otherwise well tailored to his personality.

FILMS AND FILMING, September, 1968

The word which sums the film up is cool – cool acting, cool direction, cool writing. Nothing is forced, everything is relaxed. Even the robbery seems quite leisurely and is, in fact, not particularly important to the story.

Bullitt handed Steve what was probably the coolest role of his career. The movie is best remembered for its exhilarating high-speed car chase
(COURTESY: WARNER BROS / SEVEN ARTS / BRITISH FILM INSTITUTE)

BULLITT

(Warner Bros-Seven Arts) 1968

'Steve and I were having lunch at a Chinese restaurant. We were
near the back, eating, not bothering anybody when this woman came
up to Steve and started writing her number on his back in lipstick.
He swore at her and she then started screaming 'he hit me, he hit me'
- it really threw him and he ran outside. Those things used to happen
to him all the time and he found it difficult to deal with'
- Tim Zinnemann

IF EVER THERE was a role that Steve McQueen was unlikely
to play, it was a cop. He was anti-establishment, took drugs
for recreation and was a devout non-conformist - almost
everything that would quash the claims of most to portray
a police detective. Although, this role wasn't just about any
cop. But for one or two differences, Frank Bullitt really was
Steve McQueen with a badge; he drives his car recklessly
fast, he confronts his superiors with contempt, he exudes cool
and commands respect from his contemporaries. *Bullitt* was
Steve's first film where his company, Solar Productions, had
sole creative responsibility and he was determined more than
ever to make a movie that would appeal to the masses.

Steve was determined to play a cop in *Bullitt* differently to how policemen were perceived in real life by increasing anti-establishment groups
(COURTESY: WARNER BROS / SEVEN ARTS / BRITISH FILM INSTITUTE)

Warner Brothers financed the film, which was the first of a six-picture deal. His long-time friend and colleague Robert Relyea was brought in by Steve to become Solar's executive producer, and he was present when McQueen decided to make *Bullitt*. "We had been at Warner's for about three months," recalls Relyea, "and when a studio make these deals, they expect productivity. So one night Steve and I were chatting at one of our offices and we knew we had to move on something, whatever it was, and Steve said, 'I think we better do the cop thing, because we're in the midst of anti-war demonstrations, anti-authority movements and the drug culture and I think I can do something different'." That 'something different' was revealed months later...

Steve looked up at the promotion poster for *Bullitt* and said to Relyea: "See, that's what I mean." He was referring to the turtle-neck, because in those days a cop wouldn't wear anything except a shirt and tie. McQueen's perceptive awareness of how life really was on the street, which had stayed with him since his youth, allowed him to create a character that reflected the political and social state of America with sublime accuracy. In achieving this, portraying a cop of such revolutionary ethics endeared him to the movie world. Even the rebellious kids, who rejected authority in favour of love and peace, now looked at the police in a different light, believing them to be not all bad. *Bullitt* left scars - socially and mentally. The film was shot entirely on location in San Francisco and director of photography William Fraker felt the feeling in the city complemented

Steve and his leading lady, English actress Jacqueline Bisset,
share a moment on location in San Francisco. She denied that
they had an affair during the movie
(COURTESY: WARNER BROS / SEVEN ARTS / THE
KOBAL COLLECTION)

their production. "During that film, it was the height of the revolution. The Haight-Ashbury section of the city had all the flower people and love people there. That whole movement originated in San Francisco - it was a very exciting and romantic time and we were all generated by that enthusiasm and excitement, which I think, moved into the picture."

Solar Productions was the empire that Steve desired, which would supposedly ensure life-time security for the McQueen family, so when the six-picture deal was signed with Warner Brothers, the future looked rosy. *Bullitt*, based on the novel *Mute Witness* by Robert L. Pike, was negotiated with company head Jack Warner, who gave his blessing to the project and was prepared to allow Solar total freedom with how they wished to make the film. But before shooting began, Warner sold the studio to Seven Arts and with that deal, came a new head – and he had his own plans. "There were philosophical differences between ourselves and the new management," said Relyea. "From what was supposed to be a six-picture deal became a one-picture deal, as they *invited* us to leave when *Bullitt* was complete. That's how they say it in Hollywood, but in the real world I say we were fired. It was a question of style and new management moving in and wanting to have their signature on things." Before the picture began, there were attempts made to salvage the deal when a meeting was set up in San Francisco, but the studio executives were not keen on Solar's plea for total independence - they wanted input and lots of it. A compromise was never going to be reached, so Steve was now devoted on making *Bullitt* a success and proving a point to the headstrong hierarchy - which he did to perfection.

Solar were able to get their hands on the rights to the *Mute Witness* book courtesy of a young agent by the name of John Flaxman, who worked at Steve's management company William Morris. Flaxman's job was to sift through books and screenplays and decide what material was potentially bankable and which could lead to a hit movie. He had already collaborated with writer Alan Trustman on *The Thomas Crown Affair* and he once again called in the same writer to see what he could do to adapt Robert L. Pike's book to the screen. The movie that became *Bullitt* was so different to the book that Trustman was later given the chance to claim his screenplay as an original but that would have cost another $50,000 to pay off Pike, so they settled for an adaptation.

"The *Bullitt* story has never been told and John Flaxman is clearly responsible for *Bullitt*," Trustman commented. "I was looking for an adaptation and was introduced to Pike, who was very pleasant to me, though he owed me a great deal because his book was about a 67-year-old Jewish detective in New York City. There was no character of Bullitt, no girl, there was no Mustang, no car chase, no airport chase, no hospital chase. When I read Pike's book I told Flaxman, 'This is ridiculous, I can't adapt this, there's nothing there'. And he said, 'Well write an original and we will say it's an adaptation.

So I wrote *Bullitt*, in one day. I started at four o'clock on a Saturday afternoon after returning home from the Harvard football game and finished at one o'clock on Sunday lunch time, before the New York Giants went on television, as I am very much a football fan."

Once the project landed in Steve's hands he needed some cajoling and persuading first from his wife Neile, as he then felt it would be a public relations disaster if he were to play a cop. He knew his value on the street with the hip kids and figured that if he portrayed a cop they would "turn against me so fast it would make your head spin". But that was before he realised he could play a cop 'Steve McQueen-style'. Before he went to work on the character, there was still much to be done on the business front.

"Ernie Pintoff, the director who worked mainly in animation, initially gave me *Mute Witness* to read to see if I felt it would make a good movie," Flaxman recalled. "In doing that job I realised how the best film-makers chose the lesser-known books to do a movie out of. It was never the best-sellers that got made. And they knew they would also be able to buy the rights much cheaper, too. *Mute Witness* wasn't a great book but had a germ of an idea and I gave it to Trustman and he agreed with me. He subsequently wrote the script and it was rejected by ten different film companies – they all felt it was a television movie. But my feeling was that if they got the right director and the right star, it would make a good movie. I couldn't get anywhere with it. Eventually I was introduced to Phil D'Antoni and he also saw merit in Trustman's script and we did a deal where he took on the rights for *Mute Witness*. The rest is history, as they say."

Flaxman's job was then done, but before bowing out of the project altogether he met McQueen in New York, while various contracts were being thrashed out. Steve was paid $1 million, while Flaxman negotiated a $5,000 upfront fee for Trustman plus 14 per cent of the gross. It was a deal which almost gave William Morris boss Abe Lastfogel a heart attack. He couldn't grasp that his young agent had clawed in $100,000 from United Artists for Trustman on *The Thomas Crown Affair*, yet was getting nowhere near that for *Bullitt*. But Lastfogel reluctantly supported Flaxman's gut instinct and it proved to be shrewd business as Trustman subsequently settled a dispute with Warner Brothers that pocketed him around $2 million and, subsequently, the William Morris Agency $200,000. The agency also collected commissions from Steve and producer Phil D'Antoni, who they had introduced to the property. Flaxman left the WMA after just ten months out of annoyance at his lowly salary, despite him creating *The Thomas Crown Affair* and *Bullitt* from nothing.

While D'Antoni would later express his gratitude to Flaxman for involving him with *Mute Witness*, or *Bullitt*, he would not have been so gracious during production when he and Steve were sometimes at loggerheads. Their relationship deteriorated so much at one point that Lastfogel had to intervene to smooth matters and allow the production to continue.

"Steve McQueen gave Phil D'Antoni a lot of problems while shooting the picture," Flaxman reflected. "When I met Steve he had the limpest handshake I have ever gotten. You see this tough guy in the movies but I thought he was a gentle soul. But I realise there are a lot of people who had trouble with him and wouldn't agree with me on that. At one time during *Bullitt*, McQueen banned Phil from the set! Can you believe that? The star banning the producer from the set! Phil went back to Abe Lastfogel and told him what was happening and the advice was that Steve did not have the right to do that and Phil was to go back and produce the movie – but in a way that would not upset Steve. Things improved, but McQueen still threatened to quit the picture several times."

For Tim Zinnemann, son of legendary film-maker Fred, the film was his big break and he has since become a respected producer. As first assistant director, Tim soon developed a strong rapport with McQueen. He said: "I thought Steve was a very big star and it was a thrill for me to be working on the project. I felt he was very focused and that he had a better idea than anyone else of what he wanted to accomplish with *Bullitt*. We tried to be very innovative with things like location shooting, camera mounts and so on and Steve was heavily and creatively involved. Warner's, though, had no belief in the project. At the time, the studio bosses didn't perceive this film to be anything but a sort of pot-boiler police drama and I don't think people imagined that it was going to do any business particularly. They basically tolerated it because Steve was the star. We were all young and very gung-ho and really wanted to prove the studio wrong."

STEVE McQUEEN: THE COOLER KING

Englishman Peter Yates was brought in to direct his first American film after his work on *Robbery* had impressed all concerned, including Relyea. "There were a couple of things that we really liked. Peter had tremendous enthusiasm and he had a real good slant on *Bullitt* from the beginning." Yates and McQueen shared similar qualities, according to cinematographer William Fraker: "Peter was honest and there was never any bullshit about him - like Steve in a way." The scene in *Robbery* that sold McQueen on Yates was a car chase sequence. Such footage became a major influence on the legendary car chase in *Bullitt* that still captivates audiences today. With Steve driving his Ford Mustang down the hills of San Francisco at breakneck speed, came a startled audience reaction. Never before had a car chase been captured on film in a manner so exhilarating, which revolutionised the industry by occupying eleven minutes of screen time. "The chases down those steep roads have been done to death now, but at that time, it was a fresh idea," says Relyea.

Several can claim to have had significant input in the chase. Producer Phil D'Antoni was a major influence who went on to master the genre, producing *The French Connection* in 1971, which also included an exciting car chase and won five Academy Awards. Writer Alan Trustman adamantly claims he was the one who conceived the idea for a car chase in *Bullitt*, before others adapted it, or improved it or increased its importance to the movie. "Everybody has claimed credit for the chase but I was the one who spent the summer of 1954 heading up and down those San Francisco hills in my Ford, flying through the intersections at three o'clock in the morning," Trustman affirmed. "That was not in my original screenplay but as soon as they told me San Francisco was to be the location, I wrote it in. And you had to give Steve something physical for him to involve himself in – machinery or horses. Norman Jewison explained that to me. That was the reason why they were so excited about the dune buggy and polo scenes in *The Thomas Crown Affair*.

"I asked them if they realised that if you drove a car like a Mustang down those hills at three o'clock in the morning it will take off in the air and they thought that was wonderful and McQueen went ballistic with excitement and made it known right then that he wanted to drive some of it himself. So I did two rewrites on that basis."

Second scriptwriter Harry Kleiner was another leading contributor. He originally sent McQueen a script of a western, but due to Steve's commitment to *Bullitt*, nothing materialised. Although, when the final draft by Trustman was frowned upon, Steve went back to Kleiner with a semi-script and said, 'Make it work if you can.'

The story itself is confusing, about a witness who is placed under police protection by Walter Chalmers (Robert Vaughn), and it is the task of Lieutenant Frank Bullitt to see that he comes to no harm in order for him to give evidence for The State against The Mob. In suspicious circumstances though, he is killed and Bullitt then hides

STEVE McQUEEN: THE COOLER KING

his dead body in an effort to catch the killer and untangle the mystery. Kleiner said: "If I made a straight story-line it would become too predictable, so I wanted to include a sub-story."

Kleiner's writing predecessor on *Bullitt*, Trustman, was annoyed with the amount of changes that were made to his original screenplay and the constant tinkering culminated in the breakdown of his relationship with director Peter Yates and subsequently his exit from the film. "From the outset, I was involved in the discussion when they were looking for a director," Trustman said. "I loved Peter Yates's work in *Robbery* but he was their third choice. It just so happens that the others who were ahead of him didn't answer their phone when they were called and Peter did answer his phone even though they got him out of bed at his home in the UK, when they called in the middle of the night. I thought it was preposterous that they would rule two guys out through not answering their phone but that's how it was in those days. Peter had a car chase in *Robbery* and I fell in love with what he did there by putting a camera on the following car. It was sad that my relationship with Peter became uncomfortable as he kept changing the script, notably the girl's character and my ending. I had an ending where the girl was shot at the end. Finally I blew up and said I wanted out. Kleiner then came in and made more cuts on the girl character. Strangely, though, when they screened the picture in New York I liked it. I then walked up to Peter and, even though four or five people stood up to prevent a fistfight, I thanked him for making a wonderful movie out of my mediocre screenplay."

McQueen naturally liked the idea of the chase, and as soon as plans for the scene were afoot, all pre-production discussions were dominated by it. Cinematographer William Fraker met Yates for dinner, the night he agreed to work on the picture, and well remembers their conversation. "I had seen *Robbery* and thought what Peter had done with those Jaguars was phenomenal. I asked him how he did it and he told me, quite modestly. We then started talking about how we could improve the car chase in *Bullitt* and how important it would become. Sure enough, that was the night we decided to shoot everything at 24 frames normal, but speed up the cars. We put cameras inside the cars to get a reaction and it worked beautifully. It brought the audience into the front seat with the driver and instead of being an observer they participated in the chase, which helped to make it so exciting."

Steve added a different concept to the scene when he said to Yates very simplistically, "Let's remember that we're making a western here; we're not going to strap our guns on but we are going to strap our cars on." This theory is understood just prior to the chase when both he and Bill Hickman, the stunt man driving the villain's Dodge Charger, put on their seat-belts as if to say 'let the battle commence'.

Casting was in the hands of Yates, McQueen, Relyea and D'Antoni. Only the leading lady Jacqueline Bisset was officially interviewed and tested, as roles were secured pretty much on reputation. "I felt like I was a girl among a lot of guys," Bisset said. "I hadn't seen much of Steve before we worked together though had seen a couple of his movies like *The Magnificent Seven* and *The Thomas Crown Affair*, and *Papillon* a few years after *Bullitt*. But I never knew too much about him.

"The first time I met Steve was when I had to test with him. I was a little scared and I took my friendly hairdresser along for support. Steve was extremely friendly, smiling a lot and was very open. I cannot remember the scene we had to do together but everything at that stage was awesome to me; there was a real big fear level on my part. I had worked with Frank Sinatra by that point (on *The Detective*), who was a legend and hallowed ground itself, and Orson Welles (on *Casino Royale*). So although I had been in films with big names by that stage (when she was 23), it wasn't that that bothered me but more understanding the process of getting into a part. I felt acting was a lot simpler than what people made it out to be. There was always a lot of chat going on about acting. I didn't have a lot to do in the film but Peter Yates asked me to move to San Francisco for a few weeks before shooting began 'to get into the feeling of it all', which I didn't quite understand because I felt I could get into the feeling of my part without doing that.

"But when we started to shoot Steve was well into the project and always very, very busy with it being his first picture as a main producer. Steve always seemed hyper; he was never all that chatty. He was very cool in his role, but to get to that relaxed stage you have to get things organised, especially as a producer, and my feeling is that he was always hyper and pre-occupied. He was running from one person to another, talking and worrying about things. Steve often spoke in this American dude talk and I really didn't understand what he was saying sometimes – I just nodded, as he spoke about 'soul-chicks and dudes'. I still don't know what a soul-chick is!"

Previous books on McQueen have said during the course of shooting this movie, he had an affair with Bisset, though did not offer any evidence to support the claim. It is fact that Steve's then wife Neile wrote in her memoir that she considered Bisset the most beautiful of all of Steve's leading ladies, though at no point did she ever reveal anything about her husband sleeping with Bisset, who wished to put the record straight here.

"No, we did not have an affair," revealed Bisset, who stayed at a rented San Francisco apartment throughout filming. "People write things and have done for many years. Yes he was handsome, friendly and nice and there was a little bit of teasing, but nothing happened. There were no groupies around either, as has been suggested before."

Bisset added: "I was in a relationship in Los Angeles and didn't want to hang around in San Francisco more than I had to. I was on my own frequently. I might do a scene in the morning and then go back to my flat. I had a lot of meals around town with Steve, along with Peter (Yates) and Phil (D'Antoni); we were always going to different restaurants.

That was very much the fun part for me because I would literally be waiting around for ages before I ever did anything.
We ate a lot at a nice Italian restaurant called Vanessi's and it
was always good fun with those guys. I remember us clam-
bering into to some tiny car and I felt I was hanging with the
big guys."

Bisset also commented that Neile "was around quite a lot"
and was "a nice lady, always seemed very cheerful, secure
and like a happy woman."

Other than Bisset, as far as casting went, Steve wanted
Robert Vaughn, his old friend from *The Magnificent Seven*,
to co-star. Vaughn had just completed the successful television series *The Man from U.N.C.L.E.* and wasn't overly
impressed with the project that McQueen was offering him.
He recalled: "I read this script that Steve had sent me and I
told him it was shit and asked him if he really wanted to be
doing it, considering it was his first film as a producer." At
his persuasive best McQueen replied: "The guy that's going
to direct is Peter Yates who's just come off a real hot movie
in England and I think it could be an exciting film, I'd like
you to do it." Vaughn, still unconvinced, asked Steve to
send it back after a re-write. Following several line changes
and an increase in salary – that wasn't requested – Vaughn
then consented to do it. Simon Oakland was also hired, an
actor Steve remembered from *The Sand Pebbles*, along with
Steve's close friend Don Gordon, who played Bullitt's sidekick, and a young Robert Duvall, who had studied at the
Neighbourhood Playhouse in New York like Steve.

Prior to shooting, Kleiner had serious problems with the script to overcome and there was little pre-production time to make changes, following his late appointment. He said: "Steve had made a contractual obligation with Warner's to begin the picture on a particular date in San Francisco and when that day arrived we barely had a script. We just hoped we could pull the chestnut out of the fire before it burned." This was no easy task. Kleiner managed to stay a day ahead of production throughout the picture and sometimes wrote a scene that had already been shot! *Bullitt* was that intense. "The problem with the original script was that it just didn't work for McQueen," Kleiner said, "because he had rigid ideas about what he wanted to do. Steve was finicky, and as he was the star, I straddled the script to match his persona."

Steve told Kleiner, "I don't want to talk, give the speeches to the guys in the pressed suits, I'd rather react." Getting Steve to talk was a headache for the writer, but he soon learned how good McQueen was at reacting and knew he had to give the bulk of the dialogue to the supporting actors. "Despite the problems, he wasn't difficult to work with at all - he was very straight," Kleiner admitted. "He'd try things and was very much involved in saying what he could and couldn't do."

Bisset acknowledged the script problems were on-going throughout. "I was frequently going between LA and San Francisco and I was aware that there were script issues going on but I was never privy to those conversations," she recalled.

"I had nothing to do with that stuff, and was just told 'these are your lines' and I would do the scene."

The one scene that Bisset did have a problem with, in terms of its content in relation to the scene, was when her character Cathy asks Bullitt, after seeing a dead body while he is on a case, 'What will happen to us in time, Frank?' To which, he replies, 'Time starts now.' Bisset was not comfortable with it, but Steve and Peter Yates both knew they had to move on with the rewrite they had committed to. "That was a very difficult scene and I actually didn't like it at all, but only because I had great difficulty with it," she recalled. "I felt that my character wasn't really needed as it was such a man's piece and I remember thinking does it really need my character here? The relationship of that woman in that man's story...I always felt that I'm not sure if this character of mine should be here. Those deep lines slightly bothered me because he (Bullitt) was a guy who was potentially losing his life every day and his female companion, my character, was asking those questions. She was caring but slightly annoying. Presumably when you're in love with a policeman you have to take it as it comes. But I suppose I was the aesthetic part of his life."

Despite the extra responsibility of producing, Steve's appetite for fun never wavered. His passion for bikes was imperishable, which created a potential clash with studio bosses who had issued orders that there was to be no riding motorcycles, as a serious accident to their star could destroy the picture. Considering he was driving in the picture at ridiculous speeds, this was an odd request. Steve was never good at taking orders and he came up with a plan that would allow him and Don Gordon to ride their motorcycles without inducing the wrath of Warner Brothers. Gordon fondly recalled: "Steve knew that we had to be cool otherwise the movie people would go crazy, so he hired a truck and had our bikes secretly transported to San Francisco. There, he rented out this garage where we stored the bikes. After we'd shoot, we would go and have something to eat, then clean up and meet at the garage at midnight, where we'd get on our bikes and go riding. We had a real neat time, especially as we knew we were having fun with the producers."

Steve also developed a friendship with Tim Zinnemann. The two shared many laughs, but also, many tense moments. "We were having lunch one day at a Chinese restaurant in San Francisco," recalls Zinnemann. "We were near the back, eating, not bothering anybody when this woman came up to Steve and started writing her number on his back in lipstick. He turned around and swore at her and she then started screaming 'he hit me, he hit me' - it really threw him and he ran outside. Those things used to happen to him all the time and he found it difficult to deal with. He wanted people to respect his privacy but they never did and it made him more private. Some actors bask in the glory of adulation and stardom, though I'm not saying Steve never did that, he just didn't want to be shaking hands, signing autographs and so on. He freaked at being in a crowd of people who were all after him."

Jacqueline Bisset also observed that element to Steve's personality, in which he despised having his privacy compromised. "Whenever we were rehearsing or planning scenes, there would always be Peter Yates, Phil D'Antoni, Steve and the writer Harry Kleiner, with me also trailing along," she recalled. "We would go and eat at different restaurants and Steve would always insist on booking a closed-off room in the restaurant because he liked to be quite private. He certainly didn't like to be caught up with the crowds and would always eat with his back to wherever people were. And whenever he was in a public place his bike was never far away so he could escape. He was cat-like, ready to run all the time, in case he got 'tackled'. He really was magnificent on that bike and at one with it. He was very famous at that time and liked to be in charge of his own entrances and exits. Steve was never one to be standing round talking amongst a crowd."

Don Gordon agrees that his popularity was massive at that time. "He had a magnetism to women, men *and* children - people liked him a lot. He would walk down the street in Paris and they would go bananas. I don't think people today realise just how big a star he was. When we were shooting in San Francisco, the crowds were astronomical - they were so big the police had a hard time controlling them."

Professionally, the angle of *Bullitt* is very defined, which was always the intention of McQueen and Yates. Zinnemann said: "We had lenses made specifically for the picture and used faster film stock than we do now. The idea was to shoot at low light levels and give a documentary feel." A similar approach has since been adopted in later movies such as *Seven* starring Brad Pitt and Morgan Freeman. "There was a lot of inventiveness on Peter Yates's part," Relyea said. "The original story from the book was based in Boston, but Peter and Steve moved it to San Francisco believing it to be more photogenic. We were on a location scout in San Francisco and Peter looked down at the city from the top of this building and said, 'It's nothing but gas stations and liquor stores.' Compared to London it would have been much different. He hadn't seen the city before so to have created what he did was terrific." William Fraker added: "The car chase has since become indigenous to San Francisco. It really was brilliant of Peter to take advantage of the hills and so forth - those cars literally flew through the air. It's all real, there were no camera gimmicks; everything was filmed normal."

A great deal of preparation went into the chase scene. The original sequence was set up by the stunt co-ordinator but was thrown out because it was considered too similar to past films like *It's a Mad, Mad, Mad, Mad World*. *Bullitt* had to innovate in every sense. Acquiring permission from the city authorities to close off roads was difficult initially. City chiefs were concerned that the police force was going to be portrayed in a negative way, but their fears were soon allayed. There were conditions though before the green light was given. The main one being that a certain percentage of black people had to be used in the movie, as the city had made a campaign promise to employ more of them. This was overcome by using a lot of black extras and once they did that, the film crew basically had the run of the city and the political head was then able to say that he had fulfilled his promise. Rehearsals were impossible on the streets, but they did manage to practise the chase on an abandoned airfield outside of San Francisco. Says Relyea: "Steve and Bill Hickman would go out and drive for several hours to get confidence in each other. At the airfield, if they had to swerve and go running off, there was no danger because there was all the space in the world." Hickman's work as the lead stunt driver so impressed producer D'Antoni that he hired him for *The French Connection*, which Steve rejected, having been offered the role that eventually went to Gene Hackman.

The trial runs of the chase were choreographed many times to minimise the prospect of danger, but when shooting began for real on the streets, there were still many hazards that caused concern amongst the crew. Zinnemann recalled one specific instance that could have resulted in fatal circumstances. "In the shot where the cars are jumping down the hill before they go around a corner, right behind the camera there was a kindergarten and loads of kids were pressed right up against this fence trying to take a look. I kept shouting at them to get back, because if one of the cars had rolled over it would have flattened about fifty kids."

There were more worries for the crew, as residents' garages backed out onto the road. Two policemen were provided to help maintain order (there would be more like 202 nowadays) so that the chase could be filmed safely, but even then, it was still a severely hazardous shoot. Relyea said: "We walked every foot of that chase. At night, we would go to tomorrow's location and say to the two officers, 'We'll do this piece from here to there' and we would discuss what we were going to do. Then, when we went to shoot, everybody in the crew including the wardrobe man and the script supervisor, hid behind a hedge some place to make sure some guy didn't come out of a side street or alley. Still we almost had an accident. This damn garage door popped open and a gentleman backed his car right out. The two cars split him one on each side and by the time we got to him, his mouth was hanging open (in shock)!"

There were two Mustangs and two Chargers used in the filming for safety reasons. One would be for jumps and the other for high speed. After the constant battering throughout production, things eventually took their toll. Steve's Mustang, which was used for jumps, completely gave out and the other closely followed: "At the end of the chase after the explosion at the gas station, the Mustang used for high speed, skids and goes into a ditch," said Relyea. "If you look closely the right front wheel is wobbling like a bird's broken wing. That car had said, 'I don't know about you, but I'm finished.' The axle had obviously snapped."

To Steve, the cat and mouse shooting at speeds in excess of a 100mph was fun, to the point where he was annoyed when his friend Bud Ekins (who also did *the* motorcycle jump in *The Great Escape*) drove the Mustang for air jumps. William Fraker, in the camera car parallel to Steve's Mustang, was reluctantly exposed to ridiculously high speeds. He said: "I had got used to the sound of the pitch of the tyres at a certain speed; I knew when we were going 90mph because of the sound. But in the shot by the marina, the pitch got higher and higher and I knew we were going much faster than normal. When we finished the shot, I got out and ran round to the camera car driver and said, 'You mother...how fast?' 'What do you mean Billy?' he said. 'The pitch of the tyres got higher...' 'Okay, we were going 124.' I was ready to kill him."

Before the completion of the chase sequence, the picture went over-budget and the studio demanded they wrapped things up in San Francisco and finish the film on the back lot at Warner Brothers - chase included, to prevent any further loss as they saw it. Steve refused to comply, naturally, believing it ridiculous to return to Los Angeles and he was eventually given permission to stay on and finish the movie in San Francisco. Considering the conflict Solar had endured with the studio, including the break-up of the multi-picture deal, it would have been easy for McQueen to say 'to hell with them' but he remained calm throughout, focusing solely on the success of *Bullitt*. He even invited the president of the studio up to San Francisco, to view some of the film. The reply was uncompromising and swift as Relyea remembered: "They declined our offer and said to go ahead with the picture and as soon as it was complete, could we give them our parking spots back." Comments of this sort were later regretted when box-office reaction was contrary to how Warner's expected. The punters flocked to the movies to view Steve McQueen as the cop in the turtle-neck who defied all but justice.

Steve's dare-devil stunt work wowed the crew during *Bullitt* and it didn't end with the car chase, as he was also involved in a genuinely dangerous scene when he had to run under and then lie beneath a Boeing 727 passenger jet, starting out for take-off. The plane was part of a nor-mal, scheduled flight in the evening for the public. Already over-budget, the film could not afford to arrange anything special, which would have been a further expense to the picture. Crew members were concerned for Steve's safety, as he was to embark on a stunt that took perfect timing in avoiding the wheels and the incredible heat from the jets, and endless amounts of courage. "That scene was particu-larly tough on Steve because he had an ear-drum problem and the noise from that damn thing was incredible," com-mented Relyea. It was a shot excellently photographed by cameraman Fraker, who had to work in limited light and make sure he got this stunt right first time as there would be no second chances. Fraker was also impressed with Steve's bravery, which he believed was in keeping with the charac-ter that he portrayed. "Steve never showed any fear at all, he always had his act together. He really knew who Frank Bullitt was and how he wanted him to be."

Bullitt became one of Steve's greatest successes and was his fifth box-office hit in a row. Once again, his acting was overlooked by the Academy, but the film was nominated for Best Sound, while Frank Keller won the Academy Award for Best Editor. Everyone associated with the film was proud to achieve what they did, against adversity of the highest order. Tim Zinnemann confessed: "Everybody was trying to do their best work; we were all really stretching ourselves. The film broke a lot of new ground and I'm proud to have been involved with it. I believe, for its day, it was as good as you can do something of that kind." Robert Vaughn echoed: "I was obviously wrong in my original estimations of *Bullitt*, as it turned out to be one of the highest grossing movies of 1968." Vaughn is certain the film ensured him work for the next ten years and he is not the least bit surprised that the legend of the movie still lives on: "It has to do with the car chase mainly, as the story is pretty hard to understand, but if you don't study the plot too much it's definitely an exciting picture." First scriptwriter Alan Trustman maintains that the confusion surrounding the plot was deliberate. "You have to hold the audience in their seats," he said, "because they know if they go out the room for popcorn or go to the bathroom they won't understand the plot. The plot is logical but you have to work it out or have someone tell it to you."

It was the first occasion in which William Fraker had worked with Steve and by the end of the movie, he understood why McQueen was the number one star of that time: "Steve was sensational, he was always on time, forever professional, worked hard and was innovative, always thinking, and he brought a hell of a lot to the picture. When I went to France for the Cannes festival, I spoke to the marketing director of Warner Brothers and he told me that *Bullitt* was one of the biggest opening grosses in the history of France for an American film." In the first seven days it made $1million. It was huge, *Bullitt* opened and never closed, making an estimated $42 million world-wide, but some believe it was much more. Writer Alan Trustman commented: "Eventually, *Bullitt* made so much money that Warner Brothers pulled it from general release and packaged it with *Bonnie and Clyde* and split the revenues and costs attributed to each picture to try and hide the profits it made."

John Flaxman, the rookie William Morris agent who was the first to facilitate this movie, was optimistic about its commercial value as soon as he saw the finished version. "The first showing of *Bullitt* (before its official October 17 release) was at Radio City Hall in New York at 10am and Phil D'Antoni, who was so nervous, invited me along," Flaxman recalled. "As soon as I saw the movie with that car chase I thought to myself, 'Phil D'Antoni and Alan Trustman are going to be so rich I can't believe it'. Phil is such a gentleman that he came to me afterwards and offered me two and a half per cent of his share of the profits because he felt I deserved it. But I was only doing my job and turned down his kind offer. I hoped there would be other projects we would work on together but that never happened."

Steve's second-in-command Relyea feels the authenticity of the San Francisco location shooting had a major input into the film's success. "That hotel really was a hotel – it was not a set and the elevator really was an elevator in that cheesy hotel. In fact, when we brought in two police experts to help us with the bullet holes and the body markings after the killing, the one guy said, 'You know, I did one of these a couple of months ago in this same room, but it wasn't for a movie'. To examine the picture critically you would probably find some holes that you could drive a truck through. However, once we were committed to it, we always believed in the project."

McQueen was already one of the world's most eminent movie stars prior to *Bullitt*. But this picture created a legend out of the star.

Main Credits:

Cast: Steve McQueen (as Lt. Frank Bullitt), Jacqueline Bisset, Robert Vaughn, Don Gordon, Simon Oakland, Norman Fell, Robert Duvall, Georg Stanford Brown, Justin Tarr, Carl Reindel, Felice Orlandi, Vic Tayback, Robert Lipton and more.

Director:	Peter Yates
(Assistant)	Tim Zinnemann, Walter Hill (second assistant, uncredited)
Producer:	Philip D'Antoni, Robert Relyea (Executive)
Cinematographer:	William A. Fraker
Writers:	Alan Trustman, Harry Kleiner, based on the book *Mute Witness* by Robert L. Pike
Editor:	Frank P. Keller
Wardrobe:	Theadora Van Runkle

Make-Up: Emile La Vigne
Music: Lalo Schifrin

REVIEWS:

THE DAILY CINEMA, December 20th, 1968

Fast moving, brilliantly photographed and strikingly composed - a director's piece de resistance. The audience do not so much observe the action as participate like so many flies on the wall overhearing but not understanding. And here lies the problem for the mass audience. Technically and artistically speaking, the film is outstanding and it will delight everyone who appreciates those qualities...The high spot of the film is undoubtedly the magnificently exciting car chase through the streets of San Francisco: and the well publicised information that it is really Steve McQueen at the wheel gives the emotional involvement of watching a Grand Prix. Steve McQueen adds another perfectly observed portrayal to his repertoire of cool characters.

VARIETY, October 16th, 1968

Conflict between police sleuthing and political expediency is the essence of *Bullitt,* an extremely well-made crime melodrama filmed in Frisco. Steve McQueen delivers a very strong performance as a detective seeking a man whom Robert Vaughn, ambitious politico, would exploit for selfish motives. Highlighted by one of the most exciting auto chase sequences seen in years, the film was produced by McQueen's Solar Productions with Robert Relyea as executive producer and Phil D'Antoni as producer. Good scripting and excellent direction by Peter Yates maintain deliberately low-key but mounting suspense.

MOVIE PICTURE HERALD, October 23, 1968
The hero of *Bullitt* is a lieutenant on the police force in San Francisco of rather unconventional dress - he wears turtle-necks on the job - but of behaviour patterns otherwise quite consistent with protagonists that have gone before in this type of gangster melodrama. Steve McQueen plays the title role (first name Frank) in the tight-lipped, stern visage manner that has endeared him to millions.

NEW YORK TIMES, October 18th, 1968
Bullitt, which opened yesterday at the Music Hall, is a terrific movie, just right for Steve McQueen - fast, well-acted, written the way people talk. The plot is dense with detail about the way things work: hospitals, police, young politicians with futures, gangsters, airports, love affairs, traffic, dingy hotels. There are a lot of Negroes cast, for a change in plausible roles. The setting, in San Francisco, is solidly there, and the ending should satisfy fans from *Dragnet* to *Camus*. There are excellent chases, one around and under jet aircraft taking off by night, the other, by car, over the San Francisco hills. The car chase in particular is comic and straight. (Nobody drives better than Steve McQueen). McQueen, quietly stealing a newspaper because he hasn't got the dime or exchanging just the right look with a Negro surgeon who understands, or even

delivering a line that consoles and sums up the situation with his girl (played by Jacqueline Bisset) embodies his special kind of aware, existential cool - less taut and hardshell than Bogart, less lost and adrift than Mastroianni, a little of both. Television has almost stolen the genre, or made it unserious, but *Bullitt* tightens and reclaims it for the movies. McQueen simply gets better all the time.

MONTHLY FILM BULLETIN, January, 1969

There is an eleven minute car chase which must surely be among the most exciting ever filmed (certainly outdoing the one in Yates' last film, *Robbery*), with the cars taking off like ski-jumpers over the plunging San Francisco hills and heading, all sparks flying, for the freeway and a quite splendiferous crash.

The Reivers was another change of pace for Steve, a risk in
some ways, but it was quite a well-received adventure movie
(COURTESY: CINEMA CENTRE)

THE REIVERS

(Cinema Centre) 1969

'I don't think Steve ever wanted to do a film – it was like pulling teeth. He had this funny idea that his next picture was going to be a disaster and nobody would want to see him again'
– Robert Relyea

STEVE WAS NOW the hottest property in Hollywood and his name alone guaranteed success at the box-office. His previous five movies had all enjoyed great financial rewards and there was no reason why his next vehicle should not also. However, the choice for his follow-up picture to *Bullitt* was ambitious if not peculiar. *The Reivers*, based on a Pulitzer Prize-winning novel by William Faulkner, was a family adventure-cum-comedy; certainly not a genre that Steve McQueen would normally be associated with. He was determined to prove that his range went further than action movies. "You can get stale, doing the same stuff over and over. It was time for me to stretch a little," McQueen said. It was a brave move and a change of direction that most hardened McQueen fans did not welcome. However, *The Thomas Crown Affair* was out of his normal range, yet he performed, bringing his own personality to a relatively incongruous role. Assistant director Tim Zinnemann had his own opinions as to why Steve opted for this film. "I think in the back of his mind he always wanted to do things a bit more literate and Faulkner was obviously a great writer. The fact that he went on to do Ibsen showed he was trying to stretch himself and not just get pigeon-holed, doing the kind of movies that he had done before like *The Great Escape*."

Harriet Ravetch (credited as Harriet Frank Jr.), half of the Oscar-nominated writing team along with her husband Irving Ravetch, also felt that Steve was yearning to stretch out as an actor; to show that he could play other roles and not just the tough cop, cocky poker player or rugged western hero. "For this movie, and like with *An Enemy of the People* later on, there was no question that Steve was very much interested in casting a wider range as an actor and being considered an actor who had amplitude," Ravetch commented. "This was our first personal encounter with Steve and certainly my first impression was that here was a man in need of a change, with a desire to emerge. He was very much interested in enlarging his range as an actor and finding a way to express the inner man."

Now under the wings of Cinema Centre, after the collapse of the Warner Brothers multi-picture deal, the choice of film had to be swift. It was a project that excited him and frightened him at the same time. "For Steve, who didn't want to do anything in case it might be a mistake, this one really was a strange choice," Robert Relyea, business partner and executive producer, said. "He used to say, 'Steve McQueen in a Faulkner movie? Nobody's gonna ever believe that.' He was very sensitive about it, he knew it was a challenge but accepted it." Steve was worried the studio's publicity department would try and sell *The Reivers* as a typical Steve McQueen movie – which it wasn't. Their first ad campaign said, 'Here he comes, rolling at you again' and that was just what Steve didn't want. "Whether you like the film or not, Steve was certainly honest about it," Relyea added. Even with his adoring, global fan base, McQueen was still insecure about his acting and always believed his 'fairytale' would, one day, be taken away from him. Subsequently, this paranoia created a reluctance to work sometimes. "I don't think Steve ever wanted to do a film – it was like pulling teeth. He had this funny idea that his next picture was going to be a disaster and nobody would want to see him again," Relyea said. "It was, 'How about we do nothing and buy some more time' rather than, 'Let's get stuck into this.' You can understand his reservations with *The Reivers*, because he was so far out of his normal character. Steve was concerned that people would think, 'What's McQueen doing playing this country slicker?' That worried him a lot."

Steve was not satisfied with the overall result. He regretted his decision to retry comedy. "After *Soldier in the Rain* I promised myself I'd never tackle another comic role," he told author William F. Nolan. "Yet here I was, hamming and grinning and strutting away down there in Mississippi. It seemed the right thing to do at the time, after *Crown* and *Bullitt*, but I ended up not liking it pretty damn much."

The story is set in the Deep South at the turn of the century and features McQueen as Boon Hogganbeck and Rupert Crosse as Ned – the two of them are The Reivers (old-fashioned slang for rascals). Incidentally, Crosse was nominated for an Academy Award for Best Supporting Actor.

Boon is a man who has never lost his childish appetite for adventure, and this is never more apparent than when he 'borrows' a shiny-new, 1905 Winton Flyer, bright yellow in appearance with dazzling brass trims. Tim Zinnemann considered there to be a certain resemblance between Steve and Boon. "Steve was very boyish, like Boon Hogganbeck in that sense, with his love for speed and things mechanical, but his boyishness was part of his charm." Along with 12-year-old Lucius (played by Mitch Vogel), the two reivers enjoy an eventful ride from Mississippi into Memphis, Tennessee – an experience the youngster will never forget. He is caught up in defending the honour of a prostitute (played by co-star Sharon Farrell) in a brothel, confronts a mean sheriff in a jail and has to win a horse race in order to win back the Winton Flyer that has been lost by Ned in a bet.

Sharon Farrell was the female lead, playing the role of a whorehouse beauty named Corrie. While Boon and Corrie were romantically involved, the intimacy continued off-camera also as McQueen and Farrell embarked on a steamy affair that would continue sporadically until the mid-seventies when Steve was still officially married to Ali. Steve was not only producer and male lead to Farrell but soon also became a trusted friend, someone she was able to confide in about her personal relationship and health issues. She even told him about a miscarriage she had had on the set after the first day of shooting, when she did not know who else to talk to. Sharon had started bleeding the night before the miscarriage though did not know she was pregnant at that time or who the father was for that matter. On discovering the pregnancy, she knew it was either her husband's Ron DeBlasio or Bruce Lee's, who was her lover and 'the one' for her. (Interestingly, Bruce Lee and Steve were friends though neither knew the other was having an affair with Sharon).

Steve was not present on the first day of shooting, when Sharon endured her lowest moment. After a tough day's shoot, which included her lunch-time miscarriage, she then felt pressured into posing for a photo after a request by director Mark Rydell, that would lead to a painting of her character Corrie for the set. It was all too much for her but Sharon went along with it, fearing being fired if she didn't. After this painful ordeal, Steve soon became the shoulder she so needed to cry on and he boosted her confidence when she was low. Once totally at ease with Steve, the intimacy increased when they fell into bed in an apartment that Steve had arranged for her – after he teased her playfully.

Farrell said: "Steve and I were not turned on by each other in the beginning. His protective caveman hormones were activated by what Mark did to me. And my primal 'woman in distress being saved by a man' feelings took over and it all turned into a sexual thing. The magic was finally unleashed when he said, 'Do you want to get kinky? Do you want to see my penis? You do, don't you, and I want you to see it. Show me your breasts.' He took out his swollen penis, which was hard and stiff and said, 'Look how beautiful it is, look, it's a German Helmet,' then he laughed. He peeled my clothes off and then we washed each other down in this big tub and Jacuzzi, while laughing like children. We explored one another's bodies and then he picked me up dripping wet and carried me to the big bed where we made love until we were completely exhausted.

"We had good times on *The Reivers*. Steve made things fun."

The one time, though, when the situation was definitely not fun was when his wife Neile arrived on the set. Only a woman's intuition can tell the guilt on the face of a woman who has been sleeping with her husband – and Neile had it.

"The first time his wife visited the set, I practically ran into her," Farrell recalled. "I came out of my dressing room and there she was, face to face, staring right at me. No words, just that penetrating stare. I felt that she knew. I was so ashamed. I couldn't handle his betrayal to his wife any more than I could handle Bruce's before (after she had an affair with Bruce Lee on *Marlowe*). I knew then and there that whatever this was between Steve and I wasn't going to go anywhere."

Their affair was never as full on as it was on *The Reivers*, but Steve and Sharon did continue to see one another occasionally. The last time they got together was purely by accident in Beverly Hills. Steve was sporting a full beard for his role in Ibsen's *An Enemy of the People* and had put on weight also, as he flaked out in a semi-retirement in the mid-seventies. "He was staying at the Beverly Hills Hotel, though I figured he and Ali MacGraw had broken up, but he never mentioned her or anything about his personal life," she recalled. "Here I was in a hotel suite having an illicit encounter with one man, while in an unhappy relationship with another (her third husband Steve Salkin). I just dismissed all caution and Steve and I made love as if neither of us had a care in the world. We didn't even use any protection, though I had not expected to have sex that day. I felt lost and I guess Steve had his own reasons for needing some escapist sexual recreation.

"Later he told me he had a problem with, maybe, cancer. I begged him to go down to the Livingston Clinic in San Diego. I told him about my friend Joan Hackett and Cherie the hairdresser on *The Reivers*, and all that I had learned from them about their battles with cancer. He laid there and

Teenage actor Mitch Vogel with Steve and Sharon Farrell,
whose affair with Steve went on into the 1970s
(COURTESY: CINEMA CENTRE / SHARON FARRELL)

we smoked cigars together and I said, "You'll have to give up these things, you know."

He said, "That settles it. I will never go."

The picture, shot in and around the small town of Carrolton, Mississippi, portrays how blacks were particularly suppressed in that part of the country. The film company discovered that even in 1969, the state was still a little stuck in its ways with regard to their feelings on race relations. For black actor Rupert Crosse, it was an opportunity to flaunt the freedom he had, and he took delight in demonstrating this to the disapproving townies, which caused friction for the cast and crew in such an intimate location. Explains Tim Zinnemann: "We had to be very careful because Rupert was having an affair with a white woman – and it almost got him killed. It was a time when things were still very tense down there and you daren't step out of line otherwise you would disappear. Rupert was acting up quite publicly, and in this little town, the locals couldn't believe that we the film company could let a black man get away with that kind of behaviour."

On one occasion when Steve and Robert Relyea were having dinner in a local restaurant, they got talking to a couple of black waiters, with whom they enjoyed many laughs and good conversation. Steve invited them to attend a private showing of *Bullitt* the following night in the town's only theatre, which was strictly for whites only. They reassured the guys and told them that Mr. Crosse would be there, but their efforts were in vain. Says Relyea, "On the night, I didn't see these two guys so I went out into the street and I could see them opposite in an alley, all dressed up and ready to go to the show. When they saw me, they backed off into the shadows. I walked over to speak to them but they had disappeared into the night. I guess they took the attitude of 'when you guys are gone we still have to live here'." Steve, who stood strongly against racism, actually had one line in the movie where he had to refer to Crosse as a "nigger". Steve was a little apprehensive about it, after all he was the one who encouraged more blacks to be involved in *Bullitt* only a year earlier. But as Harriet Ravetch reasons, this was a movie set in the early 1900s and it was a word that was then used widely. "I don't recall that it was much of an issue," she recalled. "It was a different time in America and the movie was a period piece. It seemed to be the correct choice at that moment, though I am not sure we would do it today."

Steve, who constantly fought writers throughout his career in a bid to lose dialogue and instead be given more licence to express himself with a reaction, did have serious problems with other aspects of his script. And he was not slow in making the experienced writing team aware of his feelings. Steve was largely respectful of the writers because he knew they had worked with his long-time friend and rival Paul Newman on three movies (*Hud, Hombre* and *The Long Hot Summer*), and gotten along extremely well. The films had been received equally as

340

good. Yet that respect only extended so far, but as Harriet Ravetch recalled, a feisty riposte to Steve's movie star gripes could be enough to win his favour. "Dialogue was not his best friend and there were a few scrapes about it," she said. "I once arrogantly told Steve to speak the words he was being paid to speak. That got a nod of respect and our screenplay was spoken word for word. Another time, it was late when the phone rang at the hotel. He said he felt combative about certain script issues. I calmly said, 'I'll meet you on the street corner at midnight and we will settle it the old fashioned way! It made Steve laugh and it became a source of humour between us." A male screenwriter using these words probably would not have received the same response; but Steve admired her spirit and upfront nature.

The situation among the cast, crew and townspeople was far less tense when Steve arrived for the first time in the town, which consisted of about 300 people. Excited crowds formed outside the hotel where the film crew were staying and their chants for photographs and autographs were loud enough to alert the police. However, their authority had little impact on matters. Desperate measures were needed in order to restore calm, and Steve was the man to do it. "Steve went over and addressed them all and said, 'All these people have to get up early for work and need to sleep," Relyea recalled, "so if you can all leave us alone and respect our privacy, I'll make sure you get your autographs and a chance to visit the set, so can you please go home.'

Everyone then departed, when the police couldn't even get them to move."

Shooting was not always a pleasurable experience as there was an obvious personality clash between Steve and director Mark Rydell, who had known Steve from the Actors Studio in the fifties. The damning verse to this chapter was the fact that Rydell once dated Neile before Steve swept her off her feet and married her. "The fact that Mark used to go out with Neile in those days undoubtedly caused the friction," says Tim Zinnemann. With this history in mind and knowing how much it riled Steve, it is strange that Rydell was hired in the first place, but professionalism came first. Steve and Relyea had viewed Mark's one and only feature, *The Fox*, and loved it. Relyea remembers the initial meeting with Rydell. "While we were filming *Bullitt* in San Francisco, Mark came out with his agent and the Ravetch's. I met with them to talk about Steve's concerns et cetera. While all this was going on, Steve bless his heart, never volunteered to me that he and Mark had been in New York at the Actors Studio together and that Mark used to go out with Neile all those years before. I had no idea of this prior relationship and it wasn't until we started shooting that I found out.

"This previous history did not help matters between them. These were two guys that used to go to the deli with Neile and who used to take the subway together. All of a sudden the whole crew is going 'Yes sir, no sir' to Mark and I think Steve still saw Mark as the guy he used to eat with in New York." Their disputes were frequent and the unpleasant atmosphere set in like an incurable disease. Rumours floated that Steve tried to get Rydell fired. Relyea refutes this: "I have heard about those stories but I don't ever remember Steve purposely trying to get somebody fired on that picture; he never walked away from any picture saying I don't want to work with that director again. The director may have said he wouldn't want to work with Steve again but not the other way."

As assistant director and as a personal friend to Steve and Mark Rydell, *The Reivers* proved to be a real headache for Tim Zinnemann. "Their rows were very public and it got to the point where Steve would only talk to Mark through me. Mark would be standing next to me and Steve would say to me, 'Tell the director I want to do this,' or 'Tell the director I want to do that,' as a way of trying to humiliate Mark. It was very unpleasant and I didn't particularly enjoy being in the middle of it, especially as I was working for Mark."

Relyea, who had worked with Steve on four movies prior to *The Reivers*, felt not all of McQueen's antagonism towards the director was out of personal malice, although he does accept their relationship degenerated as the picture went on. "Steve was naturally anti-authority, it was in his character, so all this treatment wasn't purely for Mark Rydell. It could easily have been Norman Jewison or anybody. Although it eventually got to the stage where instead of Steve saying, 'I'm doing my job I expect you to do yours,' to 'I can't do my job and yours'." After the closeness the Solar production camp had experienced on *Bullitt*, this picture failed miserably to foster a similar feeling. "With *Bullitt*, it felt as though we were all going down the same road," offers Zinnemann, "but with *The Reivers*, it was just as though we were executing a script."

As shooting progressed, Steve became increasingly insecure about his character. Such feelings led him to believe the movie would not provide the refreshing career change he had originally envisaged. Despite this, he never let on his inner concerns. "He was a very macho guy and would never allow himself to be weak in front of other people," says Tim Zinnemann. In the event, the picture did moderate business and received generally warm reviews.

"The film never received the box-office attention it deserved in my humble opinion," Farrell said. "One of the main reasons was due to marketing and distribution failures. It belonged to Cinema Center Films Group which was in the process of selling out. The company had three wonderfully acclaimed films in release at the same time: *The Boys in the Band*, *Something for Everyone* with Angela Lansbury and Michael York, and of course *The Reivers*. All three movies fell through the cracks. Studio heads have big egos and the new crowd wanted to put their money and reputations behind their own productions."

At the Premiere, Steve settled his differences with Mark Rydell and congratulated him on a job well done; though, deep down, he was relieved the project was now complete. It was time to focus on a subject that was a lot closer to his heart and one which he could be proud of – this materialised into *Le Mans*.

Main Credits:

Cast: Steve McQueen (as Boon Hogganbeck), Sharon Farrell, Ruth White, Michael Constantine, Clifton James, Juano Hernandez, Lonny Chapman, Will Geer, Rupert Crosse, Mitch Vogel, Diane Shalet, Pat Randall, Diane Ladd, Ellen Geer, Dub Taylor, Billy Green Bush, Burgess Meredith (narrator) and more.

Director:	Mark Rydell
(Assistant)	Tim Zinnemann
Producer:	Irving Ravetch, Robert Relyea (executive)
(Associate Producer)	Rick Rosenberg
Cinematographer:	Richard Moore
Writers:	Irving Ravetch and Harriet Frank Jr., based on the novel by William Faulkner
Editor:	Thomas Stanford

Wardrobe:	Joanne Haas, Alan Levine, Theadora Van Runkle
Make-Up:	Emile LaVigne
Music:	John Williams

REVIEWS:

VARIETY, November 26th, 1969
Steve McQueen's name and the fact that *Reivers* is basically an entertaining, deftly executed entertainment will draw a good audience, but the film adaptation of Nobel Prize winner William Faulkner's last novel is an economically touch and go proposition...McQueen gives a lively characterisation that suggests he will have a long career as a character actor after his sexy allure thins.

THE HOLLYWOOD REPORTER, November, 26th, 1969
In the best Disney tradition, the first Steve McQueen film for the entire family, is the perfect holiday entertainment, realised through excellent production, performance, direction and the year's best totality of casting.

MOVIE PICTURE HERALD, November, 1969
McQueen's role represents a change of pace for him – not so much in the type of character (he has played 'rascals" before) as in the type of film. He handles the part with vigour and a nice sense of comedy in it. And he certainly fits into the milieu.

FILM DAILY, December 3rd, 1969

There are lively and tender moments in the film, which add up to strong entertainment. There are other moments that strain credibility in behalf of dramatic effect...As usual McQueen gives a performance of rugged masculine appeal.

Steve with son Chad during a break on *Le Mans*, which was
the greatest disappointment of his career and had significant
implications on his life
(COURTESY: CINEMA CENTRE)

LE MANS

(Cinema Centre / National General) 1971

'It was nothing but trouble and a project that should never have been started. Steve is wearing a driver's mask, helmet and racing round a block and the people watching don't know that's McQueen - it could have been a stand-in. The picture was a disaster to begin with' – Harry Kleiner

FOR STEVE, CREATING the definitive motor racing movie had long been a dream of his. Ever since his stardom grew enough for him to visualise such an idea in realistic terms, Steve was adamant one day he would fulfil this ambition. Before *Le Mans* came about, there had already been previous developments on his racing drama concept. Initially, proceedings began in 1966, in association with close industry friend and director John Sturges. With Steve McQueen starring and John Sturges directing the first film about motor racing, hot box-office reaction was expected. The movie was to be called *Day of the Champion,* which Warner Brothers had financed. Shooting was planned to commence as soon as Steve's commitments on *The Sand Pebbles* ended. In the meantime, Sturges was working tirelessly in capturing racing footage for *Day of the Champion*. From this moment events degenerated and, quite suddenly, Steve's dream became of the pipe variety. *The Sand Pebbles* went over schedule and director Robert Wise generously committed to Warner Brothers that he would release Steve as soon as his duties were complete in South East Asia.

But in this time MGM had financed their own racing picture called *Grand Prix*, to star McQueen's friend and neighbour, James Garner and John Frankenheimer as director. Steve had been the preferred choice to play the lead in *Grand Prix*, before he and Sturges began to collaborate on *Day of the Champion*, but there were creative differences between Steve and the producers and they each went their separate ways.

Grand Prix experienced far less trouble than its rival movie; coupled with McQueen's non-availability, Warner Brothers anticipated a hefty financial loss if they released a racing picture right after *Grand Prix*, and they promptly ordered Sturges to shut down all developments on *Day of the Champion*. This was a massive blow to Steve, who had been passionate about everything to do with it. Robert Relyea, who had worked previously with the star, had been involved with the project and admitted it was a huge disappointment for all concerned, particularly for Steve. What hurt him more was that Garner, an actor, friend and neighbour, was taking the part that was initially pegged for him. Garner, aware that Steve had turned the film down, still graciously called Steve to explain that he was taking the role. Steve wished him all the best, but only after a long and uncomfortable silence on the line. Steve, who always regarded loyalty as a prime quality in a friend, never spoke to Garner for years after.

When Steve and Relyea became business partners at Solar two years later, the bitter pill still hadn't digested, and further racing movie plans surfaced once more. "We had a meeting with Stan Kamen and Abe Lastfogel from William Morris as soon as we went into business together," recalls Relyea. "I said to them that because none of us are good losers, one day we will make a movie about racing and that will probably be the end of this company and the relationship. Then we all had a big laugh; but it turned out not to be very funny."

When actors involve themselves in projects like these, with cars, bikes, planes whatever, they are sometimes seen as the typical Hollywood star showboating on camera while dabbling in one of his passing hobbies. This was something that Steve was always very conscious of, even off-camera in his own time. He would never use his movie star appeal to win over fellow drivers. In fact, he resented anybody who described him as a movie star when he was behind the wheel. His passion for racing was such that it meant more to him than a mere hobby. Steve wanted to be recognised in the racing fraternity as a serious driver and be respected accordingly; not an actor who was just having fun with speed. As he used to say to driver Derek Bell, who worked on the film, "You know, I'm not an actor, I just play myself."

Steve won the respect of his race car contemporaries with his
driving ability. But few appreciated *Le Mans* as a movie, and
saw it instead as a bland race documentary
(COURTESY: CINEMA CENTRE)

Opinion on the track, generally, was very complimentary towards McQueen's driving. In the late fifties, the aspiring film star met British racer Stirling Moss, and the two developed a friendship that spanned several years. "We had a common shared interest," says Moss. "He was very enthusiastic about racing and I think that gave us a closer bond than normal people. He was undoubtedly keen on racing. Considering he was a film star, he really was a competent driver."

A great deal of preparation and racing footage went into *Le Mans* and to achieve this, 22 professional drivers were hired as doubles to carry out certain racing scenes in the picture. One such driver was Richard Attwood, who also drove the camera car occasionally. He witnessed Steve's driving at close range and was suitably impressed. "There's no doubt that he had the ability to be a very good racing driver. The fact that he came second with Peter Revson in the 12-hour Sebring race is enough evidence." During that race, which Steve participated in as part of his preparations for *Le Mans*, he drove with a broken foot after a motor-cycle accident while filming *On Any Sunday*. He had to wear a special plaster to allow him to push on the pedals comfortably. They still won with a Porsche 908 in the 3-litre class and missed winning overall by 23 seconds to Mario Andretti's team in a 5-litre Ferrari 512.

English racing driver David Piper had first met Steve during the talks on *Day of the Champion*, and by *Le Mans* time, he was well aware of what Steve was all about as a racing authority and driver. "He was a bloody good driver," Piper said. "Steve could certainly have been a professional racing driver – he really loved cars. But the interesting thing about Steve is that he had a bit of a rough life at the beginning and he wouldn't have had enough money to go racing had he not become a film star."

The idea of the *Le Mans* movie was first born during discussions between Steve and Robert Relyea in their Solar Productions office. "When we were looking for our next property after *The Reivers*, we came up with *Le Mans* and we were determined to do a great job on it after we had got our butts kicked on *Day of the Champion,*" executive producer Relyea said. Although *Le Mans* was never going to be groundbreaking in terms of the first racing picture following the release of *Grand Prix* and then *Winning,* to McQueen it still had a definition. Says Relyea: "It was logic's idea. To tell a story about racing you have to know the field and Steve did. Racing is all about one man, one race, one time, and we had to pack it all into a drama. We both felt that the obvious way to do that would be *Le Mans*. There was never going to be anything to understand. It was just a matter of whoever wins - wins, whoever loses - loses, and whoever gets killed - gets killed."

Filming started a week after the actual 1970 Le Mans race - they had filmed location footage previously to save money on what would otherwise have been an unrealistic, unworkable shoot involving 200,000 extras. They needed that week after the 1970 race to have everything organised, with the local police obligingly closing off sections of the track for the movie. Although the concept of the picture appeared clear-cut and a certain candidate for success to McQueen and Relyea, their hope was not supported by the general consensus. John Sturges, who had also been hurt by the collapse of *Day of the Champion*, was again hired to direct after initial deliberation on the position. He had made three films previously with Steve; *Never So Few*, which put the actor's name on the Hollywood map; *The Magnificent Seven*, which was McQueen's first hit movie; and *The Great Escape*, which launched Steve's name to superstardom world-wide. Given such history between the two, there was no reason to suggest why *Le Mans* should not be their fourth hit together. Although before long, Sturges found a reason why not. He had trouble convincing Steve, who had rigid ideas for the picture, that it would be a near-documentary about motor racing. Sturges fought hard with Steve, trying to get him to see that his notion was just not bankable - or more to the point, interesting. The director wanted a story with more dialogue and human interest - just a story would have been enough. Steve, though, was not keen on compromising his racing documentary-like vision, and this focused – maybe inflexible and blinkered – attitude towards the film ultimately contributed significantly to its subsequent commercial failure.

Sceptics felt producing a movie that racing car drivers would appreciate was more important to Steve than the reaction of movie-goers. Costume designer Ray Summers commented: "Steve was just so excited that the film was to be authentic; he also loved it that he was one of the drivers. He really was determined to ensure that reality was the central theme in the picture. With seven months in France, we spent a lot of time together trying to replicate the drivers' clothes just like in real life. I contacted manufacturers in England, France and Germany so to acquire the costumes that we were looking for, to give a true international look to our drivers. Also, Steve and I mixed up this concoction of tomato and chilli sauce once and smeared it over the drivers' helmets just to make it look like they had been worn and had the odd fly squashed on them!"

For Swedish co-star Louise Edlind, *Le Mans* proved to be quite an adventure. She was a year out of drama school, had a one-year-old son, yet a separation in her marriage and a chance meeting with a film scout led to a whirlwind journey. It began with a flight to London for a meeting with Steve McQueen; a top 10 credit on this Hollywood movie; a near-fatal car crash; and a frantic love affair with the star of the picture. She had finished her studies at the Stockholm School of Drama in 1969 and having fallen pregnant soon after, Louise had little choice but to watch her friends landing parts on TV and launching exciting careers in Sweden. She wondered if she would ever have much of a career now that she was playing mum. But a freak meeting with someone who was seeking extras for *Le Mans*, resulted in her being flown to London for a short meet with Steve. Scouts were asked to find tall, blonde Swedish girls to stand around the pits, which would make for good viewing in the film. Louise had light brown hair, but could speak English, French, Swiss and German so a production aid asked if she would be keen on a speaking part in the movie. Her life would never be the same again.

"From being a wife at home with my baby and no acting work, I suddenly found myself at a hotel in a casting meeting with Steve McQueen, in May, about a month before the real Le Mans race began," Edlind commented. "That was more than I could ever have hoped for. Steve was undecided on me at first because I was tall and he never wanted his female co-stars to be taller than him because he was not the tallest guy, though he was not short either. I didn't have to read any lines; he was very brief and didn't say much. I was probably only in there with him for three minutes. I then went home thinking I wouldn't get the part but I received a call to say Mr McQueen liked me and wanted me to play the small part of his co-driver's wife. I had a very short international movie career but even now when I conduct lectures and I mention Steve McQueen, the reaction is amazing. One young Swedish actor who I met was a tough, moody type like a young Steve, and as soon as he heard about me acting in a Steve McQueen film, he just said, 'Respect, Respect'."

She reached France a week before shooting began, to get acquainted with the surroundings, while they erected 'Solar Village'. While Louise enjoyed the sudden culture change in her life from mother to Hollywood co-star, she soon had another huge experience to deal with when she was hit on by Steve and before she knew it was having an affair with him. This was at a time when Steve's marriage was falling apart. Nonetheless there was still an intention by him and Neile to salvage their relationship, at least for the sake of Terry and Chad. Neile and the children were en route to France – on the cruise liner *SS France* – while Steve was carrying on his affair with Edlind. Not that it bothered Steve. After all, for the last year or so he had pretty much explained to Neile that he needed his space to be with other women. But his complex, chauvinistic side also expected Neile to understand and put up with his ways as she was *his* 'old lady'. Edlind was introduced to Neile shortly after her arrival, with her affair with Steve still a matter of the utmost discretion for those who knew. Neile was later told about the affair and referred to Edlind in her book *My Husband, My Friend* as 'Puff of Hair'.

"Steve and I were very close for a couple of months as I got to know him maybe not very well, but rather well, and we had a good time together." Edlind recounted. "I was very flattered by Steve McQueen, of course. I was too flattered. He tried to charm all women around him and we should have been very hard, so not to fall for him. But he was very charming and I was very young, and at that time I had a little separation in my marriage. We resumed our marriage shortly after but at that time we were apart, so I was free to be with Steve.

"I knew Steve also had marital problems at the time and when I had spoken to his wife she made it known that things between them were not well. They were divorced shortly after. Obviously from my point, it was very flattering to be chased by such a famous, cool movie star, but he also had this rough way to him; he didn't talk very much. He had these looks that he would give you and the fact he was Steve McQueen – they were two big reasons to fall for him. He hardly talked and when he did talk it was as though he was just saying lines in a movie. He was not one of the big intellectuals; that's for sure. He was down-dressed, relaxed and gave me the impression then, and I still maintain now, that he was a typical working-class American who had become intelligent but was low-educated. Steve had made it in Hollywood yet he was intelligent enough to be humble about his success and that is always charming.

"It wouldn't be right to say he had no manners but he was very exciting and very rough – verbally and physically. He was polite but not too polite. He was playing with me all the time and I used to wonder, 'Does he mean this or doesn't he mean this?' He always made out he had secrets and I never knew what he meant or could never be sure if he was telling the truth. That made him exciting, not to live with, but to have a romance with. I wouldn't have wanted that continuous mystery for life – I could never have had a long-term relationship with a Hollywood star, but it was exciting for a short while."

Although Steve's primary attraction to Edlind was purely physical, she grew on him further when he came to realise how trustworthy she was at keeping a secret; and not just of their affair, but a more serious one that could have crippled the movie had it leaked out. They were both involved in a car crash before the film had started shooting and it was a miracle that neither of them nor the two men on the back seat of Steve's Porsche died that night. Steve, who was driving, and Edlind, sitting nervously in the passenger seat, were thrown out of the windscreen and over the bonnet, while the two in the back suffered worse. One of them was Steve's personal assistant Mario Iscovich, who snapped his arm, while the other, a member of the crew who worked as a press agent, broke two ribs. The greatest danger in the aftermath of the crash was keeping Steve out of jail and the movie in business. If word had leaked out into the media that this great, macho driver had nearly killed himself and three passengers, it would have spelled certain doom for Le Mans. Ironically, the movie was doomed in any case but that was not so apparent at that stage. Fortunately for Steve, all three kept the incident a secret and he was allowed to go on and make his dream project. But things might have turned out so very differently.

"It was a very bad car accident and was kept quiet because it would have been just horrible if this had come out into the Press," Edlind explained. "Steve was driving on a little, narrow road, a quiet family road I would say, and it was late at night. He came to a curl in the road and there was something in his way and as he tried to avoid this thing, the car rolled around. I remember thinking, 'Oh God, I am going to die like this', and thought of my little baby also. But I woke up on the road. We were lucky because Steve wasn't really hurt; he had some bruises but didn't cut any legs or anything like that; and I was unconscious for a very short while and felt sick and had minor shoulder pain but we were very lucky. But one of the men in the back seat who broke two ribs looked close to death. I was told he took the blame for driving the car. We weren't supposed to talk about any of this but it is so long ago now. Fortunately no other vehicles were involved and nobody saw us so we left the scene for the hotel. I was awake in bed that night thinking, 'My God I might have inner bleeding and may not wake up'. Steve and the producers kept urging me not to say anything to anyone because it would risk the whole production. Steve was supposed to be such a good driver – and he was a good driver – but if that news had got out it would not have been good for his reputation as a driver."

Edlind believes Steve was under the influence on the night, mainly drugs. Steve's racing driver buddy Derek Bell later heard lurid tales of sex and drugs within the *Le Mans* bubble, but he only ever saw evidence of the former. He was as close as anyone got to McQueen on that movie apart from his mechanic but that was the way Steve liked to play it. He compartmentalised his life and knew who he could drink with and who he couldn't drink with; who he could snort a line or pop a pill with, and who he couldn't. The racing driver fraternity enjoyed a beer and a party and the girls, but with them, drugs were out of bounds. Steve was also professional when it came to drug use or drinking if it was close to him having to race or merely shoot while driving at speeds approaching 200 miles-per-hour; he never had a death wish. But when in the company, socially, of a pretty and impressionable young co-star like Edlind and his juniors on the film crew, Steve would not have worried for a second about taking drugs.

"It was most probable that he was smoking marijuana and had taken coke on the night he was driving," Edlind recalled. "It might sound like I am trying to scandalize things but I remember the guy who sat in the back had said to Steve that he shouldn't be driving and offered to take Steve and me home. But Steve insisted he had to drive me home and would be okay so that man said he would just come with us instead. I was glad that he came because of the state Steve was in but I would have been even happier if he had have driven. At the time I thought Steve might have had too many drinks and probably shouldn't drive, as I was innocent and young then and wasn't used to that world. But looking back I really believe Steve would have been under the influence of drugs that night. He had a problem with drugs; not an everyday problem but I could see it coming. I only knew him for a short time and he was working for much of that period but I could see how his attitude was to drugs. He spoke about cocaine very casually. He would say, 'Oh that's nothing, it's good for you.' But he could not persuade me to do it. And with marijuana he'd say, 'Come on, everyone is doing it'. He had a way of trying to downplay (drugs) and made it sound like they were less dangerous.

So I could see problems coming for him. I was young and not used to those things and looking back he was probably smoking marijuana all the time when I thought they were cigarettes."

There are various reasons why *Le Mans* was not successful. Harry Kleiner, the co-writer on *Bullitt*, was credited for writing the *Le Mans* screenplay though he shared the duties with four others. He had strong theories why the movie bombed: "There were several things that destroyed the whole project: number one, the basic material wasn't there to begin with. We went into production without a script. I was basically writing for the next day, but there wasn't that much for me to write anyway. What can you say about a car doing its first lap? The lack of dialogue was a problem. I couldn't build any personal relationships that could be developed, to get away from the actual racing. I agreed with John Sturges, there should have been more human interest. When he left the picture he was relieved - in fact we all were when we left. Steve just wanted to do a film purely about racing. There were debates right from the start and Steve stood his ground very hard, saying that he wanted to do a film about racing that everybody would enjoy - but where was the personal story - that was the big problem."

Even the non-movie people such as the drivers were not blind to the weaknesses of *Le Mans*, as David Piper put it, "The cars were great and sounded beautiful, the general atmosphere in France was incredible, but obviously that does not make a good movie."

Steve had mentioned *Le Mans* to writer Alan Trustman, who he had met on *The Thomas Crown Affair*, before hiring Harry Kleiner. Trustman's instincts though on hearing Steve's vision for the movie were that it was doomed to failure unless he made it into more a triumphant racing story where he won in the end. Forever one to reject superficial storylines to appease the suits, Steve stuck to his guns – and it cost him dear.

"I felt Steve was down to earth for most of the time I knew him and that's certainly the way he liked to be portrayed on the screen," Trustman said. "But when he did *Bullitt*, he made more money than he'd ever made in his career and he started to think he owned the world, which is why he thought he could make *Le Mans* and be successful with it. It was a story about a loser and I said to Steve, 'People don't want you to be a loser. You were a loser in *The Sand Pebbles* and it killed the box-office. You were a winner in *Crown*, you were a winner in *Bullitt* and that's how people want you to be.' But he was addicted to this storyline and I reiterated that the picture would also be a loser and that it would ruin everything in his life and destroy my movie career with it. I said, 'Be a winner and I will write the picture for you'. But he was unchanged and I was right; the movie was a stinker and his life disintegrated as he lost his wife, his best friend, his agent and business empire."

McQueen's thinking was constantly about executing the definitive racing movie; and in the eyes of that field, it probably was, but it was never going to appeal to a mass audience, as it proved. It wasn't for the lack of preparation with the racing footage. Relyea and McQueen attended the 24-hour Le Mans race armed with ten cameras to obtain footage. They entered a Porsche 908, fitted it with cameras to enhance the footage and also shot the spectators in the viewing gallery, to reduce costs. Steve subsequently won the respect of his racing contemporaries, but even they observed the film's shortcomings. Says Richard Attwood, "I thought the film was very good in terms of photography and racing action, but as a film itself, it was a shambles." Relyea, having had 40 years to reflect on the picture, added: "I don't think there's anything to be ashamed of in terms of racing footage, but that doesn't make a movie." Costume designer Ray Summers ultimately felt McQueen was misguided in what he wanted to achieve from the end product. "I really believe that Steve would have taken more satisfaction out of one of his racing contemporaries complimenting the film than he would from a Hollywood movie critic. Maybe that was the problem and why John Sturges eventually left."

It was certainly clear to Derek Bell that Steve was as comfortable in a racing car, or hanging out with the drivers, as he was acting or focusing on the business of filmmaking. "He was one of us," said Bell, who also shared a small chateau with Steve along with both of their young families, for the last month of the movie. "Quite often we (the drivers) would be just sitting around having a Coca-Cola and he would come and join us and chat. He wasn't playing the prima donna, Steve just wanted to be a racing driver. He did the film because it was a reason to get into cars and race. All he wanted to do was be with cars, hence the reason why he got so involved with the film rather than just being a director on it. He was too involved in the process of driving and working with us rather than thinking, 'Oh yeah, we have to make a movie, too'." The drivers were sheltered from the production chaos going on around the film but they were not ignorant enough to realise there was very little in the way of a story. They became tired of various writers arriving on set with a pen and paper, trying to write a script, before departing days later. It was not unusual for a driver to ask, 'Where the hell has the script gone?'

Drivers also questioned the challenges they were handed on a daily basis which often called for them to re-enact footage shot at the real Le Mans race. It was almost impossible for them to be in the place on the track, ahead or behind a car they were racing at a given stage. And at racing speeds too, which Steve always insisted on. But even away from those issues and minus the human interest story, the drivers admired and respected Steve's vision, which was to recreate the reality of Le Mans. Ultimately it was a bland concept as far as a movie goes; for it is difficult to write a story interesting to the mass market about a 24-hour race where Driver A gets out of a car and Driver B gets in. Does Driver A then go off and drink coffee on some nice hotel terrace and have a laugh with his buddies? No, he would simply relax for an hour or take a bite to eat. Hardly movie-making material for those punters not overly engrossed in racing. The authenticity, though, was the real success of *Le Mans* and the drivers' input and ideas that Steve was constantly seeking were often incorporated. Steve's famous two-finger gesture to his main rival in the movie, played by Siegfried Rauch, was Derek Bell's suggestion, responding to a curiosity from Steve as to how a driver would gesticulate to his rival. As Bell says, "It was meant as a fuck off, but not in a nasty way, just as friendly banter."

Steve's creative input into *Le Mans* was significant, initially. He was obsessed with perfection and gaining the perfect shot. The precision filming required the drivers to study a sequence of film that had been shot during the real race and go back out on to the track and duplicate it. If two Ferraris, a Porsche and a Lola all went through 'White House' fifty yards apart, they had to literally do the same thing. Derek Bell remembers the dramatic lengths that Steve went to, to obtain superior photography. Bell was driving with Jo Siffert in one particular shooting run and it remained a prominent memory from his time on the picture. "Steve was doing his creative bit, while me and (Jo) Siffert were coming whistling down from Arnage to the Ford Chicane, a run of about two and a half miles. We were going at about 160mph through White House and as we come through I suddenly noticed this lunatic on the white line in the middle of the road holding a bloody great big camera. If we were three foot to the right we would have hit him. It all happened so quick; I just thought, 'Shit, what the hell was that?' Anyway, when we got out, Siffert was white as a sheet and was gesticulating in Swiss and John Sturges was there and said, 'What's the problem?'

Siffert, who was still shitting himself, told him what had happened. John then went and asked Steve, 'Who authorised putting a cameraman in the middle of the road?' And Steve said, 'I did'. And Sturges told him that he had no right to put a guy in the middle of the road and asked which cameraman he used, and Steve said: 'It was me!' That was Steve for you."

McQueen could be crazy in a manner of ways, and not always with his film producer's hat on. On a Sunday off in France, Derek Bell, Richard Attwood and Steve played like bored children while racing Porsche 911s around a tight space in Solar Village. They drove blind when passing through the plastic flaps of the food tent at 40 miles per hour. "It sounds childish and stupid and though we weren't going *that* fast, in those close confines it was pretty exciting," Bell recalled. "The place got pretty badly tore up though and come the Monday morning we were given a rollicking from the production manager Hubert Frolich, who was like a German commandant, a real tyrant. It showed our lack of responsibility and stupidity – but it was great fun!"

British driver David Piper's experience on the movie was life-changing in more ways than one. He had to have his right leg amputated from the knee down after an accident while filming. He attributes some of the blame on the lack of a script as the tragedy occurred during an afternoon racing sequence that had to be filmed purely to cover their options, and have the Ferrari 512 leading on one shoot and the Porsche 917 leading on the other. His left rear type blew out as he drove through Maison Blanc (White House) at 120 miles-per-hour and his car bounced between both guardrails before being launched up into the air and breaking in two, with his feet stuck to the pedals while his body was still strapped in at the rear. His leg was plastered up and he was flown to England, ending up in the Royal National Orthopaedic Hospital in Great Portland Street, London, via a trip to Luton to see a specialist who was on holiday. Infection eventually set in and amputation was the only option. "Steve was very good; he arranged for me to be flown back to England at night and all the drivers got into their cars with the lights either side of the plane to create a runway, so that the private plane could take off from Le Mans airport. Steve and his staff couldn't have done more to help. He came to see me in hospital with Neile and the kids later on. Steve could not have been sorrier but it was just one of those things. I imagine the mechanics didn't check the tyre pressures after lunch and one had gone soft. Steve remained in touch with me ever since, from the accident until he died." *Le Mans* was dedicated to Piper, "for his sacrifice".

Curiously, Piper's memories of the movie are more positive than negative, which says much about how he remembers working with Steve. "We had a lot of fun on that movie," Piper recalled. "There was a lot of hanging around so we used to play cards or walk along the guardrail to see how far we could walk before we fell off, and things like that. Steve was there with us in Solar Village most of the time, and he would work out every day in the gymnasium and keep himself very fit. I remember once or twice that we would be playing cards or chess and he would come out of some bushes on one of his Husqvarna trail bikes

and fly over our heads! There was a lot of fun around." The car-
nival atmosphere around Solar Village was often created by the
sounds of Simon & Garfunkel pumping out of the sound system
in the canteen at lunch breaks. There was a genuine feel-good
atmosphere; if not amongst the producers and writers.

Although Steve's creativity and sense of fun was irrepressible it mainly lasted while Sturges was around. After
a month into shooting, the director's fears for the picture
brought all the negative deliberations to a head, which
resulted in him quitting. This caused much internal friction and Relyea inadvertently blurted out the film was "out
of control", unbeknown to him that a lower-ranked studio
representative was in his office at the time. That comment
was fed back to Los Angeles and was not received kindly.
Production was shut down for a week as major executives
from Cinema Centre soon arrived, led by Bob Rosen. The
lack of a director, added to the script difficulties, escalating
budget and its going over schedule were all problems that
the studio didn't accept gracefully. Steve was given a brutal
ultimatum: CBS would close down production and cut their
losses or he could forego his $750,000 salary and percentage
of the gross profits. Understandably, Steve would later refer
to this movie as a "bloodbath".

Even facing a financial catastrophe, Steve did not wish to
lose face amongst his driving contemporaries whose respect he
had earned so well and therefore, making his dream movie for
nothing was a more palatable option than it not being made at
all, especially on the back of the *Day of the Champion* disaster and

the fact Paul Newman (*Winning*) and James Garner (*Grand Prix*) had by now made racing films. "They had run out of money and CBS came in and took it over and Steve was losing his shirt on it," said Bell, who became a close friend of Steve's during the movie and beyond. "It must have cost them bloody millions. Steve lost all his money, but had also put so much time and effort into it. There was a different atmosphere then. Steve did have a slightly different mental approach and didn't seem as interested but he still loved his cars and whenever we did any driving he still got very excited." On the changing of the guard in the director, Bell added: "As John Sturges exited, we were sent home for a week, and when we came back Lee Katzin had arrived. Lee was a typical 'we need more blood, more action' kind of TV director; whereas John was more of a traditional film-maker with *The Magnificent Seven* and *The Great Escape* behind him."

Katzin's sole responsibility and directive was to get the movie finished and back to LA for editing, in as little time as possible. There may have been disagreements prior to this appointment, but from here on, the problems multiplied. Steve's grip on his 'baby' had now loosened to the point of release. To say he was disheartened would be an understatement. Relyea said: "He believed in the project until the studio took the production over and said: 'Now we're going to finish it off.' From then on, he became merely a worker as opposed to a creator. Lee Katzin came with orders from the studio to direct as best he could to economically finish the movie. Steve didn't try to manipulate him, he just didn't acknowledge him. If Lee had an idea, Steve would say, 'Well, it's not what I wanted to do, but you tell me where to stand and what to say and I'll do it.' By that time Steve just did what the studio said."

McQueen's spirit had been destroyed and he gave up on his dream. The arrival of Katzin and his orders from the hierarchy coincided with the departure of Steve's belief and passion for the movie. "When you're on a collision course for disaster, everybody feels it," said writer Harry Kleiner. "Then you have problems with the star, the director, the script - the whole production is affected. It was nothing but trouble and was a project that should never have been started. Steve is wearing a drivers mask, helmet whatever and racing round a block so to speak - and the people watching don't know that's McQueen - it could have been a stand-in. The picture was a disaster to begin with. No matter what you do, if the basic material is not there, the project is going to fail. I soon realised that, but after *Bullitt* I felt a certain loyalty to Steve."

That loyalty from Kleiner was also the reason he collaborated with Steve on *Yucatan* from 1969 to 1971. The film was about a group of thieves who head to Mexico to find centuries-old treasure buried beneath the Yucatan Peninsula. With the eventual failure of *Le Mans* and the financial collapse of Solar, McQueen and CBS agreed not to proceed with *Yucatan*, which might have been a classic. Steve never did make that film.

Louise Edlind was a rookie actress on the film but even she could see how brittle the storyline was and how disorganised the whole production became. "There wasn't any story, there was hardly any dialogue at all, and the lines that Steve had were poor little three or four words here and there," she commented. "There were no conversations, though I realise he was not a dialogue actor. I can remember being given new scripts all the time; they changed pages and said today we are going to shoot this and then they changed it. They often changed plans on the day of shooting. There was not much organisation. But Steve did not complain – he was very professional with the way he kept his feelings private. He must have been very disappointed inside, but he wanted people to still believe he was engaged in the movie. But most knew that he had lost interest as time went on. He wanted it to turn out well because he had money in it but his creative energy was not the same as the film went on."

If the pain from the issues surrounding the movie was not tough enough, Steve had problems with more serious implications going on back at his chateau, for he and Neile had possibly their worst-ever row that culminated in him putting his gun to her head. This was not an argument based on a single incident, mind. This had been brewing and brewing. Steve could not understand that she knew of so many affairs that he had had over the course of their marriage, yet remained faithful to him. This one night in France at their chateau, with the children sleeping in other bedrooms, he quizzed her on her fidelity over and over and she was tired and sleepy and just kept denying any unfaithfulness, hoping he would drop the subject and she could fall back to sleep. But he was never one to let anything drop and somehow managed to persuade her to take a snort of cocaine even though she was dead against the use of drugs, despite knowing that her husband was a habitual marijuana smoker and coke user. She took it to shut Steve up more than anything, but soon she was wide awake and found herself being lured into Steve's game.

The more he interrogated her on her faithfulness, the less resistant she became as the coke overpowered the sleeping tablet she had earlier consumed. Eventually her resolve snapped and she admitted to one brief affair. Steve was incensed and hours of interrogation and physical and verbal abuse followed. He threatened her with a pistol, pointing it at her head until she blabbed the name of the man with whom she had cheated on him with. It was the charming actor Maximilian Schell. That affair only happened after Neile had grown tired of Steve's infidelity and partying and it was her way of hitting back. She needed to feel wanted and attractive again. But in Steve's world, he was allowed to enjoy himself but Neile was not and had to play the loyal, dutiful wife at home with the kids. For the 15 or so years they were married, she played that role pretty much throughout. And Steve loved her for it and totally appreciated the rock-steady foundation she and the children gave to his crazy life where outside of their house he was a superstar who everyone wanted a piece of, which frightened the hell out of him in one way but fuelled his ego and reduced his insecurities in another. Here in France, their troubles came to a head, though these interrogations from Steve would continue for many nights and, later, months. Although they tried to salvage their marriage – even using psychiatrists – their divorce went through on 24 April, 1972.

Derek Bell (paid $100 a day) and his wife and two young children shared a small house with the McQueen's for the last month of the film but he genuinely did not see any evidence of their faltering marriage. "I had no idea at all of their problems. I never got any impression of anything like that between them. Steve was always the same to me. Maybe he got back with Neile at night in their home and he was pissed off and would pop a pill. They used to walk around hand in hand in the day and I never had any feeling that he wasn't close to her. And I knew him as well as anybody on that film, maybe with the exception of Haig (Altounian) his mechanic, because they were both from California. But I got to know him as well as anybody. He never made any snide comments about his wife. I know he used to screw some of the girls on the movie but then we all did. There were a few around. There was lots of female interest around for Steve; I see it all the time, women who just want to sleep with famous people. They are star-fuckers and you wonder how they get on with the rest of their lives when they grow out of that and have kids. But they do go through a period when that's what they want to do."

Even co-star Louise Edlind, who had a two-month affair with Steve during the movie, is honest enough to acknowledge she would not have been the only woman Steve was seeing then. "I was realistic and knew that what I see is not the whole truth," she said. "Of course he was probably with other women during the time I was seeing him." Steve's marriage was at an all-time low behind closed doors, but he performed an admirable job in somehow bottling up his feelings, appearing as the same old Steve to those that knew him and hung out with him every day during *Le Mans*. "It must have been quite difficult for him with those issues going on," said David Piper, "but he never brought his problems on to the set with him."

The combination of Steve's faltering marriage and the picture falling in on him took its toll eventually and he lost his energy for what had been his dream project for the last five years. Steve and Neile took off for Casablanca after an invitation from Princess Lalla Nezha. It may have been a break from the stresses of the set but he still carried the weight of the collapsing movie on his shoulders more than anyone. The trip to Morocco hardly provided the magic to repair their marriage either. By the time they returned, his relationship with Louise Edlind was over, though he thanked her for her discretion with the car crash. They may not have been lovers any more but she was still close enough as a friend to Steve to detect how his body language had changed from the outset of *Le Mans*. "The air went out of the production when he came back from Casablanca," she said. "Steve McQueen had by then lost interest in the film. I got the feeling he just wanted to get it done and that's one of the reasons why the film didn't come out very well. When we started, Steve was full of enthusiasm and was telling me '*Grand Prix* was bullshit – I'm going to make a much better movie'. But after Casablanca, he had lost that passion.

"It was a tough time for Steve," added Edlind. "I think he was trying to salvage his marriage but at the same time, he didn't like the manuscript and he had seen the original director John Sturges leave the film – they didn't cooperate with one another very well so it was a difficult relationship. Then the new director came in, he was young and nice, but he was not very experienced. Steve started turning up late on set and gave some funny excuses like he had been speaking to his astrologer and things like that. Lee (Katzin) was nice but far too inexperienced to tell Steve McQueen what to do or ask him why he was late. Maybe the pressure of his marriage and the problems on the film turned Steve."

That marital pressure increased when, two weeks after returning from Casablanca, Neile learned she was pregnant; this at a time when they were heading for certain divorce. Such news can reunite couples but Steve carried resentment towards his long-suffering wife which failed to dissipate even on hearing about the possibility of a third child. The revelation of her one and only affair was still fresh in his mind and it had turned him so against her that nothing could soothe his anger. It took Neile three weeks to pluck up enough courage to tell him the news: "Steve looked at me disbelievingly," she wrote in her memoir. "'What am I supposed to say?' Steve said. 'Hey, groovy, baby? You got some nerve you know that?' And swiftly before I could react to his words, he had pulled me by my T-shirt and had sat me on the bed. 'Whose is it woman?' he taunted. 'Are you gonna tell me or are you gonna sit there and lie?' Tears started to well up in my eyes and Steve became more abusive. 'Oh don't give me that shit! How am I supposed to believe it's mine!' His words were dagger thrusts. He raised his hand to slap me, but instead he took a deep breath and abruptly released me, then marched quickly out of the bedroom." Neile was advised that abortions were not permitted in France and that she needed to travel to London. Steve did not accompany Neile to the clinic and instead the amiable set decorator Phil Abramson went along to hold her hand and treat her to Chinese food on the night. While this domestic heartache was going on, behind the scenes CBS continued to bulldoze their way to a completion of *Le Mans*. At the end, there was no wrap party. This was not a time for celebration.

CBS hired their own editors to cut the movie having not been overly impressed with the progress that had been made in France. They had 22 hours of race footage to plough through. Although Robert Relyea was invited to contribute, he felt it was more a smokescreen designed to keep Steve happy so he would cooperate with the promotion campaign they had in mind, while Cinema Centre could say it had carried out its moral duty. One of those editors installed by CBS to make some sense of the footage that had been shot in France was Donald Ernst. He and John M. Woodcock had the odious task of editing the entire movie from Los Angeles, though they were looked in on, once, by one of the original editors Ghislaine Desjonqueres and Steve also visited them, once, to check on their progress. "The only time I met Steve was when we were dubbing the film," Ernst recalled. "He came by one day when we were dubbing at Paramount Studios in Hollywood to say hello and see how we were doing. He was only there the one day. He was very nice and told us we were doing a great job; he didn't seem upset. It was only a social visit really. In fact John and I had a volleyball court set up in the studio which we would play in between takes and Steve had a game with us while he was there." Ernst and Woodcock barely knew where to start their edit and were sympathetic to the early advice of the departed director John Sturges, who pleaded for more of a story than just a car race. But this was Ernst's first feature film credit and he was just excited to be involved.

"It was a very difficult film to edit," commented Ernst. "The lack of story was quite a problem. What little story there was confused, and it was difficult to try and let the audience know what was going on with the dialogue and the racing. I edited mainly the dialogue scenes and scenes around the pits. John edited mainly the racing scenes and I thought he did a fabulous job, because we received the film without *any* editing having been done. Whether there was any editing done in France I don't know. But if there was it was undone and we started from scratch. Lee Katzin was mainly responsible for the final editing, but Bob Rosen had much input. Overall, there wasn't enough story to keep your interest so the film did seem very long. John and I wanted to put some narration with the film to clear up the confusion, but we didn't get to do that." On the legacy of the movie, Ernst added: "I ran the DVD of the film for my 11-year-old grandson very recently. He did get confused and seemed bored. Although, he told his grandfather he loved the film!"

Without too great a surprise, *Le Mans* became one of Steve's biggest flops of his career, and undoubtedly the one that hurt him most. It premiered in June, 1971 in Indianapolis, fittingly, and grossed $19 million worldwide, but that was way down on expectation. And profits were slim after the $7.5 million budget was blown. "I think the failure of *Le Mans* had a greater impact on him than anybody realised," says Relyea. "You have to remember the temporary defeat he suffered on *Day of the Champion*, to a guy who is extremely competitive. So when he made this film on his favourite subject, with him in control and around all of his racing colleagues, for it not to succeed had a massive affect on him. When any project close to you doesn't succeed it hurts, but this was taking it to an extreme. It hurt him a lot and, knowing the man, I think it soured him for quite a while. After being a respected figure in the racing world he felt embarrassed after *Le Mans* and it was tough for him to take."

Relyea was reminded of the difficulties in making a commercially appealing racing picture when he was at Paramount years later. The studio financed *Days of Thunder*, which boasted a blockbuster line-up. Still it bombed. "If I had to mortgage my house and bet on a picture doing good business that would have been it," says Relyea. "With Tom Cruise starring, Ridley Scott directing, Simpson and Bruckheimer producing and Bob Towne writing the screenplay, it was a sure hit, but it didn't do any business. I'm not saying nobody has ever made a good film about racing, I just think it's extremely difficult." The large-scale failure of *Le Mans* not only soured Steve, but it also soured his relationship with Relyea and led to the break-up of his business empire, Solar, which ceased thereafter to be an active production company. Its executives Relyea and Jack Reddish left the company with immediate effect.

"After *Le Mans*, Steve and I didn't communicate," Relyea revealed. "After some time had passed, though, he did come into my office and he would eat his sandwich on my couch, but the conversations were always strained." *Le Mans*, then, saw to the end of his company, his wealth and most importantly, his marriage and day to day family life. After this film, he was starting over again in more ways than one.

However any racing enthusiast, movie critic, fan, or whoever may choose to judge *Le Mans*, its legacy as a cult film and especially as a commercial entity should not be forgotten. Steve's seemingly everlasting appeal has meant that Steve McQueen the brand is strong into the current day. And the multi-million dollar industry that surrounds Le Mans the race is certainly well aware of that. "There's no other actor that has left a legacy like that," Derek Bell commented. "Everywhere you go, there's something, people in McQueen jackets or T-shirts, McQueen watches. It's astonishing just what an impact Steve McQueen and *Le Mans* had on the world; one of the greatest actors, in one of the greatest races in one of the greatest cars. I bet 50 per cent of the merchandise that gets sold at the Le Mans event is to do with the McQueen era."

And as David Piper concludes, even though he felt let down by the movie itself and by the virtually unknown co-stars supporting McQueen, he is adamant that Steve should be saluted for what he tried to achieve. "*Le Mans* had to be genuine; Steve didn't want to cut any corners. His heart was in the right place; he was a purist. He loved racing and didn't want any easy walkovers or anything like that, he was determined to make this movie the hard way."

Main Credits:

Cast: Steve McQueen (as Michael Delaney), Siegfried Rauch, Elga Andersen, Ronald Leigh-Hunt, Fred Haltiner, Luc Merenda, Christopher Waite, Louise Edlind, Angelo Infanti, Jean-Claude Bercq, Michele Scalera and more.

Director:	Lee H. Katzin
(Assistant)	Les Sheldon
Producer:	Jack N. Reddish, Robert E. Relyea (executive), Robert L. Rosen (production executive)
(Associate Producer)	Alan Levine
Cinematographer:	Rene Guissart, Robert B. Hauser
Writer:	An original screenplay by Harry Kleiner
Editors:	John M. Woodcock, Donald W. Ernst, Ghislaine Desjonqueres
Wardrobe:	Ray Summers
Make-Up:	Emile LaVigne
Music:	Michael Legrand

REVIEWS:

THE NEW YORK TIMES, June 24th, 1971

Let's say this for Steve McQueen, a noted speed wheeler off the screen: The actor, who is the only familiar name in the cast, looks perfectly at home behind his wheels here. But the star's exchange of monosyllabic utterances and long, meaningful stares with other drivers, and especially with Elga Andersen, a sensitive-faced blonde, add up to tepid, monotonous drama during the two-day race intervals. Dramatically, the picture is a bore.

VARIETY, June 16th, 1971

Marked by some spectacular car-racing footage, *Le Mans* is a successful attempt to escape the pot-boiler of prior films on same subject. Herein, the solution was to establish a documentary mood and enhance it via cinematic technique, and the gambit works for enough of the pic to make the Cinema Centre Films presentation a solid bet for general action throughout the summer season. Steve McQueen stars (and races), looking better than he ever has before.

THE HOLLYWOOD REPORTER, June 15th, 1971

Within 25 minutes of this hour and 46 minute movie the race begins and until the last 15 minutes or so, the film details nothing but the race. In this area it is extremely skilful. It creates and maintains a real competition, and it highlights the nature of the race with some of the most spectacular crashes ever recorded on film...McQueen's performance is laconic; he can't have more than ten lines of dialogue that may be considered revealing. It is a role that demands a star's aura otherwise interest goes by default to the machines.

Steve funded *On Any Sunday* to the tune of $313,000 as executive producer and cameo performer, but was rewarded with an Academy Award-nominated documentary on his beloved sport of motorcycling
(COURTESY: BRUCE BROWN FILMS LLC)

ON ANY SUNDAY

(Cinema 5) 1971

'Steve could never drive past a kid hitch-hiking without picking him up. That was just his nature. He spent time in reform school and never forgot how tough it was to be a kid'
– Bob Bagley

STEVE'S ASSOCIATION WITH *On Any Sunday* - an appealing and light-hearted documentary about motorcycling - was merely as cameo performer and investor, or co-producer. The idea came from Bruce Brown, a multi-skilled independent film-maker and a symbol of free-wheeling sixties' California. His upfront approach impressed and subsequently convinced McQueen and his Solar business sidekick Robert Relyea to support his idea, both financially – to the tune of $313,000 – and professionally. Brown had already made *The Endless Summer* - a highly successful documentary about surfing, which was received warmly by non-surfing types as well as those who had a love for the waves. His passion for a project and innovative approach were qualities that McQueen and Relyea admired.

Steve had lots of fun making this movie and was always
at ease around biking people. From the left, Mert Lawwill,
Steve, Bob Bagley, Malcolm Smith and Bruce Brown
(COURTESY: BRUCE BROWN FILMS LLC)

Brown had never met McQueen previously but it did not deter him from calling McQueen's Solar office to arrange a meeting with him, Relyea and Jack Reddish. Steve had seen *The Endless Summer* and agreed to talk to Brown and hear him out. Steve was intrigued by Brown's unique approach to film-making and was amazed that somebody could make a film like *The Endless Summer* and be so successful with it. Their meeting, though, was brief:

Brown: "Steve, I want to make a movie about bikes, and make it my way.

McQueen: "God that would be great Bruce, to make a film about motorcycle racing in the style of *The Endless Summer*. But what do you want me to do?'

Brown: "Put up the money."

McQueen: (laughs) "I make movies, I don't finance them."

Brown: "Bummer, then you can't be in my movie."

McQueen: "Ok, let me think about it."

Brown received a phone call the next day from Steve, who said, 'It's a great idea, I'm in, let's go for it man.' McQueen committed to investing the whole budget for 50 per cent of the equity in the picture. "Steve was a motorcycle person and he saw the potential in the movie," commented Bob Bagley, who was Brown's right-hand man as head of production and cinematographer, among other roles. "Most people who meet Bruce see that he is such a straightforward, honest guy and I don't know anybody who doesn't like him. But equally,

Steve was a fabulous partner and allowed us to film anything we wanted. If we had any ideas that (we wanted to do) that involved him, he was happy to cooperate. He was a super guy and similar to Bruce in so many ways."

Brown had secured his star, though he might never have managed a meeting with Steve had it not been for *The Endless Summer*, which cost just $50,000 and went on to gross in excess of $30 million. Brown's raw honesty and authenticity to make a movie *his* way were qualities that Steve admired in him. "He was so green," explains Relyea, "that he put the package together in his own unique way and released the film on his own. It became a great hit." That was it in a nutshell, but Brown's plight to reach the stage he was at by the time *On Any Sunday* came after a painstaking journey of self-belief and unstinting determination to succeed.

The Endless Summer began as a lecture film and Bruce toured all the surfing hotbeds of the world, projecting it to audiences in the UK, South Africa, Australia, New Zealand and France. Attendance numbers were healthy as they appreciated Brown's talent as a storyteller – he was always more interested in talking about the people than the waves. His films had a humorous feeling to them. Initially it was a stage-show as Bruce narrated his film live from stage while simultaneously playing the pre-recorded music track on a tape recorder.

He considered releasing *The Endless Summer* to theatres throughout America. Hollywood was not interested – viewing it as a surfing film that would not appeal widely enough, to the non-surf types. His critics also doubted the film would do any business more than 25 miles from the nearest ocean. After having many doors slammed in his face, Bruce opted to show the film as far away from the ocean as possible and took it to Wichita, Kansas, located smack-bang in the middle of America. He disproved Hollywood's scepticism by promoting and showing it for two weeks to sell-out crowds.

He then flew to New York to meet with Don Rugoff, who owned the distribution company Cinema 5. He liked the idea but told Bruce "Wichita ain't New York', and wanted evidence *The Endless Summer* was marketable. With the firm belief his film would sell anywhere, Brown invested his savings to make it suitable for a theatrical release. He then rented the Kips Bay Theatre in New York to show-case his film to one of the toughest non-surfing communities in the US. If it was successful there, it was sure to be a hit anywhere. First, he spoke to a close friend and renowned network sports caster Bud Palmer, who offered to help out by inviting all his influential friends and colleagues to view it. The idea was to market the picture to the wealthy and well-connected who could open doors and spread the word. They turned up in their limousines and could not get enough of the movie. *The Endless Summer* subsequently broke all audience records at the Kips Bay Theatre and Bruce was quickly being interviewed on such esteemed television programmes as the Johnny Carson show and receiving rave reviews in prestigious media like Time magazine. Bruce Brown was soon to be a millionaire, as *The Endless Summer* became one of the record cost-to-profit movies ever made.

Don Rugoff came back to Bruce after this hullabaloo, and subsequently bought the distribution rights. Unlike other companies, he did not wish to change anything whereas others were demanding more girls, more sex, more everything. Bruce was not one to be dictated to by the establishment, an attitude that later endeared him to the eternal rebel Steve McQueen. Bruce rejected dozens of offers to make a sequel to *The Endless Summer*. He didn't want to make another surfing movie. Over the years he had become interested in dirt bikes and competed in a variety of amateur events. He had been interested in bikes ever since *The Great Escape* in 1963, when Steve did his bike chase and jump. Bruce was sold on bikes thereafter. "He realised there were similarities between surfers and motorcycle racers as both were misunderstood and maligned by the general public," said Bob Bagley. "Bruce wanted to add a kind of hip, down to earth authenticity in his picture and that's where Steve McQueen came in."

As director, producer, editor, writer and cameraman, Brown was able to force his personality on to *On Any Sunday* and knew what angle would attract a wider audience, than just motorcyclists. Robert Relyea explained: "With these kinds of pictures there is the danger that they will only appeal to a certain audience, but unlike *Le Mans*, you will get more people watching *On Any Sunday* for the novelty value. It was fun and had heart, just like *The Endless Summer* did. You can bet the people who watched that were not just surfers."

Steve was preparing for *Le Mans* when this picture was commissioned, but *On Any Sunday* required minimal input from him. However, McQueen was entered into the Elsinore Grand Prix by Brown, in order to obtain footage of his racing that would be used in the film. It was a week before he raced at Sebring, in preparation for *Le Mans*, and it was here that *On Any Sunday* experienced its first hitch, though it affected *Le Mans* much more, with its considerably higher budget.

"Steve not only competed but broke his foot in the process," Bagley recalled. "Doing damage to a guy with Steve McQueen's value at that time was pretty scary. We gathered at Bruce's house after this event and Steve decided to call his agent – at a time when there was a lot of preparation going on behind the scenes to make *Le Mans*. He told his agent, 'I think I might have broken my foot,' which was a hell of an understatement as his foot was the size of a basketball. Steve then repeated himself by saying, 'Actually, I know I have broken my foot'."

Suddenly preparations for the multi-million dollar picture in France were up in the air. Brown had the difficult job of telling Robert Relyea about Steve's accident, and Relyea had an even greater task of informing Cinema Centre, which was producing *Le Mans*. CBS was outraged, that their star had acted so irresponsibly by involving himself with a motorcycle race only a week before Sebring. In any event, it all worked out fine and Brown had the footage of Steve he needed.

Steve with biking champions Mert Lawwill and
Malcolm Smith during *On Any Sunday*
(COURTESY: BRUCE BROWN FILMS LLC)

It would have been easy for Steve to dominate the screen in the documentary, but that would have been counter-productive to Brown's vision. "Steve never intended to be anything more than a cameo," says Relyea, "and if he had have appeared more, then it would have been contrary to Bruce's approach. He wanted to show how motorcycling appeals to all sorts of people and so, it was then better to show the weekend warrior falling off his bike rather than dwell on the Hollywood superstar whom everyone knows is a motorcycle expert." Steve, though, was also supportive of showing his own fallibilities.

"During one sequence," Bagley remembered, "Steve fell off his bike in the desert a couple of times and Bruce asked him, 'Do you want me to leave that in?' And Steve said, 'Hell yeah, that's what it's all about.' Steve really was not interested in projecting himself as Mr Perfect; he wanted the audience to see he fell off his bike like the next guy."

But Steve really was an expert; good enough to have represented the USA in the 1964 motocross World Trials in East Germany. Steve could so easily have been a racer that acted as opposed to an actor that raced. Don Gordon, his friend and fellow actor, felt McQueen's skill on a bike was superior. "He was a hell of a bike rider. I used to watch him race and he was real good. If he wasn't an actor, he could have been really big in either bike racing or automobile racing. Steve was very talented."

The most respected motorcycle organisation in the US posthumously added Steve into their Hall of Fame in 1999 –

STEVE McQUEEN: THE COOLER KING

because of his ability as a rider, but also for the interest and
excitement in the sport that he sparked. Steve McQueen
was, and still is, a great marketing tool for motor-cycling
the world over. "*The Great Escape* certainly put McQueen
on the radar of motorcyclists throughout America," said
Jeff Heininger, Chairman of the American Motorcycle
Heritage Foundation, which oversees the AMA Motorcycle
Hall of Fame. "But it was Bruce Brown's Academy Award-
nominated *On Any Sunday*, which featured McQueen and
the exploits of his riding friends Malcolm Smith and Mert
Lawwill, who were legends in their own right, which ele-
vated McQueen to icon status for generations to come. *On
Any Sunday* became the raison d'être for motorcyclists of
that generation and it inspired future generations of motorcyclists as well – many of whom are also enshrined in the
Hall of Fame."

Although Steve would have been well aware of Lawwill's
talents given that he was a multiple champion, they did
not strike up a friendship until they came together on this
movie. It was not until after filming *On Any Sunday*, though,
that Lawwill really saw Steve's true value as a friend. Says
Lawwill, "A couple of years after the film I had a very bad
racing accident in upstate Washington when I hit a rider that
had fallen and smashed my hand into my bike, while my
body was still going through the air, exposing the bone. I
went to hospital and the doctor said, 'Well, it's smashed so
bad there's nothing we can really do, so in the morning I will
fuse you from the knuckle to the elbow, so think about how

394

you want your hand shaped because that's the way it's going to be for the rest of your life. '

"I wanted a second opinion though the doctor insisted anyone else would tell me the same thing and that I was wasting my time. By the time I left Washington state and got to San Francisco, Steve McQueen had heard about my accident and he called me up and said his doctor was doing a seminar in town and that I should go see him with the x-rays. Steve set that up, so I went to see him and he held the x-rays against the light and told me I had big problems but recommended another surgeon in LA who was better at this than he was. I called Steve after and told him the latest and explained I had just got over a fall at Daytona at 150 and had not made much money so I was just going to stick with my local doctor and hope for the best with the amputation.

"Steve was adamant and said, 'No.' He wouldn't hear of it. He bought me a ticket so that I could fly down there to LA; he had a driver pick me up from the airport to take me to this hand specialist. Next morning he started the operations and the surgery went on for many hours. The surgeon basically carved out a new hand, saying this pile of pieces is going to be this bone and that pile of pieces is going to be that bone. It was such a complicated procedure that it was used in a medical journal afterwards – and Steve set all that up. In total I had five operations and I never received a single bill, ever. Steve paid for everything, and he even let me stay at his house in Brentwood while I was rehabilitating. We became very good friends. I have heard the stories about Steve being tight but in my case he was totally the opposite. I kept thinking, 'When am I going to get my bill?' But later I found out that Steve had paid for them all. The costs would have run into tens of thousands. The surgery was a total success and Steve saved me another six years of my racing career and enabled me to stay involved with racing afterwards."

It was Lawwill's good fortune that he and Steve hit it off so well during *On Any Sunday*; without that connection the former biking champion concedes he would have been significantly disabled for the last 40 years. "My good fortune was all down to *On Any Sunday* because without that Steve and I would never have met.

"When he invited me to stay at his house in Brentwood, while I was doing my rehab, it was an amazing experience. I got to know his wife Neile and they would fix me breakfast every morning and I was just so well looked after. The house was awesome. It had little guest quarters attached to it and that's where I stayed." By this time, Steve was ensconced in the sex and drugs revolution, when he would make full use of his movie star attraction to the many female admirers he met anywhere he went. Subsequently by this juncture, Steve and Neile's marriage was on its last legs.

Lawwill detected some frostiness at the McQueen household during his visits and thought they were playing happy families somewhat. "I think they put on a happy face for my sake but I could hear them arguing about stuff a lot," he commented. "I think Steve was quite sensitive to many things; but in my case he was just a great guy. He even called me just to wish me Merry Christmas sometime after we finished film-ing *On Any Sunday*."

Steve was famously tight-fisted with his money throughout his life, often failing to have so much as a dime in his pocket when it came to pay a restaurant bill. But, as Lawwill discovered and as befitted the unpredictable Steve McQueen, Bob Bagley also viewed him as an excep-tionally generous, warm-hearted man. "He could never drive past a kid hitch-hiking without picking them up," Bagley recounted. "That was just his nature. He spent time in reform school and he never forgot how tough it was to be a kid. Occasionally, we would be driving along and would stop off for a meal-to-go. Bruce and myself would buy a burger and Steve would buy three or four. Bruce asked him one day, 'Steve, how come you buy so many burgers, you can only eat one?' And Steve reasoned that he remembered what it was like to be poor and he'd rather have too many than not enough. But the sub-reason to that would be seen when we got back on the road. If he saw two kids sitting around on the sidewalk, he would give them those extra two hamburgers. That was the kind guy he was. He had great enthusiasm for life in general. Another time, he was driving his pickup with Mert and Malcolm and he asked them, 'Hey, do you guys like chilli dogs?' They said they did. The next thing, he does this screeching U-turn and drives about 40 miles out of his way to show them this diner that he liked so much that 'had the best chilli dogs in the world'. Steve was just a genuine guy."

Steve with biking champion Mert Lawwill, whose left
hand was generously saved because of Steve's care and,
ultimately, money
(COURTESY: BRUCE BROWN FILMS LLC)

The passion Steve had for bikes (and cars) was almost unhealthy; sometimes he thought about nothing else. Many believed McQueen committed to *On Any Sunday* purely on the fact he was a compulsive motorcyclist - but that wasn't the case. "That was part of it," admitted Relyea, "but the other part was, Steve wasn't stupid, he knew that that kind of investment could be a shrewd one. With Steve McQueen appearing in this low-budget film, it really was 'potential on legs' and he realised that." Steve enjoyed his time contributing to *On Any Sunday* and it was not unusual for him to compose hand-written letters in pencil to Bruce Brown. "The one letter that stands out," recalled Bagley, "was when Steve wrote, 'Bruce, you don't know how lucky you are to make a movie the way you want with no interference from studios, or anyone." That would prove to be a poignant issue, just months before CBS took over production on *Le Mans* due mainly to script and budget problems – after Steve led the way with his vision. Steve's only line of dialogue in *On Any Sunday* was, "Every time I start thinking of the world as all bad, then I start seeing some people out here having a good time on their motorcycles - it makes me take another look."

In *On Any Sunday*, the brief pictures of Steve riding in the desert with his buddies, reveals how at peace he was when on his bike. "Steve was a world-class motor-cycle racer," said former car racing buddy and assistant director Kurt Neumann Jr. "We both were very good at racing cars but I have to say with motorcycles he was outstanding. He wasn't put off even though he went face first into a tree once in the Isle of Man, when he used to race with Bud Ekins, Cliff Coleman and that crowd." Don Gordon remembered the days he used to go riding with Steve and how competitive he was. "I was dirt riding with him one day and I passed him, then he really cranked it on and came past me as though I was standing still, because he thought I was racing with him. He wanted to compete - 'Come on, let's do it then,' he'd say."

Steve was more comfortable when just one of the boys, hanging out, as opposed to being a movie star when confronted by photographers, writers and executives. Although, he could become irritated if he wasn't recognised for too long, like the times he would remove a false beard if too long had elapsed without him being hassled for a photo or an autograph. It could be tiresome for him, being a movie star in demand 24-7, but he knew it was still a lot cooler than being an everyman. Mert Lawwill recalled one moment during the filming of *On Any Sunday*, which exposed Steve's occasional insecurities, though in a humorous way on this occasion "We were down at Bruce's house at Dana Point and me and Steve were staying in the kids' room, which had bunk beds in it. Anyway, Steve and I walked into this room and it was covered all over in posters of myself, Dick Mann and other motorcycle stars. Steve looked round and said, 'Don't these guys ever go to the movies?' I think he felt a little left out! But that was fun – I don't suppose many people can say they've shared bunk beds with a movie star like Steve McQueen."

Steve was rarely a good loser; it was just as well then that his investment in *On Any Sunday* proved a shrewd one. Bruce Brown, the original beach-boy, usually decorated in sandals, jeans and Hawaiian shirts, created an entertaining yet informative piece, according to Robert Relyea: "It only did mediocre business in Hollywood terms, but it was successful for a low-budget picture. Bruce did it to his own drummer and made a great job of it. It still plays on Cable all the time."

The relative success of the film still failed to change Brown's laid-back culture, though Relyea pointed out that he did have to buy himself a pair of conventional 'shiny shoes' for the Premiere in Westwood, Los Angeles. Mert Lawwill remembered: "When Bruce asked me if I wanted to be in a film about motorcycling my attitude was, 'Sure, why not,' but I didn't know at the time that it would become so big. That's a credit to the way Bruce made that film. He didn't do the Hollywood thing, he made it as real and authentic as it could be and people enjoyed it for that. My mother-in-law saw me in *On Any Sunday* on the big screen and began to have more respect for what I did as a job.

"And of course if it had not been for *On Any Sunday* I would probably never have met Steve McQueen, who was just such a cool, down to earth guy. I will never forget the day we shot the beach scenes (after Steve convinced the Army General to open up Camp Pendleton in Southern California to Bruce and his cameras for the movie). On the way back, we loaded the bikes into the back of Steve's beaten-up old pick-up and drove out of the base. Just then we saw this young soldier hitch-hiking and Steve said, 'Let's pick him up.' He got in the car with us and he kept giving Steve a strange look and after a while Steve said to him, 'Yeah that's right kid, I am Steve.' I told the kid, 'Don't bother telling anyone about this, as nobody's going to believe you'!"

Main Credits:

Cast:	Mert Lawwill, Malcolm Smith, Steve McQueen (as himself)
Director:	Bruce Brown (and narrator)
Producer:	Bruce Brown, (executive) Steve McQueen
Cinematographers:	Robert Bagley (and production manager), Bruce Brown, Don Shoemaker, Mark Zavad
Writer:	Bruce Brown
Editors:	Don Shoemaker
Music:	Dominic Frontiere

REVIEWS:

MONTHLY FILM BULLETIN, April, 1972
An excellent feature-length survey of various kinds of motorcycling sport in America: road-racing, dirt track, moto-cross (with its rough and tumble over bumps in mud and dust), sidecar, drag, hill climb (in which after seven years a rider actually

succeeds in reaching the top of the notorious Widowmaker), trail riding, desert racing, and even - in Quebec - racing on ice.

VARIETY, July 21st, 1971

On Any Sunday may do for motorcycle racing what *Endless Summer* did for surfing. Produced by the same Bruce Brown who approached his new endeavour as a labour of love - and hopefully for the same boff and buff response that made his 1966 surfing pic a top fave not only with buffs but general public as well. *Sunday* is an exciting documentary of one of the most dangerous of sports. McQueen's prowess as a racer is demonstrated time and again and his name should spark interest in a film that alone stands as a spectacular piece of film-making.

THE HOLLYWOOD REPORTER, July 14th, 1971

Action is the essential element of the film, but Brown is more interested in people than in machinery. The action revolves around three interesting men: Malcolm Smith, the top-ranking amateur in nearly every form of motorcycle competition; Mert Lawwill, the leading professional; and Steve McQueen, who is much more than a dabbler in the sport. It must have been a temptation to concentrate on McQueen, but Brown has given the featured role to Smith, whose cockeyed grin charmingly disguises his incredible competitive skill.

TIME MAGAZINE, July 1971

One of the ten best films of the year

Steve enjoying a beer on the set of *Junior Bonner,* which was one of his favourite movies despite its lack of commercial success
(COURTESY: ABC /THE KOBAL COLLECTION)

JUNIOR BONNER

(A B C - C i n e r a m a) 1 9 7 2

'Whether you were a hairdresser, an extra, the star or the daughter of the director, if Steve liked you, that was it, you'd probably get hit on by Steve. He was a ladies man and he usually got what he wanted' – Mary Murphy

STEVE LOVED EVERYTHING about *Junior Bonner*: the script, the theme, the cast, he even appreciated the fiery director, Sam Peckinpah. Box-office reaction, though, was not so excitable. This was one of the few movies Steve made that didn't make any money. But that disappointment was overshadowed by the professional satisfaction he got out of the film. At a time when his 15-and-a-half-year marriage with first wife Neile was on the brink of collapse and when his career-long dream of making a racing film (*Le Mans*) had bombed, this picture did wonders for his morale and succeeded to lift his spirits at a low time in his life.

The movie derived from a screenplay by Jeb Rosebrook, who had sent a treatment to producer Joe Wizan. The producer was instantly taken on the idea. Junior Bonner is an ageing rodeo star and returns to his hometown for the Prescott annual rodeo, unable to suppress his determination to win it one more time, and to win enough money to be able to fly his dreamer of a father to Australia. He was surprised at how things had changed and how modernisation transformed this once honest, happy town of the Old West. During his stay, Junior meets up with his family again, and it is the close bond he has with his father that provides a central theme. Co-star Mary Murphy, who played Junior's sister-in-law and who co-starred alongside Marlon Brando in *The Wild One*, said: "It was a story that Steve adored, I guess because of the father-son relationship. Sam and I discussed it and we both felt that was the reason why he liked the film so much, as Steve never had that in his life."

Producer Wizan soon considered Rosebrook's script a bankable prospect and immediately paid the writer an advance to complete the script. "I have a weakness for father-son or mentor-pupil relationship stories," said Wizan. It wasn't until Marty Baum, head of ABC Pictures, telephoned Wizan that things began to happen. "I'm short on material," Baum told the producer. "Do you have anything for me?" Wizan immediately mentioned *Junior Bonner*, though explained it couldn't be made for six months as he was committed to *Prime Cut* starring Lee Marvin and Gene Hackman. Baum refused to let this script sleep and, after reading it himself, began preparations in April 1971. The first task was to free Wizan for the near future. After contacting the agents for Hackman and Marvin, the two actors gave Wizan their blessing to work on *Junior Bonner* immediately. There was still one big problem confronting

ABC: the picture had to be cast in two months because they needed shooting to coincide with the annual Prescott rodeo in the July. It was a hopeless situation. However, in one week in April, things started looking up. For the part of Junior Bonner, there was only one man Wizan had in mind - Steve McQueen. Freddie Fields, Steve's agent, soon received a script and a then career-high offer of $850,000 for McQueen to star. "I was told that Steve became the highest paid movie star in the world at that time," scriptwriter Jeb Rosebrook said. "This movie went a little over-budget (which was $2.5 million) and I suppose Steve's huge salary might have had something to do with that."

Wizan remembered just how enthusiastic Steve was to make this film and the financial aspect was not his driving motivation, more the story. "Steve got the script on the Monday and committed to it on the Thursday," Wizan said. "Most actors usually keep you waiting for two months. Steve called me straight after he read the script and said he loved it. 'I'm in. Just get a good director', he told me."

The producer carried out Steve's wish to the letter by securing Sam Peckinpah, whose reputation was on the up following his work on *The Wild Bunch*. There were more problems to overcome though, before Peckinpah could commit. He had just directed a movie for Baum called *Straw Dogs*, which they were editing in London. It was decided, without too much deliberation, that his editing team would have to finish their work in Prescott, Arizona. "Within a week, we had Steve and Sam," Wizan said proudly. Wizan was also heavily involved with the screenplay as he would give Rosebrook his feedback every time he sent him

12-page clumps during the script process. Wizan was making *Jeremiah Johnson* with Robert Redford at the time in Utah.

The Peckinpah-McQueen combination was one of the hottest a studio might find then. Despite their respective talents though, ABC might so easily have bought a whole lot of trouble for they had worked together before briefly on *The Cincinnati Kid* in 1965 when Sam was fired just four days into shooting. The producer, Martin Ransohoff, executed the decision but Sam felt Steve had contributed to his dismissal and certainly failed to speak up for him. So, for the early part of *Junior Bonner*, both were suspicious of the other. Co-star Mary Murphy, who shared an intimate relationship with Peckinpah, commented: "Sam came to me and said, 'I've got to be nice to this guy or he's going to throw me off the picture'." Another co-star Barbara Leigh noticed how both tolerated yet respected the other. "Steve and Sam had a strange relationship. Both knew just how far to push the other and the boundaries – they made it work."

Although Sam was a bigger name after *The Wild Bunch*, Steve still called the shots on *Junior Bonner*. "What had happened on *The Cincinnati Kid* almost ruined Sam's career," Murphy commented. "To have a big star like Steve McQueen help throw him off the picture was just terrible. He was like that; if Steve didn't like you, you were gone." There was an implicit atmosphere initially, though it soon dispersed. Both men were opinionated, outspoken and extremely passionate about their work. Steve was famous for being hard on directors, though Sam was even more infamous for his on-set verbal outbursts. Notes Wizan: "Sam used to blow up on a set just to stir the pot - it livens' things up. Sam's problem was that he was a perfectionist to the very end and if anybody wasn't a hundred per cent, he'd fire them on the spot. It wasn't out of ego or being an asshole, it came out of a desire that everyone put in as much as he was - and he put in his life."

Steve was equally committed to this project. Newt Arnold was first assistant director and went on to work on another two McQueen films and another three with Peckinpah. He came to understand both extremely well. "I found Steve wonderful to work with and I got along with him very well. He was exceptionally professional, very creative and always concentrated on his work - he was extremely focused. He and Sam shared a very good relationship, as both were strong-willed. They had their share of disagreements, but the centre line of their relationship was very solid. The only time people got in trouble with Sam was if they tried to lie to him or blame other people for their own mistakes. He was very straight and upfront and willing to help anybody if they approached him with a problem. Steve had a similar personality and as a result, they got on very well." Bill Pierce was one of five members serving the Motion Picture Development Commission for Arizona and instrumental in taking *Junior Bonner* to Prescott. He was also chairman of the Prescott rodeo for ten years and became a valuable Mr Fix-it to Steve and Sam throughout the ten-week shoot. "They never had a loving relationship," he observed. "It was just very business-like."

Steve relaxing on the set of *Junior Bonner* with co-star and
girlfriend Barbara Leigh
(COURTESY: ABC / BARBARA LEIGH)

Before shooting began, Sam, Steve and Joe Wizan met in Palm Springs at the end of May to discuss the script. Writer Jeb Rosebrook joined them later. During the meeting, Steve showed his magnanimous side and resisted any effort to expand his role. "This is a family movie and everybody's part is as important as mine," he told the producer and director. "Although I'm Junior Bonner, the star, this has to be it for me. If we're going to work on something, let's work on the father or the mother." Other preparations included completing the cast. For the part of Junior's father, Ace Bonner, Robert Preston was assigned. First, he met with McQueen, Wizan and Marty Baum in a Los Angeles restaurant - an occasion that was to cause a few anxious feelings as the producer explained. "At the time Steve was 41 and Robert was about 65. When Preston walked in the restaurant we nearly had a heart attack because he looked younger than Steve! He was the youngest looking 60-year-old you'll ever see. We had to age him in the movie." For the other key roles, Ida Lupino was brought in to play Junior's mother, and Mary Murphy was married to Junior's brother, played by Joe Don Baker. Veteran actor Ben Johnson also co-starred.

Steve knew he had to up his game around the likes of Preston and Lupino, and he came to realise that these old pro's would not tolerate any movie star bullshit. Writer Jeb Rosebrook recalls a rehearsal one day when Steve acted up and soon came to regret it. "I can recall one real awkward instance," Rosebrook said, "and that was when Steve wanted to change his lines in the scene where Steve met his mother, played by Ida Lupino. I think the reason that Steve was difficult on this particular day was because he had apparently wanted to call a meeting the night before but because we had all been working so hard that day we all went out to dinner, and maybe he was a bit pissed off that he couldn't find anybody. I think he was trying to be difficult that day to teach us all a lesson. He kept trying to change his lines and Ida, being a real professional, knew all of her lines. At the end of that day we had barely shot anything because of these issues that Steve had raised. As we left, Ida turned to Steve and said, 'Hey mister, you had better learn your lines otherwise you're going to be eating a hell of a lot of apple pie tomorrow.' Steve came back the next day, went to work and we never had a single problem."

The role of Junior's girlfriend, for the love interest, was provided by Barbara Leigh, replacing an actress who had been Peckinpah's number one choice for the part, Tiffany Bolling. The producers came up with a cover story to excuse Bolling from the movie but the real reason was for McQueen to have his first choice close by. "Steve and I were lovers before the movie and the only reason I got the part was so he could be with me during the shoot," Leigh admitted. She was sixteen years younger than Steve and her first memories of him were from a movie that he was mostly embarrassed by, *The Blob*. She admired his quirkiness in that flick but was a keen sci-fi fan in any case. Fourteen years on, Steve was no longer a rookie actor trying to make it in Hollywood but now a household movie icon on a global level. Perhaps on a par, ironically, with another megastar Elvis Presley, who Leigh was still privately dating by the time she started work on *Junior Bonner*. Leigh, a stunning brunette, was also hooked up with film studio executive James T. Aubrey – Steve became the third tip in a love triangle. Her presence on this movie, at a time when Steve's marriage to Neile was on the rocks, could only result one way – in a frenzied romance, which was relatively short but almost inevitable. It made Elvis Presley mad as hell when she was later forced to admit during a strained telephone conversation that she was 'dating' Steve and she could not entertain a visit from him to Arizona when he had proposed to see her there. The singer was not used to rejection.

Steve and Barbara first met at a script-reading in Joe Wizan's Los Angeles office, along with Sam Peckinpah and writer Jeb Rosebrook. She had not been pre-warned that the star of the movie would also be there. Steve's easy-going, laid-back nature put her at ease. His presence was not exactly an intimidating one, even though she had seen him on the big screen many times before. "When I walked into that office I did not know that Steve McQueen would be there, not until I saw him sitting there in a chair," Barbara recalled. "I was surprised but his demeanor was one of a regular guy, not a movie star. He wore jeans and sandals, a T-shirt, nothing like his image on the big screen of his more sophisticated movies. And he was shorter than I had imagined he would be; he wasn't a big guy, just slim and about five-foot-ten - though he may have been quoted taller, he wasn't." Her twenty minute audition seemed to have ended in failure when Steve jogged after her to the parking lot to say she probably wouldn't get the part. The real reason he pursued her was to ask her to dinner that evening, an invitation she felt compelled to accept, despite her lack of attraction to him at that stage – the idea of dating Steve was sexier than the act itself, initially. "I wasn't attracted to him in that reading," Leigh commented. "I didn't think of us together, and he wasn't even my favorite movie star. I would have chosen Gary Cooper from *The Fountainhead* or Gregory Peck in *The Omen*. I was in love with older men, and to me, no one was more sexy then Gary Cooper as Howard Roark in *The Fountainhead*."

The physical attraction soon developed for Barbara, especially having bonded so well on their first date that night at a Malibu restaurant when discovering that they were both abandoned early by their father's, spent time in children's homes and were raised by mother's who were largely unfit for purpose. That connection only served to bring them closer. Steve and Neile were separated but not divorced at this time, while Barbara was involved with two other men, Elvis and James Aubrey. Barbara was upfront with Steve about only one of them at first – not Elvis, who was married to Precilla at the time and so appreciated her discretion.

Barbara did not ask to be in the awkward but rather incredible position she was in but nonetheless appreciated the uniqueness of two-timing the world's most famous singer and one of the movie industry's most charismatic icons. She detected marked differences between them both. "When Steve started romancing me, he didn't seem like a movie star, not like Elvis Presley. Of course he was; but he didn't act it when we were alone. He had a lot of country in him, not that he was, growing up back East, but he had that down to earth nature, down-dressed, he cussed, smoked pot, drank beer and loved showing off his choice of hobbies – fast cars and fast bikes." On the bizarre love triangle that had developed, she added: "Steve knew about Jim Aubrey from the beginning but I didn't tell him about Elvis out of respect, as he was still married. I didn't really share my relationship with Elvis with anyone. Not until we were on location and Elvis decided he wanted to visit me, when I was living with Steve in his rented house under the Prescott mountains. It was a shock to Steve but ultimately he won, and Elvis didn't, so what did he care? That might have made me seem more appealing knowing that two other well-known men also wanted my affection. It did, however, change my relationship with Elvis, as he was not used to anyone saying 'no'. Jim Aubrey was exactly as the character Howard Roark. He knew I loved him, he just waited till everything passed. You might say he had as big of an ego as they did, maybe more, given he was privileged and educated. Educated people may have huge egos as movie stars but I have learned they hide it better."

Steve was careful not to expose the new woman in his life to his children when they visited him at weekends in Prescott, but for most of her six-week shoot she vacated her room at the film crew's hotel and accompanied him at his rented house on Country Club Drive. Their relationship was far from secret on location. "All I would say is that she never used the room that I rented out for her, so what does that tell you?" said Bill Pierce. "I wouldn't say Steve and Barbara looked very close from where I was standing; it was strictly physical. They were together within a day of her arriving on the set as a replacement. There were a lot of women who would have wanted to get with Steve in Prescott but he kept himself to himself for the most part and people respected his privacy, so he was able to do as he pleased in his own time."

They would leave and arrive on set together as a matter of routine. While Peckinpah was polite to Barbara, probably for Steve's sake as much as anything, he wasn't overly friendly initially as she was not even his second choice for the part of Charmagne. The director even berated Barbara through a megaphone in her first scene at the rodeo. Steve, not wanting to see his girlfriend humiliated on set, immediately took over direction and Peckinpah did not interfere. The director was a no-nonsense, hard-drinking but respected filmmaker but recognised Steve was the boss on-set. Peckinpah always had the memory of *The Cincinnati Kid* wedged in the back of his mind. While he liked and enjoyed Steve's company, he always fostered an element of fear at Steve's executive power. During the course of making this film, though, Sam and Barbara became friends.

Steve and Barbara enjoyed a romantic, idyllic time together in Prescott. Their relationship was happy enough for her to even contemplate something that millions of women across the world would have been disbelieving at – she thought about ending her relationship with Elvis to be more permanent with Steve, who eventually floated the idea of them living together, this after they returned from location. "I have great, fond memories of Steve and me getting up each morning, with Steve having tea while sitting on the front porch before being picked up by the man who drove his personal trailer and cooked our breakfast; always scrambled eggs with salsa! Nights were ours alone, and we made love a lot. It's fair to say that there were times when I felt Steve was the man for me on location. He was the only one. Then I got back to LA and James and Elvis were both there, and slowly they both crept back into my head and heart."

The true test of their relationship would always come once filming had ceased. While she was able to renew her ties with the demanding but charming Elvis Presley and the suave executive James Aubrey, Steve was still trying to work out whether his marriage was salvageable, genuinely or just to keep it alive for the children's sake. Steve and Barbara maintained their relationship after the movie was shot though, and caught up with one another again at Steve's house in Palm Springs. They rode bikes in the desert, drank beers under the hot sun and cooled off in his pool and continued to enjoy each other's company, especially physically. But Barbara's lifestyle, executed so fulsomely with her three famous boyfriends, ultimately caught up with her. She was presented with an unthinkable dilemma when she became pregnant with Steve's baby. Then at 26 and with no parents to turn to for sensible, sensitive and loving advice, she handled her predicament alone, and opted for an abortion. She saw her future with James Aubrey, not Steve. The movie icon never did get to know that it was his baby, which would have been the third child he always wanted (in his subsequent second marriage to Ali MacGraw, she would suffer a tragic miscarriage and Steve never would have a third child. His first wife Neile also aborted a pregnancy during the filming of *Le Mans* in 1970, with Steve's firm blessing after their relationship had hit the rocks). Barbara told him the baby was James Aubrey's, who had actually undergone a vasectomy years prior. Ironically, to make Barbara's predicament even tougher, Steve showed such compassion and a sweetness that belied his tough-guy screen persona during her pregnancy and subsequent abortion. He was the perfect friend. They drifted apart soon after, as Ali MacGraw came into his life. Barbara and James eventually split, also.

Junior Bonner had been literally thrown together. "In the six weeks before the July 4th rodeo, we cast it, prepared it and were shooting on the 4th with nine cameras," beamed Wizan. "We had to move this fast because of the Prescott rodeo and parade; it wasn't something we could have recreated." The Prescott location provided great authenticity, though it was also a potential hazard to cast and crew. "Prescott could be a rough town," remembered Wizan.

"On a Friday night at the Palace Bar, which was usually very busy, the place would always erupt into a free-for-all - just like the bar brawl in the film. We warned Steve that it wouldn't be a good idea for him to go there, as they'd love to kick the shit out of a movie star. McQueen just said, 'Well if that's the way it is, so be it. I'm still going.' And he did. He walked in just like a regular old guy and the funny thing is they loved him!" Incidentally, the white Cadillac Steve drives in the film was gifted to the owner of the Palace Bar after the movie, according to Bill Pierce, and has since been sold on several times but remains in Prescott, appearing now and again at the annual rodeo.

After the demoralising failure of *Le Mans* and with it the disintegration of his business empire, and away from the strain of his faltering marriage, *Junior Bonner* was a breath of fresh air for Steve. He saw it as an opportunity to return to the fundamentals of his trade: "I'm tired of being the Chief. I just want to be an Indian," he commented. The Steve McQueen of old could be a pain in the ass for producers, directors and executives, demanding script re-writes, asking to see the dailies, taking off in his car or on his bike without permission. This picture saw a marked change in his professional outlook. On the first day of shooting, he told Wizan: "I won't be going to dailies. Let me know how it's going." And to Peckinpah, he said: "Just let me be an actor and direct me." His know-how of film-making and what worked for him was too much to simply ignore, so he did contribute ideas; everything on screen always had to be natural and believable with Steve. However, his new, easy-going attitude was certainly most apparent. "Steve was really into this picture and was determined to do his best work," said Wizan. "After the problems he had had on *Le Mans*, I think he was glad to purely concentrate on his acting and he did a fine job too. I'm sure this would be one of his favourite movies."

Steve was famous for playing the all-action, heroic tough guy. Junior Bonner was still a rugged man of action, but this role required an extra quality that we hadn't seen much of before. It needed deep sensitivity, as the relationship between Junior and his father was a close one. They didn't see much of one another but their compatibility ensured a love and respect that went further than with Junior's brother. Steve and Robert Preston played off each other well. There was humour, affection and mutual respect. Newt Arnold said: "Steve was a very intelligent actor who would not get into all the details of his background training and acting classes when approaching a new character. His basic intelligence allowed him to focus on variations of his characters, although you might find similarities in his approach to various films, but that is bound to happen as his personality was so specific and dominant."

His character warranted a great deal of stunt work and as usual, Steve was keen to carry some of them off himself. In particular, he spent a lot of time on horseback and doing farm-type work as Peckinpah had asked Steve to perfect this aspect of the character. Steve accepted this, realising it could only improve the picture, and he did all of his own horse-riding in the movie, which earned him an honorary membership in the Stuntman's Association. McQueen couldn't take on the wild bulls in the rodeo, as insurance rules prevented him. But there was nothing he wouldn't do if he thought it would improve authenticity. "He prepared very conscientiously to get into his part," Arnold said. "Steve probably did more of his own stunts than most actors. He was very athletic and I'd say that he did at least 25 per cent of his own stunt work in *Junior Bonner* - and he was happy to do more. The bull riding was done with trained men who doubled for Steve, as we couldn't take risks where our main star was concerned. If anything happened it would have been a disaster for the film and his personal safety." One of the stunts Steve and Robert Preston were happy to carry out was during the cow-milking scene, which played out pretty comically, but it was considered as rough a stunt as Steve could be allowed to do. "They were thrown around a little bit but the cows were more afraid of those two guys than they were afraid of the cows," Bill Pierce added. "I'm not trying to demean Steve because I know how he did a lot of things a lot of us couldn't do like that driving on *Le Mans* and *Bullitt*, but this wasn't his thing. He even told me that although he had done his share of westerns he didn't like horses all that much. He said, 'I can control a machine, but I can't control an animal'."

Off-camera Steve was never too busy to appreciate the value of women, even with Barbara Leigh at his side for the most part. McQueen always had a reputation as being a ladies man, and now with a marital separation to deal with, he had more licence to stray. Barbara came on set later and left two weeks before shooting ceased, so Steve wasn't always taken for. "He started on me almost immediately," said Mary Murphy, "but I got scared and resisted (his advances). The thing is, whether you were a hairdresser, an extra, the star or the daughter of the director, if Steve liked you, that was it, you'd probably get hit on by Steve. He was a ladies man and he usually got what he wanted. But I declined. It was not an honour because many women got hit on by Steve. I saw him trying it on with quite a few women on the film but it was kind of funny as he was so shameless about hitting on so many in such an intimate environment. It was an ego thing, as if it was his set as he was the star and so he should have *his* women. I was certainly taken by him because he was adorable. He was always running around with his shirt off and he had a tremendous sexual magnetism in person and on screen. Like Marlon Brando, the attraction was instinctive rather than intellectual. Steve was not the type who would send you flowers or court you, it was just a flirting thing and he'd see how you reacted. He would rarely put himself in the position where he might be rejected."

Even Barbara Leigh, who was his love at this time, accepts that Steve may well have looked elsewhere for female companionship, though given the intimate times they shared while she was there in Prescott, this would almost certainly have been at times before she had arrived on location or when she had departed. "I am sure that Steve made as many passes as he felt like. After all, he was Steve McQueen – he could do what he wanted," Leigh said. Despite witnessing Steve's frequent sexual antics at close range, Murphy felt he still had deep feelings for Neile and considered her to be a very strong woman in tolerating those aspects of Steve's personality. "He must have had an arrangement with Nellie. She always forgave his indiscretions, knowing he would always come back to *her*. I feel that if Steve had simply just had an affair with Ali MacGraw and gone back to Neile, he'd have been better for it. That may sound harsh, but Neile was good for him; she gave him space, let him go, do his thing and was his steadying force."

Jeb Rosebrook was on location for the entire shoot and he was aware Steve and Barbara were close in Prescott, but he still heard how the star was not against trying his luck with other women on the set. "We had to shoot once on a Sunday, which was unusual because we normally shot Monday to Saturday. Anyway, Steve always had his driver and his Winnebago. There was this one girl he liked who worked in the office and she was buddies with one of the hairdressers or something like that. What I heard from gossip on the set was that he wanted both of them to go with him in his Winnebago but they declined, and that was that. I was not privy to a lot of what Steve got up to but I do remember that day. It wouldn't have bothered Steve though, he'd have just moved on to the next."

If Steve wasn't working, or womanising, he was probably on his dirt bike across the Arizona terrain. He was happy to be acquainted with Bill Pierce, the local Mr Fix-it and chairman of the rodeo. Says Pierce, "Steve brought his mechanic over from California and two of his motocross bikes, so I was able to get an old bike track reopened because a friend of mine owned it but had closed it down when some people got hurt. For about four nights a week, Steve would drop by and pick up my teenage son and they would go out and ride bikes together. My boy enjoyed it and wasn't at all awe-struck, and much of that has to do with the way Steve was. On-screen Steve was very professional, very demanding and wanted things his way. Off-screen he was a really neat guy to deal with. We rode along on my motorcycle also and I kept saying to him, 'Do you want to drive, but he would say, 'No, you carry on, I'm fine back here'. We both puffed cigarettes like crazy and had good times."

Pierce even made a cameo appearance in the movie and received a special dedication in the closing credits. His contribution began with sourcing Steve's accommodation after he pointed out that he required total privacy because he was going through a divorce. His can-do attitude was duly appreciated by Steve, Sam and the producers. One of his jobs was to collect Steve's weekly salary from the film company and deliver it to him. He had earned Steve's trust that much. "My dual role (local movie board executive and rodeo chairman) meant I became a pretty important guy for the film people to know," Pierce said. "I got things done, whether it involved setting up scenes to shoot, closing off roads or getting three semi-truck-loads of dust delivered to dry up the mud that the rains caused one day. The only thing I would not do was procure women for Sam Peckinpah at night. He didn't have other people call me to do that, he was able to ask me himself, but I also got phone calls from other people who were either uptown or downtown. I wouldn't get involved in that."

Pierce could see how colourful a character Peckinpah was from his first meet with him, when they were to scout locations together before shooting began. "I went to meet Sam and his associates at their hotel and there were about four or five people just milling around in Sam's room. Sam was lying on the bed and next to him was a half-full glass of Martell brandy – and this was nine in the morning!" On his other experiences in Prescott for Hollywood movies, he said: "We had a few stars down here over the years like Peter and Henry Fonda, Debbie Reynolds and Michael Sarrazin but I enjoyed Steve more than any. I have to say though that my all-time hero is John Wayne and we got close to getting *The Shootist* here, which was his last movie. But they ran out of money and had to film it on the studio lot. I would have died to have gotten John Wayne here. But I'm happy we had Steve! He was a real neat guy."

Junior Bonner was one of Steve's least successful films commercially, though professionally it was one of his best. Moviegoers saw another side to him. He proved he wasn't all about shooting guns, driving fast, playing the rebel and all these similar characterisations associated with him. The experienced cast surrounding Steve helped his performance; so often it forces another dimension from an actor's repertoire. "There's no question the better the people you're with, the better you are," Murphy added. "They make you listen and more creative. It makes a gigantic difference. Any actor that doesn't want to act with great talent has to be paranoid," something Steve was often described as. Things had obviously changed.

However well McQueen performed on this movie in one of his most believable and sensitive roles yet, it's a fact that *Junior Bonner* just never appealed to the masses. One theory was that audiences had had their fill of these types of pictures after a saturation of rodeo films came all at the same time with *When the Legends Die* (Richard Widmark), *J.W. Coop* (Cliff Robertson) and *The Honkers* (James Coburn). Its commercial failure upset Steve. Says Barbara Leigh, "Steve was disappointed that *Junior Bonner* wasn't a big hit at the time, but looking back, no real rodeo film was. Nowadays, the movie is more appreciated and I think he would be happy about that. The way I see it is that people are fickle: they can like something one day and dislike it another. Who wouldn't want every movie they help create be a success? He strived for the best and he mostly got it right." Many people considered it too slow, lacking the usual drive and excitement of a typical McQueen or Peckipah vehicle. As Peckinpah later said, referring to *Junior Bonner*, 'I made a movie where nobody got shot – and nobody went to see it'. Both of their former glories had now effectively become their downfall, in failing to churn out another all-action drama in the shape of *Bullitt* or *The Great Escape*, or *The Wild Bunch* in the case of Peckinpah.

Another aspect to hinder box-office reaction after its release on August 1, 1971 was the limited distribution it received. Says Murphy: "Word of mouth is a great power-house in America. When there has been a lot of publicity and hype, a film can do good business when it opens, but if you don't get people saying, 'Have you seen this?' and so on, interest will peter out. What they do nowadays to over-come that is open the film in a thousand theatres on the first day and consequently, that's when the big bucks roll in. That didn't happen in the seventies." Steve cared for and appreci-ated *Junior Bonner* so much that he offered to buy into the picture such was his concern at its distribution process. "He adored the theme of family values and just wanted every-body to see the movie," said Wizan.

It was a rewarding time for most on the film and Wizan remembers the two months in Prescott with tremendous warmth. "The film was the greatest experience of my life in every way because I made two very good friends with Steve and Sam and I miss them both terribly (Wizan has since passed away in 2011). There's never been anybody like either of them. I've never met two more loyal human beings than those gentlemen. They were crazy, Sam really crazy, but both guys cared deeply for what they were doing. Both were committed to loyalty, friendship and right and wrong."

Main Credits:

Cast: Steve McQueen (as Junior Bonner), Robert Preston, Ida Lupino, Ben Johnson, Joe Don Baker, Barbara Leigh, Mary

Murphy, Bill McKinney, Dub Taylor, Sandra Deel, Don 'Red' Barry, Charles H. Gray, Matthew Peckinpah and more.

Director:	Sam Peckinpah
(Assistants)	Newt Arnold, Frank Baur, Malcolm R. Harding
Producer:	Joe Wizan
(Associate Producer)	Mickey Borofsky
Cinematographer:	Lucien Ballard
Writer:	An original screenplay by Jeb Rosebrook
Editor:	Robert Wolfe, Frank Santillo
Wardrobe:	Eddie Armand; James M. George (men); Pat L. Barto (women)
Make-Up:	Donald W. Roberson
Music:	Jerry Fielding

REVIEWS:

NEW YORK TIMES, August 3rd, 1972

The movie is made to order for both McQueen and Preston, but the loveliest performance is that of Miss Lupino, whose first screen appearance this is in something like 17 years. *Junior Bonner*, which looks like a rodeo film and sounds like a rodeo film, is a superior family comedy in disguise.

FILMS AND FILMING, September, 1972

The role of Junior gives McQueen one of his best opportunities for that understatement and rough-hewn charm which have made him by far the most interesting of the current crop of screen personalities - like all the great American male stars he is a man of experience with the suggestion of a small boy struggling to be heard. Gable had it, Cooper had it, Paul Newman has it, and McQueen - who gave a beautifully judged portrayal of a sixteen-year-old boy in *Nevada Smith* when already in his thirties, would seem to have polished the type into a guy with an urge to lick the machine, car, motor bike and so on - in the same way his predecessors licked the rustler and the Injun. Albeit he has frequently voiced a strange loathing for our four-footed friends, he walks, talks and looks like a man who has spent a life-time in the saddle. After *Bullitt* and *Le Mans* this looks like a return to the grass roots.

MONTHLY FILM BULLETIN, August, 1972

Credit should go to Jeb Rosebrook's admirable script and to the cast (Steve McQueen, in particular, gives an astonishingly fine performance), but most of all to the almost hallucinating density with which Sam Peckinpah and Lucien Ballard present the town of Prescott (the film was shot on location there), all dressed up for its annual Fourth of July celebration, homely and welcoming and yet somehow dead. One scene in particular – the lengthy sequence in the saloon which manages to dovetail public and private celebrations, songs, dances, fights, reconcilliations and promising sexual encounters into one perfectly choreographed, unbroken whole – is probably the best thing Peckinpah has ever done, displaying everything he has learned in the way of techniquesince the days of *Guns in the Afternoon,* all kept under perfect control.

The Getaway saw a return to box-office success for Steve after
starring in three commercial flops
(COURTESY: NATIONAL GENERAL)

THE GETAWAY

(National General) 1972

'There was a good chemistry between Steve and Ali. That was quite clear. Their affair did begin on the movie after all so it's only natural that they'd be very intimate during that time. I think Steve was a hard guy for women to say 'no' to'
– Jack Petty

ALI MACGRAW'S FIRST recollection of Steve McQueen is watching him in New York's Radio City Music Hall when he played the cool, police lieutenant in *Bullitt*. Eight years his junior, she felt an instant attraction to him like that of a school crush. Little did she know four years later, he would become her leading man, her lover and eventual husband. For, when they came together to star in *The Getaway* as Mr. and Mrs. 'Doc' McCoy, a sexual chemistry instantly connected between them. By this time, Steve was split from wife Neile, though Ali was still married to movie producer Robert Evans. Any external complications they brought to the affair appeared irrelevant, as passion was the driving force. As soon as Ali agreed to be in *The Getaway*, she was slightly reluctant

431

STEVE McQUEEN: THE COOLER KING

as she had wanted to play Daisy in F. Scott Fitzgerald's *The Great Gatsby* instead. But there was another reason for her deliberations before accepting director Sam Peckinpah's offer of *The Getaway*. "The real reason I hesitated was that I knew I was going to get in some serious trouble with Steve," Ali commented. "There would be no avoiding it. He was recently separated, and free, and I was scared of my own overwhelming attraction to him. What I chose to see in Steve from the very start was survival. He was, even when our relationship was deteriorating badly, the person I would most choose to be with in a life-or-death situation."

This relationship was never likely to be your standard affair. Steve was as complex, macho and chauvinistic as men came; while Ali was cultured and appreciated opera and museums and generally a life that Steve had never seen. Rather than compromise the habits of their personal lives, Ali chose to fit with Steve's way.

During the three months of filming *The Getaway* in early 1972, their behaviour mirrored the way the rest of their time together would pass. "I walked the nasty razor's edge between occasional moments of sanity and remorse on the one side and, on the other, feverish excitement," Ali wrote in her memoir *Moving Pictures*. The times when Steve was angry with her for any particular reason, he would sometimes hit back at her by picking up one or more of the many groupies that littered the movie set. One night at a local party, Steve drank heavily and began to cavort with two beautiful women who constantly surrounded him, right under the unbelieving glances of Ali, who painfully looked on. Ali later heard the same two bimbos in the next apartment to hers, with Steve. It was an excruciating evening for her, but she soon became accustomed to Steve's unpredictability. But for every moment of anguish, there was a moment of romance and happiness. "From a romantic point of view, I saw him as the one who would chop down trees to make the fire that would keep away the wild animals and the one who would pull fish out of the stream so that we wouldn't starve to death if we were marooned." You could say Ali was wasting her romantic fantasies on the wrong man, though this was not entirely true about Steve; he could be very affectionate and romantic as he could chauvinistic and spiteful. This is what made Steve McQueen the complex, troubled individual he undoubtedly was.

From his inside view of proceedings, make-up man Jack Petty - who had also worked on *The Cincinnati Kid* and *The Sand Pebbles* - felt there was an obvious instant attraction between Steve and Ali. "There was a good chemistry between them," Petty said. "That was quite clear. Their affair did begin on the movie after all so it's only natural that they'd be very intimate during that time. I think Steve was a hard guy for women to say 'no' to."

Script supervisor Michael Preece, who later directed 62 episodes of *Dallas* among other notable TV shows, was one of those amongst the crew who was a little puzzled by the getting together of Steve and Ali. "That was something I didn't understand because I really liked her a lot; in fact no one could understand it," Preece reflected. "At first he was seeing her secretly. There was a town south of El Paso – Juarez in Mexico – and they were actually sneaking over the border quite a bit at first. Her husband, Bob Evans, kept flying down to Texas to find out what was going on. It was a sneaky affair. Nobody on the movie could quite believe it at first because she was such an outgoing, nice girl and Steve was not that nice, from what I saw anyway. They didn't carry on openly until the last month of the picture when they could be seen going out together and by that time her husband knew what was going on.

"Even though they were ultimately affectionate as a couple, I didn't quite get it," Preece added. "He was a good looking guy but the feeling on the set was that she fell for him because he was so macho and famous."

Costume designer Ray Summers, who had worked on *Le Mans* and who had also been a casual friend of Steve's during the early part of his career, felt that Ali and Steve conducted their affair in as responsible a manner as could be and didn't flaunt their relationship. "It gradually became obvious that something was going on," he recalled. "They spent a lot of time together, which was understandable given that they were playing husband and wife in the movie, but as a couple off-screen they were very discreet. They were never off in a corner holding hands and giggling; Steve and Ali had a very good and happy working relationship and anything more than that they kept quite private."

Second unit director and associate producer Gordon T. Dawson, who worked on six Peckinpah movies, observed that their relationship "became obvious" three weeks into shooting. He felt the occasional presence of Bob Evans on location was the most uncomfortable aspect to the affair. It created panic amongst the crew, as they did their best not to unwittingly divulge any information that the leading man and leading lady were carrying on behind his back. "It wasn't really a surprise when they moved into together during the picture," Dawson recalled. "The only time things got real awkward was when we found out Bob Evans was coming to town and then it was a case of 'Where do we hide Steve and Ali?' We were all on message that if Bob asked where they were, nobody knew. It was awkward."

Peckinpah was not unhappy his lead stars were getting it on, as he was committed to the authenticity of the picture and if they could bring their off-camera chemistry into their screen roles, all the better. What he didn't want was for them to break up during the picture and create a destructive atmosphere. "Sam was always great with actors and he respected Steve a lot, though he did not consider Ali the consummate actress," said Michael Preece. "I know Sam liked Ali personally but as an actress he didn't care for her and used to say he wished he'd hired Mariette Hartley (who starred in *Ride the High Country* with Peckinpah in 1962). There were one or two scenes that Sam had to shoot many times and he used to say, 'This is quite difficult.' But Steve was always right on the money, though Sam gave him the freedom to change the odd line here and there. He would tell Steve, 'Say it your way as long as it makes sense.'"

Steve and Ali MacGraw fell in love on location in Texas
during the making of *The Getaway* and were married in the
following year
(COURTESY: NATIONAL GENERAL)

The movie is featured around husband and wife, Doc
and Carol McCoy. After serving time for armed robbery, Doc
realises his freedom will not be given back through good
behaviour and that desperate measures are called for. He has

his wife fix a deal with corrupt politician, Jack Benyon, who is also an influential member of the parole board. The outcome is that in return for his freedom, Doc must lead a heist of a small but cash-infested Texan bank. After the robbery, he is then to split the cash with Benyon before making for Mexico. En route, Doc encounters several double crosses in a fast-moving picture that sees shoot-outs, explosions, car chases and a little romance too.

David Foster and Mitchell Brower produced the film, in association with National General and First Artists, who Steve had joined in 1971 along with Paul Newman, Sidney Poitier and Barbara Streisand. Dustin Hoffman was added a year later. With this production company, set up by Steve's agent Freddie Fields, McQueen was obliged to make three movies costing no more than $3 million each. The main benefit was the extra creative control he was afforded, as the First Artists contract allowed him final cut; a clause that supposedly angered Peckinpah, who was said to have felt his authority had been compromised when Steve made minor changes to the picture. Gordon Dawson believes that was not the case. "Steve and Sam got on just great," commented Dawson. "But Sam was always terrific with his leading man, whether it was Charlton Heston, William Holden or Steve McQueen. There was a lot of mutual respect. I hear the stories about Steve having more creative input but Steve and Sam were so on the same page during production that I don't know of any problems. The only time Steve exerted his authority was during post-production when Jerry Fielding had written a beautiful score and Steve was instrumental in getting rid of it and instead using Quincy Jones' score (because Ali was a fan of Quincy). That upset Sam and was a bone of contention because Sam and Jerry had worked together a lot."

Hairdresser Kathy Blondell, a niece of actress Joan Blondell who had co-starred with Steve in *The Cincinnati Kid*, also felt Steve never tried to undermine the director with his contractual power. "I did not ever have the feeling that Sam was not in charge and when they spoke I believed it was always for the good of the movie," she recalled. "I never saw any power-plays by Steve. I thought their relationship was great. Sam was a strong director and Steve a strong actor but both enjoyed and respected each other's talent and were not afraid to discuss differences and come to terms that suited the situation."

The Getaway was a project always intended for Steve as he and Foster had been friends for a long time and Steve had encouraged him to come up with a suitable property for him to star in. *The Getaway* was it. Also drafted in to play key roles were Ben Johnson, Al Lettieri, Sally Struthers and Slim Pickens. Before Ali MacGraw was signed, after her successes in *Goodbye, Columbus* and *Love Story*. Peckinpah was secured to direct. Originally, Peter Bogdanovich was to direct, but a conflict of other movie commitments led the producers and McQueen to favour Peckinpah, who had read the book by

Jim Thompson and was excited at the prospect of directing the movie.

Despite their occasional clashes of ego and hot-tempered rows, Steve and Sam had both enjoyed working with one another on *Junior Bonner* and were ready to continue their relationship in Texas, where the picture was to be shot. McQueen once said of Peckinpah: "I feel that Sam Peckinpah is an exceptional film-maker. He is a little bit hard on himself sometimes, and I worry about him for that. But I have great respect for anyone as committed as Sam is to his work. He surrounds himself with people who are honest and who are personally committed to what he does. Sam makes a personal commitment to his work, and I feel that a man isn't worth a shit unless he has." On McQueen, Peckinpah commented: "We fought all the time. I never met an actor - a good actor - that I didn't fight with. And McQueen was one of the best. He was very, very under-rated. He was very tough, very, very, very good. He thought *Junior Bonner* was the best thing he'd ever done; well we really worked on that. And *Getaway*, too, we worked at."

They were two of Hollywood's toughest characters, but having worked well together on *Junior Bonner* months earlier, they understood one another. They occasionally feuded but those moments never lingered and they moved on. Noted co-star Bo Hopkins: "I never saw any serious friction between them. They both wanted to make a good movie so

I think in the end they reached a compromise." Make-up artist Jack Petty felt they were both straight talkers who commanded honesty and respect from each other and their co-workers. "Steve and Sam were alike in the way that if they thought you were a jerk they wouldn't tell anyone else, they would tell you to your face." Costume designer Ray Summers echoed: "Both Sam and Steve were men's men. I really believe that if they weren't in the important roles that each had on the picture, they'd have become best buddies. I'm not suggesting they never had a beer together because they did, but they had to keep a certain distance for professional reasons."

Gordon Dawson was introduced to Steve by Peckinpah at the Formosa Café in Los Angeles during pre-production. He remembers how united everyone was in their vision for the movie, especially Steve who was determined to follow the commercial failures of *Le Mans* and *Junior Bonner* with a box-office hit. "It was a great first meeting with a lot of mutual respect," Dawson said. "We all wanted the same thing which was to make a great picture and pull in the same direction. The thing I remember most about Steve then was just how down to earth he was. I have met a lot of actors in my time but he was as down to earth as any. He left the meeting with the words, 'Let's cut a fat hog!' He was very motivated to make this a great picture – we all were. In fact, of all the Peckinpah pictures I did, *The Getaway* was the most difficult logistically but the smoothest-run ever and a lot of that was to do with Sam and Steve, who was a total professional. He knew his lines, he hit his mark and he was never late or bitched about working late. You can't say much better about an actor than that. He really did his job."

Steve's First Artists' connection proved a major benefit early into the production. Dawson, charged with the responsibility of scouting locations and shooting arty footage such as the deer in the prison sequence, secured the prison location in Huntsville for a dollar a day and the use of prisoners as extras. But he was only able to achieve that much because of Steve's influence and celebrity network. "Steve McQueen was instrumental in me being able to secure that prison location," Dawson recalled. "When I went to meet the warden with Warren Skaaren (executive director of the Texas Film Commission) he was not too crazy about having a load of movie folks inside of his prison. But Warren found out that the warden's daughter was a huge Barbara Streisand fan so we went back and got Steve to talk to Barbara, and she sent five or six personally autographed pictures with messages like 'Dear Debbie, I know you will be a star' and stuff like that. When we handed the package to the warden he had tears in his eyes and became the biggest hero to his daughter he ever could have been. So because of the connection between Steve and Barbara we were able to secure the prison and do whatever the hell we liked. The only concession was, the night before we went in, they told us that they would not entertain any negotiations should there be a hostage situation and that even if Steve was taken by the prisoners, it would be a shoot to kill scenario. If we could not accept that, we could not go into the prison, but Steve just said, 'Let's go in and get it done.'

Shooting began in February, 1972 in Huntsville, Texas, with the prison scenes. Although there was some apprehension about the safety and security of the cast and crew, especially Steve, with real-life prisoners in their midst, it was ironic that the lead star's well-being was ultimately threatened not by any cons but by a pack of bloodhounds. Recalls Gordon Dawson: "Steve was in a wagon in the prison grounds that was being pulled by a horse as they were on their way to a work detail. It was a long shot from afar so the camera and crew were way, way back by the fence. It was a beautiful shot and as soon as Sam shouted 'Cut', Steve jumped out of the wagon and started walking towards the camera. Suddenly out of nowhere come all these bloodhounds, going after him because they're taught if any prisoner in white uniform breaks away from the group they should go after him. So Steve had to run for his life and I have never seen a man run so fast. He kept going until he climbed the fence and by that time the handlers had caught up with the dogs, but for a few seconds it was a pretty scary situation for Steve. Having 'Spanky' inside the prison made for a few interesting moments. He was okay with it most of the time though he sure was frightened when he had all those dogs up his ass!"

Steve was otherwise relaxed about his safety in the prison and was frequently seen chatting with inmates. He gave them time and listened to their stories. Steve had after all been in junior detention and understood what it was like to be caged, effectively. He was content in the environment, though as Dawson quipped, "When he found out that all the extras they gave us were from the gay unit he didn't like that very much. He thought he was working with all the hardened cons!" Many of the extras were trustees, though that still did not guarantee anything. One crew member was in the prison grounds one day and got talking to a young man about bodybuilding and then casually asked why he was there. 'I murdered my wife,' he replied. 'If I'm a good boy I'll be out in 14 years.' It was a reality check. The crew were also warned by prison guards not to carry certain items on them like a pencil or ruler as they could be used as weapons. The location was certainly authentic.

Steve's focus on making a believable, critically-acclaimed movie was never in doubt. He even went to some peculiar lengths to ensure that crew members were doing their jobs. "Steve tested people to see if you were on his side," Preece recalled. "I remember the scene when he got out of prison and his wife was picking him up; he was holding a bag, like a doctor's bag. We had shot part of the scene and just as we were about to resume to complete it, I saw him move the bag from one foot to the other foot. And before Sam could shout 'Action' he yelled at me to ask which foot his bag was on in the earlier footage. We obviously didn't have the video technology in 1972 that we have today so it wasn't easily known. But fortunately I had made a note about which foot it was next to. He said, 'Are you sure', shouting over at me in front of lots of people. I said, 'Yeah, I'm positive.' He said, 'Well, you'd better be right.' I am 100 per cent confident that he knew the answer and he was testing me, as one of my roles was continuity as well as keeping a script on me in case one of the actors forgot his lines. Steve was sharp though and rarely forgot his."

Late into pre-production, it was learned that Ali didn't know how to drive, which came as a bombshell given that her character was to perform most of the driving scenes. So on the day before shooting began, as the crew stood around on a dirt-base parking lot next to a large pond, Steve took it upon himself to give her a driving lesson Steve McQueen style. Predictably, it was a hair-raising and costly exercise. "It was amazing that nobody realised she did not know how to drive," Gordon Dawson commented, "but she had recently come from a modelling career in New York. We knew we had to give her a crash course in driving and Steve then told us, reassuringly, 'Don't worry, I will get Ali in a car and make sure she will soon be at ease about it.' So we're all standing about with the picture car, a Mercury, which will be used for the first shot the next morning. Then all of a sudden Steve puts Ali in this car, starts it up, puts it in gear and speeds off so that all these rocks and mud flies up, heads up this grassy hill and on to a freeway, over the median (central reservation), over the other side of the freeway, gets a little air as he leaves the freeway and doubles back down the slope towards us, hits the parking lot at about 60 miles an hour, puts the car into a four-wheel spin and takes it right into the pond. So, a day before shooting, we had our leading man, leading lady and picture car sinking into this god damn pond. I think Steve wanted to stop at speed just before the pond but he overdid it and a few guys standing around had to jump in after them. There was never any real danger but it was quite a spectacle. That was Steve's way of putting Ali at ease inside a car!"

It was one of many instances on the movie when Steve showcased his maniacal love for speed. It was his release. He would often take his car out for a spin in the early hours and burn some serious rubber around San Marcos, where they filmed the bank robbery and the connecting sequences. Fortunately for Steve and the producers, the local police department was sympathetic. Many off-duty police officers worked on the movie in a traffic or road management capacity so anytime Steve broke the law, they tended to look the other way. That was until the local police chief spoke to Peckinpah and Dawson about Steve's new trick which was to drive the wrong way down some of their one-way streets. "He did it that often the local cops nicknamed him 'Wrong way Steve'," Dawson said. "I was asked to have a quiet word with him to cut it out, and he would lay low for a few days but would then start all over again.

"That was just Steve for you. He was crazy about anything on wheels. And he was the same even on the set. Sometimes you had to work him with a butterfly net because he always wanted to take off. We would be all set to roll and we'd say, 'Where's Spanky?' and somebody would pipe up and say he just took off on a motorcycle. That actually happened on the set. A kid was hanging around on his dirt bike and Steve went up to him and said, 'Hey kid, give me a ride on your bike. The next thing you know he's tearing off into the desert and returns about half an hour later. The kid was thrilled because Steve McQueen was riding his bike and Steve came back and signed a photo for him. That was Steve – very spontaneous. He had this tough guy persona but the Steve I knew was a kid. He lived to have fun."

Officially, Steve was advised that he couldn't ride his motorcycle while under contract to the film company - a rule he came up against on several occasions. It wasn't something that he ever accepted kindly and when he saw co-star Bo Hopkins riding a motorcycle during the first few days of shooting, he immediately approached the director and expressed his annoyance. "How come Boo (the name he called him) gets to ride and I don't?" To which Peckinpah replied, "Well, if he gets killed it ain't gonna affect the picture, but if you get killed we're sunk!" Hopkins didn't appreciate the director's honesty too much but at least Steve understood their position – even if he didn't always listen.

Assistant director Newt Arnold, who had worked on *Junior Bonner*, got along well with Steve on a professional level but was not friendly on a social footing. Until, that is, Arnold caught Steve's attention on location in Texas. Arnold wore an eye-patch after a childhood accident and it surprised McQueen that this guy was a more than useful motorcyclist. "We became a lot closer on *The Getaway*," recalls Arnold, "because one day I had to modify something in the background of this out-of-town location. And when I borrowed this bike belonging to one of the crew members to zip across and do what I had to do, Steve looked astonished: 'Jesus, I didn't know you could ride,' he said. 'Sure,' I said. 'There are lots of one-eyed motorcyclists!' From that point on, we got on much better but were never close because he had his own circle of friends."

While Steve spent most of his social time with Ali or stuntmen buddies, he would occasionally invite crew members out for dinner who he had grown to like on the set. But because of his intimidating presence, a dinner date with the most famous movie star in the world was not always as attractive a proposition as it might sound. Michael Preece recalled: "I was in my hotel room with my wife in Huntsville – where we were filming the prison scenes – and the sound man knocked on my door. When I let him in he was nervously clutching a bottle of vodka. He said that he was hiding, as Steve wanted to have dinner with him. I wondered what the problem was as most people would love to be invited out by the star, but it was not something he was keen to do. He stayed in my room for over an hour and we could hear Steve calling out for this guy down the hall. About a month later the same thing happened to me. My wife and I were sitting in my room and Steve McQueen was at our door wanting us to go to dinner with him. We hid until he left. He had problems getting people to just go out to a normal dinner with him. I said to my wife that night, 'I can't believe we are hiding from Steve McQueen!' because if Marlon Brando or Charlton Heston had asked us out we'd have been there. I worked with Brando on a few movies and he was a very funny guy. He had a great sense of humour about himself and other people. You could joke with him and I don't think anyone felt comfortable to have a joke with Steve. I don't think McQueen was as smart as Brando and perhaps Steve was a little sensitive about that. Many people who say Steve McQueen was the greatest guy in the world never met him – he really wasn't. To this day I can watch him in movies over and over again, but in person I just didn't want to sit and listen to him for a whole dinner."

Not everyone though was against the idea of dining with Steve. Pop star Elton John came to El Paso to play at the Sun Bowl on April 29, 1972. Earlier in the day he stopped by the set and shared some lunch with Steve. Most of the crew nervously kept their distance. But by the time the singer left, he generously supplied dozens of free tickets to the cast and crew for them to attend his show that night. "We all went to watch him play, including Steve and Ali, and Steve's son Chad," Preece said. "Elton was playing at the edge of the infield, and there were a lot of people there. It was a sold-out concert (stadium capacity now stands at 51,500) and we were all sitting as a group in the stands after taking a bus to the stadium. Most of the cast and crew were there. Elton was singing great, everyone was enjoying it and then there was a thing at the end of his concert where he invites the VIPs to stand around his podium to create a finale finish. Steve and Ali left at that time because he thought that all these people charging down from the stands were coming to get his autograph. I saw what was happening and kept my eye on Steve and found it kind of funny that they were running behind the stage on this football field but nobody was chasing after them, which must have puzzled Steve and Ali. I was laughing because they were stood there with Steve holding Chad's hand and there

STEVE McQUEEN: THE COOLER KING

was nobody around them. The crowd were only interested in singing along with Elton. They took the bus back to the hotel on their own so the whole cast and crew had to wait around for about an hour while the bus driver came back for the rest of us."

Steve and the film company were even less impressed with the behaviour of co-star Al Lettieri, who carried on in real life as his character Rudy Butler might do. He was a crude, big-drinking, big-coking brute of a man who played a great role in the picture but his off-screen conduct was frightening to many and Steve subsequently distanced himself from him. "He got us into trouble big time," Dawson recalled. "He was a big cocaine head. But Steve stayed out of it and was not a part of any of that. Al was having an affair with (co-star) Sally Struthers and that came apart right in the middle of the movie and she left to go to LA. Before she came back, Al let it be known that he was going to kill her. They got back together, though. But he was a crazy, big, powerful tough guy. He was exactly like his character in the picture. We had a guy standing by on the set with a hypo (needle) so if Al made any false moves this guy would hit him and knock him down. We were so concerned about him that we had a few guys from the Juarez mafia come visit the set and have a discussion with him about his behaviour. There was no trouble but when that's going on in the middle of a day's work it makes things pretty interesting."

While Lettieri misbehaved, many others on the cast and crew did not exactly carry on like innocent pussy cats.

Peckinpah's movies were always big-drinking affairs but this one went much further. "Steve celebrated his 42nd birthday during *The Getaway* and the crew had 42 shots of amyl nitrate (or poppers) inserted into his cake – with one candle!" Preece commented. "The drug was used for the rush it gave during sex. And there was also a serious amount of marijuana involved on that movie. When we got to El Paso there was a huge mail sack full of the stuff delivered to the production office. It was maybe 40 kilos in weight, with paper and twine all around it. Marijuana was very prevalent on the set."

The Getaway had one of the most laid-back, dope-smoking crews that ever worked on a Hollywood movie. Ray Summers recalled: "There were a hell of a lot of parties down there in Texas for the cast and crew but Steve usually stayed away and kept himself to himself pretty much. He was a very private person and would only occasionally hang out with us. He just didn't like to be bothered too much; Steve preferred his own space." But when he did choose to join in with the fun, Bo Hopkins remembers that he was just like one of the boys. "We used to go downtown and get something to eat and have a drink, then visit the local all-girl college they had. We had a lot of fun," said Hopkins. "I had always liked his work and the dare-devil in him. Steve liked to live on the edge, which kept him going - he loved challenges. I enjoyed watching him work as he always knew exactly what he wanted to do when he came in."

On a professional level, Newt Arnold concluded: "Steve was friendly with pretty much everybody who was involved with the picture. People say he could be awkward, but from what I saw he was extremely down-to-earth and an outstanding professional. *The Getaway* was probably the most enjoyable film that I have ever worked on and much of the reason for that is down to Steve."

Main Credits:

Cast: Steve McQueen (as Carter 'Doc' McCoy), Ali MacGraw, Ben Johnson, Sally Struthers, Al Lettieri, Slim Pickens, Richard Bright, Jack Dodson, Dub Taylor, Bo Hopkins, Roy Jenson, John Bryson, Bill Hart, Tom Runyon, Whitney Jones and more.

Director:	Sam Peckinpah
(Assistants)	Newt Arnold, Ron Wright
Producer:	Mitchell Brower, David Foster
(Associate Producer)	Gordon T. Dawson (and second unit director)
Cinematographer:	Lucien Ballard
Writer:	Screenplay by Walter Hill, based on Jim Thompson's novel
Editor:	Robert L. Wolfe
Wardrobe:	Ray Summers (supervisor)
Make-Up:	Jack Petty, Al Fleming
Music:	Quincy Jones

REVIEW:

THE NEW YORK TIMES, December 20th, 1972

For all his reputation as a director of action and violence (*Straw Dogs*), Peckinpah is most effective and most eloquent when dealing with themes of love and loss, which are as apparent in the super-bloody *The Wild Bunch* as in the quieter *The Ballad of Cable Hogue* and this year's ruefully comic *Junior Bonner*. The action and the violence of *The Getaway* are supported by no particular themes whatsoever. The movie just unravels.

Steve was surprisingly overlooked for an Academy Award
nomination for what was one of his best performances
in *Papillon*. Some felt it was because he had upset the
establishment too much during his career
(COURTESY: ALLIED ARTISTS / BRITISH FILM INSTITUTE)

PAPILLON

(Allied Artists) 1973

'McQueen was totally impossible...After saying he'd do the movie he tried everything he could to get out of it because he was having more fun with Ali MacGraw and his children...He made every effort not to make the movie and said some ridiculous things like his CIA friends told him it wasn't safe to go to Jamaica as he may get assassinated'
– Lorenzo Semple Jr.

ALONG WITH *SAND PEBBLES, Papillon* the best and most demanding movie Steve ever made. He brought a tremendous amount to his character and belied his former reputation to a certain extent, in executing the role with superb acting skills. In past movies, Steve was usually praised for his natural screen magnetism and presence, but was rarely credited as a great *actor*. But in *Papillon*, there was another side to Steve McQueen. Director of Photography Fred Koenekamp noted: "This was a different part for Steve. He wasn't playing a macho cop detective, running around chasing people or chasing cars, this really was a picture to act in and he did it and proved what a natural

455

he was." Co-star Don Gordon was a personal friend of Steve's and knew that McQueen was particularly satisfied with the film. "He was very proud of his work in *Papillon* and not many people realise that. He worked very hard and very seriously at his craft; McQueen poured a lot of himself into that film." Koenekamp added: "I think he probably worked harder as an actor than he'd ever done before. It was a very demanding role, particularly towards the end of the picture when he is an old man."

Papillon is based on the book by Henri Charriere. The compelling true story tells of his unyielding spirit to escape the torturous life sentence he was ordered to serve in French Guiana, under the strict laws of the French penal system. He was charged with the murder of a pimp, though he claimed he was innocent. The movie portrays events with unrelenting emotion, as McQueen gives a powerful characterisation of Charriere, while Dustin Hoffman plays his good friend and fellow escapee Louis Dega - a role enlarged by the third and last script-writer Dalton Trumbo, who wrote the screenplay for *Spartacus*. Although 150 minutes in length, the picture maintains interest. Just when you think the film is nearing its end, another chapter of adventure unfolds, with stunning scenery of the location setting of Jamaica, and Spain before it. They wanted to film in France where Charriere's book was set but the French government opposed its criticism of the French penal system, so the production was shifted to Northern Spain.

Steve and Dustin Hoffman may have shared an
uncomfortable relationship off-screen, but on-screen they
were sensational as prison buddies
(COURTESY: ALLIED ARTISTS /
THE KOBAL COLLECTION)

In keeping with the exploits of Charriere, McQueen sports a tattoo of a butterfly on his chest - the symbol of freedom hence his nickname (Papillon). We learn at the beginning of the film that those attempting escape will be punished to two years in solitary confinement; a second escape will merit five years of similar treatment - which exists to break the spirit of the prisoner mentally and physically to the point of inhumanity; three escapes means the guillotine. Such threats of barbarity do little to dampen the plans of Papillon, whose sole aspiration in life is only to find freedom once more. In his efforts to achieve this, he escapes twice, only to be recaptured on both occasions, to suffer the respective penalties. After his release from the five-year stretch, we see a frail, white-haired McQueen who has been reduced to unthinkable living conditions, having to consume the insects who were his only cell mates, for food. Still, following the harrowing ordeal, when Papillon is shipped out to Devil's Island to supposedly see out his life, thoughts of freedom remain. He meets his friend Dega on the island whom he tries to persuade to join him in his final make or break attempt at escape. But in the end, he departs single-handedly and sails away through shark-infested water on a raft made from coconut shells, and cries "I'm still here you bastards" - the only line remaining from the original script by the uncredited William Goldman.

Papillon was rejected by the large studios and only Allied Artists were prepared to take on its $15 million budget. Thanks to company president and chairman Emanuel

L. Wolf, Allied was on its way back from being an ailing organisation at that time. He had resuscitated it with movies like *Last Summer* and *Cabaret,* and later *Papillon.* His secret was looking for material that was unloved and unwanted by the likes of 20th Century Fox, Warner Brothers and Columbia. Independent producers would approach Allied after being turned down everywhere else – and Wolf knew it but embraced his company's role as an alternative studio. Such a producer Robert Dorfmann had purchased the rights to Charriere's book at a cost of $500,000 and had identified Steve McQueen and Dustin Hoffman as a mouth-watering star duo. Steve was hot again after *The Getaway,* with the box-office failures of *Le Mans* and *Junior Bonner* well behind him. Hoffman was seven years younger than Steve and had not yet reached the legendary status of his more senior co-star but had still clocked up impressive credits such as *The Graduate* (1966), *Midnight Cowboy* (1969) and more recently *Straw Dogs* (1971). Dorfmann's recruitment of acclaimed director Franklin J. Schaffner, who was also a producer on *Papillon,* helped to package a combination that greatly appealed to Allied, which eventually trimmed the final budget to just under $13.5 million.

Allied Artists' head Wolf soon realised what he was taking on with Steve: "We made a deal with Steve McQueen that he was to get a million bucks," Wolf commented, "but then he went and got divorced and had agreed to give his wife a million and didn't want to use his own money so he got Robert Dorfmann to give him another million bucks and in doing so gave up his profit participation rights out of the foreign revenues. Dorfmann then brought Dustin on board with my help after he had got Steve himself. I didn't like Dorfmann for many reasons but the good thing he had done before I got involved, apart from bringing in Steve McQueen, was securing a very good director in Franklin Schaffner."

Steve secured himself a $2 million fee plus his percentage of the gross profits for domestic sales. Schaffner was paid $850,000 upfront and Dustin Hoffman earned $1.25 million. It was one of the strongest-backed pictures of that era, financially. After his belated "double my money or I'm off" demand, McQueen was paid the most ever given to a star of any movie. Even Hoffman received more than half of what he would normally have banked at that time in his career. But Dorfmann wanted him happy and secure, so gave him more. Wolf allowed Dorfmann to collect the lions' share of the foreign revenues, while he got what he wanted. "It was agreed that Allied would distribute the picture in the US and Canada and would also have control of production and final cut, final cast, final script, final going to the bathroom," said Wolf. "Dorfmann could not disagree as nobody else wanted to take on the picture."

Lorenzo Semple Jr. was brought in by Dorfmann to write the screenplay when original screenwriter Goldman was axed. The final script was predominantly a work by Semple and Dalton Trumbo, though Schaffner himself rewrote many lines, too. Semple went on to write such films as *King Kong,*

Flash Gordon and *Never Say Never Again*. Coincidentally, his play *The Golden Fleecing* was also made into a movie that starred Steve McQueen in 1961, *The Honeymoon Machine*. He remembers how Steve became disinterested with *Papillon* during pre-production discussions, which caused great anxiety for Dorfmann: "McQueen was totally impossible throughout the whole thing. After saying he'd do the movie, he then tried everything he could to get out of it, because he was having more fun running around with Ali MacGraw and his children." Steve's attitude was a great concern to Dorfmann as there had been no contract signed at this stage and the very thought of McQueen walking out on the picture was an exasperating prospect. The producer had raised funds around the world to partly finance the project, before Allied Artists took on the majority of the costs. That initial funding was generated purely on the strength of McQueen's involvement.

"This is why he was irresponsible to then try and get out of it after all this money had been spent," Semple added. "He made every effort not to make the movie and said some ridiculous things like his CIA friends had told him it wasn't safe to go to Jamaica as he may get assassinated and what would his children do without him. When I met him, in a big meeting with Dorfmann and Frank (Schaffner), he said, 'Listen guys, do you really want to make this movie? I'd rather be riding around the desert with my kids.' Dorfmann nearly fell off his chair as he would probably have gone to jail if they didn't make the film. Steve was being a bit naughty." Eventually, McQueen was made aware of the strenuous preparations that had taken place to ensure that *Papillon* was made. He then poured his heart and soul in to the movie - allaying the producer's fears at the same time.

Steve became a problem to Wolf, also, and though the executive producer appreciated the kudos and box-office power that he gave to the movie, he knew he would be in for an uncomfortable ride. "I thought Steve was a great actor, a terrific personality – the on-screen chemistry between him and Dustin was fantastic," Wolf commented. "It's just that as a person, he was very difficult. Not a nice guy. I would say he was the perfect pain in the ass. Everything I had to do with the guy was exaggerated. For instance, when we shifted to Jamaica, after the shoot in Spain had wrapped, we had a ship reach Jamaica with all the props and materials for the set. Straight away Steve put up a big tantrum and insisted that his motorbikes were loaded off the ship before anything else. They were right at the back of everything, but he had his way and it cost us about a day of shooting."

It's curious that the majority of industry colleagues remember Steve warmly, of his down-to-earth nature, of his loyalty to his friends, even impressed by his trained magnetism to women, irrespective of morality. Director of photography Fred Koenekamp and editor Robert Swink, who both worked on *Papillon*, never had a negative word to say about Steve. But ask Wolf and you hear a totally disparate version. There is no doubt that impression derived from Steve's instinctive resentment towards hierarchies. Wolf represented 'The Establishment' – he was 'a suit'. As buddy-buddy as Wolf tried to be with Steve, it didn't matter and the studio boss knew it: "There's no question Steve saw me as 'one of them', he'd never allow himself to be pally with a studio boss. Even at times when we were relaxed – the few occasions that was the case – he was still on his guard. He had obviously had some other bad experiences with studios and unfortunately he related that same image to me. He saw me as a studio head and since he knew I had all the controls for the picture, like final cut and so on, I was the threat to him in many ways. And he was not a guy who liked to be controlled. He was very much of a free spirit."

Papillon brought Schaffner together with Steve for the first time. There were few problems as Schaffner knew how to deal with strong-minded, hard-willed actors. Schaffner was born in Tokyo but moved to America during his youth and served in the US Navy in World War II. It was after his time in the military that he began a near 30-year association with movies, going on to become the Academy Award winner for Best Director on *Patton* in 1970. Cinematographer Fred Koenekamp worked with him over 20 years and said it wasn't hard to see why he and Steve got along. "I loved Frank Schaffner, he was the best director that I ever worked with and he got on well with Steve, too. Frank was an easy guy to get along with; he never yelled on a set, he never

STEVE McQUEEN: THE COOLER KING

pushed people, he knew exactly what he wanted and was always totally prepared, so I think he made it easy on actors. He'd chit-chat, talk about a scene, rehearse it and that would be it - he never became nasty." Editor on *Papillon* was Robert Swink, who was nominated for three Academy Awards in his career and worked with legendary film-maker William Wyler for 25 years. Swink noticed how Schaffner's understated way of directing brought the best out in Steve. "Frank was a bundle of nerves when he worked, very uptight, but he didn't let it show too much and it never seemed to bother him. He and Steve became quite close. The great thing about Frank was that you could go to him and say, 'Why don't you shoot from this angle or that angle?' He would listen and be prepared to use ideas from others. He was not proud and never out to get praise, and I think Steve recognised that humility."

Schaffner knew exactly how to interact with Steve: entertain his ideas, involve him in the many script changes that he himself wrote in, but ultimately he had a quiet command of the set and Steve knew to respect him. Said Wolf, "I recall the scene where Steve had to scrap around in that dark cell looking for bugs...well, just before Frank was ready to shout roll 'em, Steve spends about five to ten minutes telling Frank how we should shoot the scene. Frank listened to him very patiently and let him finish his idea and then said, 'Thanks for that Steve, very interesting, but here's where we are', and he then did it his way and got Steve straight back into the picture. Steve was a very difficult guy to handle but Schaffner handled him perfectly."

The screen partnership of Steve McQueen and Dustin Hoffman was one that worked beautifully in the movie: McQueen's sturdy, captivating presence was complemented by the trained skill of Hoffman, who had lost weight to befit the role of Dega - the bespectacled wimp known as the best counterfeiter in France. Like on *The Magnificent Seven*, Steve attracted attention for a supposed rift with his co-star - but roles were now reversed from *Seven* when *he* was the minor relation, to Yul Brynner. Co-star Don Gordon dismissed talk of a rift but said there was healthy competition between Steve and his younger co-star. "At that point, Steve was not young, but Dustin was and he could sniff him snapping at his ass," Gordon commented. "There was this young guy who was virtually growling, but I think Steve saw it as a kind of game. A lot of people want to get serious about this crap, but though acting is serious business, it's not brain surgery, you're not saving somebody's life - you're acting. You should have a good time at it, work hard at it and be serious about it - Steve was all those things, but he also had a sense of fun. He saw Dustin for what he was - a young actor trying to make his way in the world. Anyone that says he saw him as a threat has got to be kidding as McQueen was never threatened by anybody; at that stage his attitude was, 'Ah fuck it.' He was very laid-back and what you saw on screen was exactly his persona (in real life)."

Hoffman's superior range of acting skills did lead Steve to question whether the industry was moving away from the macho tough guys. Some years before, after a moment of deep contemplation, he asked Neile one evening after they had watched *The Graduate* together, 'What's going to happen to guys like (Paul) Newman and me?' And then he explained his reasoning, intimating that Hoffman offered something much different to Hollywood than what he and fellow blue-eyed boy Newman had been for the last decade or so. 'God, baby, I can't believe this guy's going to be a movie star, can you? I mean, he is one ugly cat. Good actor, yeah, but he sure is homely.'

Cinematographer Fred Koenekamp maintains the McQueen-Hoffman relationship was always very professional. "I thought they got along real well. I've heard the stories about them not getting on, but I disagree totally. As a cameraman you can't get any closer to the actors and I felt things couldn't have gone any smoother. I give Dustin a lot of credit because he's such a good actor; I feel he brought a lot out of Steve. When Steve and Dustin wanted to talk about something in the picture, they would get together in the evening and meet at Frank's house - that wasn't unusual. Like Steve, Dustin was also strong-minded who had his own ideas about the film too, which helped Steve to work harder. It was real healthy competition and they pushed each other to great heights."

Editor Swink, though, saw things from a different angle and he could sense a little bitterness on Hoffman's part. He recalled: "Dustin Hoffman used to come in to the projection room, usually before everyone else arrived, and look at the rushes every night. He and I would sit and talk about the film. I can remember him saying, 'I can't get the upper hand on Steve, I always try, but all he has to do is blink his eyes or scratch his ear and he takes the scene from me.' I sensed Dustin was slightly jealous of Steve, although there was no reason for him to be, because he did a hell of a job too. He just never had the same box-office appeal at that time like Steve did, who I think had a bit more charisma about him - people just seemed to like him better and Dustin knew it."

Swink could not recall Steve ever going to view the rushes, preferring instead to ride his motorcycle. Some directors would not have believed this, of the actor who *demanded* to see the dailies during *The Cincinnati Kid* - driving Norman Jewison to despair - a regular story of the old McQueen. Now though, in his early forties, he had matured as an actor and was more prepared to put his faith in the director. "By the time Steve did *Papillon*, it was a master-class," said LeVar Burton, who later worked with Steve on his final movie *The Hunter* and who had been a huge admirer of his films. "He went toe to toe with Dustin Hoffman, who was kicking butt, but Steve was right there in every frame. Steve was brilliant in *Papillon*. You couldn't get the better of Steve – he would out-honest you!"

Executive producer Emanuel Wolf concurs that on this movie it was Hoffman, certainly not McQueen, who was paranoid and insecure. "Dustin would sit there and study the dailies for an hour or two every day, watching what he had shot that day. He really was a professional and took his acting extremely seriously. But Dustin was kind of scared of Steve and was intimidated by him physically and by his manner also. Filming *Papillon* with Steve was quite unpleasant for him. He tried to avoid him as much as he could. On the other hand, Steve took a liking to Dustin and wanted to become buddies with him. The more Steve tried to be friendly, the more Dustin was hiding. I can think of an example of that frustration that was eating away at Dustin, during the last scene of the movie when Steve says goodbye to Dustin's character and they embrace. Well, Dustin had made his mind up that he was going to have some fun and bite Steve McQueen on the neck – and run. Either Dustin or Franklin Schaffner told me that, I can't remember who. But anyhow, when it came to the take he lost his courage and didn't go through with it."

While on location in Jamaica for the greater part of the picture, having already spent a month in Spain, Steve felt content with life alongside new love Ali MacGraw - whom he married on July 13, 1973. The couple lived in a traditional Jamaican house rented by the studio, with a garden filled with exotic flowers and they were afforded a personal cook to prepare native delights for them - usually fresh fish. Steve also had his weightlifting equipment moved in to keep him in shape and he was living his own version of paradise. As Ali recounted in her memoirs

Moving Pictures, life was sweet: "When we were not on the set we listened to music, took long walks in the woods and on the beach, and generally behaved like two people on a lazy honeymoon. Steve discovered the Jamaican beer Red Stripe, and ganja, and when he wasn't working he was very relaxed indeed."

Fred Koenekamp had not met Steve before *Papillon*, but he soon developed a good friendship with him. In Spain, things were still a little tense as producer Dorfmann scrambled to complete his financial obligations. But once those issues were settled, the atmosphere among cast and crew eased. "It took a little while for me to get to know Steve and vice-versa, though I never usually got too close to actors - but in the case of Steve, he and I really hit it off down there in Jamaica," Koenekamp said. "I liked the kind of person he was: he was macho - yes, he was a man's man, but he was a fun guy who enjoyed all the good things and fun in life. We were on the same wavelength." Away from the set, Saturday night parties became a regular thing and were seen as a good way to unwind from the strenuous six-day shooting schedule. Cast and crew members all took their turn as host. Koenekamp said: "The last party we had was actually thrown by Steve - it was a kind of wrap party and was a lot of fun. He was a darned good host and a great person to be around."

Prior to the fun and games in the Caribbean, those financial problems in Spain caused great tension and at one point even caused shooting to cease. McQueen and

Hoffman still received their pay as normal, but the others were affected by the hitch, as one of the executive producers backing the film failed to deliver the promised funds. Koenekamp recalled: "They gave us money to live on but our pay cheques never came through. People among the crew wanted to know what was going on, as they were ready to go home." Schaffner, though, reassured all concerned and promised that everything would work out okay. He was a man people trusted and when he displayed his faith in the movie, the spirit improved. The extra money was found from other sources, after editor Robert Swink constructed an eighteen-minute exploitation reel of footage from the film, with music added for exhibition purposes. Armed with the reel, Schaffner then went to Germany and France to unearth the required investors, which he did successfully. "That first month in Spain was spooky," Koenekamp admitted. "What you don't want to be doing when you're on location is sitting around - that costs money. It started out rough but finished terrific. Once all those problems settled down we had a wonderful time."

One of the more light-hearted scenes in the movie saw McQueen and Hoffman wrestling with an alligator (although the mouth was tied), when a prison guard orders them to kill it. Splashing around in the Jamaican mud swamps, the two stars looked more like Laurel and Hardy than two huge movie stars, such was the entertaining manner in which they approached the scene. Schaffner was perplexed at how to shoot the sequence, but it was the two stars of the picture that were in greater trouble. Fred Koenekamp witnessed events from close range: "Steve and Dustin really got into it, I was amazed. The conditions were so swampy and God damn awful with bugs and mosquitoes, but boy, when they started chasing that thing around and then it turned and started chasing them - it was crazy. Frankly, if the tail had whacked one of those guys it could have hurt them bad, but I suspect they loved every minute of it - Steve especially." The main prison camp used in Jamaica was a duplicate of the original one that Henri Charriere was at. The set decorator even copied the places where they slept. It was typical of a production where realism and authenticity was everything. The scenery at the beginning and end of the picture really *is* footage of Devil's Island. For the farewell sequence between Papillon and Dega, they used a carbon copy prison, because the real Devil's Island in French Guiana was said to be destroyed and crawling with rats.

When the location work was complete, *Papillon* hit the cutting room back in Los Angeles, where Swink worked tirelessly to edit and polish the final package, which was not an easy task. "We had a problem with length," Swink revealed. "I think we still released it too long, but it was such nice footage that we left it in. I don't know whether that worked for or against the picture." When in the cutting room, shortly after midday, Swink was visited by the director and Steve to check how things were progressing.

After their discussions McQueen suggested a spot of lunch at a local restaurant. Swink naturally agreed, thinking the hottest movie star in town who was paid $2million for *Papillon* and the director, who was paid $850,000, would foot the bill. Swink recalled: "We got to the diner and ate very well, but when the bill came Steve said, 'I've only got two dollars and I have to buy gas for my car to get home.' Schaffner then said he didn't bring any money, so I was the only one there with any cash and I got stung for the whole lunch. I thought it was funny that Steve McQueen - the biggest movie star in Hollywood - would be driving around with only a gallon of gas in his car and just two dollars in his pocket!"

This tight-fistedness was not an unusual claim against Steve. His tough background, post-reform school, post-marine corps, saw him hustling around night spots in New York, playing poker to earn his beer and spaghetti money. So when fame and wealth arrived, he sometimes had difficulties with financial generosity – though he could surprise.

Papillon was afforded two Premieres: an East Coast function in New York, which Steve did not attend, and one on the West Coast, when Steve attended with Ali MacGraw. Ironically, having banked his $2 million fee for the movie, and with a share of the revenues for the domestic sales, Steve's finances were well and truly back on track. However, this wealth and newfound security did not alter his old habits.

Says Wolf, "We laid on a beautiful suite at the Beverly Wilshire Hotel for Steve and Ali and a chauffeur-driven car, so they could be taken from the hotel to the theatre for the Premiere and then on to the party afterwards. Well, half an hour after the thing was supposed to start, everyone was there at the theatre apart from Steve and Ali. I'm getting real nervous by now and wondering what's going on. About then he pulls up outside of the theatre in his *own* car. We meet up inside and while I'm trying to get him to sit down so we can get on with the show, he starts telling me that he had gone out and spent a lot of money on his tuxedo for this function. 'Are you going to reimburse me for that?' he asks. I said, 'Fine Steve, we will reimburse you, just please sit down so we can see the movie.' Then he said, 'And what about Ali's dress?' Again I said, 'No problem, we will take care of it'. This conversation is going on with lots of people milling around nearby, and they are probably thinking we are having a real deep and technical debate about something to do with the film; not about his clothing costs! Anyway, later on in the night I discovered why Steve was late. I had got talking to the hotel manager and he revealed to me that Steve had insisted on downgrading his room from the suite to a small room as he thought he had to pay for it; and the same with the chauffeur-driven limousine. He didn't realise it was all paid for. We took it for granted that he knew he would be treated like the star that he undoubtedly was. The hotel manager did not feel it was his place to tell Steve and kept out of it, which you can't blame him for, especially as Steve was an intimidating guy and a huge movie star so he was naturally scared to question Steve's motives. I don't think Steve realised how intimidating his presence could be on people; not in a nasty way, just because he was such a big star. I'm not a psychologist but, because of his tough upbringing, I think he was uncomfortable in this sort of environment and in some ways did not feel deserving of this kind of lavish treatment."

Later that evening, at the Los Angeles Premiere, Dustin Hoffman's parents Harry and Lil came to understand why their son had experienced difficulty with the legend that was Steve McQueen. They had a long drive home but before making an early exit, they approached their friend Emanuel Wolf with a favour. He recalled: "I knew Dustin's Mum and Dad pretty well; they came as my guests and sat on my table. They came to me and said they would like to meet the star of the film, Steve McQueen, as they had never met him. At this time Steve was intensely involved in a conversation with Doctor Jonas Salk, the famous medical researcher, Jonas's wife and Ali MacGraw. I went over apologetically, interrupted Steve and asked if he could say a quick hello to Dustin's Mum and Dad, who were just leaving. Steve turned around and asked them, 'What's wrong with your son? He never returns my phone calls!' With that he got up and walked away. That was the lovely Steve McQueen at his charming best. But that's how Steve was. One second he's being gracious and nice and chatting with Doctor Salk and his wife. And when I introduce him to Dustin's Mum and Dad, he acts like that, with these nice, older people."

Despite the funding problems that *Papillon* encountered, the movie flourished at the box-office, earning in excess of $50 million, providing a healthy return to the investors who had demanded their chunk of the profits, not to mention to stakeholders like Allied Artists, McQueen, Schaffner and especially Dorfmann. Allied were innovative and aggressive with their marketing of the film: Shortly after *Papillon* opened on December 16, 1973, there was the Super Bowl at Rice Stadium in Houston, Texas between Minnesota Vikings and Miami Dolphins. Allied Artists opted to take the unprecedented step for a motion picture and buy the first advertisement at the Super Bowl, which set them back $250,000 for a 30 second commercial, and another $75,000 for producing the ad (these costs were additional to the $13.462 million production costs). Their tactics seemed to pay off as *Papillon* was the fourth-highest grossing picture that year behind (No.1) *The Exorcist*, (2) *The Sting* and (3) *Amercian Graffiti*. It was opened to 450 theatres domestically. Studio chief Wolf had seen their production of *Cabaret* earn ten Oscar nominations, yet *Papillon* was more successful than *Cabaret* commercially but received just one Academy Award for Best Original Score. Steve's powerful characterisation of Charriere was ignored by the Academy's panel of judges. "Whatever anyone might say about Steve, he and Dustin on this movie were pretty marvellous and should have received more recognition," said Wolf.

STEVE McQUEEN: THE COOLER KING

"Part of the reason was the antagonism that Steve had built up among the Academy members. Steve was not all that popular in some circles."

Allied Artists and Dorfmann should have been living off *Papillon* for years but they ended up in court over a television rights dispute. Says Wolf, "I did not like Mr Dorfmann. He was the main producer and had put together the basic elements like the book rights, the stars and the director. But he was a slippery slope, this guy. For example, when we sold the TV rights, it was a tremendous deal and probably would have been the biggest package ever on network television, with *Cabaret* and *Papillon* packaged together. We had all the distribution rights in the US and Canada yet Dorfmann went out and sold the rights that he did not have to CBS for network television. We got into a big lawsuit over it and he cost us and himself millions of dollars. The problem was we were a small network so I couldn't go and upset CBS even though they had bought the rights off Dorfmann illegitimately. It's a cottage industry and we didn't want to upset anyone so we had to do a compromise deal where all three major networks had certain broadcast rights to the movies. It obviously diluted the value quite a lot. We had a lot of money owing to Dorfmann, the son of a bitch, and so we got him round a table to settle everything. And when we had him face to face I turned to him and asked, 'Robert, why did you do this? This is the contract saying clearly what you have and what you get?' And he said, 'Manny, a contract is merely an agreement to agree.' I nearly hit the guy."

Youngsters in particular flocked to see the movie as it was an aspiring, anti-establishment film. Steve may not have been rewarded by the Academy (though he earned a Golden Globe nomination), but his performance left a strong impression on those that had previously doubted his acting skills. Fred Koenekamp reflected: "I've often thought that *Papillon* is the best thing that Steve ever did acting-wise." Script-writer Lorenzo Semple was another to admire his work. "After everything that had gone on before it and how Steve had acted, in any event *Papillon* was a great movie and Steve gave a wonderful performance. I couldn't imagine anybody else that could have done better."

Main Credits:

Cast: Steve McQueen (as Papillon), Dustin Hoffman, Victor Jory, Don Gordon, Anthony Zerbe, Robert Deman, Woodrow Parfrey, Bill Mumy, George Coulouris, Ratna Assan, William Smithers, Val Avery, Gregory Sierra, Vic Tayback, Mills Watson and more.

Director:	Franklin J. Schaffner
(Assistants)	Jose Lopez Rodero, Kuki Lopez Rodero

Producers:	Robert Dorfmann, Franklin J. Schaffner, Emanuel L. Wolfe (executive),
(Assistant Producer)	Robert O'Kaplan
Cinematographer:	Fred Koenekamp
Writers:	Dalton Trumbo and Lorenzo Semple Jr., based on the book by Henri Charriere
Editor:	Robert Swink
Wardrobe:	Mickey Sherrard, Tony Pueo
Make-Up:	Charles Schram
Music:	Jerry Goldsmith

REVIEWS:

VARIETY, December 12th, 1973

McQueen has thrown himself into the part with at least as much verve as he did for Robert Wise in *The Sand Pebbles*, and with equally strong results. That is likely no accident, for both directors are noted for going beyond the superficial. In McQueen's more conventional films, there is enough running and jumping and action to gloss over the character loopholes. Herein, and as much as the script allows, McQueen has become Charriere, in an outstanding performance.

FILMS & FILMING, April, 1974

Steve McQueen has never acted better than he does as Charriere...From an initial sturdiness, we watch the man lose physical stamina, and McQueen makes us believe that he is really losing it. The best sequence in the whole film is Charriere's first long spell of solitary confinement, when the actor's known personality is merged remarkably with the grit of the person he portrays, exercising in the cell and forcing down unpalatable food to keep up his strength and his will to escape.

Steve only came into *The Towering Inferno* halfway through
the film but, according to colleagues, he made such
an impact that it never mattered
(COURTESY: 20th CENTURY FOX / WARNER BROS / BFI)

THE TOWERING INFERNO

(20th Century Fox-Warner Bros) 1974

'After Steve's tiny part in Somebody Up There Likes Me, he was very happy about the fact that he was vying for top billing with Paul Newman. He got a real kick out of that'
– Robert Vaughn

IRWIN ALLEN'S PRODUCTION of *The Towering Inferno* is regarded as one of the greatest disaster movies of all time. With an all-star cast, all-action drama and impressive special effects, it ranks alongside its genre contemporaries such as *The Poseidon Adventure* (also by Allen), *Jaws* and the more recent *Titanic*. Financed by 20th Century Fox and Warner Brothers, it had the financial muscle to assemble a greatly distinguished cast. Initially both studios were meeting for a head-on collision, but they decided to combine their respective projects - *The Glass Inferno* by Thomas M. Scortia and Frank M. Robinson, and *The Tower* by Richard Martin Stern. Two disaster films competing against one another, both about blazing tower blocks, could never have enjoyed prolonged box-office success, so it became logical for the two production giants to team up. In doing so, they could afford to sign one of the most celebrated casts ever and pay Steve McQueen $1 million plus 7.5 per cent of the gross profits – his most lucrative pay cheque ever, including future residual payments. The cast included Robert Vaughn, Fred Astaire (who earned an Academy Award nomination for Best Supporting Actor), William Holden, Faye Dunaway, Robert Wagner, Jennifer Jones, Richard Chamberlain, Susan Blakely, O.J. Simpson and Paul Newman – who shared top billing with Steve.

The professional relationship between McQueen and Newman was a significant hidden agenda that lent so much to the film. Casting the two most celebrated and exciting screen actors of their time was always going to be a sure bet for success. Since 1956, when Steve was a $19 a day extra in *Somebody Up There Likes Me* - when Newman had top billing, Steve always aspired to the moment he would be viewed on the same level as Newman. It wasn't out of dislike or jealousy; his feelings were borne purely out of a natural, tenacious desire to be an equal. He even insisted that 12 more lines of dialogue be added to his character in *The Towering Inferno* so that he and Newman would have the same amount of lines. Curious, given that he spent most of his career trying to lose lines, and react instead.

Co-star Robert Vaughn said: "After Steve's tiny part in *Somebody Up There Likes Me*, he was very happy about the fact that he was vying for top billing with Paul. He got a real kick out of that." After hits like *The Sand Pebbles*, *Bullitt* and *Papillon*, McQueen had been as big a star as Newman for the previous decade, though he had to actually share the same space as Newman before he could believe, himself, that he was as big. Such illustrates the respect he had for Newman - who was five years his senior - as he forever measured his own acting ability and stardom against his rival. "McQueen was just naturally competitive with everybody – I mean absolutely everybody," says close friend Don Gordon, who also co-starred *in The Towering Inferno*. "Paul was more laid-back, a wonderful man and Steve appreciated him and liked him. He respected Paul's talent." Vaughn agreed: "They got along very well. They were friendly and were joking a lot. I think Steve was very happy at this time and not just because he finally got to share top billing with Paul; he had just married Ali MacGraw and I could sense that he was happy at that time."

Steve and Paul formed the modern-day 'tough guy' duo, just like Cagney and Bogart had captivated audiences years earlier. Both were macho, both could bring steel to a character with the minimal amount of effort. It was a studio's dream-ticket to line up these guys on the same picture, and the results were inevitably successful, reflected by Steve's eventual earnings from the film of around $14 million. Steve therefore was able to take things easy after this movie and he even considered retiring.

"They were two different kinds of actors," noted Jeff Corey, who appeared with Steve in *The Cincinnati Kid* and with Paul in *Butch Cassidy and The Sundance Kid*. "There was a wildness in Steve that served him well, but Paul was laid-back by nature and he knew how to make that work for him. They were both very gifted. Steve was really ballsy and he liked working with his own, strong, masculinity and libido – people found that attractive. Paul, who was another speed demon, was also exciting on screen without being outwardly macho - like Steve." The two stars linked up perfectly, according to Fred Koenekamp, who won the Academy Award for Best Cinematography. "I thought they complimented each other because they both have different styles, with Paul the more serious-minded while Steve is purely macho – he loved being that Fire Chief." Assistant director Newt Arnold believes the picture would have been equally successful if the casting had been different. "If you inverted the roles of Steve and Paul, you would still have had two excellent performances. Either one of them could have played any of the two parts. They were that good."

The one aspect that constantly surfaced in Steve's career was how well suited he was to the majority of his characters. Nobody could have played any better the surly, anti-establishment soldier in *Hell Is for Heroes*, the cocky, wise-cracking prisoner *in The Great Escape*, the super-cool, non-conformist cop in *Bullitt* or even the tough sailor in *The Sand Pebbles*. *The Towering Inferno* was another example. He played the Fire Chief and was very convincing in the kind of macho role that he was synonymous with. As Chief Michael O'Hallorhan, Steve is introduced mid-way through the movie – an initial concern of his – helping his crews fight a blazing 138-storey tower block, designed by an architect played by Newman. As the fire spreads, Newman joins forces with McQueen, to combat the unrelenting inferno that was caused by an electrical fault. Steve was initially offered the role of the architect but felt he was more suited to the Fire Chief. And he knew how to best project himself in the movie.

Says co-star Susan Blakely, "Steve asked for the brim on his fireman's helmet to be cut back as he didn't want his bright blue eyes to be shadowed! He was told by the wardrobe department that if they changed his they would have to change everyone's. To which he replied, 'then change 'em!' Steve really knew what worked for him."

Steve took an excitable relish from the research involved in getting into character. He was assigned personal assistance in the shape of Peter Lucarelli, a Battalion Chief of the Los Angeles City Fire Department. Lucarelli, one of the movie's credited technical advisers, was not paid a salary for his expertise and had to use up his annual vacation allowance to spend such a long time in pre-production and on the movie shoot, which totalled around 70 days from May to October of 1974. It was not unusual for him to be with Steve or on the set for ten hours and then have to go into work and turn in a long shift with the LAFD. But his experiences with Steve McQueen rewarded him enough, as his student was appreciative of his advice and a keen pupil who was intent on doing justice to the Fire Service as a profession, by being as realistic as possible with his portrayal of the Fire Chief.

Steve and Paul Newman could have shared top billing on
Butch Cassidy and the Sundance Kid had they not disagreed on
the billing. But they came together five years later as two of
the biggest movie stars of their time
(COURTESY: 20th CENTURY FOX / WARNER BROS /
THE KOBAL COLLECTION)

"Our first encounter was in a production meeting in Irwin Allen's office at the 20th Century Fox Studios in Hollywood," Lucarelli recalled. "All of the producers, directors, writers, set designers and other key staff were in attendance. Steve was getting measured in Wardrobe and Irwin had asked him to stop by to specifically meet me and to briefly discuss our relationship during the production. When Steve walked into the room, there was that aura that indicates that someone special is in our midst and one could actually sense his impact on all in attendance. Steve was in casual clothes: denim jeans, tennis shoes, long sleeve collared shirt – and had a full growth beard and long hair. After introductions, Steve asked to talk with me and we left the main meeting room for a small office to chat.

"Steve must have sensed something in my eyes as he quickly indicated that the beard would come off and long hair cut for the movie. He explained that he needed the 'disguise' so that he could lead a somewhat normal life in public. He was extremely personable and friendly. We discussed my experience in the Fire Service and how it would relate to the movie. He was relaxed and indicated that he looked forward to our relationship during the production and asked me to make him one promise. He asked that anytime during the production that he was doing something in his role that would make the public laugh or think less of the fire-fighting profession, he wanted me to immediately notify him. Of course, he had my promise and gratitude for his approach to his role as a Fire Chief.

"Steve was perfect for the role. His popularity, acting ability and commitment to delivering the message was outstanding. I saw my involvement as an opportunity to get some very important life safety issues to the public regarding fires in high-rise buildings. Steve was totally on-board with the safety measures and was very serious that the public absorbed the messages. While there was some theatrical licence that had to be implemented in certain scenes, I believe that the reaction and feedback from the public was positive."

Lucarelli kept his promise to Steve and never failed to hide his discomfort if ever he thought a scene was being set up in a way that was more Hollywood than reality. Steve hated anything phoney and was always committed to authenticity. Despite their personal agreement, producer Irwin Allen was not always so pleased with Lucarelli's trained eye that identified drama over reality (though Allen did always put the safety of cast and crew before anything). On the very first day of filming, Steve and Paul Newman were in the room where the water storage tanks were located above the blaze. They were setting C-4 charges to blow up the tanks and thus put out the fire. Lucarelli was standing next to director John Guillermin and during the middle of the scene, Steve stood up and yelled 'Cut'. He walked over to his Fire Service adviser and asked what was wrong, for he intuitively saw a look on Lucarelli's face that indicated he was not comfortable with the scene. Lucarelli told Steve that with the amount of fire that was supposed to be below them in the building, there was not enough smoke in the scene to make it realistic. Irwin Allen was soon in on the debate and Steve quickly explained to the producer what the issue was and left for his dressing room, expecting things to be put right. An exasperated Allen invited Lucarelli to take a walk around the sound stage with him. He put his arm around his shoulders and diplomatically said how he appreciated his observations, but shared that he had over $14 million invested in the movie and that his two most expensive investments, McQueen and Newman, were key to obtaining a healthy return. "So Chief," Allen said to Lucarelli, "if people can't see Paul Newman's and Steve McQueen's infamous blue eyes because there's too much smoke, we are not going to sell any f****** tickets. Do you understand?" Lucarelli understood but pointed out his earlier promise to Steve. "Irwin was keen for us to work together and he persuaded me to agree to some theatrical licence and I accepted this. Irwin was somewhat intimidated by Steve and I did occasionally receive phone calls from him late at night to discuss the next day's shooting schedule, asking if I observed any issues for Steve with the script."

Never had Steve felt more at home with a role. Cinematographer Fred Koenekamp, who had made a good friendship with Steve on *Papillon* the previous year, recalled when Steve interrupted a pre-production meeting to speed off to a major fire that had broken out at Samuel Goldwyn

Studios in Hollywood. "He was keen to get involved and learn the ins and outs of the job. He really got a kick out of those moments. Consequently, he knew his character inside out and he worked really hard to make a success of the picture."

It was Steve who brought the blaze to the attention of Lucarelli, who was attending a meeting in Irwin Allen's office. The lead star called Lucarelli at the producer's office and informed him of the fire and asked if he and Ali could ride along with him to the incident. Steve was on the lot in Wardrobe while being fitted for his uniforms, but on hearing of the blaze, there was only one thing he wanted to do and it had nothing to do with his costume. He drove to the production meeting, with his disguise beard now gone and sporting a new haircut, and he and Ali jumped into Lucarelli's two-door Toyota Corona before heading off to the fire. It was a very serious incident and by the time they reached the blaze, a large sound stage had already been completely destroyed and the fire was extending into a two-storey office building that was adjacent to the sound stage.

"I took Steve and Ali to the LAFD command post and we observed the actions that were taking place and I explained to Steve why and how the tactics were being utilized and deployed," Lucarelli recalled. "He was taking it all in and asking excellent questions. Then he asked me if he could go into the building with the fire-fighters. At that point, I observed

the fire was pretty much confined to the attic of the building and the fire-fighters were making good progress. I borrowed some protective gear from an Engineer who was oper-
ating a pumper. I found a very experienced Captain who had
worked for me and was about to enter the operations on the
second floor and asked him to take Steve with him and keep
a very close eye on him. Steve and the Captain climbed a fire
ladder into a second floor window and proceeded to join in
attacking the overhead fire. Within ten minutes the fire was
extinguished and most of the office building had been saved
from total ruin. I was with Ali at the command post and
closely monitored, through radio communications, the activities in the overall fire and especially what was happening on
the second floor of the office building. Steve emerged at the
second floor window with a huge smile, though somewhat
sooty-faced, and quickly descended the ladder to the command post." Around this time a photographer took photos
of Steve and one of those pictures appeared in the next issue
of Time. When Irwin Allen became aware of what happened
at the fire, he was furious and let his technical adviser know
in no uncertain terms. Lucarelli accepted he was wrong to
allow Steve to enter the burning building though the megastar would have been hard to say 'no' to. Allen explained that
if something had happened to Steve it could have massively
impacted the production, and at a very high cost, too. While
Lucarelli knew he was wrong he also knew Steve was in
safe hands and had used his own experience to ascertain the

level of danger. Steve was desperate for a 'debrief' on his first fire-fight later that evening.

"Steve indicated to me that he was very hungry, which is very common among fire-fighters after being involved in a blaze and he asked if I could join he and Ali for dinner before we went back to Fox Studios to retrieve his vehicle," Lucarelli remembered. "We piled back into my Toyota and headed for Melrose Avenue and one of the best Italian res-taurants in Los Angeles. We were early for what is consid-ered the dinner hour. As we pulled up to the valet parking station, the Toyota received very little attention – until Ali and Steve got out. He shared with me that he and Ali visited the restaurant often. We were led to a nice private booth. I could detect the odour of smoke from Steve's clothes and after he cleaned up, we had a nice dinner. Steve was still exuberant and recounted with pride going down the hall-way with the crew and pulling down a ceiling to make sure that the fire did not get behind them and trap their exit. He shared the feeling of having hot water cascade down from the attic area and how he worked his way onto the attack fire hose line that was knocking down the fire. After the dinner and taking Steve and Ali back to the studio, I reported to my command and worked the balance of the shift until eight the next morning!"

Although an exceptional cast had been assembled for this film, it can sometimes be counter-productive, as big stars rarely enjoy sharing the limelight. This can cause fierce competition on a set. There were rumours of some jealousies boiling over, particularly William Holden, but there were no unsavoury incidents according to Koenekamp. "I never felt there was any competitiveness amongst the cast, mainly because there were about six really big stars who all had completely different roles to play; not like on *Papillon* where they're all prisoners. The spirit on this film was not as close purely because we all went home after work as the majority of the movie was filmed in Hollywood. Only the outdoor sequences were filmed on location in San Francisco. On location there's more a chance of bonding with the cast and crew as you may have a drink or have dinner together."

Co-star Susan Blakeley concurred: "There was a good camaraderie. Paul Newman especially had a fabulous sense of humour and style about him; he was such a generous actor to be around. He had a place on the beach in San Francisco that he rented out and he invited us all out there. Most of the cast went along and it was a real fun occasion. Paul was so friendly and outgoing. For someone of his stature I was just so impressed that he included everyone like that in his social life. Paul was always so nice to everybody who came up to him."

Steve did 'friendly' in his own way. He may not have been as outwardly smiley and jovial as Newman but he did charm people in his own, cool, man-of-few-words way. Blakely recalled how he shrewdly and helpfully advised her during their first meet. "I met Steve right at the beginning when I was introduced to Irwin Allen and then again when I went for a make-up test early on. Irwin wanted me to wear my hair down but I felt that because I was playing the daughter of a wealthy businessman (Holden) and was being cheated on by Richard Chamberlain's character, I should have a certain down-dressed look that probably didn't show off my best features. So I looked slightly dowdy. I took things way too seriously and the first thing that Steve said to me was, 'You don't have to have them make you look like that.' I explained to Steve that my look was totally my choice and he looked at me like I was an idiot and of course he was right. His take was, 'What are you doing kid, play up your assets.' Steve was smart and was looking out for me in his own way as he knew it would be a popular movie and it was a chance to get people to like me. But I just didn't think like that in those days – I was a model fresh out of New York and didn't have a clue about the industry. But Steve was just so savvy about what it meant and took to be a movie star. He wanted me to look sexier and cuter and he was right."

The very presence of McQueen and Newman, along with the other star names, was one of the reasons why the young Blakely accepted the part. She added: "I only got the part as a replacement so I was literally thrown in. If I had time to read the script I probably would have turned it down. But as soon as they said Steve McQueen and Paul Newman are in it, I couldn't agree quickly enough. Paul Newman was my major crush growing up so I was very shy around him.

But he put me at ease very quickly; he was such a generous human being. It was difficult for me because I was shy so to be surrounded by so many of these great actors... I was not exactly speaking up; I was in awe and felt inhibited. Fred Astaire was so friendly and so humble. It was funny because during making the film I saw a Fred Astaire movie package in my hotel room. When I returned to the set I could barely speak to him!"

Precautions were taken to prevent any potential movie star tantrums. To make sure nobody felt slighted with regard to the size of their dressing room, the studios decided to have fifteen identical dressing rooms built – all with a toilet, a sink, a bed and so on. One media story that surfaced, though, told how William Holden felt undermined by his one-dimensional part, which consisted mainly of rushing around the roof-top restaurant, comforting guests and answering the telephone for updates of the inferno's behaviour. It was also reported that Holden didn't particularly appreciate third billing behind two younger actors than he. Assistant director Newt Arnold refuted these rumours. "Bill Holden was a joy to work with. He was never unhappy at having two younger guys cast above him. He knew what was what and what his character was all about in the picture. His supposed unhappiness was never an issue and was never demonstrated in his personal attitude. He got along beautifully with everyone. Those stories just prove the desperation of the Press in trying to concoct problems that just didn't occur."

The one undoubted personality clash that did occur on the movie was between producer Irwin Allen and director John Guillermin. "Maybe it was professional jealousy, but Irwin always wanted people to know that he was the producer and in charge of things," Arnold observed. "Irwin was terrific at producing movies, but he wasn't as good at dealing with people."

For Steve, once he had his initial pay and script demands adhered to, there was no conflict with anybody. The only issue he was adamant about was getting first billing ahead of Paul Newman. However, this was something Newman could not accept. Subsequently, it was agreed they would share top billing with Steve's name appearing first on the left-hand side of the screen and Paul's slightly higher on the right. The laid-back Newman was more carefree about whichever option he ended up with and the final decision of the billing placement was down to Steve, being led by the advice of his agent Freddie Fields. "I personally thought Paul had the better credit as his name was higher but people look at it differently," commented Susan Blakely. "Ultimately, they both knew the movie would be good for them because it would be a populist kind of picture, not to mention their record-breaking salaries."

The picture was a huge, financial hit for Steve, but he earned his money sincerely, executing a great deal of his own stunts once again. Along with Newman, he featured in the climax sequence of the movie, when it is decided the best method to quell the blaze is to blow up the water tanks above the restaurant and suffocate the fire with 10,000 gal-lons of water. It was a precarious stunt and was a potential danger with such an amount of water involved. "We had a wonderful special effects crew and it was beautifully set up and pre-rehearsed, pre-discussed and everybody knew what was going to happen and when," Newt Arnold said. "There's always a potential hazard when you're dealing with materials like that, but Steve and Paul loved every minute of it."

At 44, Steve was by now a Hollywood veteran. It was a good time for him professionally and financially. *Inferno* was his third straight hit at the box-office and he now had enough cash to not have to worry about working again, taking his cut of the gross profits into consideration. "From 1974 to the time he died, Steve hardly worked," Robert Vaughn said. "I think he basically lived off the profits from *The Towering Inferno* as he had a great big percentage."

Although the picture was a harmonious experience for Steve and everyone connected with it, there was one distress-ing event during the making of the picture that affected Steve greatly, but it had nothing to do with the movie. Steve was tak-ing a rest with Ali MacGraw in between scenes one day on the lot at 20th Century Fox when something terrible happened: both sitting next to one another, Ali looked down to find she was sitting in a pool of blood. Steve frantically rushed her to the nearest hospital to discover that Ali had had a miscarriage. They were unaware of the pregnancy. Says Ali, "It was very disturbing, and Steve in particular was very upset. He always felt that if we had a child, we could save our marriage." After the miscarriage, their relationship gradually degenerated. At this time they were sharing their luxury beach house in Trancas, northern Malibu with Steve's son Chad and Ali's son Joshua.

One of their neighbours was Ryan O'Neal, who had starred opposite Ali in the smash hit *Love Story* in 1970, and who also made *Driver* in 1978, which Steve turned down. On one visit to O'Neal's home in 1975, the two opinionated actors almost came to blows after one of Steve's most significant career choices was pointedly questioned.

Says PR mogul Steve Jaffe, who was present during the heated conversation: "It was only the second time I had met Steve after accompanying him and his family to the Academy Awards in 1971. This time we were at Ryan's house on Carbon Beach in Malibu, on the Pacific Coast Highway. Ryan and Steve had this very spirited discussion on films. Around this time, I believe Ryan was preparing to make *Barry Lyndon* with Stanley Kubrick. Anyway, this discussion became quite fraught when Ryan confronted Steve by saying, 'Why did you do that picture, *The Towering Inferno*?' The implication was that it was beneath a big star to do a film like that. The question gave no credence to the fact that Paul Newman and all the other great stars that were in it also did the film. McQueen was really angry at this question and I genuinely thought he was going to hit Ryan. He took a deep breath, calmed down, stepped back and said, 'I did it for my kids' annuity.' That was his defence. It certainly was not a kind thing for Ryan to say and Steve was embarrassed. I personally just thought it was a nice thing what Steve did for his kids. He really took care of his family and, though he would not have had any concept that he would die early at this point, he knew this movie would give a chunk of money to his family that would make things easier on them."

With Steve's career at an all-time financial high and with Ali just about content as housewife and mother, putting her career on a prolonged hold, it should have been happy days for them. However, such a scenario facilitated a time in Steve's life when things stagnated - his marriage, his career, his life. *The Towering Inferno* was the last major film that Steve made for five years. On his return to movie making and after an inevitable divorce (that officially went through in 1978), his vibrancy was gone and the old McQueen spark was lost forever.

Main Credits:

Cast: Steve McQueen (as Fire Chief Michael O'Hallorhan), Paul Newman, William Holden, Faye Dunaway, Fred Astaire, Susan Blakely, Richard Chamberlain, Jennifer Jones, O.J. Simpson, Robert Vaughn, Robert Wagner, Susan Flannery, Sheila Mathews, Norman Burton, Jack Collins, Don Gordon, Felton Perry, Gregory Sierra and more.

Director:	John Guillermin
(Assistant)	Newt Arnold
Producer:	Irwin Allen

(Associate Producer) Sidney Marshall

Cinematographer: Fred J. Koenekamp

Writer: Stirling Silliphant, based on the novels *The Tower* by Richard Martin Stern, and *The Glass Inferno* by Thomas N. Scortia and Frank M. Robinson

Editors: Carl Kress, Harold F. Kress

Wardrobe: Paul Zastupnevich (designer)

Make-Up: Emile LaVigne, Monte Westmore

Music: John Williams

REVIEWS:

VARIETY, December 18th, 1974

Within the action-adventure spectrum is located the disaster, or multiple-jeopardy picture – call it what you will – and one of the greatest yet made is *The Towering Inferno*...McQueen and Newman are perfect in their roles.

MOVIE, December, 1974

There are a lot of stars in *The Towering Inferno* and they are an exceptionally charismatic lot. This is not an opinion of Newman, McQueen, Dunaway and the rest, but merely factual – they are major stars and it is part of the phenomenon of stars that people identify with them. If these identification figures are in peril, you feel the peril too...Casting both Paul Newman and Steve McQueen is a masterstroke. Throughout the film we see pairs of dauntless, piercing blue eyes. They come to constitute a central motif in the film. Those eyes are a feature of Newman and McQueen's images, but meaningfully exchanged looks between men are an important element in the narrative of *The Towering Inferno*.

Steve in a scene with Swedish co-star Bibi Andersson. This
peculiar choice for a movie by Steve won respect for his
bravery in opting for a film quite unlike anything he had
acted in before, but it was largely criticised as
being too 'un-McQueen-like'
(COURTESY: WARNER BROS / THE KOBAL COLLECTION)

An Enemy of the People

(First Artists-Warner Bros) 1978

'I sometimes feel that people get carried away when they say how difficult Steve McQueen was. Being difficult can translate as being very professional, which is how I viewed him'
– William Tuttle

THE WEIGHTY PERCENTAGE that Steve received from the gross profits of *The Towering Inferno* afforded him not only a wealth in dollars but a lifestyle that was totally free of work pressures. He had made enough money from that one movie to allow him to lead a life of complete tranquillity and solitude, devoid of his reluctant connections with Hollywood. He lived a withdrawn lifestyle for two years after *Inferno,* almost like that of a hermit. So long as he was surrounded by his beloved family, Steve was happy. Steve resided at his beautiful beach house in Trancas, in northern Malibu with Ali, Chad and Ali's son Joshua, and didn't want anything to do with bright lights and rolling cameras. He also saw his daughter,

Terry, frequently as she stayed with Neile after the divorce. Steve simply cherished his peaceful existence where he was bothered by nobody and could just wander the Trancas market unnoticed, with a bottle of his favourite beer in his hand and contentment in his heart. New scripts still came in, but his crazy take-it-or-leave-it demands of at least a $3 million fee and $1 million to merely read the script frightened most producers off.

One industry figure who was faced with McQueen's ultimatum was Francis Ford Coppola. He approached McQueen for the lead part in *Apocalypse Now* in 1975. After being offered $1.5 million, McQueen accepted but then asked for the same amount on completion. When they inevitably failed to agree terms and location schedules, Coppola suggested a smaller role that would consist of just three weeks work. "Okay," said McQueen, "but my price still stands!" He wanted $3 million for just three weeks trade. This was Steve's way of saying, 'Look, I'm not too bothered whether I get the part or not. I don't need the work.' He was happy with the life he had and acting was not important to him at this point. That was until his beach-bum-style existence became unbearable for Ali, who was the dutiful wife throughout and turned down all work offered her because that was Steve's wish. Ali's eventual outburst of frustration had the desired effect and pushed Steve into work again. He decided on an unusual property to return with: Henrik Ibsen's 1882 play, *An Enemy of the People*, which he planned to adapt for the screen.

Under the guise of First Artists, the production company he shared with Barbara Streisand, Paul Newman, Dustin Hoffman and Sidney Poitier, Steve poured himself into this project, which many observers thought inappropriate and too literate for Steve McQueen. Like with *The Thomas Crown Affair*, all the negative vibes just fuelled his spirit to prove the doubters wrong. Warner Brothers took on the major financial responsibilities, and it was to be a move they very much regretted. People were used to McQueen as the cool, macho, tough; what they saw in this film was an overweight, heavily bearded McQueen who looked beyond his 46 years.

"First Artists and Warner Brothers both wanted him to do another all-action movie," commented editor Sheldon Kahn. "They weren't ready for Steve to do an Ibsen adaptation, even though Steve could do anything he wanted according to his contract. So I don't think the studios were 100 per cent behind this picture. We didn't even preview the picture to get an audience's reaction (which was normal practice) in the event, after we had finishing shooting and editing. Simply, people just wanted to see Steve in a war movie, riding his motorcycle, trying to get away from the Nazis. They weren't ready for him to do a serious role or the kind of picture that *An Enemy of the People* was."

Steve knew the film was a massive gamble and that it might be the biggest mistake he ever made; but that didn't seem important to him. What *was* important was the theme and the classic material that he knew would stretch his acting skills. Under the direction of George Schaefer, he plays

Thomas Stockmann, a doctor in a small Norwegian village. He discovers that the town's 'healing waters' have been polluted by harmful wastes from a local tannery. He promptly sets out on a one man crusade to tell the whole village in hope that his findings will be heard. Led by a mayor (played by Charles Durning) who thinks with his pocket, the town's people turn against Stockmann and wish his outburst to remain under the proverbial carpet, as such a controversy would surely reach tourists and cost the village substantial income from this essential trade. It becomes the familiar tale of how monetary greed can cloud people's minds even when health is at stake. The mayor continues to disparage Stockmann's findings and encourages the villagers to turn against him, making him 'The Enemy of the People'. Eventual repercussions see his home stoned, his wife (played by Swedish actress Bibi Andersson) insulted and his children also impacted by the scandal that Stockmann refuses to ignore, much to his cost. McQueen fell in love with the ethics of this one man fighting the whole establishment. Steve was constantly attracted to the underdog or to the man fighting a hierarchy.

Sheldon Kahn revealed that Steve was well aware of the opposition and negativity surrounding his choosing of this picture. Kahn had been hired to the movie but was informed by producer Phil Parslow that he just needed to meet with Steve to rubberstamp his appointment. It was a painless exercise for the youngster, who had made his name on *One Flew Over the Cuckoo's Nest*, but it was also a revealing one as Steve spoke of the difficulty he would have in opening people's minds to accept him in such a different role; compared to Frank Bullitt or Captain Virgil Hilts.

"I had to visit Steve in his trailer on the lot and this was a big thing for me then as *Papillon* was one of my favourite movies, and *The Great Escape* also," Kahn recalled. "Those two pictures come to my mind like, boom, automatically when I think of Steve. I remember when I saw *Papillion*, I was just so impressed with his performance, and Dustin Hoffman's too. I was blown away and have never understood why Steve was not even nominated for an Academy Award for that picture. That was how I viewed Steve then but he knew that was how everyone else saw him.

"When we came to chat in his trailer Steve did most of the talking. He told me how he saw this movie, how he saw his role and what he was looking for in the story. He knew that the people who had gone to all his movies might not be in favour of seeing him do this part as the good doctor. He knew it was a gamble, but he wanted to do it and he had the right under his contract with First Artists to do it, so he did it. I sat there and agreed with him as I had read the story many years ago and I thought he was absolutely right in what direction he wanted to go. I was quietly munching on a carrot and after ten or 15 minutes Steve said, 'I like you very much and they like you so I would like you to do the picture.' That was the start of my relationship with Steve."

Despite the similarities between McQueen and Stockmann, his unfamiliar appearance and the incongruous vehicle which he chose as his comeback movie after *The Towering Inferno*, combined to form a sure box-office bomb. Swedish co-star Bibi Andersson, getting her first break in a Hollywood production, was a little surprised at Steve's decision to produce an Ibsen story. "I assumed that the only reason why he had chosen this play was because of the title, as he was a rebellious person himself," she said. "He obviously wanted to prove to people that he could do Ibsen as well as his normal action films, which he did as well as anyone." Bibi not only felt puzzled at Steve's choice to make *An Enemy of the People*; she was also perplexed why a good looking actor famous for his rugged charm would want to conceal his face. Says Andersson, "I had seen a few of Steve's movies before I met him but not that many. I always thought he was very sexy and very handsome, which is why I couldn't understand why he wanted to cover his face in this film with that great big beard. It was very stupid of him to have that beard, because people need to see a star's face, especially when you are as big a movie star as Steve was. In this film he relied too much on using his eyes to act; you need more than that. However, it was certainly very courageous of him; maybe he thought the beard made him look more Norwegian!"

Actress and model Barbara Leigh had not seen Steve since they split, amicably, following their romance before, during and after the filming of *Junior Bonner* in 1971. But Steve surprised her with a call out of nowhere with an invitation for her to go and visit him, while he was preparing to make *Enemy*. He was staying at the Beverly Wilshire Hotel in Los Angles at the time: Leigh was stunned by the appearance of the aged, overweight, bearded man who opened the door of his room to her. "That was the last time I saw Steve, when he was preparing for *An Enemy of the People*," she said. "He was in a strange place – he looked like Heidi's grandfather on the Swiss mountains. But that's not how I care to remember him. When I think of Steve, I remember him as the man alone with me in his rented house at the foot of Prescott Mountains hanging out laughing, loving and of us being a happy, normal couple."

Right from the beginning of preparations on the picture, Steve, as executive producer, was the overriding influence connected with the project. He assigned George Schaefer as director and instructed him to hire the best talent available to befit such a literate property. It was an extremely brave move by Steve given that he hadn't acted in a theatre-like production since *A Hatful of Rain* in 1956. Schaefer warned him of the dangers that his co-stars could very well steal the film from beneath him with their superior experience with such expansive material. "If I can't cut it, it'll be my funeral," Steve exclaimed fearlessly.

Ultimately, it was Steve's production company making the film so he wanted his co-stars to stand out, even if they were superior to him. McQueen could be a devious, clever actor who knew how to steal scenes and win fans but he also knew when his co-stars were making a film he was connected with, better. Rather like the way Frank Sinatra had acted when Steve was the hungry co-star in *Never So Few*. Roles had now reversed.

His determination to make an overwhelming success of the picture was never in doubt; the end result, though, was way short of even the most modest expectations. Bibi Andersson felt Steve was too inflexible on the set and too proud to hear ideas from his colleagues. She recalled: "We rehearsed for three weeks and in that time I remember once when I wanted to talk something over with Steve and Schaefer. I approached them and Steve got very angry and said, 'You're not Bergman and you're not in Sweden now - this is Hollywood!' He basically told me shut up and be quiet, which I didn't like very much. I understand that once you're shooting for real you don't want to be experimenting, but this was rehearsals and the time to try things out. I had done plays and had read Ibsen and I felt that I had something to offer, but no one really wanted to listen. I pointed out to Steve that it concerned him too and eventually he listened. I didn't realise that he was deaf in one ear and because of this he would sometimes mis-interpret things. I think that was one of the things that made him a little paranoid about situations.

"When he wanted to be, though, he could also be very sweet. There was a time during the film when I was feeling very down and missing home; the whole Hollywood thing was not really an enjoyable experience for me. Steve saw that I was down and the very next day he bought me this ten-gear bicycle so that I could ride it around the lot. That was the other, sweet, caring side to him. He was basically a very nice man away from work and very sweet. Even on the lot he could be very nice, once he got over his paranoia. Steve was too over-sensitive and it didn't suit him at all."

On that two-sidedness to Steve's character, Sheldon Kahn added: "That was Steve; he could be complex like that but he's also one of the nicest people I have ever met in the industry. When we finished the movie and were almost done with the dubbing and mixing, he gave me his black push bike that he used to ride around the studio. That was a nice little gift and I thought it was very generous of him." The only occasion when Steve took a more serious, disapproving attitude with Kahn was when the young editor was nominated for an award in Britain for his work on *One Flew Over the Cuckoo's Nest*. "I wanted to go over to the UK but Steve said he didn't want me to go because we were in the final throes of *An Enemy of the People* and he needed me around so I didn't go. Although it would have been a wonderful trip, I understood his reasons and didn't go. Steve was just passionate about us all making this picture the best it could be and I accepted that."

After *The Towering Inferno*, McQueen's fans had to wait nearly four years for his follow-up due to his sabbatical, and the eventual glimpse after all that time was a major shock, or, nearer the truth, a major disappointment. The role was a great departure for Steve and in trying to put the ghost to rest that he could not do properties other than action-adventure pictures, he became a victim of his own success. Steve, though, was an immensely principled person and even when his career and reputation was on the line, he remained true to his beliefs about what he wanted to do and what the material stood for.

An Enemy of the People promised to be rewarding professionally but never financially. Indeed, many studios would not go near the film, believing it to be lacking significantly in box-office potential. Warner Brothers failed to try and make it work, after the picture was shot in Hollywood in 1976. They decided to shelve the picture from mass distribution for eighteen months, which was a ruthless decision but one which Warner executives felt was the right one. Their deciding vote on its likely global failure was made after the picture was shown for two months in eight major U.S. cities: a campaign which had attracted a poor response from the public. Steve even contributed towards the publicity by making a rare public appearance at Loyola Marymount film school with critic Charles Champlin. Still, interest surrounding the project was not enough to persuade Warner Brothers to release the film and be confident of its success. Steve was deeply hurt by Warner's lack of faith in the project and criticised their narrow-mindedness, in judging what Steve McQueen was and was not good at. He felt the studio failed to recognise the relevance of the picture's content and how ideal it was for movie audiences of its day. Warner's simply thought, 'McQueen doing Ibsen: forty pounds overweight and with a great big beard. Who wants to see that?'

"They want me on the screen with a gun in my hand," bemoaned Steve. "The full macho bit. McQueen the rebel; the cool killer; same crap I've been into for years. But this time I'm going in a different direction. When you get right down to it, though, I'm still playing a non-conformist, because that's what Stockmann is. He's a guy that won't back down when the whole town's against him. He stands alone for what he knows is right, and he's strong because of that. Sure, it was written nearly a century ago, but the theme ties right into the problems we face today with polluted lakes and poisoned air and chemicals in our food. That's what attracted me to this play, the message it carries - that we need to take personal responsibility for what's happening around us. That's what Ibsen was saying."

William Tuttle was make-up artist on the movie and had the difficult role in converting the cast to a 19th century look. Tuttle had already worked on three McQueen movies - *Never So Few*, *The Honeymoon Machine* and *The Cincinnati Kid* - during his 37-year career at MGM. He had never got to know Steve though, until *An Enemy of the People*, and it was a relationship he was glad to make. "I had heard that Steve could be tough to work with and that he gave film crews all kinds of trouble," said Tuttle, "but I think that he just wanted perfection. He was a very meticulous person and because of that he could be demanding, but people shouldn't criticise him for that. I sometimes feel that people get carried away when they say how difficult Steve McQueen was. Being difficult can translate as being very professional, which is how I viewed him. I enjoyed working with him a lot."

This was a picture that demanded a huge departure from his normal characters, and Steve's former industry colleagues acknowledged his boldness to tackle such a project, even if they didn't agree with his decision to be in it. Says Tim Zinnemann, who worked with Steve on *Bullitt* and *The Reivers*: "I thought he had a niche as a star in pictures like *The Great Escape*, *The Magnificent Seven*, *The Thomas Crown Affair* and *Bullitt*. That was his genre and an area he was naturally good at. I don't think his doing Ibsen was his strong suit; it was to prove something to himself as he was always pushing himself as an actor. You have to admire him for trying." The sentiment that Steve wanted to make this film to prove a point was highlighted further when Steve said to Tuttle on the set: "Bill, I'm gonna show Newman and Redford that I can do other things too!" His competitiveness possessed him once more, like in *Le Mans* and *The Reivers* - other risky projects where he placed great faith. He was so determined to show that his range went further than action movies involving cars and guns, that he virtually waived the prospect of box-office success in favour of chasing professional respect.

Eli Wallach, a keen student of the theatre himself, noted: "Steve's yearnings were still to go back and do things with literary quality. I certainly appreciated what he was trying to do, even though it didn't work out for him." It wasn't that McQueen had took on too much personally; it was more his choice to make a film that was far better suited to the stage than it was to the screen. The picture carried powerful dialogue but movie audiences can be impatient in their need for action. This is one area where *An Enemy of the People* was never going to win, but Steve gave everything to make it work.

"I don't think it was a typical Steve McQueen movie," conceded Tuttle, "but he was very anxious to do this, very dedicated to the whole idea. He gave his heart and soul and I thought he did an admirable job. I think it was just the fact he was so far away from his usual characters, where he had gained his popularity - that it didn't catch on. He had been typed so much that he really went out on a limb for this one. It's a damn shame it never came off."

Main Credits:

Cast: Steve McQueen (as Dr. Thomas Stockmann), Charles Durning, Bibi Andersson, Richard Dysart, Michael Cristofer, Michael Higgins, Eric Christmas, Robin Pearson Rose, Richard Bradford, John Levin, Ham Larsen, Louise Hoven and more.

Director:	George Schaefer
(Assistant)	Jack Aldworth
Producer:	George Schaefer, Steve McQueen (executive)
(Associate Producer)	Philip Parslow
Cinematographer:	Paul Lohmann
Writer:	Screenplay by Alexander Jacobs, based on Arthur Miller's adaptation of the Henrik Ibsen play *En Folkefiende*
Editor:	Sheldon Kahn
Wardrobe:	Noel Taylor
Make-Up:	William Tuttle, Tom Tuttle
Music:	Leonard Rosenman

REVIEWS:

VARIETY, August 30th, 1978

Transferring stage works to the screen has always been a procedure fraught with peril, and *An Enemy of the People* fails to avoid the obvious pitfalls. With the unusual casting of Steve McQueen in the title role, the First Artists production faces a rocky commercial road. Warner Bros. has kept this film under wraps for more than a year and a half until its World Film Festival prem last weekend in Montreal. The reasons are apparent... Director George Schaefer does his best to eliminate the usual dull blocking of filmed plays, but he's hamstrung by the casting of McQueen himself. The problem has nothing to do with the abandonment of a successful action adventure image, but rather the unsuitability of this particular actor to this particular role...As a feature film this seems destined for art houses, college bookings and a generally academic audience, far, far from the paying crowds.

FILMS AND FILMING, December, 1978

A curiously hirsute Steve McQueen takes the screen. With a mane of hair, a luxuriant beard and a moustache to go with it, plus a pair of very round spectacles with thin rims, he could call to mind one of yesterday's hippies or Henrik Ibsen. And no doubt the latter impression is what he intends, for *An Enemy of the People* did contain in its central portrait of Dr. Stockmann, whom McQueen portrays, some passing autobiographical references to the playwright himself... McQueen is dedicated in his representation of Stockmann, and he gets especially strong support from Charles Durning as his venal brother the mayor.

Steve had a lot of passion for the story behind *Tom Horn* and
cared deeply about doing justice to the memory of his character,
who he felt had been wronged by the authorities
(COURTESY: WARNER BROS)

TOM HORN

(Warner Bros) 1980

'Steve said he slept on Horn's grave until they communicated'
– Bud Shrake

WITH THE EXCEPTION of *Le Mans,* Steve never had more enthusiasm for a project than he did for *Tom Horn.* The film is based on a true story and taken from the book: *Life of Tom Horn, Government Scout and Interpreter,* written by himself. In reading the book, McQueen developed a deep admiration for Horn, who lived a colourful life in the Old West before his ill-fated death in 1903. Cinematographer Fred Koenekamp, who first worked with Steve on *Papillon,* remembered a conversation he had with Steve when he was sought for the picture. "He wanted to do *Tom Horn* real bad and he gave me the book and a script and he called me a couple of times asking if I'd be interested in working with him on the movie. Unfortunately it never worked out, as I got involved with another film. But Steve was so enthusiastic about that project; there was something about the part that he really liked."

Some aspects of Horn's life mirrored the tough and adventurous childhood that Steve had been through himself: At fourteen, Horn ran away from home and went to work on a railroad and drove for a stagecoach company; he lived with Apache Indians for a time; he was a silver miner in Tombstone; he fought in Cuba; was a cowboy and rodeo star; he was a famed cavalry scout when he brought the legendary Geronimo to captivity and was finally a hired gunman and bounty hunter for a group of ranchers troubled by rustlers.

The movie deals with Horn's final occupation. He rides into a Wyoming town with his reputation preceding him, and is soon hired by villagers to rid the place of cattle thieves. Horn's gesture in answering a desperate request from cattle-rancher John Coble becomes his downfall. His unscrupulous methods in fighting the rustlers shock the town and they promptly turn their backs on him when he is supposedly framed for the murder of a young boy. Writer Thomas McGuane drafted the first script but it was thrown out because of its excessive length. Bud Shrake, later famous for his work on golf books, was then given the task of streamlining a good, but over-long script. He said: "When Steve gave me the script I thought it was going to be an easy job and just throw half of it away. But it wasn't that simple as McGuane had written scenes thirty pages long when they could have been three, so I had to do a re-write, but using most of his original material."

The working relationship between Shrake and Steve flourished. Both men understood one another. It was obvious right from their first meeting at Steve's Beverly Wilshire Hotel apartment in Los Angeles that they would get along. Though meant to be informal, the writer's short-term destiny was on the line and whether the job was his or not all depended on Steve's evaluation as he was not only the star of the movie but an executive producer also. Shrake, with his broad Texan accent, didn't care a great deal for these get-togethers and was initially reluctant to attend. He recalled: "I just wore a pair of old Levi's, a beat-up old shirt and an old corduroy cowboy hat. When I walked in to meet Steve I realised I had out-dressed him on the down-side - he had on roughly the same clothes as I did, so we had an instant rapport."

Not far into their discussions, Steve got a call from a studio executive who was waiting for him in a lower-level restaurant. McQueen was wanted for another project after *Tom Horn*. "Excuse me for a few minutes, I just have to go and pick up a million bucks," he coolly announced to Shrake, which was the figure he told him he was demanding just to read a script - *Tai-pan* in this case. On his return half an hour later, Shrake curiously asked whether he would make the picture. "Shit, no!" came the swift reply from the much-hunted movie star. In reality, Steve did consider the project seriously, but the location shoot in Hong Kong didn't appeal to him, especially with his increasing health problems.

Shrake visited Steve at his beach-house in Malibu four times a week over a six-month period to work a script that McQueen felt comfortable with. Sometimes producer Fred

Weintraub would accompany him. "Let's go and throw some peanuts to the gorilla," Weintraub would say, before embarking on their visit to the McQueen residence. The first time Shrake went to Steve's house, Weintraub issued some advice to the unsuspecting writer: "When you're in these meetings with Steve, don't get angry or upset at anything he says. In fact, don't pay any attention to what he says - just pay attention to what he does." It was a friendly warning; the producer knew how Steve liked to test people he was unsure of. Shrake, however, soon found his own way to deal with Steve. "I really enjoyed his company," says Shrake. "A lot of people had trouble with him and said all kinds of things, but I never saw any of that. When I was around him he was a really good fella. He was honest and up-front and didn't see any reason why he had to lie to anybody."

Steve never appreciated interference from studio executives, whom he viewed cautiously, and he was never afraid to speak candidly to them. Shrake remembers when McQueen fought hard to maintain the picture's integrity when Warner bosses wanted to change the ending. They strongly opposed the idea that the star of the picture would die from hanging. The executives figured the prospect of Steve McQueen dying would have a dampening impact at the box-office. They suggested the film should end when Tom escapes from jail and heads for the mountains. "We can run a little line saying that Tom Horn was later captured and hanged," a studio exec proffered. Steve had none of it – and got his way. McQueen was forever striving for realism, but Shrake feels there was another reason for Steve's stubbornness to leave the ending as it was. "His last speech as Tom Horn were Tom's very words in front of the crowd before the gallows sprang, which said: 'I've never seen such a pasty-faced bunch of sheriffs in all my life,' then they hanged him. I think Steve knew he was very ill at the time and thought that might be his last speech on Hollywood." Although Steve *was* later confirmed as having an incurable cancer, he went on to make another movie - *The Hunter.*

Shrake said Steve's overwhelming interest in Tom Horn the man was obsessive. "He wanted to talk constantly about *Tom Horn* the movie in detail; he cared deeply about it. He had a vision of what he wanted it to be and look like. I think this might have been Steve's favourite movie. He had the book *The Life of Tom Horn* on him all the time and he had it memorized. I know he loved that movie."

Co-star Bert Williams, who played the judge that sentences Horn to death, echoed Shrake's opinion on Steve's creativity: "He had a great visionary mind and a great story mind. At one point they thought about scrapping the film after it had been shot because the original editor couldn't follow the thinking that was going on in Steve's mind. Instead they brought in another editor who was able to capture his thinking."

Shrake had many disagreements, bordering on full scale arguments, about the script with Steve as they sat discussing the picture in Malibu. McQueen enjoyed their debates in the knowledge that it was all for the good of the movie. More often than not, Steve would win out because he had an amazing secret that he eventually allowed Bud to share. Says Shrake, "Whenever Steve and I got into an argument about the script he would go: 'Well, Tom says it's this way.' The first time he said that I went, 'Tom who?' Steve said, 'Tom Horn.' It turns out Steve had found Tom Horn's grave somewhere outside of Denver (Old Pioneer Cemetery in Boulder) and spent I don't know how many nights sleeping on it! Steve said he slept on Horn's grave until they communicated and Tom Horn told him that he didn't kill any kids or do the things they said he did. So when Steve and I ever got into an argument about the script, Steve would say, 'Tom told me it was the other way'. I couldn't argue with him because he'd already talked to the guy!" That 'conversation' occurred during a road-trip with his third wife-to-be Barbara Minty, who never shared Steve's sympathy for Horn. Barbara wrote in her wonderfully colorful memoir *The Last Mile* that she felt Horn was "guilty as sin", though only through a hunch.

The film, which began shooting in January 1979, was a complicated affair from the start. If it wasn't experiencing budget problems or script problems, then there were issues with directors. In total *Tom Horn* saw four directors involved at some point. Don Siegel, who had worked with Steve on *Hell Is For Heroes*, was briefly linked with the project initially before Elliot Silverstein was hired. Silverstein was best known for making *Cat Ballou* starring Jane Fonda and Lee Marvin. However, his time on this movie was spent with considerably less success. His concept of what *Tom Horn* should be about clashed with Steve's, who saw more of an action-adventure vehicle as opposed to Silverstein's deep and meaningful relationship story between Horn and Geronimo. Furthermore, Silverstein struggled to find peace with the producer Fred Weintraub, who eventually fired him. Shrake remembered: "Elliot was the director when I came in. He was quite an intelligent sort of guy, where as Fred was more like an East Coast nightclub operator, though he was a real good guy, but their personalities just clashed."

Next was James Guercio. He was an unknown quantity as far as making Hollywood movies went, but he managed to talk his way into Steve's confidence and as executive producer and star of the picture, Steve's opinion went a long way. It wasn't long before Guercio exercised his weight as director and persuaded Steve to make changes to the script, which had been approved by Weintraub, McQueen and Warner Brothers. Shrake had by now returned to his home in Texas but he received a telephone call from Steve asking him to catch a red-eye to Ketchum, Idaho. When Shrake arrived, he was greeted by Barbara Minty, who informed the writer that Steve was working a nearby field on his tractor. When he finished his agricultural duties, McQueen said to Shrake: "There's somebody I'd like you to meet." That was James Guercio, who soon exerted his authority on the scriptwriter. Says Bud, "We got talking about the movie and

Guercio turns to me and starts telling me about all these changes he'd like to make to the script. I said I wouldn't do it, as it was suicide; everything had already been approved. We then got into a big argument and Guercio fired me. Steve went outside to think for a while and when he came back he said, 'Bud, I'm sorry but Jim's my director and I'm going to have to trust him'." Shrake then called the producer informing him of the absurd events in Idaho. Weintraub, conscious of the ever-escalating budget, knew full well there would be no more alterations to the script. "Don't pay any attention to Guercio, I'll deal with him. Just don't say anything to make Steve mad and get out of there," Weintraub advised on the telephone.

This was the start of a short and bumpy ride for the director. Two weeks into shooting in Arizona, Steve also experienced professional differences with Guercio, which resulted in his departure. Second assistant director Ed Milkovich recalled: "It was quite mystical how he left. Jim had a meeting with Fred and Steve at lunch then, afterwards, he just drove off in his motor home and we were all standing there with no director. Guercio was quite bitter about how he was forced out." Bert Williams felt sympathetic towards the director, who had made his name making music videos. "Steve and Guercio didn't get along on a lot of things because Guercio was a different kind of director that Steve was used to working with. Jim was more of an artistic director and he didn't really have a chance as Weintraub backed Steve on most things."

At that stage, Steve would have liked nothing more than to direct the picture himself but the Directors Guild of America had a rule in place that prevented anyone already employed on a project from taking over the reins. This meant the arrival of a fourth and final director - William Wiard. He had no previous experience in feature films, only television work. He came recommended by James Garner who had worked with Wiard on *The Rockford Files*. Steve's passion for the film was such that it didn't matter who the director was - he was the creative force behind everything and though the credits may not list Steve as director, he generally was. "Steve wanted a puppet director he could manipulate," Williams said. "Bill Wiard was basically a figurehead. Steve was an actor-director and was fantastic at both. If he would have lived on, he may have been one of *the* great directors but he didn't have that much time left in his life."

Although McQueen was regarded as number one on the set, Milkovich is adamant he never became arrogant or a dictator. "By then I was twenty-five and had been around some pretty big stars and I found Steve to be the best behaved of any of them. Sure he had his opinions and could be as stubborn as the day is long, but he would listen to people and would sometimes change his thoughts in midstream. Like if cameraman John Alonzo said, 'Steve it would be better if we shot it this way,' Steve would say, 'Okay - I always listen to the cinema-photographer' as he called them. I adored him. Just to be around him was quite unique. He was bigger than life on one side and on the

STEVE McQUEEN: THE COOLER KING

other he was just a regular guy. He loved to ride this pick-up truck, put chains on it and pull things out of the mud. If anything got stuck, he'd be the first one there, telling the drivers where to hook up the chains. That was the most fun he had on the picture. He was a unique guy and I feel fortunate that in my career I had an opportunity to work closely with him."

Williams, a former world diving champion, knew Steve before the film as they shared a common interest in motor-cycles. He still rode well into his seventies and visited Steve at his temporary home at the hangar in Oxnard, near Santa Paula once, and was thrilled to see McQueen's exquisite collection of planes and motorcycles. This bond, though, counted for nothing as far as the movie went. Steve didn't even know Williams had been cast and later discovered Guercio had hired him. "I know you've done a lot of stage acting Bert, but I want you to forget all that," McQueen preached to the actor. Steve took a firm grip of proceedings, as only he really knew what he was trying to create. His vision of *Tom Horn* was so defined and personal that many fell in with his directives.

Williams had always held Steve in high regard as an actor, but as soon as they started work together, his respect for Steve went much further, despite inducing his criticism on the set. He recalled: "On my first take as the Judge, I gave this great stage-like monologue while Tom Horn is up in court. The extras, the crew, everyone applauded me, but Steve said, 'Bert, you're missing the point. You've got to remember that you're railroading me. You know it and I know it. Speak to me like a father speaks to his son, patronize me, and maybe spit out a bit of tobacco, that'll be a nice touch.' He really knew what he wanted. He was a good film-maker and had a nice, low-key way of being powerful."

Steve's control on the set never stopped with the actors; the stuntmen were also accountable. As a man known for doing many of his own stunts, Steve was in a valid position to demand stunt work of the highest order. He had no time for amateurs. Says Williams, "He took all the stuntmen cowboys up to this ranch and had them ride; going through tests to make sure they weren't bullshitting him about the riding. He put them through a routine with his stunt coordinator. They had them jumping logs, going through roughage, going over rocks and at hard pace, so if they were kidding as a rider they were going to be found out. Steve was that professional."

Although Steve was dedicated to making a resounding success of *Tom Horn*, he also knew when it was time to unwind and allow the cast and crew breathing space from a tough shoot, during one of Arizona's coldest winters. Milkovich, who struck up a good friendship with Steve, recalled some frightful moments when he would take him for a ride in his pick-up truck over the bumpy Arizona terrain. "You can't believe what a phenomenal driver Steve McQueen was. Every once in a while I'd ride out with him and I used to live in fear. He'd push the pedal to the metal along these mountain dirt roads, upon to this plateau and he would say 'let's take the short cut' - it was total panic on my part. Butt in the air the whole deal, but man could he drive. Anything you put him on - motorcycles, four-wheel drives, race-cars; he was just amazing. He had a great sense of fun. It was his idea to throw a roller-skating party for the cast and crew, which we did one weekend in Tuscon. Steve was there, skating away with Barbara Minty and was quite good as a matter of fact. He was like a 48-year-old six-year-old, like a big kid, but with a gigantic heart."

Not only did Steve initiate the fun, he was occasionally the butt of it. There was a joke running through the set at his expense. He had innocently remarked to one of the crew, with good intentions, 'I'm gonna go rough it and live in the wild on *Tom Horn*.' Eventually it took a small army to help him. Steve's version of roughing it by the time they were through included staying in a 26-foot Winnebago motor home, electrical stations, radio receiving towers and a pen for his dog! They were, though, genuinely in the wild, in Patagonia, Arizona. It was hardly roughing it, but he did spurn the offer of a swanky hotel. The outcome nonetheless was a well-worn parody known as 'Camp Horn' - a line Steve would hear a lot of. Incidentally, Steve's beloved dog Junior, who he took on as a stray, disappeared for good during the three-month shoot and it was then that Barbara saw Steve cry for the first time. Almost two decades earlier on the set of *Hell Is for Heroes*, director Don Siegel had tried all kinds of tricks to squeeze a tear from Steve to no avail, yet the loss of his four-legged companion genuinely hurt him.

Budget problems were never far away on *Tom Horn*. Heavy financial cuts were forced on a picture that started out with a $6 million budget but was slashed. The lengthy pre-production stage, including researching, script re-writes and problems with directors, caused the movie to suffer as a consequence. Although Steve was delighted with the finished article, the money troubles added a frenetic element that rushed particular scenes and stages, when under more relaxed circumstances a more polished job may have been executed according to Shrake. "By the time we got to shoot the movie, they had just about run out of money. The first twenty minutes of the script was about Tom Horn dealing with Geronimo, but due to the financial problems Fred Weintraub picked up the script and tore out the first twenty pages. They couldn't afford to shoot it. 'We'll start when Tom rides into town,' Weintraub pronounced. Steve was okay about it; he didn't like it, but he understood the situation."

Milkovich acknowledged the budget troubles, but felt the spirit on the set never dipped as a result. "Financially, it was a chore from the word go. The movie eventually had to be scaled down to fit the budget. But the fact we were located in the middle of nowhere on the Mexican border, with nothing in sight as far as the eye could see, made us bond together. There was a bit more tension by the time we got to Tuscon, but even then those moments were overshadowed by the fun stuff." Perhaps Steve's happiest time while working on the movie was announcing news of co-star Richard Farnsworth's Academy Award nomination for *Comes A Horseman*. They were miles from civilization, but when Milkovich visited the nearest gas station he was able to communicate with their office in Tuscon. They informed him of the good news from Hollywood regarding Farnsworth. "Instead of announcing it I went to Steve and told him first," Milkovich said. "He was so tickled that I got him a bullhorn and he stopped everything on the set. He was so thrilled that he got to make the announcement, as Dick didn't even know himself at that point. As it happened he got to find out the same time as all the extras, all the crew and all the stand-arounds. That was the happiest day ever during the picture.'

At this point of McQueen's career, his health was on the wane, although it was to become more obvious on his next film. Still, in *Tom Horn* it is clearly visible to see a man in pain; minus the graceful movement he was so famously associated with, carrying extra weight and looking considerably older from *The Towering Inferno* shot only five years before. Williams noted: "In the running scene where he is trying to escape, he didn't look right and his belly was swollen. I thought, 'Wow, that's not Steve the way I know him.' He was a courageous guy." Milkovich saw no significant reason to consider Steve ill, but there was a moment that made him suspicious. "I heard him arguing with the studio regarding his next film, *The Hunter*. Steve was adamant at not wanting to take a physical. That didn't mean much to me at the time but after I wondered, 'Did he know that he was ill then?'

The reason I never got concerned was the fact that he was jogging most mornings on this set and he was also considering elaborate plans to make *Tai-pan*. I *know* he wasn't planning on checking out."

Tom Horn bombed at the box-office and a whole host of reasons were given. All valid arguments and explanations offered included: The release of a two-part TV movie, *Mr Horn*, shown the previous year; the number of westerns released shortly before: *Breakheart Pass, Comes A Horseman* and *The Electric Horseman*; the suggestion that the western genre had by now run its course and, notwithstanding, the sadly altered state of Steve's physical posture. However, *Tom Horn* was one of Steve's best performances. He exerted tremendous depth and gave the impression he knew what the character was about. Summing up the film, Williams said, "*Tom Horn* is now a cult movie. That means it's extraordinary and will never die."

Main Credits:

Cast: Steve McQueen (as Tom Horn), Linda Evans, Richard Farnsworth, Billy Green Bush, Slim Pickens, Peter Canon, Elisha Cook Jr., Roy Jenson, James Kline, Geoffrey Lewis, Harry Northup, Steve Oliver, Bill Thurman, Bert Williams, Bobby Bass and more.

Director:	William Wiard
(Assistant)	Cliff Coleman, (second assistant) Ed Milkovich
Producer:	Fred Weintraub

(Associate Producer)	Michael Rachmil, Sandra Weintraub, (executive) Steve McQueen
Cinematographer:	John Alonzo
Writers:	Thomas McGuane and Bud Shrake, based on the book *Life of Tom Horn, Government Scout and Interpreter*
Editor:	George Grenvile
Wardrobe:	Luster Bayless
Make-Up:	Del Armstrong
Music:	Ernest Gold

REVIEWS:

FILMS & FILMING, April, 1980

Steve McQueen looking suitably aged and moving with a stooped jerky gait far removed from the lithe prowl we remember from earlier days, gives us a Tom Horn who has seen much and knows he has little left to see. It is a stunning comeback for a star who seems to have eschewed his real trade in recent years, apart from the seemingly deliberate aberration of *An Enemy of the People*...McQueen at 50 is, of course, a very much older Tom Horn and one must be grateful that a genuine star - there are very few left - has designed to come out of semi-retirement to give us another example of that naturalness which almost surpasses reality.

MOTION PICTURE PRODUCT DIGEST, June 11th, 1980
McQueen still projects a powerful presence on the screen. His weather-beaten face has a lot of 'character' in it: now all he needs is an acting role of some scope.

NEW YORK TIMES, May 23rd, 1980
Tom Horn has a number of things to recommend it, chief among them the redoubtable Steve McQueen. Mr. McQueen makes his return to the screen after too long a hiatus.

THE HOLLYWOOD REPORTER, March 28th, 1980
Steve McQueen, after a six-year absence, returns to the main-stream of film-making in a role that fits his persona like a well-worn saddle, as an Old West gunman who understands triggers but not trickery...McQueen takes to the western milieu as comfortably as Wayne, Cooper or Eastwood ever did, and *Tom Horn* takes advantage of that partnership.

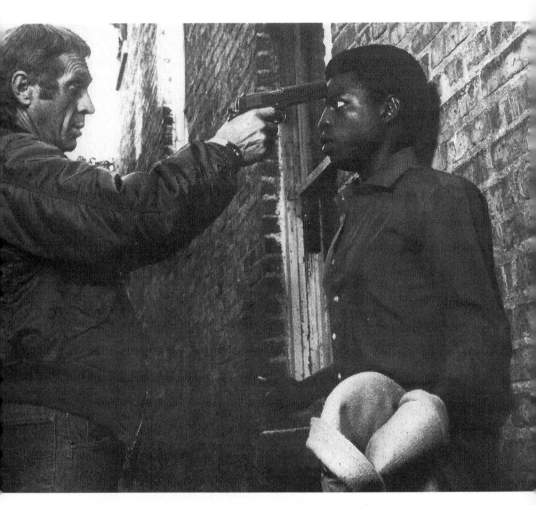

Steve in a scene with LeVar Burton, who he enjoyed
mentoring and was actually influential in earning
him a part in the picture
(COURTESY: PARAMOUNT PICTURES)

THE HUNTER

(Paramount) 1980

'I felt towards the end of the movie that he was tired. He was still fun, but there was a difference in him and he was definitely not the same Steve I knew from Papillon. I had no idea it (cancer) was that close to taking him' – Fred Koenekamp

WHEN SHOOTING OF *The Hunter* closed on November 28th 1979, little did the world realise that Steve McQueen, a symbol of masculinity and an icon to millions, would never appear on a movie set again. There were rumours of his faltering health, but his life was a tale of rumours - mostly unfounded - so most chose to ignore what they didn't really want to believe. Steve long denied the reports of his ill-health so fans preferred not to believe that the man they idolised as 'The Cooler King' and 'The Cincinnati Kid' was terminally ill, as he approached his fiftieth birthday. But, the rumours *were* true. He would be dead within a year. Steve McQueen was dying of cancer and there was nothing that could be done, even though he fought it all the way. The fatal news was confirmed to Steve by doctors less than a month after the picture was shot. Before and during the movie, he sensed he had a problem and considered which doctor to approach, with confidentiality being his number one concern. While shooting *The Hunter*, though, his fears remained a secret. Steve didn't want anybody's sympathy. He just wanted to be treated as the same old Steve that everybody knew. But there were clues known only with the benefit of hindsight that Steve McQueen knew this movie would be his last.

"Look, he was on the wane, he was on the backhand side of his life, but he knew it and was trying to squeeze every last ounce out of it as he could," said co-star LeVar Burton, who Steve had warmed to in a mentor-pupil way. He had made sure Burton was cast in the film after being blown away by his portrayal of Kunta Kinte in the television series *Roots*. "If you caught him in a moment you could tell that he was tired. But he was feeling good most of the time and was ready to kick up some dust. He loved playing the bounty hunter, Ralph Thorson. I think he related with the character and thought it was the perfect time in his life to say, 'I'm too old for this shit!' He relished delivering that line. 'I'm too old...for...this...shit!' That was it in a nutshell for Steve, encapsulated, at that point in his life. He had been doing this a long time. Steve was incredibly self-aware. Look at the way he chose to set himself up as an incompetent driver in *The Hunter*, when the world knew he was a great racing car driver. Isn't that great; to leave that as a part of his legacy? It's a completely and conscious bowing out. He turns all those things about his image on their heads, and he's got his tongue in his cheek and he's grinning all the way. He was really feeling that way in his life: 'I'm too old for this shit.' I would be surprised if this being his last film did not occupy a good part of his mind."

Director of photography Fred Koenekamp added, on Steve's condition then: "When we started *The Hunter*, I had no idea Steve was ill. To me he looked good, though he did have a personal therapist working with him on the set. The rumours that he had cancer were flying around but I sure never asked him if they were true. I felt towards the end of the movie that he was tired. He was still fun, but there was a difference in him and he was definitely not the same Steve I knew from *Papillon*. I had no idea it was that close to taking him."

Right from the moment producer Mort Engleberg offered him the starring role of *The Hunter*, Steve looked at the vehicle favourably. In the film he was to portray a bounty hunter, coincidentally the same role he played as Josh Randall when making his name on television in *Wanted: Dead or Alive*, 22 years earlier. As pre-production generated momentum, certain things that Steve did and words he spoke, are now clear signs that he realised *The Hunter* would be his final movie. While working on *Tom Horn*, Steve gave a gigantic hint to scriptwriter Bud Shrake of the condition he was in, while discussing *The Hunter*. "He told me that he was going to do that film and that he was going to give his $3 million fee straight to his wife Barbara and his two children," Shrake said. "After he died I could then see what he meant. He knew he was over with and that it was his last big pay day, which he would give to his heirs."

Steve had a lot of enthusiasm for this project. Even with his dyslexia, which could make reading a slow exercise, he read Christopher Keane's biography on Thorson in a single sitting and knew thereafter that he just had to make this movie. He wasn't a producer on it but when Steve McQueen wanted something at this stage of his career, he made damned sure he got it. Subsequently he had a significant influence on the cast and crew and surrounded himself with old friends, like co-stars Ben Johnson (*Junior Bonner* and The *Getaway*) and Eli Wallach (*The Magnificent Seven*), cinematographer Fred Koenekamp (*Papillon* and *The Towering Inferno*), his long-time stunt double Loren Janes, while he made his son Chad a production assistant and wife-to-be Barbara Minty was there with him all the way too. He even hired people he had less history with, like the female lead Kathryn Harrold, and those he had a hunch for, such as the exciting acting talents of LeVar Burton. The cast was thin in the way of well-known celebrities. Much depended on the McQueen name with regard to box-office appeal. Wallach took second billing, though his part was basically a cameo appearance. It was more an excuse to meet up with an old friend and get paid for it. "The producer called me and said he had a part in a Steve McQueen film and that he would like me to do it," said Wallach. "I thought what a nice thing, to have a reunion with Steve after twenty years, so I flew out and did it. There was a huge weight of responsibility on Steve's shoulders, but Steve always carried the load of a picture, he wasn't a supporting actor, he was *the* star." Koenekamp echoed: "The picture relied solely on Steve as nobody else's role was as important in the script as his part. He *was* the bounty hunter."

McQueen took a great deal of satisfaction in mentoring Burton, whose promising career later became known more for his role as Geordi La Forge in *Star Trek: The Next Generation*. Burton plays Tommy Price in *The Hunter* - an amusing delinquent who Thorson takes in, along with several others that have been on the wrong side of the law. Burton was thrilled to work with his hero and was one of a small number to attend his funeral the following year. "The first time I met Steve was in his garage at his beach house in Malibu," Burton recounted. "I went there with my manager at the time Delores Robertson as she was friends with Ali (MacGraw), before Steve had met Barbara. Steve had asked to meet me. He was there with his head under a hood in a motor when I walked in; we just hung out and talked. He told me he was looking to do a new picture and he wanted me to be in it. I said, 'Sure!' What do you say when Steve McQueen says he wants you to act with him? So I was in *The Hunter* simply because Steve wanted me there. My role of Tommy Price was expanded from the original script purely because Steve wanted this young kid to be noticed. So they wrote more stuff in. It was an incredible time for me. I was just so overawed. I had seen *Papillon, Bullitt, The Great Escape, The Thomas Crown Affair,*

I had seen them all. I never saw anything of the complex Steve McQueen that people talk about. It was hard for me to be in Steve's presence without being aware of all the history he left behind on film. It was impossible for me to sit there in his presence and not think of *The Magnificent Seven* or some of those iconic moments in movies that he was a part of, burning memories into my psyche. He was a huge part of my childhood."

This was a happy movie for Steve, especially now that he was sharing his life with his beloved Barbara, with whom he shared one adventure after another. On arriving in Chicago for the location shoot, they were pleasantly surprised by the lavishness of their suite that Paramount had hired for them at the Drake Hotel. But as soon as Steve learned that the rest of the cast and crew were 'roughing it' at the less-grand Holiday Inn downtown, he insisted they checked out immediately and joined 'his people'. "That's Steve McQueen, man," Burton said. "He did *An Enemy of the People* at the end of his career. But in real life he was A Man of the People. He was one of us and always identified with the working guy." It mattered little where Barbara and Steve resided at this time, for they were so in love that a marble floor against a frayed carpet in their hotel room was the least of their concerns. The lead make-up artist on *The Hunter*, John M. Elliott, observed how smitten they were as a couple. "They seemed very close and good together," he recalled. "She was great for him. I first met her when I went up to Steve's place at the airplane hangar in Santa Paula to discuss his ideas for *The*

Hunter, his character and how he wanted to look. He didn't look ill to me at the time; he looked a little tired when we started shooting, but you would never know that he was as sick as he was. He never made a fuss about anything; he was just a good guy."

McQueen began *The Hunter* in September 1979 as normal; at least it appeared that way to everyone else. Only later did his lack of energy and agility become clearer. Before shooting began, Steve went through all the usual pre-production routines like script meetings, final casting discussions and on how he was going to look. Hairdresser Bren Plaistowe was then a 26-year-old blonde, pretty newcomer to Hollywood – a self-proclaimed Goldie Hawn lookalike. She struck up a close bond with Steve though initially could barely recognise him. "I met Steve two months before the movie when I went to see him at his hangar in Santa Paula," she recalled. "I walked into this garage and there was a very old man with greying hair and a very long beard. And when this man turned around it was Steve. I was there to get his hair right and cut his beard down for *The Hunter*. He said, 'Yeah, I don't really want to work anymore but there's this old biplane I want to buy so I need to earn some money!' When I went back a couple of weeks later he had shaved this beard into a goatee. I said, 'Steve, they want you back, they want Steve back. Shave your beard off, it looks ugly.' I just wanted to tell him that the public had missed him. He agreed to lose the beard and have a new haircut but he said he wanted his hair cutting out on the runway so he could watch the planes go by. So there I was cutting Steve's hair on the runway at his home. While I was there this lady started walking towards us and the closer she got I thought, 'Wow, here comes Ali MacGraw, I thought they weren't together anymore.' But you know what, it wasn't Ali, it was Barbara Minty. They looked so alike. Barbara was nice and we went roller skating together a couple of times."

Buzz Kulik was brought in to direct, as a replacement for co-writer Peter Hyams, who later directed *Time Cop* with Jean-Claude Van Damme and *End of Days* with Arnold Schwarzenegger. Kulik was also unaware of any medical problems troubling Steve. It was near-impossible for him to know that the all-action, gung-ho star of movies like *Bullitt* and *The Towering Inferno* was struggling with a life-threatening illness. Although, in hindsight, Buzz felt there were moments that showed the extent of his cancer. "Every once in a while something would happen that seemed a little peculiar," Kulik said. "He always told me that he had a collapsed lung which was caused from being in the water too long when he made *Papillon*. He worked with his personal trainer every morning to build up his stamina, but there were certain physical things that made me wonder. I remember a chase scene when he had to jump over some cars and chase a guy up these steps. When I said 'Cut' he didn't come back and I wandered around the corner where he was, to find him leaning against a building, gasping for breath, nearly passing out. I said 'Are you okay?' 'Yeah I'm alright, just give me a minute,' he said. In retrospect after his illness was known, I remembered those instances and thought he must have been quite ill. It didn't really affect his performance though, but he sure did struggle with those chase scenes."

It was during the shoot of those chase scenes that LeVar Burton saw another fascinating side to McQueen: "It was wild at times when we shot on the streets, as when you put Steve McQueen in the middle of Chicago it's going to draw a crowd," Burton commented. "I marvelled and learned a lot from him, just being around Steve. I could not help but just learn stuff. On this one particular day, we're out there with the people and I had done *Roots* so I'm signing autographs and I look over and Steve is NOT signing autographs. I thought, 'Ok, what's going on here?' He was shaking hands and talking to people and eventually the crowd disperses and we all go back to work. So later I asked him, 'What's the deal? You don't sign autographs...' He said, 'Well Burty (he always called me Burty), I've been doing this a long time and I've come to the conclusion that what people are after is evidence of the moment. They want to be able to say, "I was there, I met him." And in my view instead of me standing there with my head buried, scribbling my name on a piece of paper, my time is better spent making eye contact, shaking a hand, saying a kind word, because nine times out of ten that piece of paper is going to end up crumpled in a drawer in the kitchen. It's all about the moment, Burty, that's important.' I thought that's a beautiful philosophy but only a man like Steve McQueen can get away with not signing autographs because he commands this presence and respect. He had figured it out. He worked out that as long as this routine is going to be a part of my life I am going to make it work for me. The natural assumption that people jumped to was, 'What an asshole, that Steve McQueen.' But he was just so human, so compassionate and sympathetic that he wanted their experience to be better."

Similarly, despite refusing all Press interviews for the previous eight years, he agreed to be interviewed by a kid that worked for a school magazine in Los Angeles, when the location work returned to California near the end of the picture. The boy was bold enough to approach McQueen direct and was told to prepare a list of questions and return later that evening. He got his interview simply because Steve liked kids. His permanent Press agents Rogers & Cowan and the publicist on the movie were aghast; for different reasons. While Warren Cowan had the biggest magazines and newspapers in the world breaking down their door for interviews with McQueen, the movie star decides to give an interview to a school kid. Equally, that would have been a good news story and positive publicity for The Hunter but Steve never did these generous acts to win approval through the media. He did them because HE wanted to do them.

Steve never did direct in his career but word had got out that he basically had sole creative control of his previous two films and that The Hunter would follow a similar pattern. Had it not been for opposition from the Directors

Guild, Steve would have directed *Tom Horn* and *The Hunter*. They had a ruling that an actor already cast cannot take over as director once the film had started. But Steve was well aware of his deteriorating physical state and wanted to make this picture *his* way. Peter Hyams wrote the initial screenplay based on the book about the colourful character that was bounty hunter Ralph 'Papa' Thorson, who was deemed to have apprehended more than 5,000 criminals in his lifetime. It was soon agreed that Hyams would also direct after he had met with Steve and gained his blessing. "The first time Steve and I met was to discuss the film in Alice's restaurant in Malibu," Hyams recalled. "We talked for a long time about what he wanted and what he was looking for. He kept telling me how much he wanted to be directed and the stories I'd heard at how difficult he was weren't true. He told me I was the man to direct him and why. I think he was trying to allay some of my fears and he was also sizing me up. He said to me: 'You look me right in the eye - I like that'."

Following the meeting, Hyams then researched Thorson closely for the benefit of the script. He spent a great deal of time with him and his wife, at his house, hanging out with him. Hyams lived in his pocket to develop a screenplay that would smack of realism. During this time, he was in constant touch with Steve. Mort Engleberg was the producer but Steve McQueen had significant influence and many key decisions were down to him.

Hyams and McQueen met regularly to discuss the script and Hyams found it a stimulating experience to be in such close proximity with a man he idolised. "He was a fascinating guy just for the fact that he was Steve McQueen. We spoke about some of his old films like *Bullitt* and *The Great Escape* in particular; I tried to use some of his former characters as analogies. He never really enjoyed talking about his old films; he was kind of modest like that. But he really knew what worked for him. He'd say, 'A man's got to know his limitations' – good movie stars know themselves better than anyone what works best for them. When you're writing a script for Steve McQueen, you don't give him pages and pages of dialogue. He was a great reactor who could say more with a smile, a squint or with the turn of his head." Conversation was never dull with Steve, who had so many idiosyncrasies. Hyams continued: "We'd sit there talking and he would be chewing tobacco, spitting it into a glass and by the end of the meeting this glass would be half full of tobacco juice!"

While the script was taking shape, Hyams and McQueen began to clash over their own ideas concerning which direction the movie should go. Relations were never unpleasant, but both had different angles on the story. Hyams revealed: "As months passed, it became clear that Steve and I just didn't see the same movie. My ideas for Thorson were a lot more harder-edged than Steve's. He had a lot of ideas that I didn't like and I'm sure he didn't like some of mine. Eventually, he didn't want me to make that movie. Unfortunately, I wasn't qualified to argue what Steve McQueen was and was not good at. I'm just disappointed I never got to do a film with Steve. It wasn't an acrimonious end, he just saw me as a man who wouldn't be told by him how to make the movie." The situation had arrived, which Steve had tried to convince Hyams never would occur; that he wasn't in total control and that he wanted to be directed. "Like a complete schmuck I believed him," laughed Hyams. The same old chestnut of Steve realising that it could be his last film, which had plagued him also on *Tom Horn* was surfacing again.

"I think at that time of his life he didn't *'not'* want to be in control of his films," Hyams reasoned. "During the making of that movie, he knew he was ill, so maybe that element affected his feelings about it." Hyams' departure was regretfully received by Engleberg, who was a close friend to the writer, but the film and McQueen's wishes had to come before sentiment. Hyams explained: "Mort and I had been friends before the film and I know he was not happy that things didn't work out. It was a personal thing for Mort, as you don't like to see somebody you care for go through an unpleasant time as I did - and it was very unpleasant. When you've written something and you're then unable to make it, it's kind of like somebody taking your baby from you."

Buzz Kulik was then drafted in to direct, but his decision to work with McQueen was not an easy one. He knew Steve in the fifties when they were both involved with television together, both eager to make a living out of the industry. Kulik thought little of McQueen in those days and considered him to be an ill-mannered jerk with only a hint of acting ability. "I thought he was a pain in the ass, quite frankly," Kulik recalled. "He was very young after coming in from New York where he had made a name for himself very quickly. It was not a happy experience because of Steve's cocky attitude, so when I was offered *The Hunter* I was concerned because of my experiences with him years before. But I liked the script and I also liked Mort Engleberg very much, so I decided to jump in."

Buzz recalled a conversation with Steve in the late fifties when the two met at the 20th Century Fox studios after Steve had made a big splash on *Wanted: Dead or Alive*. The young McQueen was gaining in confidence and was sure where his career was headed. "Buzz," he said, "I'm gonna be a big star." Kulik was shocked and quietly made fun of his misplaced arrogance. "I went back to my wife and said, 'Do you remember that Steve McQueen - the guy I had all that trouble with - well he told me he's going to be a big star; what a joke.' By then he was still young and inexperienced but he was always ambitious and a very instinctive actor." Twenty years on, the two men barely spoke a word of the past and enjoyed an excellent working relationship. There was no conflict and only a healthy camaraderie and respect. Whatever reputation Steve had earned during his career, Kulik knew he was fortunate enough to be working closely with Steve at a time in his life when he wasn't there to exorcise demons. He had lived that part of his life. He was content to just show up, hit his lines and do his job. "Steve and I just hit it off so well," Kulik said. "I felt he had mellowed and that his young lady was good for him. There was no doubt he had also matured as an actor. He was an outstandingly bright guy who had learned a lot in his movie-making career. I thought he had made a number of very good films, especially *Bullitt*, which was an extraordinarily well made and well-acted film."

The Hunter's chief subject Ralph 'Papa' Thorson was technical adviser and had a cameo role as a bartender in the picture. He impressed all the crew with tales from his eventful life. The stories within the film appear far-fetched at times, with the car and combine harvester doing battle in the corn field, but all such moments were taken from the book. Steve soon got into character after meeting Thorson. With his typical originality and inventiveness, McQueen added a few of his own ideas to the part of Thorson: he decided to drive his car clumsily; Steve also brought his own personality into the script by making Thorson a keen collector, of toys especially. Kulik said: "The toys were solely Steve's idea, they were very expensive, we spent $35,000 on them if I remember rightly and I thought we got precious little use out of them. In fact the day after we finished shooting, Steve drove a truck on to the lot and took them all home!" Fred Koenekamp was not aware of Steve's fondness for toys and this soon became a shared interest. On display in the Koenekamp residence, just outside of Los Angeles, are model fire engines bought from all around the world. He was delighted when Steve brought in some of his toys for props. The two men chatted like young kids discussing their latest Christmas gifts. "Steve had a lot of input on that movie with all the little gimmicks he came up with like the toys." said Koenekamp. "He was trying to make that part a character he believed in and liked."

The movie required a lot of stunt work on location around Chicago and Steve was well known for performing the majority of his own stunts, but now he thought it was the time to stop. He told the director prior to shooting: "I'm not doing stunts any more, I'm too old. You've got Loren Janes, who's a great double for me - let him do them." It was an attempt by Steve to take things easy and conserve his energy, but his deeper, competitive spirit soon got the better of him, as Kulik recalled. "When Steve told me he wasn't doing stunts, it was typical of a guy that age, no real surprise. Then, all of a sudden, he seemed to have a change of heart." The most dangerous scene called for Thorson to lie on top of a city 'L' train moving at normal speed, while it went under a tunnel with only two feet of clearance. The crew experimented first by placing a stick on the train to clarify the gap between the train and the tunnel roof. It was the kind of stunt most actors would happily leave to his double, but not McQueen. Says Kulik, "I was going to film it another way using a stunt man, but as soon as he saw me on the train lining up the shot, he said: 'If you're up there, I'm up there.' His natural competitiveness came through. He did a number of things like that at the last minute."

While on location, Steve was working hard with his personal trainer and close friend Pat Johnson, trying to take good care of himself – as he had done through most of his career until the mid-seventies when semi-retirement beckoned. "You could tell he was taking better care of himself at this time," Steve's hairdresser Bren Plaistowe noted. "He didn't seem to be drinking all that much, he didn't do drugs anymore and he was eating well. He might have been a little crazy when he was younger but not by this stage of his life, when he was eating bran muffins and healthy things like that. It was almost impossible to tell that he was ill at that time. He mentioned how tired he was feeling a few times, but I just put that down to the location work, not all that long after he had filmed *Tom Horn* also."

One crew member alleged that Steve was reluctant to spend much time around Plaistowe because she was promiscuous towards him and he was not keen to be surrounded by that kind of behaviour, or temptation maybe, when he was in love with his wife-to-be, Barbara Minty. The Steve McQueen of old would not have thought twice about bedding a pretty blonde crew member – his career was littered with such occasions. Neile, his long-term first wife was well accustomed to it. But this was a different, more content and mature Steve McQueen from those days. "There was a little bit of sexual tension between us," Plaistowe commented. "We felt it; there was a bond. But we were professional and didn't act on it. I was married and he was in love with Barbara, but if it was another time and another place I think we would have enjoyed one another's company. We had just the one moment, when we were on the tram, or 'the L' as they're known in Chicago. Steve looked at me and said in this slow, quiet voice, 'If I wasn't nearly married...' I said, 'M-i-s-t-e-r M-c-Q-u-e-e-n!' I never called him that but you could say we had a moment. But that was as close as we came to anything happening between us. I was attractive and young and, at 26, I was 20 years younger than most hairstylists in those days. Steve just exuded sexuality; he was a man's man and most certainly a lady's man. The combination of the two was very exciting. He was just a very cool, low-key person."

While on location, Steve would often go out for dinner with certain members of the cast and crew. In fact he was universally well liked because he made it his business to know the names of people as lowly as the grip or the electrician and would often greet them daily by their first name. Buzz Kulik, meantime, was present on more than one occasion when Steve exhibited the rebellious but lovable rogue-like behaviour that endeared him to so many. "We'd have a few beers and some food and by the time it came to paying the bill, Steve used to say, 'Put it on my account' and then he'd sign Robert Redford's name on the cheque - and get away with it."

Although Steve was famous for being tight-fisted over the years, these were different times. He never enjoyed giving autographs but as principal photography began in the slum area of Chicago on Kenmore Street, he was generous in so many ways. He had 2,000 signed eight-by-ten glossy photos distributed to locals; after observing the lack of sporting resources there he gave his buddy and stunt double Loren Janes a bundle of cash with orders to go out and buy hundreds of baseballs, bats, mitts and footballs for the local kids, with strict direction to leave them on a nearby sports field for the kids to claim and use; and he donated a significant cash amount to the local church, and even persuaded Mort Engleberg to match his donation. None of these gestures, though, came close to what he did for a local teenage girl by the name of Karen Wilson. With no father to speak of, she was the breadwinner for her family. Steve was especially interested in the plight of this girl.

"We visited Karen's mother deep in a ghetto neighbourhood, where we found her and her entire family living in squalor," explained Barbara Minty, in her excellent, warmly-written book *The Last Mile*. "It didn't take long for Steve to get down to business. 'We'd like to take Karen back with us to California, put her in a good school so that she has a chance to get out of here'," he told Karen's ill mother, who was apparently offended at first and said no. Gradually she came to realise the excellent opportunity awaiting her daughter, like a gift from God, and she changed her mind. Despite Steve's other kind deeds, this particular act even took Barbara by surprise. "Once *The Hunter* wrapped, we enrolled her in a private boarding school in nearby Ojai," added Barbara. "The school was a prestigious one and everyone that went there was either rich or spoiled. Karen was neither. Her grades were not up to par, but that was understandable given her background. She was a bright kid and the school's administration loved her free spirit and the fact she was a thankful and appreciative child, so they accepted her. They also gave her the extra attention she needed and her grades improved almost immediately. On weekends, we picked Karen up from school and brought her back to our home so she could have some sense of normality. Almost a year after we became her legal guardians, Karen's mother passed away in June 1980. Steve and I personally saw to it that she graduated High School." Years later, Karen was married with four children and working in Los Angeles.

Steve did not want to publicize what he and Barbara had done for Karen. He liked good PR, of course he did. After all, he used publicists throughout his career. But he would never have made such a humane, compassionate gesture as this just for good media coverage. Steve cared for her; he simply loved children. He never knew his father and he empathized with Karen. Because his own childhood was so tough he liked to make a positive difference to kids' lives where he could, though this was something altogether different. A small number on the set did come to discover what Steve and Barbara had done for Karen, as it wasn't unusual for Barbara to be holding her hand behind the scenes. "Hardly anybody else on the set knew anything about it," John Elliott recalled. "I knew at the time but that was only because I was one on one with Steve for an hour every morning and we would talk a lot. Make-up artists have a different dynamic with actors than anyone else on the set. I didn't tell anybody else what Steve had told me. But it was no surprise to me because it just seemed pretty consistent with his character as he was such a nice man. He did that from the heart. It was a really, really special thing that Steve did. It was terrible neighbourhood where she had been living." Hairdresser Bren Plaistowe was also aware of what Steve had done for Karen, and was equally shocked at his generosity and warm-heartedness. "I couldn't believe it when they actually took her home," she recounted. "It wasn't announced and was kept quite private. I do remember her being around and Barbara taking this little girl by the hand and walking around with her. She looked really thin and you could tell that she had already had a hard life. Living anywhere in that area would not have been a pleasant life for her. But Steve took her out of that. He saved her."

The Hunter was released in the U.S. on August 1, 1980 to a decent reception but not one that gave Paramount the kind of profits they had hoped for. From a budget of $8 million, it made $37million world-wide ($16.6 million domestically). Steve's performance contained his usual presence, but critics noted an unusual lack of energy and awkwardness in his work. He carried a persistent cough by now and his movements in action sequences were certainly devoid of the grace we had become accustomed to, more resembling a man that was hurting. "The film did alright, it grossed well enough, but I think Steve's illness and subsequent death had a lot to do with the picture not being received as well as it should have been around the world," Kulik said. "He went into hospital when we were cutting the film and died not long after its release. Those at Paramount and myself thought his death squashed the interest surrounding the movie."

Audience reaction could have followed two paths: the one where they rush to see Steve McQueen in his final movie or where they would prefer to mourn the passing of Hollywood's most exhilarating actor by choosing not to view him as a tired man. The latter seemed to apply. But his legacy was there for all. Whether he was leading the Germans a merry dance on his Triumph motorcycle in *The Great Escape* or whether he was fighting flames as the heroic Fire Chief in *The Towering Inferno*, Steve McQueen will always remain one of the coolest movie stars ever. Fittingly, the last words he ever uttered in his movie career were: 'God bless you.'

"He was the King of Cool," added Burton. "There was nobody cooler than Steve McQueen, nobody. And he was very honest and told me he was baffled by the appeal. He said, 'I'm just a kid who was on the wrong side of the tracks, had a hunch, got working and here I am. I don't get it, but I'm lucky as hell'."

Main Credits:

Cast: Steve McQueen (as Ralph 'Papa' Thorson), Eli Wallach, Kathryn Harrold, LeVar Burton, Ben Johnson, Richard Venture, Tracey Walter, Thomas Rosales Jr., Teddy Wilson, Ray Bickel, Bobby Bass, Karl Schueneman and more.

Director:	Buzz Kulik
(Assistant)	Richard Learman, Robert Dahlin (second assistant)
Producer:	Mort Engleberg

Cinematographer:	Fred J. Koenekamp
Writers:	Peter Hyams, Ted Leighton, based on the life story of bounty hunter Ralph Thorson, written by Christopher Keane
Editor:	Robert L. Wolfe
Wardrobe:	Denita Del Signore (women); Tommy Welsh (men)
Make-Up:	John Elliott
Music:	Michael Legrand
Technical Advisor:	Ralph Thorson

REVIEWS:

THE HOLLYWOOD REPORTER, July 28th, 1980

The new Steve McQueen movie, *The Hunter*, reminded me a lot of a Chinese family-style dinner - something from Column A (*Bullitt*), something from Column B (*The Getaway*), something from Column C (*The French Connection*). You mix'em and match'em - and in two hours, you're hungry again. But not, I'm afraid, for another *Hunter's* stew...What I find so distressing about this Paramount release is the realisation that without McQueen's participation, it would probably never have been made - and the world would not be any the poorer.

MOVIETONE NEWS, March 13th, 1981

It's a neat idea for Steve McQueen, who started his career playing a bounty hunter on TV, to confront his own image by playing an ageing contemporary bounty hunter in a sort of '*Bullitt* Grows Old' adventure film.

Steve McQueen at his very best, in *Papillon*
(COURTESY: ALLIED ARTISTS /
BRITISH FILM INSTITUTE)

REFLECTIONS OF STEVE McQUEEN

'I've heard people say that he played himself, but in real life I never saw in front of me the guy who's on the screen. I saw an intense guy who clearly had a hard time getting up there after his early childhood. He overcame a lot of very difficult things in his life to achieve what he did.'
– Emanuel L. Wolf

'STEVE WAS a very big star and was serious box-office. And he was also great to work with. I worked with George C. Scott for 37 years but also John Wayne and Steve, and they were very similar in how they were just so famous that they were constantly hunted down by fans and it therefore made them become very private people.'
— **Del Acevedo** (Make-Up Artist on *Nevada Smith* & *The Sand Pebbles*)

'WHEN ACTORS are born and raised in the theatre, like Steve was, it is hard to master the screen, but Steve did - he was born

STEVE MCQUEEN: THE COOLER KING

to be a movie star. It is unbelievable to think that he never won an Oscar in his career. He only ever received one Oscar nomination and he should certainly have received more; maybe he slept with somebody's wife and upset the wrong people, I don't know. He was badly under-rated as an actor. Steve really had a spark and was quite unique. He didn't play by the Hollywood rules, he danced to his own drummer and I always found him charming.'

— **Edie Adams** (Co-Star on *Love with the Proper Stranger* & neighbour in Malibu)

❧

'WHEN I got the job to work on *Tom Horn*, I thought 'Oh no, I haven't got to work with this guy again have I?' because after three months with him on *The Thomas Crown Affair* he got to be fairly trying. Every time he needed making up he'd say, 'Oh no not again, mumble, grumble et cetera.' I got on okay with Steve but there was a certain way to handle him. When he moaned I'd say to him, 'Well I don't care what you look like; it's your face on the screen.' Then he'd say, 'If that's the way it is, you had better make me look good then.' You just had to kid him along. Underneath that hard exterior, he wasn't a bad sport - it was just self-consciousness and ego.'

— **Del Armstrong** (Make-Up Artist on *The Thomas Crown Affair* & *Tom Horn*)

❧

'I THINK Steve would have projected through and become one of the outstanding older character actors in the industry. As for directing, I think he had the strength, knowledge and the humour to become a very good director and would have worked very well with actors if he chose to make that switch. He had the ability to stimulate people, which is very important. God rest his soul, too bad it didn't happen that way.'
— **Newt Arnold** (First Assistant Director on *Junior Bonner, The Getaway & The Towering Inferno*)

'STEVE WAS a magic guy in the time I knew him during the making of *On Any Sunday*. When Steve was around motorcycle guys, he was one of them. He was a good mechanic, he was an outstanding automobile driver and those skills converted well to bikes. He fitted in well with the group and everyone really liked him. Bruce (Brown) used to tease him about being a movie star and Steve just enjoyed the camaraderie. Steve, though, wasn't above playing the movie star card when it was needed like if he'd walk into a restaurant that was closing, he would remove his sunglasses and all of a sudden it wasn't closing anymore. But he never used his celebrity in an arrogant way; people just admired him and reacted to him in that way.

'Steve spoke very little about his movies but Bruce and I felt that his fame was an obstacle at times because we would be interrupted so often, but Steve gave time to his fans. He admitted it could at times get uncomfortable so Bruce asked him, 'So why don't you wear a hat and sunglasses?' And Steve said, 'Because I don't want to look like an idiot!'

'He was such a great, big movie star that people treated him differently. But it never affected him as a guy. When we came from shooting a sequence for *On Any Sunday*, we arrived at the hotel in Las Vegas. Steve parked his truck with his bikes right in front of a sign that said 'No Parking'. But these valet guys that worked there just said, 'No problem Steve, we'll watch your stuff.' But when we pulled up in the same way in our truck they told us, 'Hey guys, the parking lot is in the back.' When we told them we were with him, pointing to Steve, the response was, 'The parking lot is still in the back'.'
— **Bob Bagley** (Head of Production and Cinematographer for *On Any Sunday*)

❧

'BEFORE WORKING with Steve I had seen all his big movies like *The Magnificent Seven, The Great Escape, The Thomas Crown Affair, Bullitt*, then after *Le Mans* he did *Papillon* when I thought he was fucking brilliant, along with Dustin Hoffman. Because I knew Steve so well, I could just see him in his roles, it was just like Steve.

'Before us drivers met him on *Le Mans*, we saw him in those movies and to us he was like a real life James Bond. The things he did in movies like *The Great Escape* was just great entertainment and everyone likes to be entertained. The funny thing is he didn't want to be an actor; he wanted to be a driver. Whereas we didn't want to be an actor, we were happy driving. We were just pleased he became a part of our world.

'Steve liked us (drivers) because he knew we weren't trying to get anything out of him. Most of the people that he came into contact with were after a photo or an autograph, or wanted to upstage him or were trying to prove they were a better actor than him. We weren't like that; if anything, he wanted to upstage us as he wanted to prove himself as a driver.

'He and I rented a small chateau with our families for the last month of *Le Mans*. I remember going out in the garden and firing a .45 with him, because he had a gun with him over there. So we went out shooting in the garden, doing that sort of thing. When I look back on it I do think, 'Bloody hell, I was sharing a house with the biggest movie star in the world and the sad part is I don't remember that much because it was so normal. We really did live a normal life.

'Steve never changed. He was who he was. I met him again after the movie and had dinner in Hollywood with him and Ali MacGraw. It was an amazing experience, quite like dining out with Tom Cruise in this era I suppose. He kept saying to me, 'You have to come and ride bikes with me out in the desert', as he had a little hut out there. Sadly I wasn't a man of leisure and couldn't just say to my wife, 'Bye sweetheart, I'm just going to go and ride a bike in the desert with Steve McQueen'. I never did, but we used to keep in contact. He wrote letters to me; if only I could have kept those letters. When we changed our business premises they were accidentally thrown out with everything else. Can you imagine Steve McQueen writing a bloody letter?! It wasn't typed, he wrote it longhand.

'I think he liked me because I didn't treat him like a superstar, I treated him with respect; we all did. The tragic thing is that, years later, he phoned my office when I wasn't in and I got a message from my receptionist saying 'Mr McQueen called and he would like you to phone him back'. I didn't get around to it because I didn't know he was ill. He died three weeks later.'
— **Derek Bell** (Racing Buddy and Colleague on *Le Mans*)

'I'm glad Steve is getting some attention with this book. When he died it took a long time for him to get much attention and I was surprised by that. Steve is sadly not around to enjoy it but I'm glad books like this are being dedicated to his memory.

'I worked with Paul Newman on *When Time Ran Out*, and there were similarities between Paul and Steve. They were both good looking, very attractive, but both very different in other ways. Steve didn't say much and had a mystery about him; whereas Paul was rather jolly, jokey and had a kind of spontaneous freshness to him. He would be kind to crowds but he was similar to Steve in that he was always keen to get away into his own space; before he got into his 'I don't sign autographs mode'. I don't remember Steve ever signing an autograph.

'Ultimately, Steve was a good actor and quite a fascinating man and there are not that many men who are as intriguing as Steve. Yes he was handsome and was an exciting actor but he also had that intriguing quality about him, because of the way he went

about his business. He was quiet and you never quite knew what was going on in his head. That has a kind of sexuality and that's intriguing – you don't know too much and it gives off a kind of mystery. Nowadays people are so out there and open, you get to know too much, and I think a bit of holding back is interesting.'
— **Jacqueline Bisset** (Co-Star on *Bullitt*)

⁓

'STEVE'S ENDURING popularity is quite incredible. I have been asked to do so many interviews about Steve McQueen in the last few years but no one ever asks me about Paul Newman. It's interesting how his legacy really lives on. Maybe people prefer to know more about the bad boys, similarly with James Dean. I've done a few autograph shows and I can't believe how many people want to speak about *The Towering Inferno*. It has such a cult following and I suppose much of that has to do with Steve McQueen. I feel very lucky that I agreed to do that movie and was part of it.

'It's sad that we only had Steve for such a short period. I sometimes wonder what he would have done had he lived on. He was so very instinctive and always knew what worked for him.'
— **Susan Blakely** (Co-Star on *The Towering Inferno*)

⁓

'I WATCHED him act closely on the set of *The Getaway* one day and after they filmed this particular scene, I went to the director Sam Peckinpah and said, 'I don't get it; he doesn't look like he is doing anything.' So Sam got me to sit right under the camera one day when we were in a very tight set and said, 'Watch now, and then we will see dailies.' Again I didn't see him do much while sitting almost right in front of him. But when I went to dailies it was all there. He had an incredible magic between the camera and himself that the naked eye didn't see.

'He also had this attraction that grew on you as you were around him. And I think when he wanted to pour it on, he could. The playful part of Steve stood out for me. He considered it great fun to pick me up – probably because I didn't like it – and run around with me or stick me in a truck. I did truly like him after a rough start and did see the man who I think probably might have been just as happy being a racer as an actor, but I think we are all grateful that he gave us all those great performances.'
— **Kathy Blondell** (Make-Up Artist on *The Getaway*)

'I WAS just a kid when I worked with Steve and he was very generous to me and I learned a lot from him. Every time I am on a set and there are bright lights, Steve is there. He taught me a trick that I will never forget and something that he said he learnt when shooting *The Magnificent Seven*. 'Look directly into the light with your eyes closed and when you open them, you will be able to focus for a few seconds without squinting or blinking.' It's a technique for film acting that you only get through experience. That was a veteran passing on that knowledge. Steve was very generous with his time, with his talent, with his heart, with his money and with his influence.

'Steve is one of the great movie stars. I'm lucky enough to be able to say that I knew him as a really great guy; a really, kind and caring human being. It's not often that you can meet a hero and have them meet and surpass your expectations. I met Steve at a time in his life when he was more settled so therefore I was never disappointed by the Steve McQueen I encountered. He remained a hero and in front of my eyes his stature only increased through having a personal experience with him and that's really rare for human beings.'

— **LeVar Burton** (Co-Star on *The Hunter*)

❧

'STEVE WAS a jock; he was a man's man. When I worked with him on *The Getaway*, there were never any complaints about having to get wet or dirty or working late or anything like that, which would not have been the case with many lead stars. But Steve was a guy who was always more comfortable hanging out with stuntmen, or on his dirt bike or in a fast car. He hardly ever hung around with other actors. And he liked to drink but only Budweiser beer. He said he didn't like the taste of anything else. He told me, 'You could give me a drink blindfolded and I'd know if it wasn't Budweiser.' And all of Sam Peckinpah's pictures were drinking pictures. A lot of drinking went on. But Steve hardly ever sat around in bars at the end of the day. He would rather swap stories with stuntmen and guys like that. If we were hanging around waiting for shots, he was always talking to the stunt guys and the

drivers – he definitely didn't like to hang with management. He was a crew's crew guy.'
— **Gordon T. Dawson** (Associate Producer and Second Unit Director on *The Getaway*)

ᶜ⁄ᵒ

'WITH STEVE MCQUEEN as my co-star, it was really my first time to play opposite someone who was a great big old movie star, and that's exactly what Steve was. He was one of the best-loved actors around, one whose talent more than equalled his sizeable commercial appeal. Steve I loved. He was darling. He was daunting. Steve McQueen was an absolute professional, and he knew what was necessary technically to achieve his performance every time he got in front of the camera. Steve was all sinewy and tough, but at the same time he had such a vulnerability.'
— **Faye Dunaway** (Co-Star on *The Thomas Crown Affair & The Towering Inferno*)

ᶜ⁄ᵒ

'STEVE WAS complex and had so many different sides. There was that rough side, especially. You could tell he had struggled in his early upbringing. And I have to say I admire the way he succeeded as he did when he could have been much, much, much worse. Who knows how he may have gone if it was not for his acting?

'Later into filming *Le Mans*, I asked someone close to Steve and the movie why everyone tolerated his antics, like being late on the set and everything else. And he explained that in America they don't have any royalty but what they do have is their stars. And at that time Steve McQueen was as big as they came. He played by his own rules and there were a lot of people depending on him in terms of their own careers below him.'

— **Louise Edlind** (Co-Star on *Le Mans* and Girlfriend)

∽

'I HAD known Steve from was when I was a kid and I would see him hanging out in Bud Ekins' motorcycle shop in the early sixties. I didn't get to know him then, just from afar. But when we came together on *The Hunter* he recognised me and we hit it off well. He was just the most unpretentious man in the world. Steve was a man's man and I'm a make-up artist, so I learned how to deal with him. Steve never wanted me to touch him make-up-wise in front of people that were watching. I always had to call him around a corner to touch him up.

'He had an understated generosity. We worked at a hospital this one day and a guy was in a wheelchair after losing his legs. He was watching us film but the movie people never liked that and had to keep the public away. But rather than have some security guy move him on, Steve walked up to him and said, 'Look, I'm sorry but I am going to have to ask you to move back,' and he put $200 in his hand, which I thought was a sweet gesture. I liked Steve a lot.'

— **John M. Elliott** (Make-Up Artist on *The Hunter*)

∽

'HE WAS an awkward bloke when I first knew him on *The War Lover*, but in hindsight none of that matters because he wanted to be on top of the world and he got there. When he achieved his ambition and became the biggest star in the world, he didn't want it. It was hard to understand him because I don't even think he understood himself. He'd endured a horrible childhood, was clearly damaged and was a product of his background.

'Steve made so many wonderful films. I loved *The Thomas Crown Affair* and he was magnificent in *Papillon*; that was Steve's real talent coming out. That's the Steve I admire most and I always knew he had it. He was perfect in that and it suited his character. He could easily have been in prison than in films – there was a thin line.

'The world is a sadder place without him; I would have liked to have seen him as an older man. He had it all but the one thing he never got was the health card. It's so sad.'
— **Shirley Anne Field** (Co-Star on *The War Lover*)

∽

'HARDLY a day goes by when I don't think of Steve. We were very close and very good friends - I miss him very much. Some people will give you a smile and look real nice on screen, but when you meet them they're real bastards. But Steve was just what you saw.

'We talked about a lot of personal things. One night we had an interesting evening; it was raining, absolutely pouring with rain and about eleven at night the bell rang at my house. I opened the door and it was McQueen! He'd got his leathers on and he had his Triumph motorcycle with him. I had a bike the same as his. He said, 'Come on let's go; let's play.' So I put my leathers on and out I went. He took me to where he lived as a young man...in the rain...and this would now be about midnight. I then took him to where I'd been raised and we talked. We both had similar backgrounds and I think that's what drew us together as friends, because I understood him and he didn't have to talk too much.

'He didn't trust hardly anybody. At first, he used to play games with me by giving me a piece of information - some-thing that he'd made up which would be quite outrageous, and wait to see if it appeared in the newspapers. Of course it never would because it was nobody's business what he said to me and more importantly because he was my friend. Eventually he came to trust me and I trusted him.'

— **Don Gordon** (Co-Star in *Bullitt, Papillon* & *The Towering Inferno, and Close Friend*)

❧

'I FOUND him to be very amicable, very friendly and I had no problem with him at all when I worked with him. Steve McQueen was Steve McQueen; what you saw was what you got. He was very straightforward and had no deception about anybody or no hidden agenda. He was just grateful

to be an actor; he never thought he would be but he was. He was one of those natural actors who just played himself all the time. But he worked hard and tried to be good, as he knew little classical training. He had a natural Steve McQueen attraction and he made it work for him as best he could.'
— **John Michael Hayes** (Screenwriter on *Nevada Smith*)

ော

'INITIALLY, I had two impressions of Steve when he was training in New York: one was that he looked a very commercially usable type and also, I knew that he must have been a good actor otherwise Peggy Feury wouldn't have accepted him as a student - although I never thought he'd have the career that he did. When we worked together on *Nevada Smith*, I hadn't seen him since those New York days, but I still followed his career with interest. I would hear exploits about him being a daredevil bike-rider, which we all saw in *The Great Escape*.'
— **Pat Hingle** (Co-Star on *Nevada Smith*)

ော

'HE WAS a fascinating guy - just for the fact that he was Steve McQueen. When he spoke I'd kind of study him. It was hard to sit with him and not think of *The Great Escape*, *Bullitt*, *Love with the Proper Stranger*, *The Towering Inferno* and all these movies where he was the coolest movie star I ever saw. Although he didn't look like that at the time he was still fascinating. He might not have been a great actor, but Steve

was the most exciting and charismatic movie star of his time. I'm just disappointed that I never got to make a film with Steve McQueen, but it was certainly a thrill to spend some time with him.'
— **Peter Hyams** (Screenwriter on *The Hunter*)

ഐ

'I THINK there was nobody better than Steve, especially in his era, because he was one of the first to do really good action pictures and it was a joy to watch him work. He gave the industry something different; he brought a bit of salt and pepper to the screen. At one time the vast majority of action films were westerns and Steve started the trend of going the other way - though not against them as he did his share of westerns. He just never made the action pieces that we know today, which are pretty mindless. They might as well re-issue them but under different titles, because they're basically all the same. Steve's movies had warmth, substance and action. There was something else there besides mindless violence. *Bullitt* and *The Getaway* are great examples.'
— **L.Q. Jones** (Co-Star on *Hell Is for Heroes*)

ഐ

'STEVE IS one of the nicest people I have met in my career. I clearly remember one day in particular when my wife and two daughters, who were four and six at the time, came to

575

meet me for lunch as I wanted to show them around. I was just a young editor making my way in the industry at the time (though had already made his name on *One Flew Over the Cuckoo's Nest*). As we came out of the studio, Steve saw me while he was on this bicycle from a block away, and he shouted over, 'Hey Shelly, stay there; don't go anywhere.' He rode his bike right up to me and declared, 'I want to meet your family.'

'Given what a big star he was, my wife could not believe that he would come from a block away where he was riding his bike to say hello to us. He shook hands with my family and exchanged some small talk but it made me feel good and made them feel good. I was only a young film editor at the time and my wife turned to me afterwards and said, 'You must be doing well if a big star like Steve McQueen goes out of his way to meet us.' That's the type of memories I have of him.'

— **Sheldon Kahn** (Editor on *An Enemy of the People*)

 ⁘

'He was so young when he passed and had a lot of work left in him. My favourite Steve McQueen movie would be *Papillon*, but he also did a hell of a job on *Sand Pebbles*. In *Bullitt* when he was chasing that car, he was just terrific, and in *The Thomas Crown Affair*. To my knowledge he never made a bad film; if he did his performance made it better. He was a guy's guy actor;

I didn't like pussyfooters and Steve was a macho good guy all the time. I've often thought about who would be the modern day version of Steve and I struggle to think of one, but Brad Pitt might be close.'

— **Fred Koenekamp** (Cinematographer on *Papillon, The Towering Inferno & The Hunter*)

'I'M NOT surprised that his legend lives on. He was his own man and a strange individual who had these quirks that were very interesting, very different. I remember once at Columbia when he used to drive this beautiful old Mercedes - he wouldn't bring it onto the lot because he thought there were too many nails on the roads that the carpenters had dropped inside the gates, so he used to leave it outside on the main road and walk in. He had a number of these fascinating idiosyncrasies. He ended up living in a hangar; he took me up in a Stearman once and I thought I was going to die. Steve built a home out of this aeroplane hangar and he lived there just shortly before he died; going to that lifestyle from his gorgeous beach house in Trancas, Malibu. He was a very special individual and a lot of fun to be with.'

— **Buzz Kulik** (Director on *The Hunter*)

'THEY CALL him 'The King of Cool' and there's no question about that; he was a damned good actor. *The Thomas Crown Affair* is a good example. (Director) Norman Jewison didn't want him for that role but he was excellent in that movie, with that sexy scene between Steve and Faye Dunaway across the chess board; just brilliant. Steve was more versatile than people would give him credit for. The training he got in New York with those great teachers showed up but was not overly visible to the average eye.

'Because I knew what he was trying to do as an actor I felt he was a very responsible actor than one who just flew by the seat of his pants. Steve was very instinctual and organic. When he went into a scene he knew what it was about; the choices he made would show him off well because he was also a movie star. He wasn't just haphazard, he never walked into scenes just trying to be cool; he studied the scene and he knew the best way for Steve McQueen to play that scene. He did his homework. He may not have been a great actor but he was a very good actor. What I am saying is, he knew how to project himself on the screen as a great movie star. He's a guy from the wrong side of the tracks without (good) parents, comes to New York, wants to be an actor, becomes a movie star and a damned good one. It was quite a journey.'

— **Martin Landau** (Fellow Student at the Actor's Studio and Co-Star on *Nevada Smith*)

'WE WERE on Steve's driveway at his Brentwood home and he said to me, 'Mert, you're the luckiest guy in the world.' I was slightly stunned by that comment and asked him what he meant. He said, 'Well you're No.1 (in motocross) and have earned it and will always be No.1. But me, I'm only an actor and will only be as good as my character. That's not really me.' It was an interesting point of view. Steve was a real neat guy.

'In 1971 he was the grand marshal at the Ontario Motor Speedway; he was doing the 'Gentlemen start your motors' bit. He asked me if my wife June and I would like to accompany he and Neile. I said we'd love that and he arranged for them to send us a helicopter to take us over. But this helicopter pilot would not fly us all as he said there were too many people so Steve simply chartered his own helicopter and flew us out there. He was generous in so many ways through the time I knew him. The way he treated me was unreal.

'I had seen all his movies and he just had an aura about him. You felt lucky and excited just to be in the same room as him. But saying that, he liked to be known as one of the guys; that's until you started to forget the fact he was a movie star. Mal (Malcolm Smith) and I used to tease him and say, 'You're not really an actor, that's just the way you are.' And although that's what he used to tell other people, he also didn't want anyone to forget the hard work he had done to become a star. He'd say, 'No, I have studied hard, I'm an actor. That's my job, that's what I do.' Because he was so

easy to get along with it was sometimes not hard to forget he was a big star.'
— **Mert Lawwill** (World Champion Motorcyclist and Colleague in *On Any Sunday*)

‿

'I LOVED Steve in *The Great Escape*, he was the epitome of every American Rebel, full of himself, confident, and he was both of that in real life too. He was exactly as his character, a rowdy, bike-riding American rebel. A little bit of every young man in him, and why I think men identify with him in that movie.

'Personally, I have the best of memories with Steve. We didn't fight, didn't argue, we rode his dirt bikes in the sands of Palm Springs in our bathing suits, laughing, feeling free and that is how I think of Steve; being free to be who you are, never asking permission from anyone on how to behave, no validation from the world… just being Steve McQueen. He rules and he always will to those who love him for the man he was, the actor he was, the movies he left behind for all to enjoy.'
— **Barbara Leigh** (Co-Star on *Junior Bonner* and Girlfriend)

‿

'THE EXPERIENCE at the time was for me, wonderful and great, working with John Sturges and of course Steve. He and his wife Neile were kind and fun to be with and we kept in touch for a couple of years after the movie. I was in Munich for 16 weeks and made some splendid friends (like Steve).

'Steve and I learned our lines (together) on the set or location. There's no secret to Steve's talent – it's all up there on the screen – and was indeed a joy to watch.'
— **Angus Lennie** (Co-Star on *The Great Escape*)

❧

'STEVE WAS always looking for ways of enhancing his role in a film. In anything he ever did he always wanted to emphasize whatever character he was playing. Steve is remembered in *The Great Escape* not for playing Hilts but for the bike chase sequence.

'He was always looking for what we called 'a lot of business' to do within the scene. He would create a lot of idiosyncrasies in the scene and it can be a bit off-putting for the other person if one is fiddling around to steal the scene. But I think Steve was quite discreet with the way he did it. There was that scene when he asks Richard Attenborough how many he is planning to take out and he replies, '250?' He pulled a bit of a face and put a lot of drama into that, which was a clever way of grabbing the camera's attention. It's taking acting to the next step. Every actor tries to get as much as he can out of every scene and Steve was one of the best at it.

'I saw Steve almost every day for six months on *The Great Escape* and he was a very nice guy; he wasn't standoffish or anything like that; he was very friendly. John Sturges introduced me to Steve at a pre-shoot party at Geiselgasteig studios as we were two of the first ones to pitch up. John seemed on edge and introduced us three times and Steve picked up on it and said, 'Hey John, chill man, you've already introduced us twice!' Steve was a real nice guy and we stayed in touch after the movie.'

— **John Leyton** (Co-Star on *The Great Escape*)

❧

'I WORKED WITH Steve on and off for over six months while he was preparing for and then shooting *The Towering Inferno*. I did not sense a movie star ego with Steve. Out of necessity, Steve prized his privacy above all. I believe that one was allowed to enter his inner circle if there was trust and respect for his privacy. In fact he explained to me on the first day that I met him during a pre-production meeting, when he had a big beard and long hair, that he needed the 'disguise' so that he could lead a somewhat normal life in public. I always respected that and did not ask for one autograph during my entire six-month involvement with the movie. My brother was visiting the set one day and during a break the studio photographer was taking a picture of the two of us; Steve walked by and asked if we would like a photo with him. Of course, we accepted. Steve was extremely personable and friendly. We spent some time between scenes chatting and I was invited to his motor home on occasions when it was okay with him.

'After the conclusion of production, he and Ali invited my wife Millie and I out to dinner at a very nice, quaint, French restaurant on Melrose Avenue called Le Saint Germaine. There were no menus and Steve ordered for all of us. It was apparent that Steve and Ali were well known at the restaurant. We met in the bar and Steve ordered a Millers beer. They did not have this brand, but I noticed rather quickly that one of the parking valets was running up the street to a market, and the Millers suddenly appeared.

'Before then, I had invited Millie to the set one day to watch some of the scenes. Steve walked up and asked if this was Millie. I introduced them and they got along just great. Steve always inquired about how she was doing. I think that this occurred because of our approach in respecting their privacy. When Millie would visit the set and Steve was working, he would invite her to sit next to the camera in his director's chair, which was from *Papillion* and had the butterfly logo embroidered. It was the only chair on the set that was as high as the director's and Irwin Allen's chairs'.

'Steve appeared to be in awe of people who could lead a normal life and go anywhere and at any time and have privacy. After the production, Steve and Ali asked my wife and I to join them for a few days at, I believe, the Ventana Inn, Big Sur, California. We could not go, primarily because I had utilized all of my allowed time off for the year from my fire department work to work on the movie.'
— **Peter Lucarelli** (Technical Adviser on *The Towering Inferno*)

'IT'S KIND of hard to believe that Steve only ever received one Oscar nomination. To me he was a great actor. Before I worked with him I used to think that when an actor had a lot of dialogue he must have an important role; but Steve made me realise that being able to act without words is just as important.'

— **Mako** (Co-Star on *The Sand Pebbles*)

∾

'I REMEMBER when I was in an off-Broadway play, *A Hatful of Rain*, with Steve McQueen. On one occasion we all decided to go to a restaurant for dinner. Steve was driving and we all piled in his car – myself and several other cast members. We learned our lesson very quickly and never did that again because on the way to dinner there was a long, very steep hill. And to our fright he took it on, racing downhill at top speed. We were all terrorized! Needless to say we were all happy to still be alive after that experience and learned an important lesson: Do not ride with McQueen!'

— **Vitina Marcus** (Actress on *A Hatful of Rain* and Co-Star on *Never Love A Stranger*)

∾

'IN THE time I knew Steve, he just wanted to fit in and be one of the guys (around Santa Paula airport). I was just 20 at the time but I was a qualified flight instructor like my Dad and we both taught Steve to fly. I remember this one day when a woman who worked at the airport was a fan of his and wanted to meet him. I asked Steve and he said ok, so I brought her over to introduce them and said, 'Hey, here's that movie star you wanted to meet.' After they had a quick chat and she went away, Steve turned to me and said, 'Don't EVER do that to me again. I don't appreciate being introduced as a 'movie star.' And then he finished with the words, 'Now, you owe me a lemonade!' He had a really good way of dealing with people. He let me know he didn't like what I did but he wasn't angry – I don't think I ever saw him mad.

'Another time, when we stayed at a small motel in Portabello, I was in the swimming pool and there were a couple of girls in there also. Steve was giving me this eye contact as if to say, 'Hey, there's girls there, go and have a chat with them.' But he got up first and went over to them and said, 'Hey girls that's my flight instructor over there, you should go talk with him.' Steve didn't feel the need to identify himself as a movie star, he kind of had fun with his anonymity. He really liked to hide behind his beard.

'He did something similar when we were in a bar after a flight to Watsonville. We got talking to a few people and had dinner together. When the bill came, Steve said, 'I'll take care of this,' and he gave the waiter his credit card and said, 'but be careful, as this card belongs to Steve McQueen.

'Around that time he gave me a tour around his hangar, where he kept his extensive collection of antique motorcycles and cars. He would walk to each motorcycle and tell a detailed story about each one, when it was popular and so on. One was a mail service bike and he gave me its history – he had a wealth of knowledge. For all I knew he could have been making it up, but it was a real interesting tour. He was still passionate about bikes then and I was able to witness that for myself on another occasion. We were flying about 30 miles east from Santa Paula and there was a motorcycle track that used to be there called Indian Dunes. Steve looked down and

saw this sidecar motorcycle race and he said to me, over the headset, 'Hey is there any way we can land down there?' They did have a runway but it was private, so we went ahead and landed. Straight away a guy came over to shoo us away and then recognised McQueen and said, 'Oh, you guys can stay.' We got on the back of these dirt bikes to get a lift to the race and I asked this kid, 'Do you know who that guy is?' And he went, 'Yeah, that's Steve McQueen!' with this big grin.'
— **Pete Mason** (Steve McQueen's flight instructor)

'I HAVE a spot in my heart for this guy and it will always be there. I truly, truly adored him. He was a good man and eccentric as shit. He would choose the busiest moments to ask crazy questions. Like for instance, on *Tom Horn* when I was moving some cattle, he was adamant about knowing what the guys were having for lunch, because he wanted to take care of his crew. I said, 'Steve, the day you sit down with us and eat the same as the crew is the day I know you're really interested, now leave me alone.' He had his own cook and I knew he would never eat the same as everyone else, but he *was* genuinely interested about his crew though.

'Steve used to say to me, 'Don't ever take drugs.' I never did and was probably the weird one in Hollywood that never took drugs. As he'd tell me, he would be drinking Coors beer in a glass with ice in it. He'd say, 'I drink Coors beer because it doesn't have these other additives.' He was funny like that. Anyway, it was common knowledge that he had done drugs in his life and his whole point was, 'Don't make the same mistakes as me - been there done it.' He was charming.

'People reacted to Steve in various ways. He could intimidate you without trying because of who he was, and a lot of people reacted to him in awe. If he said, 'I'm thirsty,' five guys would run to get him a drink; or if he said, 'Today I wanna chew apple-jack tobacco,' the prop guy would go out and buy fifty cases of it! People over-reacted to him, partly because they wanted to win his favour, but also because they were intimidated by his status. He was a wealthy guy who was used to getting his own way and Steve could be very demanding and he didn't like not getting his own way. He adored me, we got along very well and I think that's because I treated him like a regular guy - he appreciated that.'
— **Ed Milkovich** (Second Assistant Director on *Tom Horn*)

'IT WASN'T only his ability as an actor (that I liked), he had an incredible personality. He had those twinkling eyes and was so marvellously handsome - he really was something. I liked him as a person; we got along very well together. I enjoyed my relationship with him and I am only sorry that he is not here today. I think he would have gone on and continued to have a *real* career because he had such a commanding personality.'
— **Walter Mirisch** (Executive Producer on *The Magnificent Seven, The Great Escape* & *The Thomas Crown Affair*)

'STEVE WAS a much better actor than he allowed himself to be after he became a major star. Once that spotlight turns on it tends to blind people, and they often lose their way. Steve isn't the first actor that's happened to, and he won't be the last. Toward the end of his life, it seemed to me he was trying to get back to being a working actor again. It's sad that he didn't have more time.'

— **Robert Mulligan** (Director of *Love with the Proper Stranger & Baby, the Rain Must Fall*)

❧

'STEVE ALWAYS seemed to have this attitude in his films that said, 'I'm going to survive whatever you throw at me.' He had that rebellious quality in an entirely different way to somebody like Marlon Brando. Steve never wanted to have a part where he was the big talker. Gary Cooper made a living out of that too. Reacting is a lot harder than it looks. Steve's eyes could express so much. He knew what his strengths were and that's how you get to become a great actor.'

— **Mary Murphy** (Co-Star on *Junior Bonner*)

❧

'STEVE IS one of those people I've worked with who's more a movie star than an actor. Although he did a fine job as an actor, he was like a John Wayne, who extended his own personality on screen, rather than create a lot of different characterisations. You knew what you were going to see with a John Wayne film and it was the same with Steve McQueen. When he tried to break out of his normal range it didn't work, like with *An Enemy of the People*.

'Steve is one of the truly great movie stars I've ever worked with. He had a quality that was very appealing and very interesting. I myself always found him interesting on screen, even if I felt his acting wasn't too good, because he had movie star quality. He had the magnetism of his own personality, which he projected on to the screen very well. People want to see it. When I was a kid I liked John Garfield, who was like Steve - a tough guy. I didn't want to see him acting any differently; if he did I'd never buy it. People compare Steve with James Cagney and Humphrey Bogart, which are not bad comparisons though they both had more range.'

— **Don Murray** (Co-Star on *Baby, the Rain Must Fall*)

'I FIRST met Steve when he came from New York as I was the assistant director at that time on Rawhide, with Clint Eastwood and Eric Fleming. I met Steve when he came out for work on westerns and things like that and eventually he obviously landed his own series (*Wanted: Dead or Alive*). But we became friends because I was racing a Lotus 11 at that time and he got into sports car racing and we both ended up driving Formula Juniors. We competed against each other so we'd see one another on weekends at those races as well as at the studios. We went our separate ways though as he began his great career and I did my own thing too. Then we met up again for *The Cincinnati Kid*.

'We never had a close relationship but we had a nice relationship whereby I knew if I needed some information on something I could always call him and he knew he could do the same. I grew up in the film business – my mother and father were in it – so I was not easily impressed. That meant I was not in awe of film stars and Steve liked that, he wanted people to talk to him like a regular guy, which is what I did. And the motor racing aspect also helped our friendship. I saw him towards the end when he came back from Mexico and he looked like Victor Buono or Sidney Greenstreet, he was completely blown up like a balloon. It was really sad to see."
— **Kurt Neumann Jr.** (Racing Buddy and Assistant Director on *The Cincinnati Kid*)

℘

'STEVE WAS darling. I just thought he was one of the neatest guys I ever met in Hollywood. Certainly one of the most exciting men I ever met, which was quite unique because most actors are pretty boring when you actually get to know them off-camera.

'He was a very fine actor and is quite rightly known as 'The King of Cool'. The motorbike chase on *The Great Escape* piqued people's interest in him and he went on to do a lot of good movies after that. I had a great deal of respect for him as a man and an actor. It's curious that he was always more comfortable around mechanics than movie stars. I think that summed up the kind of guy that he was.'
— **Chris Noel** (Co-Star on *Soldier in the Rain* and Girlfriend)

∽

'IT HAS been an interesting journey for me working on his Collection, in terms of coming to better appreciate McQueen's work. Learning both the body of work and the life behind has been the useful part of working with McQueen's total package. That he was able not only to succeed, but become an international 'icon' and remain so long after his death, after the ferocious and unexpected struggles he had growing up, is almost unfathomable. McQueen owned up to that 'sense of wonder' in many an interview.

'To pick a contribution from him to Hollywood in general, one might not go wrong with the quality of visual intensity. McQueen could do more with his facial expressions than many can do with their dialogues. He might well have been a throwback to the best of the silent-film era male stars – say, Richard Barthelmess, John Gilbert, Sessue Hayakawa, Harold Lloyd, Rudolph Valentino, or William S. Hart – who had to make their faces tell a goodly part of the tale, and succeeded.

'I can say that McQueen does now, for me, possess some of the same 'presence' that I have enjoyed in the work of my all-time favourite actor James Cagney. I do pay attention to his characters, and what they are looking like and doing, and how they are reacting. I agree with the often cited strengths and weaknesses of his body of work, but I don't think that all the weaker ones are as bad as claimed by some. *An Enemy of the People* and *Baby, the Rain Must Fall*

are, I think, a pair of wrongly-overlooked films, but he was indeed probably most heavily miscast in *Soldier in the Rain*.'
— **Steve Nontell** (of The Steve McQueen Birthplace Collection, Beech Grove Public Library, Indiana)

&

'I didn't interview Steve McQueen and it seems to me his work is summed up by the old adage: "the camera loves you or the camera doesn't." In his case it did.'
— **Sir Michael Parkinson** (Legendary Chat Show Host)

&

'THERE ARE two sides to celebrities and 99 per cent of us only get to see the actor's side of their personality on the screen. On this side Steve was a tremendous actor; he could take a role and make it look real. In *Bullitt*, gee, he was good. He made his character look real in *Junior Bonner* and had that limp nailed down - walked it all the time.

'On the personal side, Steve was a very genuine person – you could sit and talk to him about anything. He loved his kids, he liked his privacy, he respected the fact that he was an actor and that people did want his attention but on the other hand he wasn't one that chased the limelight. He just wanted to do a good job in the role he was given to act in. And he did, he studied his lines, knew his lines and was very real.'

— **William Pierce** (Friend and Executive Coordinator on *Junior Bonner*)

༄

'I SPENT a lot of time with Steve during *Le Mans*; we would go into Paris sometimes for social times. And he would lend me his airplane and pilot so that I could go and race at weekends as long as I was back on Monday. He couldn't have been more helpful. We were great friends and I still see his son Chad now.

'We (drivers) loved Steve; he was a great chum, a good friend. We had similar interests because we all loved racing and it really turned us on and turned the girls on as well. We would go to Paris with Steve and all the doors opened wherever we would go. If you were with Steve you would have some fun. A lot of girls would turn up on the set and there were some great parties on the evenings – all kinds of things were going on. It was a very exciting time.'

— **David Piper** (Racing Buddy and Colleague on *Le Mans*)

༄

'I CAN'T say enough good things about Steve McQueen, he was wonderful. I used to make Steve's coffee every morning. He liked honey in his coffee, which I had never done for anyone before so the first time I made coffee for Steve I put three teaspoons of honey in and he nearly choked. He wasn't angry, he just said with a smile, 'Maybe there's just a little too much honey.' He was very charming.

'My father died during *The Hunter* and I was around on the set trying to be as cool as I could be, but Steve was very sensitive. He didn't talk too much and wasn't all that personal but he understood people. He saw I was having tough time and he put his arm around me and his head next to mine and said, 'It's going to be a long day, huh?' He was very sweet with me.

'When I started working with him, I was going round saying to my colleagues, excitedly, 'Oh man, that's Steve McQueen'. And people would say, 'Yeah but just give it a few days,' as if to suggest he was difficult. But I never had any problems with Steve; I just thought he was probably a perfectionist and sometimes that translates to others as being difficult. I am just sad I never got work with Steve McQueen anymore.'

— **Bren Plaistowe** (Hairdresser on *The Hunter*)

ೲ

'THE GETAWAY was my first association with Steve, though I was set to work on *Love with the Proper Stranger* with him in 1963 but I broke my Achilles after falling from a ladder! There were two versions of Steve McQueen for me. I think he was one of the best film actors that ever lived. I watched the scene on *The Getaway* when he built that model out of matches in prison and at the time I said, 'This scene is boring'. But when

I saw it back on film in dailies I thought, 'My God, it's wonderful'. He was a true film actor because I didn't even see his magic when I was sitting there live watching it but his value comes over marvellously on the screen.

'But there was also a cruel side to him, which I didn't like; the way he treated people around him like his wardrobe man and his driver. We were shooting in San Marcos and Steve had a Mexican guy as his driver. One day Steve was sitting on a stool in this square with his shirt off and there were hundreds of people watching from the side. This guy brought Steve a mug of milk and a peanut butter and jelly sandwich and the guy stood there holding this tray out for a long time and Steve treated him like a lowly waiter which I didn't like. There were a few things like that which bothered me; like when he would finish a scene and would just take off and drop his jacket on the floor so his wardrobe man would have to chase after him and pick it up off the floor. I was quite pleased when this movie ended. I got along very well with the director Sam Peckinpah, though, but I would see Sam roll his eyes at Steve many times.'

— **Michael Preece** (Script Supervisor / Continuity on *The Getaway*)

❦

'I HAVE the utmost respect for anyone who achieves so much in this business, because it's very tough in Hollywood where everyone is trying to make it. Steve was a true professional, just like John Wayne when I worked with him on *In Harm's Way*. I thought John Wayne was one of those actors who just shot his scenes with a minimum amount of fuss or preparation. But I was surprised to see that he rehearsed his part as hard as anyone I've ever worked with. Steve was equally serious about his acting and was equally exciting on the screen; he cared deeply about what he was doing. It seemed to me as though people like Steve McQueen and John Wayne just acted themselves in their movies - they were so natural.'

— **Paula Prentiss** (Co-Star on *The Honeymoon Machine*)

'I FOUND Steve reasonably easy to deal with. He arrived with respect at the outset. Our previous work enabled him to know our history, to have a sense of our work, so we weren't a blank slate. He seemed to feel that he was playing at this level...

'There was no rivalry (with Paul Newman). If he secretly was competing with Paul, he kept that to himself. We did three movies with Paul and I found Paul professional, hard-working, exceedingly cooperative and collaborative. Steve was less so. Steve was good but he was more like a street kid who found his way into an acting career.

'(But) when I worked with him on *The Reivers*, I found Steve more than competent; we both found him very competent in the part. In fact, privately, this movie held a special place for my husband and me. It may have been his favourite.

I don't really have favourites but it was a particular triumph for us professionally and personally.'

— **Harriet Ravetch** (Co-Screenwriter on *The Reivers*, along with her long-time collaborator and husband Irving Ravetch. They also wrote three films for Paul Newman)

❧

"I WAS on the set of *The Reivers* as a ten-year-old and McQueen offered me my first beer but made me swear never to smoke!

'He called me Slim. We encountered one another about a decade later, shortly before he died. I had just gotten my pilot's license and he had a plane which he kept at a small airfield near Los Angeles called Santa Paula Airport. I took a friend for lunch there and Steve was in the corner booth under a baseball cap. There was a gorgeous moment for me where we recounted that beer from my youth and he asked me if I smoked and I said, 'No'. And he said, 'Well you certainly filled out, Slim.' Steve showed me his airplane or "his girl" as he called it, before he took off into the bluest sky I think I ever remember.'

— **Josh Ravetch** (Nephew of Writers' Irving and Harriet Ravetch; now a Writer/Director)

❧

'I REMEMBER Steve on the personal side for having fun and being one of the most loyal people I've ever known. I went through a rather ugly child custody trial and one day, when my children were away testifying, Steve came round as he didn't have anything to do; the real reason was that he wanted to be sure that, under all the stress, I didn't do anything goofy. Although, if anyone would have asked him what he did, he'd have said, 'Well, I was bored so I went to Bob's house.'

'When we signed the six-picture deal with Warner Brothers, one of the promotion guys asked Steve if he would pose for some photographs with company head Jack Warner. Steve told them straight out that he didn't mind but his business partners had to be there right beside him. You might say Steve was being crafty and that he was trying to keep us on side and to get more work out of us, but the truth is that Steve was naturally loyal. It was just in his character to be that way. These are the things I remember him for.

'Professionally, my impression of him stayed the same pretty much over the years I knew him - a very good guy, terribly talented but also good fun and somewhat of a rebel, to his own drummer as they say. Over the years we've watched a lot of people try to do the same things that Steve did, but it just didn't come out the same. He could clean the chamber or adjust the gun-belt and get away with it, but when people tried to do it to be like Steve McQueen it looked like just that. He really worked at his craft and he knew what he could get away with. When Steve got out of a car - he floated. When he cocked a machine gun - it looked natural. It's like with footballers - you can tell those that have been coached and those that are just natural and Steve was a natural to acting.'

— **Robert Relyea** (Friend, Industry Colleague on seven movies and Business Partner)

꙰

'WE DIDN'T get to know each other that well because he could be aloof and very professional. But I also have to say that Steve helped change my life (by taking on *Junior Bonner*). He didn't hang around with us very much. When he wasn't working I guess he was with (co-star and girlfriend) Barbara Leigh. But he was a likeable guy. In fact Steve nicknamed me Shakespeare because in certain instances I wrote too much and he liked it short. So that was my learning curve with him. It wasn't that he didn't like what I had written, just that he didn't like to say a lot of words. When Steve got ill and was in Mexico towards the end, I sent him a note just saying that I was praying for him. And I signed it "Shakespeare". I hope it brought a smile to his face.'

— **Jeb Rosebrook** (Screenwriter on *Junior Bonner*)

꙰

'I FOUND him wonderful to work with. I used to tease him about being macho with his motorcycle riding - that frequently got him very angry, though he took it in good nature. We weren't bosom buddies or anything like that because I lived in New York and he lived in California, but every time I went to LA I would see him. We would have dinner or just hang out. He lived in a real big house but he didn't look comfortable in it. There was a pool table downstairs and all the other luxuries of a Hollywood movie star. It's funny to think

that later in his life he lived in a run-down shack, or airplane hangar as it was called; I think he outgrew the other lifestyle.'
— **Arnold Schulman** (Screenwriter on *Love with the Proper Stranger*)

༄

'I REALLY enjoyed his company. We had some pretty funny adventures: the first day I went to his house in Malibu, he had about ten Ford Thunderbirds parked out front and God knows how many motorcycles in his garage and a whole string of cars and pick-up trucks. Steve was tearing apart one of his motorcycles when I got there, and after we got talking, this guy - who turns out to be his next-door neighbour from about 100 yards away - comes to the front door and says, 'Steve I've got to talk to you.' He then started bitching about all the space in the road that Steve was taking up with his cars and that he hasn't any space to park his own cars. I wasn't really paying much attention but as I turned around Steve hits this guy right on the chin, knocking him off the porch and flat on to his back. He got up yelling 'I'm going to sue you' and went back towards his house. We then went into the house and Steve turns to me and says: 'You know the trouble with that mother fucker there?' I said: 'What's his trouble?' 'The trouble with him is that he's nothing but a two-bit architect and I'm a movie star and he can't get over it.' I thought to myself, 'a two-bit architect?' The house that the guy was living in was worth at least five million bucks.

'I asked Steve if he always goes punching out his neighbours. 'No,' he said. 'The last time I had to do this was with Keith Moon (drummer from The Who rock band). He was living in the same house as that architect and I had to go tell him to turn off his music because it was keeping me awake. The next morning I went out on to my porch to get a newspaper and found that somebody had taken a shit on my porch - nobody had to tell me who it was, I knew it was Keith Moon.' 'Did you hit him?' I asked. 'No, I sent my son Chad round to sort him out but he'd already left for England.'

'Steve could also be quite paranoid. One day we were chatting in his living room, which looked out over the beach, and he suddenly got up and ran on to his back deck yelling at this person, 'Get the fuck away from here, I'm gonna get the law on to you.' Then he came back in and said, 'Fucking tourists, bothering me all the time.' I didn't say anything; to me it was just a woman walking her dog, 200 feet away, down the beach.'
— **Bud Shrake** (Screenwriter on *Tom Horn*)

∽

'I THOUGHT Steve was a very nice guy and he was particularly kind to me. When we were shooting in Europe on *Papillon*, I received a letter from my daughter who was soon to get married. She was requesting a picture of Steve McQueen. When I saw him next I told him and he said 'Okay, I'll make sure she gets it.' I then got on with it and a week had gone by when Steve grabs me by the shoulder and says, 'Hey, we've got a cameraman here, you and I are here, so let's get that picture taken.' I said, 'But she only wants a picture of you.' 'Well I want a picture of both of us,' Steve said. He stood there and held up a V sign for victory. The photographer printed it for me and my daughter got her picture. I thought that was very nice and very thoughtful of Steve, especially as I had almost forgotten about it.

'He was one of those natural actors like Gregory Peck - who I worked with on a few pictures - who were not in the same echelon as actors like Laurence Olivier or Frederic March, but they came across on screen very well. Steve had a charisma that people wanted to see on screen.'
— **Robert Swink** (Editor on *Papillon*)

౿౿

'WHEN PEOPLE talk about Steve McQueen stealing scenes, that's not because he was crafty, that is because of quality work. Steve might move from his mark by half a foot or something, so you looked at him in the shot, but he knew what he was doing. Steve McQueen was a quality actor, he hit the mark, he knew his lines and if Steve stole scenes by exposing the person he was doing the scene with, then I give him credit. He stole scenes by being great; that's fine. I had scenes with him where we changed lines but he was always on the money.

'I hear people say that he played himself; fine. He might have played himself in movies like *Bullitt* and *Le Mans*, as he knew about cars so didn't really have to stretch out. But on *The Sand Pebbles* he was a sailor and that was a whole new can

of corn and he handled the part and the costume well. He just knew what to do instinctively and by thought.'
— **Joe Turkel** (Co-Star on *The Sand Pebbles*)

∽

'IT WAS funny because after *The Magnificent Seven*, Steve and I didn't see one another because he lived in California where he made all those movies and I went back to New York where I lived. Then, twenty years on, we met again on the set of *The Hunter* and Steve and I were friendly again. Just after the film was finished I got a call from a British journalist who asked, 'Did you know Steve McQueen was very ill?' I said 'No, he wasn't ill while we were working.' I had no idea. Then it all happened so quickly - it was awful. I enjoyed acting with Steve, he was giving and we liked acting with one another. It's interesting that even though he's gone he is still a personality on the screen now; he pops up on television every once in a while and you think, 'What would he have done now?'
— **Eli Wallach** (Co-Star on *The Magnificent Seven* & *The Hunter*)

∽

'HE HAD a certain charisma that made you interested in him and he had a boyish charm and mischief about him in a very charming way. He was like Jimmy Dean without the danger, yet there was an element of surprise and unpredictability to him which makes for movie star quality. The camera had a fondness for him and he worked well on screen. I remember him with respect as audience and as a co-worker.'

— **Al Waxman** (Co-Star on *The War Lover*)

‽⁓

'I'VE NEVER worked with an actor who knew what
worked for him best as Steve did. He must have studied
himself on screen a lot because every so often I would be
rehearsing a scene and he would say to me, 'Gee Bob, I
think I could get that part over without that line and do it
with a reaction.' And he was right. He really knew what
worked for him. He would be up there as one of the best I
ever worked with (who include Gable, Cagney, Lancaster
and Newman).'

— **Robert Wise** (Director of *Somebody Up There Likes Me* & *The
Sand Pebbles*)

‽⁓

'STEVE McQUEEN was a very intense man. He would never
let anything go by casually. When you were with him you
felt that intense, driven nature but he also had this wonderful
charisma. I rarely saw him relax, but once the camera went on
he became this cool guy. There was a switch in personality.
But he had a wonderful personality for the screen that came
out so wonderfully. It was such a strange dichotomy between
the two characters: the Steve McQueen you worked with and
met and talked with, and the Steve McQueen that you saw on
the screen. They were two different people. And that made it
difficult because I never quite knew which Steve I was dealing with.

'I've heard people say that he played himself, but in real life I never saw in front of me the guy who's on the screen. I saw an intense guy who clearly had a hard time getting up there after his early childhood. He overcame a lot of very difficult things in his life to achieve what he did.'

— **Emanuel L. Wolf** (Executive Producer on *Papillon*)

'HE HAD a quality when he was in a close-up and those piercing blue eyes just burned a hole right through you. He was unique and nobody could ever imitate him or replace him. There are people today who have qualities – but never the same as Steve.'

—**Tim Zinnemann** (Assistant Director on *Bullitt* and *The Reivers*)

CHAPTER REFERENCES

HUNDREDS OF INTERVIEWS were requested to write *Steve McQueen: The Cooler King* with many industry figures, whether actors, directors, producers, writers, wardrobe designers, hairdressers, make-up artists, cinematographers, editors, first or second assistant producers or directors, friends or acquaintances of Steve no matter how brief their contact with him, and so on. It would obviously have been desirable if all of the people I applied for an interview with – usually through their agents – had granted my request so as to acquire totally exclusive material and allow me to be able to ask my own questions of their experiences with Steve McQueen. But in the real world this rarely happens. When chronicling these types of books, not everyone wishes to be interviewed. I respect anyone's choice in this regard.

However, rather than ignore other research or content material that is relevant to this book and out there in the public domain, if I felt an anecdote or account of a certain time was relevant, I have attempted to include a flavour of it. So therefore some interesting, concise observations have been taken from publications such as autobiographies of people who came into contact with Steve. I have credited the relevant publishing details below. The wonderful reference back-ups of *Wikipedia* and *imdb.com* were widely used for fact-checking, though the internet was used sparingly when I embarked on this journey. As I alluded to in my author's note. I am especially grateful to Robert Relyea for the hours he spent with me on Trans-Atlantic phone calls talking in depth about Steve and answering many, many questions I had for him on the seven movies he worked with Steve on, and more.

And I should give special mention to books penned by Steve's three wives Neile (*My Husband, My Friend*), Ali (*Moving Pictures*) and Barbara (*The Last Mile*), as I suspect there can be no greater insight of life behind the scenes than from close family.

Notes and References:

The Man Behind the Movie Star:
The author interviewed Chris Noel, Jeb Rosebrook, John Leyton, Jock Wilson, Martin Landau, Joe Turkel, LeVar Burton, Emanuel Wolf, Bill Pierce, Sharon Farrell, Barbara Leigh, Louise Edlind, Pete Mason, Robert Relyea, Don Gordon, Russell S. Doughten, Shirley Anne Field and Jeff Heininger.
Reference material was sourced from:
A Fortunate Life, Robert Vaughan's autobiography, published by JR Books, 2009
AI.com, interview with Ali MacGraw
The Garner Files, James Garner's autobiography, published by Simon & Schuster, 2011
Hello! (UK magazine), interview with Terry McQueen, May 1989

Independent on Sunday, interview with William Claxton in 1994
The Last Mile by Barbara Minty McQueen, published by Dalton Watson Fine Books, 2007
McQueen, the semi-autobiographical book by William F. Nolan, published by Congdon & Weed in 1984
Moving Pictures by Ali MacGraw, published by Bantam, 1991
My Husband, My Friend by Neile Adams McQueen, first published by Signet, 1986
Parade.com, interview with Ali MacGraw
Steve McQueen: Portrait of an American Rebel by Marshall Terrill, first published by Plexus in 1993
Steve McQueen: The Untold Story of a Bad Boy in Hollywood by Penina Spiegel, published by Collins/Fontana, 1986/87

Somebody Up There Likes Me:
The author interviewed Robert Wise and Martin Landau.
Reference material was sourced from:
My Husband, My Friend by Neile Adams McQueen, first published by Signet, 1986

Never Love A Stranger:
The author interviewed R.G. Armstrong and Emanuel L. Wolf.
Reference material was sourced from:
My Husband, My Friend by Neile Adams McQueen, first published by Signet, 1986

The Blob:
The author interviewed Russell S. Doughten and Vince Kehoe

Reference material was sourced from:

Man on the Edge, documentary by Wombat Productions, MPI Home Video, 1991

McQueen, by William F. Nolan, published by Congdon & Weed in 1984

The Great St. Louis Bank Robbery:

The author interviewed Charles Guggenheim.

Reference material was sourced from:

McQueen, by William F. Nolan, published by Congdon & Weed in 1984

Never So Few:

The author interviewed Robert Relyea and Kurt Neumann.

The Magnificent Seven:

The author interviewed Eli Wallach, Walter Mirisch, Robert Relyea, Robert Vaughn and Shirley Anne Field.

Reference material was sourced from:

A Fortunate Life, Robert Vaughan's autobiography, published by JR Books, 2009

I Thought We Were Making Movies, Not History, by Walter Mirisch, published by the University of Wisconsin Press, 2008

McQueen, by William F. Nolan, published by Congdon & Weed in 1984

My Husband, My Friend by Neile Adams McQueen, first published by Signet, 1986

The Honeymoon Machine:
The author interviewed Paula Prentiss, George Wells and Lorenzo Semple Jr.
Reference material was sourced from:
My Husband, My Friend by Neile Adams McQueen, first published by Signet, 1986
Steve McQueen: Portrait of an American Rebel by Marshall Terrill, first published by Plexus in 1993
Steve McQueen: The Untold Story of a Bad Boy in Hollywood by Penina Spiegel, published by Collins/Fontana, 1986/87

Hell Is for Heroes:
The author interviewed L.Q. Jones and Chuck Hicks
Reference material was sourced from:
Don Siegel: An Autobiography, published by Faber & Faber of London), 1993

The War Lover:
The author interviewed Al Waxman, Gary Cockrell and Shirley Anne Field.
Reference material was sourced from:
thecolumnists.com, for their interview with Philip Leacock
Robert Wagner – Pieces of my Heart, published by Hutchinson in 2009.

The Great Escape:
The author interviewed Robert Relyea, Walter Mirisch, John Leyton and Angus Lennie.
Reference material was sourced from:
Cinema 71, the French publication that sourced a quote by Charles Bronson on McQueen
The Garner Files, James Garner's autobiography, published by Simon & Schuster in 2011
I Thought We Were Making Movies, Not History, by Walter Mirisch, published by the University of Wisconsin Press, 2008

Soldier in the Rain:
The author interviewed Chris Noel, Ed Nelson and Sugar Blymyer
Reference material was sourced from:
Filming Soldier in the Rain, by Chris Noel, 2013
McQueen, by William F. Nolan, published by Congdon & Weed in 1984

Love with the Proper Stranger:
The author interviewed Arnold Schulman, Robert Mulligan, Edie Adams and Sugar Blymyer, while producer Alan J. Pakula had also agreed to be interviewed, days before his tragic and fatal car crash in 1998.
Reference material was sourced from:
My Husband, My Friend by Neile Adams McQueen, first published by Signet, 1986

Baby, the Rain Must Fall:

The author interviewed Robert Mulligan, Horton Foote, Don Murray and John Leyton.

Reference material was sourced from:

Steve McQueen: Portrait of an American Rebel by Marshall Terrill, first published by Plexus in 1993

The Cincinnati Kid:

The author interviewed Martin Ransohoff, Jeff Corey, Kurt Neumann and Ring Lardner Jr.

Reference material was sourced from:

All My Yesterday's, the autobiography from Edward G. Robinson, published by W. H. Allen, 1974.

Independent on Sunday, an interview with William Claxton in 1994

Man on the Edge, documentary by Wombat Productions, MPI Home Video, 1991

McQueen, by William F. Nolan, published by Congdon & Weed in 1984

My Husband, My Friend by Neile Adams McQueen, first published by Signet, 1986

My Story, an autobiography by Ann-Margret, published by Orion, 1994.

Steve McQueen: The Untold Story of a Bad Boy in Hollywood by Penina Spiegel, published by Collins/Fontana, 1986/87

Nevada Smith:

The author interviewed Martin Landau, John Michael Hayes, Pat Hingle and Del Acevedo.

Reference material was sourced from:
My Husband, My Friend by Neile Adams McQueen, first published by Signet, 1986

The Sand Pebbles:
The author interviewed Robert Wise, Mako, Joe Turkel and Del Acevedo
Reference material was sourced from:
Knock Wood, Candice Bergen's autobiography, published by Linden Press/Simon & Schuster, 1984

The Thomas Crown Affair:
The author interviewed Walter Mirisch, Kurt Neumann, Alan Trustman, John Flaxman, Robert Wise, Del Armstrong and Vince Kehoe
Reference material was sourced from:
I Thought We Were Making Movies, Not History, by Walter Mirisch, published by the University of Wisconsin Press, 2008
Looking For Gatsby, Faye Dunaway's autobiography, published by Simon &Schuster, 1998
McQueen, by William F. Nolan, published by Congdon & Weed in 1984
My Husband, My Friend by Neile Adams McQueen, first published by Signet, 1986
Steve McQueen: The Untold Story of a Bad Boy in Hollywood by Penina Spiegel, published by Collins/Fontana, 1986/87

Bullitt:

The author interviewed Robert Relyea, William Fraker, Robert Vaughn, Tim Zinnemann, Alan Trustman, Harry Kleiner, Don Gordon, John Flaxman and Jacqueline Bisset.

Reference material was sourced from:

My Husband, My Friend by Neile Adams McQueen, first published by Signet, 1986

Steve McQueen: Portrait of an American Rebel by Marshall Terrill, first published by Plexus in 1993

The Reivers:

The author interviewed Sharon Farrell, Robert Relyea, Tim Zinnemann and Harriet Ravetch (formerly Harriet Frank Jr.)

Reference material was sourced from:

McQueen, by William F. Nolan, published by Congdon & Weed in 1984

Steve McQueen: Portrait of an American Rebel by Marshall Terrill, first published by Plexus in 1993

Steve McQueen: The Untold Story of a Bad Boy in Hollywood by Penina Spiegel, published by Collins/Fontana, 1986/87

Le Mans:

The author interviewed Donald Ernst, Robert Relyea, Louise Edlind, David Piper, Derek Bell, Richard Attwood, Ray Summers and Harry Kleiner.

Reference material was sourced from:
The Garner Files, James Garner's autobiography, published by Simon & Schuster in 2011
My Husband, My Friend by Neile Adams McQueen, first published by Signet, 1986
Steve McQueen: Portrait of an American Rebel by Marshall Terrill, first published by Plexus in 1993

On Any Sunday:
The author interviewed Mert Lawwill, Robert Relyea, Bob Bagley, Don Gordon, Kurt Neumann, Jeff Heininger and collaborated with Bruce Brown via Bob Bagley.

Junior Bonner:
The author interviewed Joe Wizan, Jeb Rosebrook, Barbara Leigh, Mary Murphy, William Pierce and Newt Arnold.
Reference material was sourced from:
The King, McQueen And The Love Machine by Barbara Leigh, published by Xlibris in 2002

The Getaway:
The author interviewed Bo Hopkins, Kathy Blondell, Jack Petty, Newt Arnold, Gordon Dawson and Michael Preece.
Reference material was sourced from:
McQueen, by Tim Satchell, published by Sidgwick & Jackson (London), 1981
Moving Pictures by Ali MacGraw, published by Bantam, 1991

Papillon:
The author interviewed Emanuel L. Wolf, Don Gordon, Fred Koenekamp, Robert Swink and Lorenzo Semple Jr.
Reference material was sourced from:
Moving Pictures by Ali MacGraw, published by Bantam, 1991

The Towering Inferno:
The author interviewed Robert Vaughan, Susan Blakely, Newt Arnold, Steve Jaffe and Peter Lucarelli.
Reference material was sourced from:
Moving Pictures by Ali MacGraw, published by Bantam, 1991
Steve McQueen: Portrait of an American Rebel by Marshall Terrill, first published by Plexus in 1993

An Enemy of the People:
The author interviewed Bibi Andersson, Sheldon Kahn, Barbara Leigh, Tim Zinnemann and William Tuttle.
Reference material was sourced from:
McQueen, by William F. Nolan, published by Congdon & Weed in 1984

Tom Horn:
The author interviewed Bud Shrake, Bert Williams, Del Armstrong, Fred Koenkamp and Ed Milkovich.
Reference material was sourced from:
The Last Mile by Barbara Minty McQueen, published by Dalton Watson Fine Books, 2007

The Hunter:

The author interviewed LeVar Burton, Eli Wallach, Peter Hyams, Buzz Kulik, John Elliott, Fred Koenekamp and Bren Plaistowe.

Reference material was sourced from:

The Last Mile by Barbara Minty McQueen, published by Dalton Watson Fine Books, 2007

Steve McQueen: Portrait of an American Rebel by Marshall Terrill, first published by Plexus in 1993

Reflections of Steve McQueen:

All exclusively interviewed, with the exception of Faye Dunaway's quote, taken from her autobiography *Looking For Gatsby*, published by Simon & Schuster, 1998

ABOUT THE AUTHOR...

Richard Sydenham has been a journalist since 1994, working mainly in sports. This is his fourth book but first non-sports title. He has written for organisations such as the Associated Press (AP), Reuters, The Sunday/Daily Telegraph, Bloomberg and lived in Dubai for a year in 1998-99, while working for Gulf News. He is the founder of the media and sports company Big Star Creations. He enjoys the cinema, playing golf, watching and playing cricket, and is a passionate supporter of Aston Villa Football Club. Richard lives in the West Midlands with his wife and two children.

4813655R10354

Printed in Great Britain
by Amazon.co.uk, Ltd.,
Marston Gate.